COPYRIGHT LAW

By

JANE C. GINSBURG

Morton L. Janklow Professor of Literary
and Artistic Property Law
Columbia University School of Law

ROBERT A. GORMAN

Kenneth W. Gemmill Professor of Law Emeritus
University of Pennsylvania Law School

CONCEPTS AND INSIGHTS SERIES®

FOUNDATION PRESS
2012

THOMSON REUTERS™

© 2012 By THOMSON REUTERS/FOUNDATION PRESS

    1 New York Plaza, 34th Floor

    New York, NY 10004

    Phone Toll Free 1–877–888–1330

    Fax 646–424–5201

    foundation–press.com

Printed in the United States of America

ISBN 978–1–59941–251–1

Mat #40555494

With gratitude to our instructors:

*Benjamin Kaplan and Arthur R. Miller
in the classroom,*

Alan Latman in the law office,

*and to the generations of students
who have enriched our thinking about
the substance and ideals of copyright law*

PREFACE

In the years since the authors began studying and teaching copyright law, the field has emerged from what may have seemed the Elysian territory of a few artistically-inclined jurists. Copyright now, as portrayed in popular media and much of academia, unfolds on a ubiquitous battleground arraying the aging business models of "hegemonic" "content industries" against freedom of speech and the progress of technology. While this sort of caricature attests to copyright's dramatic evolution from romantic backwater to public preoccupation, it neglects a signal feature of this area of the law: Copyright inspires idealism among both those who seek to foster creativity and those who promote public access to the fruits of that creativity—indeed, the same actors often endeavor to achieve both those aspirations. Moreover, though bellicose polemics too often prevail over informed analysis, copyright abounds in intellectual fascination, and one aim of this manual is to enrich the public debate by assisting its participants—law students, teachers, lawyers, judges and other public servants—to understand the principles, content and operation of the U.S. copyright law. The law's too often excessive complexity makes a book like this one a useful contributor to rigorous discussion of legal norms, for a well-grounded appreciation of the positive law should precede the advocacy of policy goals.

Many of this book's readers are likely to be law students. While the chapters in this manual are organized to correspond with Robert A. Gorman, Jane C. Ginsburg & R. Anthony Reese, *Copyright: Cases and Materials* (8th ed. 2011), we believe that students whose teachers have chosen a different casebook, or, for that matter, those readers who consult this book as a free-standing reference, rather than as an adjunct to a law school course, will also find this book to be both stimulating and helpful.

The authors are tremendously grateful to John L. Schwab, Columbia Law School class of 2012, for expert research assistance and excellent editorial suggestions. We also express great appreciation to Prof. R. Anthony Reese, our "new" co-author on the copyright casebook, whose deep knowledge and moderating perspective have illuminated our discussions of all aspects of the field, from basic principles to the latest technological challenges.

BIBLIOGRAPHIC NOTE

The purpose of this manual is to serve as an introduction to, and a starting point for research about, the law of copyright. It cannot feasibly be minutely detailed in its text or heavily annotated in its footnotes. Fortunately, there are a number of longer works of high quality that can be recommended to serve those latter purposes. For nearly fifty years, the masterful multi-volume treatise, constantly cited by the courts, has been that of the late Professor Melville Nimmer: Melville & David Nimmer, *Nimmer on Copyright*. It has since been joined by an equally outstanding multi-volume treatise by Professor Paul Goldstein, titled simply *Copyright*. Both works are regularly updated. William F. Patry's multi-volume treatise, *Patry on Copyright*, also regularly updated, is another entrant in the lists.

There are two research services that provide current updates on copyright developments and decisions. These are published by Commerce Clearing House and by the Bureau of National Affairs (*BNA Patent, Trademark & Copyright Journal*), the latter in an online service as well. The *United States Patent Quarterly* also publishes advance sheets containing decisions in the fields of patents, trademarks, and copyright. The relatively few federal district court copyright decisions that are not published in the *Federal Supplement* can usually be found in full text in either the CCH or USPQ reports.

The Copyright Office website contains a wealth of information about the substance and administration of the Copyright Act (http://www.copyright.gov). One can find there not only the text of the Act, but also pending copyright bills, the rules and regulations promulgated by the Copyright Office, news of the activities of the Office, its very useful reports and studies, speeches and statements by the Register of Copyrights, the various application forms, informational circulars, and access to registration records.

The law journal articles written about copyright have vastly proliferated over the past decades, and are published in general law reviews as well as in an increasing number of specialty journals devoted to intellectual property or to allied fields (such as computer law and entertainment law).

Throughout this manual, the provisions of the copyright statute now in effect—the 1976 Copyright Act, most of the provisions of which went into effect on January 1, 1978—are referred to by their section numbers within title 17 of the U.S. Code.

Many courts and scholars have come to regard the report of the House Committee on the Judiciary, H.R. Rep. No. 94–1476, 94th Cong., 2d Sess. (1976), as the most comprehensive, exhaustive, and authoritative legislative source of the history and purposes of the Copyright Act. This monograph makes frequent reference to this significant document, which is denoted simply as "House Report."

Excerpts from most of the cases discussed in this book, and from the House Report, can conveniently be found in Robert A. Gorman, Jane C. Ginsburg & R. Anthony Reese, *Copyright: Cases and Materials* (8th ed. 2011).

The coverage of this manual is complete as of January 23, 2012.

SUMMARY OF CONTENTS

TABLE OF CONTENTS

COPYRIGHT LAW

Chapter 1

HISTORY AND BACKGROUND

Copyright is the law of literary and artistic property. It regulates the ownership and exercise of rights in creative works. The basic purpose of U.S. copyright is to enrich our society's wealth of culture and information. The means for doing so is to grant exclusive rights in the exploitation and marketing of a work as an incentive to those who create it. The Founding Fathers phrased this more elegantly—and provided the constitutional source for Congress's power to enact copyright laws—in Article I, section 8, clause 8 of the Constitution: "The Congress shall have power ... To promote the Progress of Science and useful Arts, by securing for limited Times to Authors and Inventors the exclusive Right to their respective Writings and Discoveries." This provision is both a source of and a limitation on Congress's power to enact copyright and patent statutes. It recognizes both the general public interest in fostering creativity, and the individual rights of creators—for limited times—over the fruits of their intellectual labors. The Framers perceived, as James Madison urged in Federalist 43, that "The utility of this power will scarcely be questioned. The copyright of authors has been solemnly adjudged, in Great Britain, to be a right of common law. The right to useful inventions seems with equal reason to belong to the inventors. The public good fully coincides in both cases with the claims of individuals. The States cannot separately make effectual provision for either of the cases, and most of them have anticipated the decision of this point, by laws passed at the instance of Congress."

Further examination of the copyright clause yields themes that recur throughout copyright law, and inform this book. Copyright may also call into play other parts of the constitution as well, notably the supremacy clause and the First Amendment, and we will consider those issues in due course. For now, however, we highlight the framework questions that emerge from the copyright clause. Does the opening phrase "to promote the progress of science" state a general aspiration for a copyright system, or does it constrain Congress' power by authorizing only laws which result in the advancement of learning? How would a court judge what kinds of legislative measures are consistent with that objective? Must Congress's measures provide incentives to create new works? To disseminate works, new or old? If the aim to progress does not generally cabin the content of copyright laws, is that goal relevant to the determination whether any particular author, work or category of work may enjoy a copyright? (Are assessments whether copyright afforded an

1

incentive to creation, or whether a work promotes knowledge, any less elusive when applied to individual authors or works rather than to the copyright system as a whole?) Does the promotion of progress play a role in the evaluation of defenses to copyright infringement? Does the promotion of progress furnish the sole rationale for copyright protection in the U.S? If not the only justification, the dominant one?

Pursuing the inquiry past the preamble, what does "limited times" mean? The phrase appears to envision a public domain free of proprietary claims, but how "limited" in time is the period of proprietorship, and how immutable is the public domain? The clause empowers Congress to "secur[e]" authors' exclusive rights; does the term imply the reinforcement of a pre-existing right? Did the Framers thus assume the existence of an author's natural property right in the fruits of his intellectual labor? And who is an "author?" The work's human creator? The person or entity who hired the human creator? The person or entity who purchased or operated the machine or device that generated the work? The rights Congress has power to secure are "exclusive;" does Congress therefore lack power to substitute in whole or in part a system of remuneration which would compensate authors but deny them the control over their works that exclusive rights afford? Finally, what is a "writing?" Does the term imply that the work must exist in some material form before a federal copyright law may cover it? Does the term exclude certain kinds of works from the subject matter of copyright? Does the term, standing alone or in conjunction with "authors," imply any threshold of creativity, quality or purpose to the work?

I. The Copyright Statutes

A. *British antecedents and the 1790 Act*

U.S. copyright law traces its source to British censorship laws of the sixteenth century. Following the invention of printing, a system of printing privileges, paired with government control over the content of the works, developed in many European States, particularly in Venice, the Papal States, and France. The governing authority, having verified the work's political and religious orthodoxy, granted the petitioner, usually a printer-bookseller, but sometimes the work's author, a time-limited monopoly over the printing, selling, and importation of copies of the work.[1] England departed from this scheme in vesting in the publish-

---

1. On printing privileges *see, e.g.*, Elizabeth Armstrong, BEFORE COPYRIGHT: THE FRENCH BOOK-PRIVILEGE SYSTEM 1498–1526 (Cambridge University Press, 1990)); Pierina Fontana, 3 INIZI DELLA PROPRIETÀ LETTERA- RIA NELLO STATO PONTIFICIO (saggio di documenti dell'Archivio vaticano) Accademie e Biblioteche d'Italia 204–21 (1929); Rudolph Hirsch, PRINTING, SELLING AND READING, 1450–1550 (1974); Angela Nuovo and Christian

ers themselves the control over the dissemination of books. In 1556, the King granted to the Stationers' Company, made up of the leading publishers of London, a monopoly over book publication, thus placing in the hands of the guild the power to restrain the publication of seditious or heretical works. Publishers were given an exclusive and perpetual right of publication of works that passed muster with the Government and the Church (by way of the Star Chamber).[2] As with many systems of printing privileges, the English monopoly primarily promoted investment in the material and labor of producing and distributing books; protecting or rewarding authors was generally an ancillary objective.[3]

After nearly a century and a half, licensing laws were left to expire and publishers sprang up independent of the Stationers' Company. The Company turned to Parliament for protective legislation and in 1710 the Statute of Anne was enacted. As we shall see, however, the resulting law was not entirely made to the Company's order. The basic philosophy and contours of the Statute of Anne have dominated the U.S. law of copyright for most of our history as a nation. Its purpose was stated to be "for the Encouragement of Learning," which was threatened by the damage done to authors and their families by unauthorized copying of their books. This purpose was to be promoted by granting to authors an exclusive right of publication to last for 21 years for existing works and for 14 years for works published in the future. Moreover, were the author still living at the end of the first 14–year term, the exclusive right would revert to the author for an additional 14 years. A condition of statutory copyright was the registration of the title at Stationers' Hall and the deposit of nine copies at official libraries.

The Statute of Anne thus became the first law explicitly and systematically to vest copyright in the work's creator. Two factors, one philosophical, one economic, motivate this shift in orientation. First, making authors the owners of the exclusive right reflects the Enlightenment tenet that property derives from labor. From ownership of the physical fruits of agricultural and other labors, it is not a long step to ownership of the incorporeal fruits of intellectual labor. Indeed, if John Locke voiced the former argument in his Treatises on Government, he

Coppens, I GIOLITO E LA STAMPA NELL'ITALIA DEL XVI SECOLO (Geneva, Droz 2005). *See also* sources cited, *infra*, note 3.

2. *See* John Feather, A HISTORY OF BRITISH PUBLISHING 31–32 (1988)(describing how the Stationers Company "became an equal partner with the Crown in the suppression of undesirable books").

3. *See, e.g.* Cyprien Bladgen, THE STATIONERS' COMPANY: A HISTORY 1403–1959 (London 1960); CAMBRIDGE HISTORY OF THE BOOK IN BRITAIN (Lotte Hellinga & J.B.

Trapp eds., 3d ed. 1998); Mark Rose, AUTHORS AND OWNERS: THE INVENTION OF COPYRIGHT (1993); John Feather, A HISTORY OF BRITISH PUBLISHING (1988). Authors could directly hold privileges, however, and in some systems of printing privileges, particularly the Papal privileges, but to a lesser extent in Venice and France as well, authors in fact frequently applied for and received monopolies over their works' publication and distribution.

made the latter in his writings on the expiration of the Licensing Act.[4] The replacement of the Licensing Act with laws vesting property rights in authors also sought to break the monopoly of the Stationers' Company by promoting the rise of other publishers with whom authors might negotiate.[5] In that respect, one may perceive the author's reversion right not only as an endeavor to ensure that authors share in the success of their works, but also as a measure to promote competition among booksellers, for the author who retrieves his rights is free to grant the second fourteen-year term to another publisher.[6]

The Statute of Anne, and the copyright laws later adopted in the former Colonies, set the stage for the Copyright and Patent Clause of the Constitution and for the enactment by the first Congress in 1790 of the first federal statutes governing copyrights and patents. After the close of the Revolution, all of the Colonies except Delaware passed laws to afford a measure of protection to authors, pursuant to a recommendation of the Continental Congress,[7] and the entreaties of Noah Webster, who tirelessly (and self-interestedly) urged that protecting authors not only responded to the claims of natural justice, but would spawn the creation of the kinds of American-oriented school books, geographies and dictionaries essential to the development of the citizenry of the new republic.[8] Webster thus coupled the cultural policy of the new nation with the recognition of authors' inherent rights in their works. Similarly, while many states patterned their statutes after the Statute of Anne, many others mingled natural rights rhetoric with the more utilitarian inspiration of the English model. For example, the preamble to the Massachusetts Act of March 17, 1783 proclaims:

> Whereas the improvement of knowledge, the progress of civilization, the public weal of the community, and the advancement of human happiness, greatly depend on the efforts of learned and ingenious persons in the various arts and sciences: As the principal encouragement such persons can have to make great and beneficial exertions of this nature, must exist in the

---

4. On these writings, see Laura Moscati, Un "Memorandum" di John Locke tra *Censorship* et *Copyright* (2003) LXXVI Rivista di storia del diritto italiano 69.

5. See Feather, *supra* note 2; Moscati, *supra* note 4; Rose, *supra* note 3.

6. On the reversion right in the Statute of Anne and its successors in British and U.S. Copyright law, see Lionel Bently and Jane C. Ginsburg, *"The sole right shall return to the Author"*: *Anglo-American Authors' Reversion Rights from the Statute of Anne to Contemporary U.S. Copyright*, 25 BERKELEY TECH. L. J. 1475 (2011).

7. 24 Journals, Continental Congress 326 (1783).

8. Noah Webster, *Origin of the Copy-Right Laws in the United States, in* A COLLECTION OF PAPERS ON POLITICAL, LITERARY AND MORAL SUBJECTS (N.Y. 1843 & B. Franklin ed. photo. reprint 1968); Jane C. Ginsburg, *A Tale of Two Copyrights: Literary Property in Revolutionary France and America, in* OF AUTHORS AND ORIGINS: ESSAYS ON COPYRIGHT LAW 131, 138–39 (Brad Sherman & Alain Strowel eds., 1994).

legal security of the fruits of their study and industry to themselves; and as such security is one of the natural rights of all men, there being no property more peculiarly a man's own than that which is procured by the labor of his mind.

Connecticut, New Hampshire, Rhode Island, North Carolina, Georgia, and New York also enacted copyright laws combining natural rights and public-benefit rationales.[9] But whatever the state copyright statute's philosophy, these laws were limited in their operation to the boundaries of each state: if an author in one state wished to obtain protection for his work throughout the other states, he was obliged to comply with a multitude of laws. The territorial limitations of state protection underlie Madison's observation that "The States cannot separately make effectual provision" for the protection of works of authorship.

The constitutional copyright clause quoted above echoes the Statute of Anne's incentive rationale, but its authorization to Congress to promote the progress of learning "by securing for limited times to authors ... the exclusive right to their ... writings" also reveals undercurrents of natural property claims, for "securing" suggests that some kind of exclusive right already inhered in works of authorship. Hence Madison's reference to copyright in Britain as "a right of common law." The clause's direction that the exclusive right be "for limited times," in the plural, may also advert to the Statute of Anne's conditional second term of copyright, and thereby implicitly endorse the author's reversion right established by the English example.

The first U.S. copyright statute adopted many features of the Statute of Anne, including the dual 14–year terms with reversion to the surviving author, and registration and deposit formalities. The rights secured were to "print, publish and vend," and the subject matter covered "any map, chart or book."

In the handful of major copyright revisions through the 1976 Act (and in the more frequent amendments since), Congress has gradually increased the kinds of works that are eligible for copyright and the kinds of exclusive rights afforded to the copyright owner. Congress has also progressively extended the period of copyright protection and reduced the significance of compliance with statutory formalities. It should be noted that Copyright protection is not limited to works of "high culture," and that its coverage embraces such mundane works as business directories and such technologically oriented works as computer programs.

9. *See* Copyright Enactments of the United States 11, 14, 18, 19, 25, 27 and 29 (Thorvald Solberg ed., 1906); Francine Crawford, *Pre–Constitutional Copyright Statutes,* 23 Bull. Copyright Soc'y 11 (1975).

B.   The Copyright Act of 1909

The Copyright Act that dominated the twentieth century was enacted in 1909. Inartfully drafted and lacking important definitions—and enacted before the invention or widespread commercial use of the phonograph, motion pictures, radio and television, the photocopy machine, the computer, and a wide array of communications media including, of course, the Internet—the 1909 Act was subjected to frequent ad hoc amendment and to unguided judicial interpretation.

A principal feature of the 1909 Act was the preservation of state copyright protection (known as common-law copyright) for unpublished works; once a work was published by dissemination to the public, however, either federal copyright formalities were satisfied or the work fell into the public domain. If the familiar copyright notice was placed on all copies of a published work, federal copyright protection attached, exclusively enforced in federal courts (provided the copyright owner registered the work in the Copyright Office prior to commencing suit). Such federal copyright lasted for 28 years and was subject to renewal upon timely registration for an additional 28 years. The most significant exclusive rights accorded to the copyright owner under the 1909 Act were those of printing or otherwise copying, of making adaptations or versions, of selling, and of publicly performing (for musical compositions, publicly performing for profit).

Although the 1909 Copyright Act is no longer in effect, it does govern important aspects of transactions that took place before the current Act's effective date of 1978, and many of those transactions continue to be a source of litigation today. Knowledge and application of the 1909 Act will therefore continue to be pertinent to resolve disputes concerning, for example, whether a work published prior to 1978 complied with statutory formalities or was thrust into the public domain,[10] and who is the owner of copyright when claims are traced back to transfers that took place while the 1909 Act was in effect.[11]

C.   The Copyright Act of 1976 and its frequent amendments

After a major effort in the Copyright Office and the Congress to restudy and revise the law, an effort lasting more than 15 years, U.S. copyright law was drastically overhauled in the Copyright Act of 1976,

---

10. *E.g.*, Estate of Martin Luther King, Jr., Inc. v. CBS, Inc., 194 F.3d 1211 (11th Cir. 1999); Academy of Motion Picture Arts & Sciences v. Creative House Promotions, Inc., 944 F.2d 1446 (9th Cir. 1991).

11. Martha Graham Sch. & Dance Found., Inc. v. Martha Graham Ctr. of Con-

temporary Dance, Inc., 380 F.3d 624 (2d Cir. 2004) (work made for hire); Forward v. Thorogood, 985 F.2d 604 (1st Cir. 1993) (transfer of physical object embodying musical work).

which in most pertinent respects took effect on January 1, 1978. That statute abolished common-law copyright and made federal copyright exclusive from the moment a work is "created," that is, "fixed in a tangible medium of expression," whether in published or unpublished form. Works then in the first term or the renewal term of copyright under the 1909 Act had their term of protection potentially extended to 75 years. Works created on or after January 1, 1978, or first published thereafter, were to be protected for 50 years after the death of the author, and corporate works were to be protected for 75 years after publication. If a work was published after January 1, 1978, it was still required to bear a copyright notice, but failure to use the notice would be subject to cure and would not necessarily thrust the work into the public domain. Congress has since eliminated the notice requirement altogether for works published after March 1, 1989. In 1998, 20 more years were added to the term of copyright for all works still under copyright protection.

The exclusive rights accorded the copyright owner under the 1976 Act are essentially the same as those given by the 1909 Act, with the addition of the right of "public display" to take account of transmissions of fixed images by television and computer. A host of intricately delineated exemptions are incorporated in the 1976 Act, so that a variety of uses of copyright-protected works may be made without securing the authorization of the copyright owner, many of them for certain nonprofit, charitable and educational purposes, and others subject to compulsory licenses providing compensation to copyright owners, but depriving them of the right to refuse to authorize the use. The well-known doctrine of fair use, judicially devised in the middle of the nineteenth century, was expressly incorporated in the text of the statute.

In almost every year of the decade after the Copyright Act was amended in 1989 to eliminate the requirement of placing a notice on all publicly distributed copies, the statute was amended further, principally in order to take account of new technological developments or to conform to the provisions of international treaties that have come increasingly to harmonize the copyright laws throughout the world. Only the most significant amendments are noted here.

In 1990 Congress granted to visual artists certain limited rights of attribution and integrity in the original physical copies of their works; expanded the rights of architects in their plans and buildings; and granted commercial-rental rights covering computer programs (as it had done in 1984 for musical recordings). In 1992 the Act was amended to provide for automatic renewal of the copyright terms of pre–1978 works then in their first term of copyright; and to ensure compensation to recording companies and performers in connection with the sale of digital recording machines and media (the Digital Audio Home Recording Act, which also expressly immunized home recording for noncommercial purposes). In 1994, Congress restored copyright protection to non-U.S. works from treaty-signatory nations (the Berne Convention and the World Trade Organization) if those works were still protected in their "countries of origin" but had never been protected here because they were first published in countries with which the U.S. then had no copyright relations, or had lost their U.S. protection because they had been published here without the notice required under the 1909 Act or had not been timely renewed under that Act. The Supreme Court in 2012 ruled that the copyright restoration law violated neither the constitutional "limited Times" proviso nor the First Amendment.[12]

In 1995 and again in 1998, Congress extended to sound recordings an exclusive right of digital public performance (e.g., by being played over the Internet), resulting in the copyright owner's full rights over interactive digital transmissions and a compulsory-license regime for most other digital transmissions. In 1998, as noted above, the term of copyright protection was extended from 75 years to 95 years (for corporate works and works published under the 1909 Act that were not yet in the public domain), and from "life plus 50" to "life plus 70" for other works created or published after January 1, 1978. In 2003 the Supreme Court sustained this "Sonny Bono Copyright Term Extension Act" against constitutional attack.[13] In 1998 Congress took a significant step beyond conventional copyright in the provisions of the Digital Millennium Copyright Act that prevent the circumvention of technological protections (such as digital encryption) of copyrighted works, and prohibit the knowing removal or alteration of "copyright management information."

II. Copyright as an Element of Intellectual Property Law

The general domain of copyright law is often misunderstood. In particular, its boundaries are often confused with those of the law of patents and trademarks. These three fields are commonly grouped together as "intellectual property," but they are quite different in important respects, which are summarized here.

The purpose of copyright and patent is to provide incentives to "promote the progress of science and useful arts" and the constitutional source of Congress's power to legislate is the Copyright and Patent Clause. The purpose of trademark law is to prevent confusion in the commercial marketplace—and thereby to ensure accurate information

12. Golan v. Holder, 132 S.Ct. 873 (2012).

13. Eldred v. Ashcroft, 537 U.S. 186 (2003).

and the maintenance of quality of goods and services—and the constitutional source of Congress's power to legislate is the Commerce Clause.

A. *Patents*

The law of patents[14] embraces the subject matter of products and processes. To be eligible for protection, an invention must be useful, and novel, and—even though it might not have been known before—also "nonobvious," that is, not reasonably anticipatable by a person versed in the current state of the pertinent art. Before a patent is issued by the Patent and Trademark Office, the invention must be determined by an examiner, after a detailed search of prior art, to satisfy these three statutory conditions. Patent protection begins only when the Office issues the patent at the end of the examining process, and the patent lasts for 20 years as measured from the date on which the patent application was initially filed.

The exclusive right granted by the patent law is much more powerful than that accorded by copyright, in two important respects. Copyright infringement requires that the work of the copyright owner have been copied, so independent origination of a similar or identical work is not an infringement; but patent infringement can arise even from a later independently created invention. Copyright gives the author exclusive rights to copy and otherwise exploit only the pattern of expression in the copyrighted work and not the underlying ideas, concepts or systems; patents protect against replication of chemical or mechanical processes as usefully embodied. For example, copyright in a book that describes a newly invented medical device will afford protection only against those who copy or closely paraphrase the author's prose depiction. It will not prevent another person from manufacturing, selling, or using the medical device; only a patent can provide that protection to the inventor.

Similarly, copyright in a computer program protects only against copying or paraphrasing the sequence of commands (whether in "source code" intelligible to humans or in "object code" which directly operates the computer). It does not prevent a person from replicating the process that the computer program implements, provided there is no copying of the program. Thus, a computer program might be designed to run certain tests and move certain machinery components in the course of producing a particular product. Copyright will prevent another from copying the program, but anyone is free—even by means of decoding the program (which has been held to be a "fair use")—to devise another method for running those tests and moving those components, perhaps manually or perhaps by devising another computer program that does

14.   35 U.S.C. §§ 101 et seq.

not track the commands or structure of the first program. If, however, the production process (which incorporates the computer program) is one that meets the requirements of novelty and nonobviousness under the patent law, a process patent can issue. This patent will preclude others who seek to use or to market the protected process, even by means of a computer program of altogether different configuration—and, indeed, even though the later program is independently originated.

In sum, copyright protection is much easier to secure and lasts much longer; patent protection is more powerful in curbing competitors. Both patent and copyright are enforced exclusively in the federal courts.[15] Appeals in patent cases are centrally channeled to the Court of Appeals for the Federal Circuit,[16] whereas the appellate channels in copyright cases are the usual, geographically dispersed ones.

B. *Trademarks*

The law of trademark protects words or pictures or other distinctive signs that identify the source of a product or service. Under state common law, a person commits the tort of unfair competition by "passing off" its product or service as that of another through deceptive or confusing use of words or pictures in identifying, advertising or packaging. The plaintiff must prove that its "mark" (or the shape or packaging of its product) has become "distinctive," i.e., has come to be identified by the consuming public principally with that person as the source of the product, and that the defendant's use of a similar mark on a similar product confuses a significant segment of the purchasing public. State and federal law permit owners of such marks to register them in a public record; such registration provides constructive notice and other advantages (typically evidentiary but some substantive). Suits under the federal Trademark Act (the Lanham Act)[17] are brought in federal court, whereas suits to enforce state common-law or statutory trademark rights may be brought in state courts. In either forum, the fundamental issues are the same: identification by the public of the mark with the plaintiff as the source (known as secondary meaning), and confusing use of the mark by the defendant on similar products or services.

Trademark rights generally begin when the mark is used in commerce (although a 1988 amendment of the Lanham Act made it possible to register a mark in the Patent and Trademark Office when there is merely "intent to use," subject to other conditions); they last so long as the mark is used and retains its secondary meaning. Some graphic

---

15. 28 U.S.C. § 1338(a).

16. *See generally* Herbert F. Schwartz, PATENT LAW AND PRACTICE (BNA Books 6th ed. 2008).

17. 15 U.S.C. §§ 1051 et seq.

works, or words in conjunction with graphic works, that function as trademarks are also eligible for copyright protection, although many are not protectible for reasons that will be discussed in the next chapter. The figure of Mickey Mouse is a particularly well-known example of an image that is protectible both by copyright and by trademark (as a symbol identifying Disney products and entertainment services). Copyright protection begins earlier, when a work is fixed in tangible form, and can be enforced against copiers even without proof of the plaintiff's use in commerce or of secondary meaning and confusion. Trademark protection is available for a longer period of time (potentially forever) and even against persons whose confusingly similar mark has been adopted independently and without copying from the plaintiff.

C.   *Copyright and Chattels*

It is, finally, useful to draw a distinction between copyright law and the body of law that regulates the ownership of tangible personal property ("chattels"). Copyright is a form of "intangible" property. The subject of copyright—such as the words of a poem or the notes of a song—can exist in the mind of the poet or composer, or can be communicated orally, without being embodied in any tangible medium. Even when thus embodied, it is possible for persons to recite a poem, sing a song, perform a play, or view a painting without having physical possession of the original physical embodiment of the creative work. (For example, the painting can be viewed by means of a reproduction as a poster or its image can be transmitted over the Internet.) The Copyright Act attempts to draw a clear distinction between the literary, musical or artistic "work" that is protected against unauthorized exploitation in various forms, and the physical object in which that work is embodied. It is possible to be the owner of one without being the owner of the other.

Although, for example, earlier copyright statutes referred to a "book" as the focus of copyright protection, the 1976 Act makes it clear that protection is for the "literary work" (i.e., the sequence of words or symbols) regardless whether the tangible medium in which that work is embodied is a book, an audio- or videodisk or in computer memory. A sculptor may create a bronze statue and sell it to another, who may in turn keep others from touching it and can place it on the back porch or in the basement; but the buyer does not have the right, accorded by copyright, to make and sell photographs or three-dimensional replicas of the statue. Those latter rights are held initially by the sculptor (as "author" of the sculptural work, under section 201(a) of the Act) and they may be retained by the sculptor despite the transfer of ownership of the physical object to another.

Section 202 of the Copyright Act expressly provides for the separation of copyright and chattel ownership, and sets forth default rules in the event of transfers:

> Ownership of a copyright, or of any of the exclusive rights under a copyright, is distinct from ownership of any material object in which the work is embodied. Transfer of ownership of any material object, including the copy or phonorecord in which the work is first fixed, does not of itself convey any rights in the copyrighted work embodied in the object; nor, in the absence of an agreement, does transfer of ownership of a copyright or of any exclusive rights under a copyright convey property rights in any material object.

There is, then, a presumption that the exclusive rights that make up the copyright are not transferred when the physical object—the manuscript, the canvas, the sculpture—is transferred. To have an effective transfer of the copyright, section 204(a) of the Copyright Act requires that there be "an instrument of conveyance, or a note or memorandum of the transfer, ... in writing and signed by the owner of the rights conveyed or such owner's duly authorized agent." In sum, copyright is transferable intangible property, but an effective voluntary transfer requires clear and signed written evidence, and will not be inferred from an outright sale of the tangible object in which the work is fixed. All of the conventional state rules of chattel ownership are applicable with regard to that object, and are almost without exception not displaced by the federal Copyright Act.

III. Copyright Office and Judicial Review

Much of the work that is done in the administration of the Copyright Act is in the hands of the Copyright Office and its head, the Register of Copyrights. The Office, *inter alia*, handles applications for copyright registration, records transfers and other documents relating to copyright, and issues regulations (in volume 37 of the Code of Federal Regulations) about such matters as ineligibility for copyright, setting and distributing fees under the various statutory compulsory-license provisions, and the mechanics of registration and deposit.

Unlike most other federal administrative agencies, which are housed within the executive branch, the Copyright Office lies technically within the Library of Congress and is thus an arm of the legislative branch; the Register is appointed by the Librarian of Congress. Nonetheless, the Office operates very much as a typical federal administrative agency, most clearly in its promulgation of regulations that are designed to implement the Copyright Act. Section 702 of the Act expressly grants that power to the Register, and other provisions of Chapter 7 give the

Register wide-ranging powers to run the Copyright Office and to be the voice of the U.S. Government in copyright matters.

An important provision in the Copyright Act with respect to the federal courts is section 701(e), which provides that (with very limited exceptions) "[A]ll actions taken by the Register of Copyrights under this title are subject to the provisions of the Administrative Procedure Act of June 11, 1946...." As with respect to judicial review of administrative agencies generally under the APA, courts give considerable deference to the regulations and other decisions and practices of the Copyright Office. Perhaps the most pertinent provision of the APA is 5 U.S.C. § 706(2)(A), which provides: "The reviewing court shall ... hold unlawful and set aside agency action, findings and conclusions found to be ... arbitrary, capricious, an abuse of discretion, or otherwise not in accordance with law...."

Thus, when the Register of Copyrights declines to register a submitted work, because the material deposited does not constitute copyrightable subject matter or because the claim is invalid for any other reason, this decision is subject to review in a federal court through application of the lenient "abuse of discretion" standard, a concession to the vast number of applications passed upon by the Copyright Office.[18] When, however, the Office registers a work, and the defendant in an infringement action asserts that the copyright is invalid, the courts treat this not as a direct and deferential review of the agency, but as a matter of law which is for the court to determine de novo.[19] This approach is buttressed by section 410(c) of the Copyright Act, which provides that a registration certificate issued within five years of first publication of a work (or before its publication) "shall constitute prima facie evidence of the validity of the copyright and of the facts stated in the certificate." In other words, although the registration is helpful as an evidentiary matter in the presentation of the plaintiff's case, it merely shifts the burden to the party challenging the validity of the copyright, an issue that then falls to the court to decide on its own.

On a wide range of issues, particularly when the application or interpretation of Copyright Office regulations or longstanding practices is called into play, courts quite uniformly give deference to the agency. This is generally viewed as dictated by the 1984 Supreme Court decision in *Chevron, U.S.A., Inc. v. Natural Resources Defense Council, Inc.*[20] Under the *Chevron* precedent, a court is to defer to an administrative agency whose interpretation of an ambivalent legislative provision is

---

18. Atari Games Corp. v. Oman, 979 F.2d 242 (D.C. Cir. 1992). *See also* Darden v. Peters, 488 F.3d 277 (4th Cir. 2007).

19. OddzOn Prods., Inc. v. Oman, 924 F.2d 346 (D.C. Cir. 1991); Coach, Inc. v. Peters, 386 F. Supp. 2d 495 (S.D.N.Y. 2005).

20. 467 U.S. 837 (1984).

"reasonable" or "permissible."[21] Courts have, for example, invoked this standard in affirming the Register's definition of terms within the complex statutory provisions delineating various compulsory licenses.[22] Even before the development of the *Chevron* standard, the Supreme Court had made it clear that courts should give weight to the statutory interpretation given by the Copyright Office, particularly when manifested in "contemporaneous and long continued construction ... by the agency charged to administer" the Act.[23]

21. *See* Broadcast Music, Inc. v. Roger Miller Music, Inc., 396 F.3d 762 (6th Cir. 2005) (holding Copyright Office's statutory interpretations are entitled to deference "if reasonable" while the Office's opinion letters are only entitled to respect if "persuasive"); Satellite Broad. & Commc'ns Ass'n of Am. v. Oman, 17 F.3d 344 (11th Cir. 1994) (court must defer even though Copyright Office interpretation disagrees with court's own earlier interpretation; regulations may be struck down only if they contradict "clear meaning" or "plain language" of the Copyright Act). *Cf.* Bonneville Int'l Corp. v. Peters, 347 F.3d 485, 490 n.9 (3d Cir. 2003) (disagreement whether to apply *Chevron* deference or so-called *Skidmore* deference).

22. Cablevision Sys. Dev. Co. v. Motion Picture Ass'n of Am., Inc., 836 F.2d 599 (D.C. Cir. 1988) (deference to "reasonable" agency interpretation is dictated both because of agency's expertise in dealing with a recurrent problem and because it is proper to allow agency to import policy choices when there is a statutory ambiguity). *See*

also Southco., Inc. v. Kanebridge Corp., 390 F.3d 276 (3d Cir. 2004) (giving deference to Copyright Office's decision to extend to part numbers the "longstanding practice of denying registration to short phrases"); Marascalco v. Fantasy, Inc., 953 F.2d 469 (9th Cir. 1991) ("We agree with the D.C. Circuit that the Register has the authority to interpret the copyright laws and that its interpretations are entitled to judicial deference if reasonable." (citing *Cablevision*, 836 F.2d at 607–10)).

23. Mazer v. Stein, 347 U.S. 201 (1954). *See also* De Sylva v. Ballentine, 351 U.S. 570 (1956) (dictum). *See* Morris v. Business Concepts, Inc., 283 F.3d 502, 505–06 (2d Cir. 2002) (agency's "specialized experience and broader investigations and information" warrant deference, even if *Chevron* standard does not apply (quoting United States v. Mead Corp., 533 U.S. 218, 220 (2001))). *But see* Cartoon Network LP v. CSC Holdings, Inc., 536 F.3d 121 (2d Cir. 2008) (declining to defer to Copyright Office's interpretation of "fixation.")

Chapter 2
THE SUBJECT MATTER OF COPYRIGHT

I. General Principles

Copyright extends to all varieties of literary, artistic and musical works. To be eligible for copyright protection, however, such works must satisfy additional criteria, which find their source in the constitutional copyright clause. Not only does this provision ensure that federal copyright may not be of perpetual duration, but it also mandates that the congressional grant of copyright be to "authors" for their "writings."

United States copyright law therefore requires that a work manifest "original authorship" in a special sense, to be discussed below, and that it be "fixed" in some tangible form. Indeed, precisely these constitutional requirements are reflected in the language of section 102(a) of the Copyright Act of 1976: "Copyright protection subsists, in accordance with this title, in original works of authorship fixed in any tangible medium of expression, now known or later developed, from which they can be perceived, reproduced, or otherwise communicated, either directly or with the aid of a machine or device."

A. *Original authorship*

The constitutional terms "author" and "writing" were given very broad interpretations by the first Congress, which in the first copyright statute, enacted in 1790, granted protection to "maps, charts and books." Those two terms were also broadly construed by the Supreme Court in two seminal, and relatively early, decisions. In *Burrow-Giles Lithographic Co. v. Sarony*,[1] decided in 1884, the Court was confronted with a constitutional challenge to Congress's inclusion of photographs in the Copyright Act. It was argued that the photographic process was a purely mechanical one requiring no authorship and that a photograph was not a "writing" as that term was conventionally understood. The Court, however, held that an author is anyone "to whom anything owes its origin," and that a writing is any "production" of an author that includes "all forms of writing, printing, engraving, etching, &c., by which the ideas in the mind of the author are given visible expression."[2] The Court noted that the photograph in litigation—a posed portrait of Oscar Wilde (reproduced on the cover of this volume)—exhibited "har-

1. 111 U.S. 53 (1884).   2. *Id.* at 58.

15

monious, characteristic, and graceful" placement of its subject and, rather than a purely mechanical reproduction, was "an original work of art, the product of plaintiff's intellectual invention, of which plaintiff is the author."[3]

Justice Holmes expanded the concept of "authorship" even further in *Bleistein v. Donaldson Lithographing Co.*,[4] in which the Supreme Court upheld copyright in a color poster drawing of circus performers. Even if the performers had been drawn from life while actually engaged in their circus endeavors, the posters would not for that reason fall outside copyright protection any more so than would a portrait painted by Velasquez or Whistler. "The copy is the personal reaction of an individual upon nature. Personality always contains something unique. It expresses its singularity even in handwriting, and a very modest grade of art has in it something irreducible, which is one man's alone. That something he may copyright...."[5] Although it was argued that the poster should be disqualified from copyright because it was a mere advertisement and not a work of "fine art" (a phrase that was then in the Copyright Act), Holmes rejected this argument in an often-cited and important passage:

> A picture is none the less a picture and none the less a subject of copyright that it is used for an advertisement....
>
> It would be a dangerous undertaking for persons trained only to the law to constitute themselves final judges of the worth of pictorial illustrations, outside of the narrowest and most obvious limits. At the one extreme, some works of genius would be sure to miss appreciation. Their very novelty would make them repulsive until the public had learned the new language in which their author spoke.... At the other end, copyright would be denied to pictures which appealed to a public less educated than the judge. Yet if they command the interest of any public, they have a commercial value—it would be bold to say that they have not an aesthetic and educational value—and the taste of any public is not to be treated with contempt.[6]

Just as Justice Holmes refused to restrict the domain of copyright to high art, other courts, similarly wary of judging the worth of literary and artistic productions, have declined to discern content-based constitutional limitations on copyrightable subject matter. Most notably, perhaps,

---

3. *Id.* at 60.

4. 188 U.S. 239 (1903). For a full examination of this decision see Diane Leenheer Zimmerman, *The Story of Bleistein v. Donaldson Lithographing Company: Originality as a Vehicle for Copyright Inclusivity, in* INTELLECTUAL PROPERTY STORIES 77 (Jane C. Ginsburg & Rochelle Cooper Dreyfuss eds., 2005).

5. *Bleistein*, 188 U.S. at 250.

6. *Id.* at 250–51.

the Fifth Circuit, in *Mitchell Bros. Film Group v. Cinema Adult Theater*,[7] rejected the defendant's endeavor to interpolate an obscenity exception into the constitutional grant of power to Congress to protect works of authorship. To the defendant's argument that pornographic films do not "promote the progress of science" and therefore fall outside Congress' purview, the court declared:

> The words of the copyright clause of the constitution do not require that *Writings* shall promote science or useful arts: they require that *Congress* shall promote those ends. It could well be argued that by passing general laws to protect all works, Congress better fulfills its designated ends than it would by denying protection to all books the contents of which were open to real or imagined objection.[8]

It is therefore well-established that "authorship" and "originality," not merit or purpose, are the requirements for copyright protection.[9] Moreover, these are readily found even in commonplace works of literature, art and music. "Originality" need not constitute an advance over the existing state of our culture. Thus, the patent requirements of "novelty" and "nonobviousness" are completely inapt in applying the law of copyright. In another well-known judicial passage, Learned Hand stated:

> [A]nticipation as such cannot invalidate a copyright. Borrowed the work must indeed not be, for a plagiarist is not himself pro tanto an "author"; but if by some magic a man who had never known it were to compose anew Keats's Ode on a Grecian Urn, he would be an "author," and, if he copyrighted it, others might not copy that poem, though they might of course copy Keats's.[10]

Indeed, even a copy of a work in the public domain—most obviously, a handmade copy of an old master painting—may be eligible for copyright protection because, as Holmes noted in *Bleistein*, it is inevitable that the copyist will bring some independent personality to his or her work. Copyright will be afforded if the copy is a "distinguishable variation," that is, if the author has contributed something more than a "merely trivial variation," something recognizably "his own." "Originality in this context 'means little more than a prohibition of actual

---

7.   604 F.2d 852 (5th Cir. 1979).

8.   *Id.* at 859–60, *quoting*, Phillips, *Copyright in Obscene Works: Some British and American Problems*, 6 ANGLO-AM.L.REV. 138, 165–66 (1977) (emphasis in original)

9.   *But see* Robert A. Gorman, *Copyright, Courts and Aesthetic Judgments: Abuse or Necessity?*, 25 COLUM. J.L. & ARTS 1 (2001).

(analyzing extent to which courts in fact honor the principle that merit is irrelevant to protection).

10.   Sheldon v. Metro–Goldwyn Pictures Corp., 81 F.2d 49, 54 (2d Cir. 1936). *See also* Feist Publ'ns, Inc. v. Rural Tel. Serv. Co., 499 U.S. 340 (1991).

copying.' No matter how poor artistically the 'author's' addition, it is enough if it be his own.''[11]

That said, what "his own" means may not be as clear as first appears. The issue calls for related inquiries into whether the creator must be a human being, and how much control the human creator must exercise over the work's creation. Put another way, to the extent the work emerges from random or automated processes, is it nonetheless a work of "authorship"?

With respect to works in whose creation machines intervened, an initial distinction is warranted between types of machine assistance. Some machines or devices, such as pens, typewriters, and word processing programs, supply the tools for creation, but are not integral to the resulting work. That work remains constant, whether it is expressed in handwriting, or on a computer printout or screen. The only "author" of the work is the creator of the expression, whatever the tools employed to express it. Thus, a federal district court has held that scanning a prior work into a computer, without otherwise modifying its content, "confer[s] no authorship" on the person doing the scanning; the work is the same, despite the machine-generated change of medium.[12]

Other machines, however—notably cameras and sound recording equipment—participate in the creation of a work that would not exist but for the medium made possible by the machinery. Pictorial images may exist in a variety of media, but photographs require cameras. A musical composition exists independently of its medium of fixation, but a sound recording must be recorded. Does it therefore follow that one who employs this machinery is not an "author," and that the author, if there is one, is the machine?

As *Burrow-Giles v. Sarony* illustrates, early challenges to the copyrightability of photographs did raise this sort of objection, coupling it with the further claim that not only is a camera a machine, it is a machine that reproduces reality; no one (other than the—capital C—Creator) can be the "author" of things in nature; therefore the photographer may be a skilled craftsperson in the manipulation of the machine, but he is no author. The Supreme Court responded that perhaps the "ordinary production of a photograph" mindlessly captured reality, but the photograph at issue showed detailed—even compulsive—composition of light effects, camera angle, costuming and posing of the subject and background. In short, Napoleon Sarony's carefully contrived image dripped Art, and amply met the Constitutional standard for the "writ-

---

11. Alfred Bell & Co. v. Catalda Fine Arts, Inc., 191 F.2d 99 (2d Cir. 1951) (quoting Hoague–Sprague Corp. v. Frank C. Meyer, Inc., 31 F.2d 583, 586 (E.D.N.Y. 1929)).

12. *See* S.T.R. Indus., Inc. v. Palmer Indus., Inc., No. 96 C 4251, 1999 WL 258455 (N.D. Ill. April 9, 1999).

ing" of an "author," in that it entailed a "form in which the ideas in the mind of the [photographer] are given visible expression."

But what of machine-assisted outputs in whose production human intervention is more attenuated? The caselaw exemplified by the Second Circuit's 1951 decision in *Bell v. Catalda*, upholding the copyrightability of mezzotint engravings of Old Master paintings, admits the possibility of what one might call "accidental authorship," creativity stumbled upon rather than summoned as an act of will. Judge Frank's exposition of unintended acts of creation, notably images generated by bad eyesight, claps of thunder, and frustrated flinging of sponges, supplies the most famous example. Admittedly, the author accomplishes an act of will when she "adopts" the accidental effect as her own, but arguably the creative act occurs at the image's genesis, not only at its subsequent acceptance. If "adoption" suffices to confer authorship, it might follow that outputs identically produced, such as words, musical notes or images randomly generated by a computer program, would differently qualify as works of authorship depending on which of several outputs the "author" selected. To require instead a human role, even if unintentional (as in *Bell v. Catalda*), at the outset as well as at the conclusion of the generative process might help avoid anomalous outcomes.[13]

B.   *Originality under the 1976 Copyright Act*

The principal source of legislative history for the 1976 Copyright Act, House Report No. 94–1476 (1976)—hereinafter referred to simply as the House Report—endorsed the expansive definition of the earlier cases. In discussing the phrase "original works of authorship" as it appears in section 102 of the Act, the House Report states that this undefined phrase "is intended to incorporate without change the standard of originality established by the courts under the present [1909] copyright statute. This standard does not include requirements of novelty, ingenuity, or esthetic merit, and there is no intention to enlarge the standard of copyright protection to require them."[14]

---

13. Not all courts are as welcoming of randomness in creative endeavors. In *Kelley v. Chicago Park District*, 635 F.3d 290 (7th Cir. 2011), the Seventh Circuit ruled that an installation of wildflowers planted in Chicago's Grant Park lacked sufficient authorship because the patterns of wildflowers primarily resulted from natural forces. The court seemed to distinguish works that incorporate living elements, such as a sculpture composed partly of plantings of flowers, from productions consisting entirely of living elements: "To the extent that seeds or seedlings can be considered a 'medium of expression,' they originate in nature, and natural forces—not the intellect of the gardener—determine their form, growth, and appearance." The court appears not to have considered whether the "gardener's" artistic vision includes the alterations nature will bring, and whether the "gardening" was designed to channel nature to that vision. In those circumstances, a distinction based on the ratio of "natural" to human-made elements may not be warranted.

14. H.R. Rep. No. 94–1476, at 51 (1976).

Despite this broad disclaimer, the Supreme Court has made explicit what was perhaps to be inferred from the earlier jurisprudence: that, in addition to the requirement of noncopying, there is a requirement that a work show some modicum of creativity before it is eligible for copyright protection. This latter requirement was delineated and applied by the Supreme Court in its very significant decision in 1991 in *Feist Publications, Inc. v. Rural Telephone Service Co.*[15] The issue there was whether a telephone company could claim a valid copyright in a white-page directory that listed names (accompanied by telephone number and town) in alphabetical order. The Court stated:

> Original, as the term is used in copyright, means only that the work was independently created by the author (as opposed to copied from other works), and that it possesses at least some minimal degree of creativity.... To be sure, the requisite level of creativity is extremely low; even a slight amount will suffice. The vast majority of works make the grade quite easily, as they possess some creative spark, "no matter how crude, humble or obvious" it might be.[16]

But the "grade" must nonetheless be "made," and in Rural Telephone's case, the Court concluded that even though the plaintiff had engaged in useful efforts, and did not copy its directory from others, "[t]he end product is a garden-variety white pages directory, devoid of even the slightest trace of creativity."[17] Alphabetical sequencing was found to be "time-honored," "commonplace," and indeed "practically inevitable."[18]

The requirement that a work, to manifest originality, must show some modicum of creativity, has been long reflected in regulations promulgated by the Copyright Office. 37 C.F.R. § 202.1(a) states:

> The following are examples of works not subject to copyright and applications for registration of such works cannot be entertained: ... Words and short phrases such as names, titles, and slogans; familiar symbols or designs; mere variations of typographic ornamentation, lettering or coloring; mere listing of ingredients or contents.

Short phrases and commonplace designs are thought to lack minimal creativity, or are likely to have been copied from others, or are too useful as literary or artistic "building blocks" for other works, so that they should be left free for others to use as well, without undue concern for inviting possible litigation.

---

15.   499 U.S. 340, 346 (1991).   **17.**   *Id.* at 362.

16.   *Id.* at 345.   **18.**   *Id.* at 363.

Not surprisingly, the decided cases manifest some difference of view as to whether the copyright claimant has manifested a "modicum of creativity" or whether the allegedly infringed materials are too short, familiar or commonplace.[19] The more a phrase is generic or descriptive, or the more it gives instructions to accomplish a functional objective, the more that courts are inclined not to permit copyright to interfere with others seeking to make practical use of the language. Courts have thus refused to extend copyright to such phrases as "priority message: contents require immediate attention".[20] But many courts (perhaps with the admonition of Justice Holmes in mind) are reluctant, not only with respect to literary and musical works,[21] but particularly in the case of graphic works—and now, computerized audiovisual works—to find particular expressions too trivial for protection.[22]

Judicial uncertainty in applying the "modicum of creativity" standard may reflect an ambiguity—present also in the Copyright Office Regulation—in the concept of "modicum." That is, is the phrase to be understood quantitatively or qualitatively? A short phrase may in fact be very creative—think of the headlines to news stories—yet also be very brief. But if brevity is the soul of wit, is it nonetheless also a bar to copyright? The "building blocks" rationale underlying the Regulation's exclusions makes sense if the objective is to prevent private claims of right in elements so basic as to belie anyone's "creation." By contrast, if

19. *Compare* Tin Pan Apple Inc. v. Miller Brewing Co., 30 U.S.P.Q.2d 1791 (S.D.N.Y. 1994) ("Hugga–Hugga" and "Brr" are "more complex than [a] single drum beat and . . . in that complexity lies, arguably at least, the fruit of creativity"), *with* Perma Greetings Inc. v. Russ Berrie & Co., 598 F. Supp. 445 (E.D. Mo. 1984) ("along the way take time to smell the flowers" not copyrightable).

20. Magic Mktg. v. Mailing Servs., 634 F. Supp. 769 (W.D. Pa. 1986). *See also* Southco, Inc. v. Kanebridge Corp., 390 F.3d 276 (3d Cir. 2004) (en banc) (holding part numbers used to assemble machine parts not copyrightable); Spilman v. Mosby–Yearbook, Inc., 115 F. Supp. 2d 148 (D. Mass. 2000) (holding grammatical alterations and "stylistic tweaking" are not copyrightable); Apple Computer v. Microsoft Corp., 799 F. Supp. 1006 (N.D. Cal. 1992) (holding phrase "Get Info," used as part of computer graphical interface, was not copyrightable).

21. For musical works, *see, e.g.,* Santrayll v. Burrell, 39 U.S.P.Q.2d 1052 (S.D.N.Y.1996) (distinctive rhythmic repetition of phrase "uh oh" held sufficiently

original to survive motion for summary judgment); Swirsky v. Carey, 376 F.3d 841 (9th Cir. 2004 (seven-note sequence in the first measure of the plaintiff's song—apparently identical to "For He's a Jolly Good Fellow" and "The Bear Went Over the Mountain"—sufficiently satisfied the minimal-creativity requirement as to warrant submitting the issue of originality to a jury). Literary works, *see, e.g.,* Innovation Ventures LLC v. N2G Distrib. Inc., 635 F. Supp. 2d 632 (E.D. Mich. 2008) (label on vitamin supplements); Sebastian Int'l, Inc. v. Consumer Contact (PTY) Ltd., 664 F. Supp. 909 (D.N.J.1987), *rev'd on other grounds,* 847 F.2d 1093 (3d Cir.1988) (shampoo label).

22. *See* Mattel, Inc. v. Goldberger Doll Mfg. Co., 365 F.3d 133 (2d Cir. 2004) (basic features of doll's face); Atari Games Corp. v. Oman, 888 F.2d 878 (D.C. Cir. 1989) (remand to Register of Copyrights, who had refused to register video game with simple artwork). *But see* John Muller & Co. v. N.Y. Arrows Soccer Team, 802 F.2d 989 (8th Cir. 1986) (soccer team logo, of arrows-within-arrows, lacking in original authorship).

the goal is simply to expel expressions that fail to cross some unstated threshold of heft regardless of their level of creativity, then it is not clear what if any sensible copyright policy the exclusion advances.

C. Fixed in a tangible medium of expression

As already noted, the additional requirement in section 102 of the Copyright Act of 1976—that works to be protectible by copyright must be "fixed in any tangible medium of expression, now known or later developed, from which they can be perceived, reproduced, or otherwise communicated, either directly or with the aid of a machine or device"—is derived from the constitutional requirement that Congress protect "writings," as that word has been liberally construed. Only rarely has the vast enlargement of the word "writings" been questioned. Justice Douglas did so, in a 1954 concurring opinion,[23] in which he stated that it was not obvious to him that "statuettes, book ends, clocks, lamps, door knockers, candlesticks, inkstands, chandeliers, piggy banks, sundials, salt and pepper shakers, fish bowls, casseroles, and ash trays," all of which had been registered for copyright in the Copyright Office, are "writings" in the constitutional sense.[24] Despite Justice Douglas's doubts, there is no question that today these objects would be eligible matter for copyright protection, subject to certain limitations on the protectibility of shapes of useful articles.[25] Moreover, the Copyright Act has since been amended so as to embrace within copyrightable subject matter such "writings" as architectural works, computer programs (even though intended to communicate only with a computer), and sound recordings (even though intended to communicate only to the human ear).

The statutory requirement that a work be "fixed" is of great significance for the application of the statute within our federal system. Federal copyright attaches immediately upon a work's "creation," i.e., when it is "fixed" for the first time, with the authority of the author, in a form that is "sufficiently permanent or stable to permit it to be perceived, reproduced, or otherwise communicated for a period of more than transitory duration."[26] Before a work is "fixed," states may grant the author protection against copying under their own statutory or common-law rules; an example would be an improvised comedic performance—or a "live" interview—being secretly taped by a member of the audience. But if, say, the comedic author has previously reduced his or her routine to writing, or captured it on an audiotape, the illicit recorder

23. Mazer v. Stein, 347 U.S. 201 (1954).
24. Id. at 221 (Douglas, J., concurring).
25. See infra pages 47–51.

26. Definitions of "created" and "fixed" in 17 U.S.C. § 101.

in the audience may be pursued only under the federal Copyright Act and only in a federal court.[27]

The statute contemplates that a work may be fixed either in a "copy" or a "phonorecord." The latter is defined in section 101 as a material object in which sounds (other than a motion picture soundtrack) are fixed and from which they can then be communicated, either directly or with the aid of a machine. Examples of a "phonorecord" are a 33–rpm vinyl disk, an audiotape, a compact disk or a computer hard-drive on which music has been recorded. A "copy" is a material object (other than a phonorecord) in which a work is fixed and from which it can be communicated. In general, a copy communicates a work to the eye, while a phonorecord communicates a work to the ear. In various situations under the statute, the distinction will matter; but fixation in either kind of tangible object is sufficient to bring a work under the federal statute.

It is important to bear in mind that once a work is "fixed," and therefore within the scope of the Copyright Act's coverage, it no longer matters for purposes of infringement whether the work was copied without authorization from a fixed or unfixed source. Fixation is the threshold which all works must cross to qualify for federal copyright protection, but once across, the work exists independently of any particular material object in which it may be concretized. Thus, for example, copying a protected dramatic work from a book containing the text of the play will infringe the work (assuming no applicable exceptions), but so will the unauthorized taping or transcription of the dialogue from a live performance of the work.

1.   Musical Performers' Fixation Right

Although the point of "creation" or "fixation" is ordinarily the focal point for dividing federal and state power to bar unauthorized copying, there is one significant exception. In 1994 Congress—implementing the treaty known as the Agreement on Trade Related Aspects of Intellectual Property (TRIPs)—enacted section 1101 of the Copyright Act, which protects against unauthorized fixing or broadcasting of "the sounds or sounds and images of a live musical performance" (what has come to be known as "bootleg" recordings or broadcasts), and against the distribution of copies or phonorecords of those unauthorized fixations. Note that section 1101 covers only the performance, not the underlying work of authorship. Thus, a "bootleg" recording of a performance that improvises a musical composition will violate the section 1101 fixation right of the players, but because the recording of the improvised musical compo-

---

27.   17 U.S.C. § 301.

sition was unauthorized, it does not count as a "fixation" for purposes of bringing the musical composition within federal copyright;[28] any claim in the composition must lie at state law. Note that section 1101 protects performances of only musical works, and not literary works as well.

Two aspects of section 1101 place it in tension with the constitutional copyright clause. First, because the provision addresses performances that, at the moment of their rendering, are not fixed with their creators' authorization, it is not clear that the statutory subject matter is a "writing" in the constitutional sense. At least, if the term implies a pre-existing, rather than incipient, concretization, then Congress may not have power, under the copyright clause, to protect unfixed works. Second, where the copyright clause empowers Congress to secure copyrights "for limited times," section 1101 lacks any express time limitation upon the enforcement of the provision. Thus, the unauthorized distribution in 2200 of a "bootleg" recording made in 2000 apparently would violate the statute. Nonetheless, courts have upheld section 1101 as an exercise of Congress's Interstate Commerce power rather than its power under the Copyright Clause of the Constitution.[29] A contentious debate continues as to whether Congress may avoid the limitations expressly set forth in the latter constitutional provision by anchoring its powers instead in the Interstate Commerce Clause. In any event, section 1101(d) provides that state common-law or statutory rights and remedies directed against such "bootlegging" of live musical performances are not meant to be annulled.

2. Special rule for transmissions—Simultaneous fixation

Under the definition of "fixed" in section 101 of the Act, a radio or television broadcast or other transmission simultaneously recorded by the broadcaster or other transmitting entity is "fixed" and thus within the coverage of the Copyright Act. For example, a television program of a professional sports event—which embodies original authorship in its camera-work and its selection of which camera images to display to the home viewer—falls within the federal Act by virtue of its recording simultaneously with its "live" transmission. Unauthorized recording or public performance of such a broadcast by others may thus constitute a federal copyright infringement.

---

28. Under the section 101 definition, "A work is "fixed" in a tangible medium of expression when its embodiment in a copy or phonorecord, *by or under the authority of the author* ..." (emphasis supplied).

29. United States v. Moghadam, 175 F.3d 1269 (11th Cir. 1999); Kiss Catalog, Ltd. v. Passport Int'l Prods., Inc., 405 F.

Supp. 2d 1169 (C.D. Cal. 2005). *See also* United States v. Martignon, 492 F.3d 140 (2d Cir. 2007) (upholding constitutionality of 18 U.S.C. § 2319A(a)(1),(3), the criminal counterpart to 17 U.S.C. § 1101, on the ground that the criminal provision was not a "copyright law").

Note that the work of authorship in this instance is the "work consisting of sounds, images, or both, that are being transmitted"—that is, the transmitted audiovisual recording of the sporting event, not the event itself. The simultaneous-fixation rule, by bringing the audiovisual recording of the game within the subject matter of copyright, makes it unlawful as a matter of federal law to copy the audiovisual work conveyed in the transmission, but it is not a violation of federal law for a third party to film the game as it is being played. (Such filming may, however, violate a variety of state laws as well as the terms and conditions of entry to the stadium.) While the baseball or football games are not themselves copyrightable, the outcome would be the same even if the subject matter of the third-party filming, such as an improvised dramatic work, were potentially copyrightable. Because the improvised play as it is being performed is not yet fixed, an audience member who smuggles a videocamera into the theater is not violating the federal copyright rights of the performer-authors because their work has not yet crossed the threshold into federal coverage. If the live improvisation is simultaneously recorded and transmitted, then the audiovisual recording is protected against copying from the transmission (assuming no applicable exceptions), but because the simultaneous-fixation doctrine covers only the audiovisual work, the copyright would not extend to the underlying literary elements. As a result, writing down the dialogue, rather than copying the images, from the transmission would not violate the federal rights of the creators of the improvisation, although it might violate state statutory or common law rights.

3. Fixation and digital media

The most significant issues arising in recent years regarding the "fixed in any tangible medium of expression" requirement have concerned new technologies. In the 1980s, a number of cases addressed challenges to the "fixed" nature of video games, typically as on view in game arcades but also as played on game consoles for home viewing. Defendants argued that the constantly changing images on the video game screen, subject to seemingly endless varieties of manipulation by the human user, rendered them "unfixed" and therefore freely subject to copying under federal law. The courts, however, consistently held to the contrary. As one court found, "[T]here is always a repetitive sequence of a substantial portion of the sights and sounds of the game, and many aspects of the display remain constant from game to game regardless of how the player operates the controls."[30]

More significantly, courts also rejected the argument that the program that creates screen displays (an application program) or that

30. Williams Elecs., Inc. v. Artic Int'l,
Inc., 685 F.2d 870 (3d Cir. 1982).

directly operates a computer (an operating-system program) is ineligible for copyright protection because it is embodied in a disk or in computer hardware that cannot be directly deciphered by a human. As to video games, it was held that "The printed circuit boards are tangible objects from which the audiovisual works may be perceived for a period of time more than transitory. That the audiovisual works cannot be viewed without a machine does not mean the works are not fixed."[31]

It was a natural step, but an important one, to hold that computer programs more generally—whether application programs or operating-system programs—are "literary works" (section 101 defines them as works "expressed in words, numbers, or other verbal or numerical symbols or indicia") that are eligible for federal copyright protection once they are "fixed" in computer hardware, such as semiconductor chips.[32] The fact that some such programs are designed to interact with the computer and not directly to generate human-readable screen displays does not negate compliance with either the "original authorship" requirement or the "fixed in a tangible medium" requirement of section 102(a) of the Act.

A question that remained after the decisions in the 1980s regarding the storage of computer programs within hardware components was whether a work is "created" (conceptualized and fixed) for purposes of federal copyright when it is entered into a computer's temporary memory, or random access memory (RAM), which is lost when the computer is shut down. Because the consequences of determining that a work is "fixed," and therefore constitutes a "copy" when it enters temporary memory are even more significant with respect to the inquiry whether making a "RAM copy" is infringing, we will address this issue in Chapter 6, in the context of what is a "copy" within the meaning of the section 106(1) exclusive right "to reproduce the work in copies."

D. Categories of works

After setting forth the requirements of original authorship and fixation in a tangible medium, section 102(a) as originally enacted in 1976 goes on to itemize a number of subject-matter categories for works of authorship, which "shall include" literary works, musical works, dramatic works, pantomimes and choreographic works, PGS (pictorial, graphic, and sculptural) works, motion pictures and other audiovisual works, and sound recordings. "Architectural works" were added in 1990. Most of these categories of works are defined in section 101. Although

---

31. Midway Mfg. Co. v. Dirkschneider, 543 F. Supp. 466 (D. Neb. 1981). *See also* Stern Elecs., Inc. v. Kaufman, 669 F.2d 852 (2d Cir. 1982).

32. Apple Computer, Inc. v. Franklin Computer Corp., 714 F.2d 1240 (3d Cir. 1983).

Congress did not intend these listed categories to exhaust its constitutional power to accord copyright protection, it appears that almost every litigated claim of copyright protection has been with respect to a work that fits comfortably within the itemized categories, and it is difficult to think of a creative fixed work that does not.

The statutory categories are very broadly defined. "Literary works," for example, are defined as "works, other than audiovisual works, expressed in words, numbers, or other verbal or numerical symbols or indicia, regardless of the nature of the material objects, such as books, periodicals, manuscripts, phonorecords, film, tapes, disks, or cards, in which they are embodied." The House Report makes it clear that by using the term "literary," Congress did not intend to import any requirement of "literary merit or qualitative value," and that the term includes such works as catalogues, directories, and other compilations of data, and that computer programs and databases are embraced within the subject matter of section 102.[33] Finally, it should be noted once again that the definition of "literary works" makes a sharp distinction between the work itself and the variety of physical forms in which it can be manifested; copyright protects only the former, while the physical object can be protected under state personal property law (which is distinct from and not preempted by the rights accorded under the federal Act).

II. The Distinction Between Idea and Expression

Copyright protects against the unauthorized copying of an author's "expression," i.e., the particular pattern of words, lines and colors, or musical notes, and not against the copying of an underlying idea. This is a principal way in which copyright "promotes the progress of science and useful arts," as contemplated by the Constitution, and is also a principal way in which the scope of copyright protection differs from that of patent protection. Although securing a copyright is easy—all that need be done is to "fix" an independently created work embodying a "modicum" of creativity—and although copyright lasts much longer than a patent, the scope of copyright protection is much "thinner" because it is limited to the expression. Although copyright protects against more than literal copying, and also bars paraphrase, abridgment and other "derivative works," it does not afford an exclusive right to ideas, methods, facts and the like, no matter how startling the discovery or arduous the effort.

A. *Development of the distinction*

The major judicial pronouncement of this principle can be found in *Baker v. Selden*,[34] decided by the Supreme Court in 1879. There, Selden wrote a book setting out a new system of bookkeeping, consisting

33. H.R. Rep. No. 94–1476, at 54 (1976).
34. 101 U.S. 99 (1879).

primarily of certain forms, with various columns and headings, embodying his system. Baker copied the forms with minor changes. Selden claimed that Baker's forms infringed his copyright; he contended that anyone using his bookkeeping system would have to use forms substantially similar to his. The Court framed the issue for decision as "whether the exclusive property in a system of book-keeping can be claimed, under the law of copyright, by means of a book in which that system is explained."[35] It held that copyright in a work that describes a practical method, system or process does not prevent others from putting that method, system or process into use; to secure such exclusive rights, the inventor must satisfy the more exacting requirements of the patent law.

> To give to the author of the book an exclusive property in the art described therein, when no examination of its novelty has ever been officially made, would be a surprise and a fraud upon the public. That is the province of letters patent, not of copyright. . . .
>
> . . . He may copyright his book, if he pleases; but that only secures to him the exclusive right of printing and publishing his book.[36]

The Court went on to hold that if it was necessary for Baker to copy Selden's forms in order to make use of the latter's unpatented accounting system, then such copying would not be a copyright infringement.

> [W]here the art [that a work] teaches cannot be used without employing the methods and diagrams used to illustrate the book, or such as are similar to them, such methods and diagrams are to be considered as necessary incidents to the art, and given therewith to the public; not given for the purpose of publication in other works explanatory of the art, but for the purpose of practical application. . . .
>
> . . . [The bookkeeping system] was not patented, and is open and free to the use of the public. And, of course, in using the art, the ruled lines and headings of accounts must necessarily be used as incident to it.[37]

Despite the Supreme Court's suggestion that the forms appended to Selden's book were subject to copyright and could be infringed by persons copying the forms for "explanatory" purposes rather than for "use," the Court somewhat confusingly concluded its decision by stating:

35. *Id.* at 101.
36. *Id.* at 102–03.
37. *Id.* at 103–04.

"The conclusion to which we have come is, that blank account-books are not the subject of copyright."[38]

Baker therefore stands for at least three important propositions in copyright law: (1) Copyright in a work does not cover ideas, concepts and systems described therein, but only the form of expression in which they are communicated; (2) if in order to duplicate or put into use an unprotected idea, concept, or system, it is necessary substantially to copy another's otherwise copyrightable expression, such copying is not an infringement; and (3) blank forms—i.e., forms used for the recording of information rather than for explanation—are not eligible for copyright.[39]

The first of these propositions, the most important, is now embodied in section 102(b) of the Copyright Act: "In no case does copyright protection for an original work of authorship extend to any idea, procedure, process, system, method of operation, concept, principle, or discovery, regardless of the form in which it is described, explained, illustrated, or embodied in such work." In the words of the House Report, section 102(b) "in no way enlarges or contracts the scope of copyright protection" under prior law; its purpose "is to restate ... that the basic dichotomy between expression and idea remains unchanged."[40]

Apart from leaving in the public domain unpatentable or unpatented processes and systems, one of the most important impacts of the idea/expression dichotomy is in the field of fictional literature. Copyright protects against the unauthorized copying or paraphrasing of a short story, novel or drama; it also bars other unauthorized "derivative works," such as abridgments and translations; and it even protects the author against the copying of a detailed story line, with its plot incidents and sequences, even though the copyist uses altogether different language for description and dialogue.[41] But copyright protection does not bar another from copying the more general patterns, themes or story ideas, or character prototypes.[42] Where the line is drawn in fictional works—and indeed in all works, including music and art—between protected expression and unprotected idea is not subject to a litmus test. As Learned Hand said: "Obviously, no principle can be stated as to when an imitator has gone beyond copying the 'idea,' and has borrowed its 'expression.' Decisions must therefore inevitably be *ad hoc*."[43]

38. *Id.* at 105.

39. For a thorough analysis of the decision and how its progeny addressed these propositions (and others), see Pamela Samuelson, *The Story of* Baker v. Selden*: Sharpening the Distinction Between Authorship and Invention, in* INTELLECTUAL PROPERTY STORIES, 159–93 (Jane C. Ginsburg and Rochelle Cooper Dreyfuss eds., 2005).

40. H.R. Rep. No. 94–1476, at 57 (1976).

41. Sheldon v. Metro–Goldwyn Pictures Corp., 81 F.2d 49 (2d Cir. 1936).

42. Nichols v. Universal Pictures Corp., 45 F.2d 119 (2d Cir. 1930).

43. Peter Pan Fabrics, Inc. v. Martin Weiner Corp., 274 F.2d 487 (2d Cir. 1960). *See generally* Mannion v. Coors Brewing Co., 377 F. Supp. 2d 444 (S.D.N.Y. 2005).

It is also generally acknowledged that the determination of how generously to mark off protectible "expression" will depend on the nature of the work, for example, whether the work is fictional or fanciful, on the one hand, or is factual or functional, on the other. In the latter works, too generous a characterization of material as protectible expression runs a greater risk of interfering with the statutory policy favoring free access to discoveries, methods, systems and the like. Because of the close interrelationship between the characterization of elements of works as "ideas" and policies supporting free copying, we suggest that "in copyright law, an 'idea' is not an epistemological concept, but a legal conclusion prompted by notions—often unarticulated and unproven—of appropriate competition. Thus, copyright doctrine attaches the label "idea" to aspects of works which, if protected, would (or, we fear, might) preclude, or render too expensive, subsequent authors' endeavors."[44]

The second principle extracted from *Baker* is that even normally protectible material in a copyright-protected work may be freely reproduced when that is necessary in order to use the underlying unprotected system. It is often said in these cases, in which there are limited expressive options, that there is a "merger" between idea and expression, and that the latter becomes unprotected as well. Courts analyze these "merger" situations in at least two different ways: one leads to the conclusion that the work, although copyrightable, is rarely susceptible to infringement; the other denies copyrightability altogether.

The former approach is exemplified in *Continental Casualty Co. v. Beardsley,*[45] in which the claim of copyright was in the text of a set of legal and business documents—a bond that had been drafted so as to cover the replacement of lost securities, along with an affidavit, a contract form, and a form of letter and board resolutions. The Court of Appeals for the Second Circuit held that the language of the forms was copyrightable because the forms were not blank as in *Baker*; but the court also held that because use of the forms necessitated copying them essentially verbatim, such copying would be permitted in order that the underlying business and legal "system" not be monopolized by way of copyright. The court thus granted a "thin" level of copyright protection:

> [The pertinent court decisions] indicate that in the fields of insurance and commerce the use of specific language in forms and documents may be so essential to accomplish a desired result and so integrated with the use of a legal or commercial

Application of the idea–expression distinction is discussed *infra* Chapter 6 (at pages 137–40).

44. Jane Ginsburg, *No "Sweat"? Copyright and Other Protection of Works of In-* *formation After* Feist v. Rural Telephone, 92 COLUM. L. REV. 338, 346 (1992).

45. 253 F.2d 702 (2d Cir. 1958).

conception that the proper standard of infringement is one which will protect as far as possible the copyrighted language and yet allow free use of the thought beneath the language. The evidence here shows that [the copyist] in so far as it has used the language of [the copyrighted] forms has done so only as incidental to its use of the underlying idea.[46]

A different and well-known formulation of the "merger" doctrine is found in the case of *Morrissey v. Procter & Gamble Co.*,[47] where the Court of Appeals for the First Circuit held certain rules of a "sweepstakes" promotional contest uncopyrightable. The court found that there were only a limited number of ways that a person could vary the statement of the contest rules while making allowable use of the unprotected contest format. It stated:

> When the uncopyrightable subject matter is very narrow, so that "the topic necessarily requires," if not only one form of expression, at best only a limited number, to permit copyrighting would mean that a party or parties, by copyrighting a mere handful of forms, could exhaust all possibilities of future use of the substance.[48]

The principle that copyright should not be extended even to "expression" when there is a finite range of ways to express an underlying subject matter has also been employed in a variety of fields, from art, where it has been held that a piece of jewelry in the shape of a bee with small jewels arrayed on its surface reflected an unprotectible "idea,"[49] to computer programs.[50]

Closely related to the distinction between protectible expression and unprotectible idea is the distinction between expression and fact. A fact, or a group of facts, no matter how significant or how laborious the effort to find it, cannot be protected by copyright against use, duplication or communication by others.[51] That facts are unprotectible is supported in part by the exclusion of any "discovery" from copyrightable subject matter by virtue of section 102(b) of the Copyright Act of 1976, and in part by the observation that no person can be said to be the "original author" of a fact which he or she uncovers. Thus, the facts—and even speculations as to facts—that are unearthed by an historian or biogra-

---

46. *Id.* at 706.

47. 379 F.2d 675 (1st Cir. 1967).

48. *Id.* at 678.

49. Herbert Rosenthal Jewelry Corp. v. Kalpakian, 446 F.2d 738 (9th Cir. 1971). *See* Mannion v. Coors Brewing Co., 377 F. Supp. 2d 444 (S.D.N.Y. 2005).

50. *See, e.g.*, Computer Assocs. Int'l v. Altai, 982 F.2d 693 (2d Cir. 1992).

51. Feist Publ'ns, Inc. v. Rural Tel. Serv. Co., 499 U.S. 340 (1991). However, when the facts are selected, coordinated, or organized in an "original" manner, the treatment of the facts can yield a protectable compilation. The issue of "compilation copyright" is discussed *infra* pages 37–41.

pher can be reiterated by a copyist, provided the latter uses his or her own expressive language to do so.[52] Although many courts under both the 1909 and 1976 Acts appeared to sustain copyright in factual research, and in data embodied in compilations, on the basis of "sweat of the brow"—the time, effort and expense invested in unearthing information—this approach has been unequivocally rejected by the Supreme Court. In *Feist Publications, Inc. v. Rural Telephone Service Co.*,[53] decided in 1991, the Court discussed the "fact/expression dichotomy" and recognized that the "thin copyright" concept followed from the nonprotectability of facts:

> This inevitably means that the copyright in a factual compilation is thin. Notwithstanding a valid copyright, a subsequent compiler remains free to use the facts contained in another's publication to aid in preparing a competing work, so long as the competing work does not feature the same selection and arrangement. . . . Facts, whether alone or as part of a compilation, are not original and therefore may not be copyrighted.[54]

The final significant *Baker* principle is its holding that "blank forms" are not copyrightable. This is reflected in the text of section 202.1(c) of the Copyright Office Regulations:

> The following are examples of works not subject to copyright and applications for registration of such works cannot be entertained: . . . blank forms, such as time cards, graph paper, account books, diaries, bank checks, scorecards, address books, report forms, order forms and the like, which are designed for recording information and do not in themselves convey information.

The rationale for excluding protection for blank forms is partly that the forms are intentionally designed to be put into use in the course of implementing an unprotectible system. Moreover, a blank form with little or no writing might be thought to lack "original authorship" as required of all copyrightable works. Not surprisingly, courts have disagreed as to whether forms containing various degrees of text and graphic design should or should not be treated as "blank" and therefore unprotectible under *Baker* and regulation 202.1.[55]

---

52. Miller v. Universal City Studios, Inc., 650 F.2d 1365 (5th Cir. 1981); Hoehling v. Universal City Studios, Inc., 618 F.2d 972 (2d Cir. 1980). For discussions of the concept of "expression" in works of history and of the *Hoehling* decision, *compare* Robert A. Gorman, *Fact or Fancy: The Implications for Copyright*, 29 J. COPYRIGHT SOC'Y 560 (1982), *with* Jane C. Ginsburg, *Sabotaging and Reconstructing History: A Com-ment on the Scope of Copyright Protection in Works of History After* Hoehling v. Universal City Studios, 29 J. COPYRIGHT SOC'Y 647 (1982).

53. 499 U.S. 340 (1991).

54. *Id.* at 349–50.

55. *Compare* Bibbero Sys. v. Colwell Sys., Inc., 893 F.2d 1104 (9th Cir. 1990), *with* Utopia Provider Sys. v. Pro–Med Clini-

B.   *Copyrightability of computer programs*

The idea-expression dichotomy—articulated by the Supreme Court in *Baker v. Selden* and by Congress in section 102(b) of the Copyright Act—and other copyright doctrines frequently applied to conventional literary and graphic works have also been applied by the courts in ruling upon the copyrightability of computer programs. Courts dealing with computer programs and screen displays have attempted to protect expressive authorship without interfering with wide access to computer features that are either functionally dictated or are at a level of abstraction warranting treatment as an "idea."

A computer program is defined in section 101 of the Act as "a set of statements or instructions to be used directly or indirectly in a computer in order to bring about a certain result" and is thus one form of "literary work" within the coverage of section 102(a). Whether expressed in so-called "source code" (written and read by a human being) or "object code" (the string of ones and zeroes meant to operate the circuitry of a computer), a computer program may embody sufficient creativity as to justify copyright. This was the intention of the Congress in 1980 when it amended the Copyright Act so as, among other things, to include the above-quoted definition, and in later amendments to the statute allowing certain copying of computer programs but only in narrowly defined circumstances.[56] The federal courts of appeals have consistently held that a computer program—the sequence of instructions, not unlike an instructional manual written for humans—is copyrightable.[57]

Baker, however, teaches that copyright protection for computer programs and related materials should be accorded with an eye toward allowing the use of the program's underlying principles. There is indeed an obvious facial tension between the definition of a computer program, intended to fall within the subject matter of copyright, and the mandate of section 102(b) that "methods of operation" shall not be given copyright protection. In any event, the House Report makes clear that copyright does not extend protection to the "methodology or processes

---

cal Sys., 596 F.3d 1313 (11th Cir. 2010). *Cf.* ABR Benefits Servs. Inc. v. NCO Group, 52 U.S.P.Q.2d 1119 (E.D. Pa. 1999) (applying Third Circuit's view that "blank forms may be copyrighted if they are sufficiently innovative that their arrangement of information is itself informative").

56.   *See* 17 U.S.C. §§ 117(a), (c).

57.   Computer Assocs. Int'l, Inc. v. Altai, Inc., 982 F.2d 693 (2d Cir. 1992); Sega Enters., Ltd. v. Accolade, Inc., 977 F.2d 1510 (9th Cir. 1992). *See also* Lexmark Intern., Inc. v. Static Control Components, Inc. 387 F.3d 522 (6th Cir. 2004). Perhaps the most illuminating discussion is to be found in the decision of the Court of Appeals for the Third Circuit in *Apple Computer, Inc. v. Franklin Computer Corp.*, 714 F.2d 1240 (3d Cir. 1983).

adopted by the programmer."[58] And, by application of the "merger" doctrine espoused in *Baker*, if the detailed sequence of instructions in a copyrighted computer program is essentially necessary to implement such an unprotected methodology or process in an efficient fashion, then the program may lawfully be copied by others in the design of other programs.[59] On the other hand, "if other programs can be written or created which perform the same function as an Apple's operating system program, then that [Apple] program is an expression of the idea and hence copyrightable."[60]

Courts have applied this analysis so as to protect not only detailed computer-program language but also what have come to be referred to as the "nonliteral" elements of computer programs. Nonliteral elements are the structural features of a program that lie somewhere between the detailed commands of the program code and an abstract statement of the functional purpose of the program. The concept is based on the jurisprudence that, in conventional literary works such as novels and plays, treats the detailed story line and incidents as protectible "expression" and the more general themes as unprotectible "ideas." The task of drawing the line between idea and expression in literary works of all kinds, including computer programs, is a demanding and somewhat unguided one.[61]

The idea-expression dichotomy also applies with respect to computer screen displays, and the same principles of "merger" or "constraints" are utilized. If the colorful action scenes depicted on a screen in connection with a video game are essentially dictated by the subject matter—e.g., the appearance of a baseball diamond or football field or racetrack—courts will not protect these elements against copying, given the limited number of ways they can be visually expressed.[62] In assessing copyrightability, the court must, however, consider the totality of the visual

---

58. H.R. Rep. No. 94–1476, at 57 (1976).

59. Perhaps the most thorough and influential treatment of the nonprotection of "ideas" embodied in computer programs, and the application of the merger doctrine in this context, is in *Computer Associates International, Inc. v. Altai, Inc.*, 982 F.2d 693 (2d Cir. 1992). *See also* Lexmark Intern., Inc. v. Static Control Components, Inc. 387 F.3d 522 (6th Cir. 2004) (discussing *Altai* and *Feist Publications, Inc. v. Rural Telephone Service Co.*, 499 U.S. 340 (1991), in holding printer toner loading program was not expressive). *But see* Lotus Dev. Corp. v. Borland Int'l., Inc., 49 F.3d 807 (1st Cir. 1995), *aff'd by an equally divided Court*, 516 U.S. 233 (1996) (holding

Altai test inappropriate in cases of literal copying of computer code).

60. *Apple Computer*, 714 F.2d at 1253.

61. *See infra* Chapter 6, Infringement.

62. Incredible Technologies, Inc. v. Virtual Technologies, Inc., 400 F.3d 1007 (7th Cir. 2005) (golf video game); Data E. USA, Inc. v. Epyx, Inc., 862 F.2d 204 (9th Cir. 1988) (karate video game); Frybarger v. IBM Corp., 812 F.2d 525 (9th Cir. 1987) (mousetrap video game) (expression that is "indispensable" or "standard" is protectible only against "virtually identical copying"). These cases invoke the *scènes à faire* doctrine typically applied in literary infringement cases involving novels, plays and films.

elements and not simply the discrete components (which might on their own be too "simple" to be protected).[63]

There is less consensus about how best to apply the idea-expression dichotomy in cases involving the copyrightability of so-called "user interface," which is the set of commands given by a human user to a computer by striking certain keys or clicking on a screen image. For any given computer program, such as an accounting spreadsheet or a tax calculator, the commands meant to be chosen by the user may number in the hundreds, and they may be grouped or clustered under dozens of headings and subheadings; thus is formed a "menu command hierarchy" or "tree." This interface is to be distinguished from the internal operations of the computer (protectible if at all by patent), the program that brings about those operations, and the screen display (the graphic presentation of the command tree on the computer monitor). Some courts have concluded that these commands, even viewed as a composite and not as individual words and keystrokes, are necessary to bring about the computer's functioning and are thus a "method of operation" falling outside the scope of copyright protection by virtue of section 102(b).[64] Other courts have concluded that, so long as these commands can be expressed and grouped together in a variety of different ways, then the way chosen by the plaintiff is "expression" and not an uncopyrightable idea or method of operation.[65]

III.   Compilations and Derivative Works

In many kinds of copyrightable works, the original authorship lies in the expression of preexisting materials. An anthologist may collect and sequence poems written by others. A scholar may translate another's play from French to English. A cataloguer may prepare a directory by gathering and organizing information about individuals or businesses. If there is original authorship manifested in the anthology, the translation, and the directory, these works are eligible for copyright protection—but only to the extent of the copyright claimant's original contributions. If the underlying poems and play are in the public domain, as are the facts in the directory, they remain in the public domain for others to copy and base their works on. If the underlying poems and play are still in copyright, their use by the anthologist and the translator does not alter the duration or ownership of that copyright.[66]

---

63. Atari Games Corp. v. Oman, 979 F.2d 242 (D.C. Cir. 1992).

64. *Lotus Dev. Corp.*, 49 F.3d 807; Mi-Tek Holdings, Inc. v. Arce Eng'g Co., 89 F.3d 1548 (11th Cir. 1996).

65. Dun & Bradstreet Software Servs., Inc. v. Grace Consulting, Inc., 307 F.3d 197 (3d Cir. 2002); Mitel, Inc. v. Iqtel, Inc., 124 F.3d 1366 (10th Cir. 1997). See also the cases upholding copyright in a detailed subject-matter taxonomy, *e.g.*, American Dental Ass'n v. Delta Dental Plans Ass'n, 126 F.3d 977 (7th Cir. 1997).

66. 17 U.S.C. § 103(b).

The anthology and the directory are examples of what the Copyright Act refers to as a "compilation." A compilation as defined in section 101 is "a work formed by the collection and assembling of preexisting materials or of data that are selected, coordinated, or arranged in such a way that the resulting work as a whole constitutes an original work of authorship." The translation is an example of what is defined in section 101 as a "derivative work":

> A "derivative work" is a work based upon one or more preexisting works, such as a translation, musical arrangement, dramatization, fictionalization, motion picture version, sound recording, art reproduction, abridgment, condensation, or any other form in which a work may be recast, transformed, or adapted. A work consisting of editorial revisions, annotations, elaborations, or other modifications which, as a whole, represent an original work of authorship, is a "derivative work."

The relationship and differences between compilations and derivative works are well described in the House Report:

> Between them the terms "compilations" and "derivative works" which are defined in section 101, comprehend every copyrightable work that employs preexisting material or data of any kind. There is necessarily some overlapping between the two, but they basically represent different concepts. A "compilation" results from a process of selecting, bringing together, organizing, and arranging previously existing material of all kinds, regardless of whether the individual items in the material have been or ever could have been subject to copyright. A "derivative work," on the other hand, requires a process of recasting, transforming, or adapting "one or more preexisting works"; the "preexisting work" must come within the general subject matter of copyright set forth in section 102, regardless of whether it is or was ever copyrighted.[67]

Because copyright protection turns upon original creation, copyright in a compilation or derivative work attaches—as noted just above—only to those original contributions made by the compiler or by the creator of the derivative work. Section 103(b) of the Copyright Act provides:

> The copyright in a compilation or derivative work extends only to the material contributed by the author of such work, as distinguished from the preexisting material employed in the work, and does not imply any exclusive right in the preexisting

67. H.R. Rep. No. 94–1476, at 57 (1976).

material. The copyright in such work is independent of, and does not affect or enlarge the scope, duration, ownership, or subsistence of, any copyright protection in the preexisting material.

Thus, a motion picture based on a classic (copyright-expired) novel will not remove the novel from the public domain; nor will it prevent another motion picture producer from basing a new film on the same novel, although the second filmmaker will be barred from copying original elements from the first film (most obviously, for example, music on the soundtrack).

Another important principle is set forth in section 103(a), which provides, in pertinent part: "[P]rotection for a work employing preexisting material in which copyright subsists does not extend to any part of the work in which such material has been used unlawfully." Thus, an unauthorized translation of a copyrighted novel will infringe the exclusive right of the novelist to make derivative works, under section 106(2); such unlawful use, which permeates the derivative translation, will render it uncopyrightable. If, however, the unauthorized use of the copyrighted novel were to take the form of, for example, a drama with music, it is likely that the music would be copyrightable, because it would not make unlawful use of the protected material in the novel. In the former example, the translator might well complain that, even though he might be an infringer, that fact does not justify denying him a claim against another who makes an unauthorized copy of *his* translation. Congress, however, has rejected that contention and has stripped the infringer of a copyright claim in his infringing material, no matter how creative it might be.[68]

In the sections that immediately follow, compilations and derivative works are considered separately.

A.   *Compilations*

It is possible for an author to gather a group of otherwise uncopyrightable elements, and by their minimally creative linkage to create a compilation that is protectible by copyright. The designer of a greeting card can pair a simple drawing on the outside with a simple phrase on the inside; it has been held that another's card will infringe the "compilation" of the two elements even though its drawing is a bit different and the copied phrase is uncopyrightable.[69] This decision pushed the concept

---

68. *See, e.g.*, Anderson v. Stallone, 11 U.S.P.Q.2D 1161 (C.D. Cal. 1989) (no copyright in screenplay for proposed "Rocky IV" film that infringes prior three "Rocky" motion pictures).

69. Roth Greeting Cards v. United Card Co., 429 F.2d 1106 (9th Cir. 1970).

of "compilation" to the brink by holding that only two coordinated elements will suffice; and it introduced an unfortunate phrase into the copyright lexicon by announcing that the "concept and feel" of the two cards were alike, so that the later card infringed (even though it is quite clear that copyright should not be deployed to protect either a concept or a feel). In any event, merely grouping disparate uncopyrightable elements will not necessarily create a "compilation"; courts have held that a compilation comes into existence only when there is some synergy among the elements.[70]

How the definition of "original work of authorship" applies to a compilation has for many years been a subject of considerable dispute. Both under the 1909 Act and the 1976 Act, a substantial number of courts had extended copyright protection to directories—even, routinely, to alphabetically organized white-page telephone directories—by giving weight (often only implicitly) to the effort, time, and expense devoted to gathering and organizing the underlying factual data that were themselves undeniably in the public domain. This rationale became known as the "sweat of the brow" or "industrious collection" theory.

In a major decision, *Feist Publications, Inc. v. Rural Telephone Service Co.*,[71] the Supreme Court in 1991 explicitly and uncategorically repudiated the "sweat of the brow" theory as inconsistent with fundamental principles of copyright (as manifested both in the Constitution and the statute) and with the specific definition of "compilation" in the 1976 Act. The Court in *Feist* defined "originality," the prerequisite to copyright protection, to require not only independent creation (i.e., noncopying) but also "some minimal degree of creativity," "some creative spark." Although the Court acknowledged that "the requisite level of creativity is extremely low" and that "even a small amount will suffice," it concluded that white-page telephone directories fail to satisfy this test.

Even the plaintiff directory compiler had conceded that the factual information contained in the book was in the public domain and unprotectible by copyright. The Court agreed; even assuming that such facts—name, telephone number, and town—were unearthed by the plaintiff, it could not claim authorship, for these facts did not "owe their origin" to, and indeed existed prior to, the plaintiff's publication.

---

70. Matthew Bender & Co. v. West Publ'g Co., 158 F.3d 674, 688 (2d Cir. 1998) (West's "editorial enhancements" in its case reports do not together constitute a copyrightable compilation, but are rather a "piling up" of trivial elements "each in its discrete way in its discrete spot"); Sem-Torq, Inc. v. K Mart Corp., 936 F.2d 851 (6th Cir. 1991) (set of five placards, to be sold as a group in department store, not a compilation).

71. 499 U.S. 340 (1991).

Nonetheless, the plaintiff claimed protection for the overall coordination and presentation of those facts. The Court therefore went on to parse the statutory definition of "compilation" and found it to compel the following conclusions: (1) merely collecting and gathering information, no matter how arduous it may be to do so, are not in themselves sufficient to warrant copyright; (2) compilations must satisfy the "originality" requirement in the same manner as all other kinds of works eligible for copyright and cannot properly be treated differently under any "sweat of the brow" theory; and, most important for the Court, (3) because the compiler of facts "can claim originality, if at all, only in the way the facts are presented," there will inevitably be some fact-based works that lack the required "minimal level of creativity" in selection, coordination, and arrangement—"a narrow category of works in which the creative spark is utterly lacking or so trivial as to be virtually nonexistent."[72]

Feist held—contrary to decades of decisions by lower courts—that the white-page telephone directory falls within that fatally flawed category. The plaintiff there might have worked hard in making a directory that was useful, but there was "insufficient creativity to make it original."[73] The Supreme Court found the selection of listings to have been obvious; so too were the book's coordination and arrangement of facts:

> [T]here is nothing remotely creative about arranging names alphabetically in a white pages directory. It is an age-old practice, firmly rooted in tradition and so commonplace that it has come to be expected as a matter of course.... It is not only unoriginal, it is practically inevitable. This time-honored tradition does not possess the minimal creative spark required by the Copyright Act and the Constitution.... Given that some works must fail [the test of originality], we cannot imagine a more likely candidate. Indeed, were we to hold that [the plaintiff's] white pages pass muster, it is hard to believe that any collection of facts could fail.[74]

Although the Court in *Feist* stated several times that the creativity requirement was a quite modest one ("no matter how crude, humble or obvious"), its reliance upon a subjective and unquantifiable standard (a modicum, a spark) has introduced an element of uncertainty—as perhaps is inherent in the matter—in drawing a line between the copyrightable and the uncreative. (This line, the Court reminds us, finds its source not simply in the statutory language of section 102(a) but also in the word "author" in the Constitution.) Thus, in what was perhaps an overzealous application of the *Feist* authorship standard, the en banc

---

72. *Id.* at 359.

73. *Id.* at 363.

74. *Id.* at 363–64.

Court of Appeals for the Eleventh Circuit held that the typical yellow-page telephone directory lacks creativity in the selection of some 7,000 classified headings (as to which there are a great number of options in nomenclature) and in the linking of some 100,000 business entities to those headings.[75]

Some sorts of familiar anthologies will almost certainly pass the test of original authorship, e.g., selecting a finite number of poems from among the entire corpus of world poetry throughout history, or from among the poets of a particular nation in a particular literary time period, or even grouped thematically (e.g., different varieties of inebriation) from a single poet. The statutory term "compilation" contemplates authorship in the manner in which preexisting works or data are "selected, coordinated, *or* arranged."[76] Although the poetry anthologies evoked above will likely pass the test for all three kinds of intellectual endeavor, authorship in only one will suffice. Similarly, the Court of Appeals for the Second Circuit has held that a comprehensive listing of 18,000 baseball cards (with information about price and the like), and a designation of 5,000 as "premium" cards, represented a copyrightable work.[77] It reached the same conclusion for the well-known directory of used-car values (the so-called *Red Book*), organized by make and model, five-year periods, and selected accessories.[78]

But the same court found that the gathering of five discrete bits of daily information regarding redeemable bonds was inadequate to justify copyright protection for the cards embodying that information.[79] And two courts of appeals have denied copyright protection to lists of numbers generated and compiled to identify product parts: fasteners such as screws in one case[80] and automotive-transmission parts in the other.[81] The courts invoked a number of theories—such as lack of originality, the idea-expression dichotomy, merger, *scènes à faire*, and short phrases—and declined to follow another circuit court's grant of copyright protection to a taxonomy taking the form of numbers used to identify various dental procedures.[82]

75. BellSouth Adver. & Publ'g Corp. v. Donnelley Info. Publ'g, Inc., 999 F.2d 1436 (11th Cir. 1993) (en banc). *But see* Key Publ'ns, Inc. v. Chinatown Today Publ'g Enters., Inc., 945 F.2d 509 (2d Cir. 1991) (classified directory of businesses of likely interest to Chinese–American community in New York City).

76. Section 101 (emphasis added).

77. Eckes v. Card Prices Update, 736 F.2d 859 (2d Cir. 1984).

78. CCC Info. Servs., Inc. v. Maclean Hunter Mkt. Reports, 44 F.3d 61 (2d Cir. 1994).

79. Financial Info., Inc. v. Moody's Investors Serv., 808 F.2d 204 (2d Cir. 1986).

80. Southco, Inc. v. Kanebridge Corp., 390 F.3d 276 (3d Cir. 2004) (en banc).

81. ATC Distrib. Group, Inc. v. Whatever It Takes Transmissions & Parts, Inc., 402 F.3d 700 (6th Cir. 2005).

82. American Dental Ass'n v. Delta Dental Plans Ass'n, 126 F.3d 977 (7th Cir. 1997).

Several cases of particular interest to law students, lawyers and judges have involved claims by the West Publishing Company of copyrightability for certain "compiled" elements of its case reporters.[83] In a case decided prior to *Feist, West Publishing Co. v. Mead Data Central, Inc.*,[84] the LEXIS computerized research service announced its intention to incorporate in its screen displays of case decisions "star pagination" reflecting all page breaks in the unofficial West federal and regional reports. West prevailed in its claim that this would constitute an infringement of its copyright in its case compilations, which the Court of Appeals for the Eighth Circuit held reflected "authorship" in the distribution, sequencing and organization of cases. A flatly contradictory decision was issued by the Second Circuit Court of Appeals several years after *Feist*, by which time the technology had moved to the point that West's competitors sought to insert West page numbers in their CD–ROM products.[85] In part because those numbers were found to derive not from West's creativity but from the mechanical layout of its pages, the court held that its competitors could copy them, and it held the earlier case in the Eighth Circuit to have been erroneously decided.[86]

The same principles that govern copyrightability of compilations will apply when the claim relates to the particularly modern-day compilation known as the computer database, which is no more than a collection of discrete factual data fixed in tangible form in a computer storage medium.

B. *Derivative works*

Although the 1991 Supreme Court decision in *Feist* has helped to eliminate much of the earlier uncertainty about the "original authorship" requirement in compilation cases, there remains a comparable uncertainty about the application of that requirement in cases involving derivative works. Derivative works require some sort of "recasting, transformation or adaptation" of underlying works within the subject matter of copyright.[87] As a threshold matter, what does it mean to

---

83. West does not claim copyright in the text of the judges' opinions and even its competitors have acknowledged West's copyright does extend to its syllabi and headnotes, along with its key-system taxonomy and its tables and indices prepared by the West staff.

84. 799 F.2d 1219 (8th Cir. 1986).

85. Matthew Bender & Co. v. West Publ'g Co., 158 F.3d 693 (2d Cir. 1998) (2–1 decision).

86. *Id.* at 707–708. In a companion case, the Second Circuit also held that West's

various "editorial enhancements" to the courthouse opinions—such as case captions, attorney information, and insertion of parallel citations—could be copied by West's competitors. Matthew Bender & Co. v. West Publ'g Co., 158 F.3d 674 (2d Cir. 1998) (2–1 decision). *See also* Skinder–Strauss Assocs. v. Massachusetts Continuing Legal Ed., Inc., 914 F. Supp. 665 (D. Mass. 1995) (holding directory of lawyers' contact information uncopyrightable).

87. *See* 17 U.S.C. § 101: "A 'derivative work' is a work based upon one or more preexisting works, such as a translation,

"recast, transform or adapt . . . one or more preexisting works"? We will later address whether the recasting, transformation or adaptation are sufficiently creative to support a copyright. While the inquiry into what constitutes a derivative work may be implicit in cases addressing the requisite level of originality, we should first ask two question: first, whether the claimant has in fact *changed* the preexisting work; and second, whether the changes introduced bear on the *work*, as opposed to its ideas or other unprotectible elements. If a novel is translated into another language or is expanded into a motion picture film, there is usually little doubt that the translation and the film fulfill both criteria; they clearly are based on the prior work's expression, and incorporate creative and "distinguishable variations" beyond the underlying novel. By contrast, in *Bridgeman Art Library, Ltd. v. Corel Corp.*,[88] the court found that Bridgeman's color transparencies which reproduced famous public domain artworks did not in any way alter the underlying works. Bridgeman attached a color correction strip to each image, ensuring that the transparency "was a genuine reflection of the original work." The court held that Bridgeman's transparencies were not copyrightable, as they were "substantially exact reproductions . . . copied from the underlying works without any avoidable addition, alteration, or transformation. Indeed, Bridgeman strives to reproduce precisely those works of art." Notwithstanding the different medium, there is no transformation where the photograph "is no more than a copy of the work of another as exact as science and technology permit."

With regard to the second inquiry, the "new matter" the putative derivative-works author introduces may well be amply creative, but the underlying material may not itself be a "work." Such would be the case, for example, of a painting depicting bottles or other noncopyrightable objects,[89] or of a motion picture based only on the ideas of a prior play.[90] The latter example clarifies the statutory definition of a derivative work as "a work based upon one or more preexisting works." "A work based upon" implies a more substantial debt to the underlying work than one merely "inspired by" its predecessor. The putative derivative work must capture the underlying work's expression, not simply "derive from" the prior work in the aesthetic or literary and artistic criticism sense, lest

---

musical arrangement, dramatization, fictionalization, motion picture version, sound recording, art reproduction, abridgment, condensation, or any other form in which a work may be recast, transformed, or adapted. A work consisting of editorial revisions, annotations, elaborations, or other modifications which, as a whole, represent an original work of authorship, is a 'derivative work'."

88. 25 F. Supp. 2d 421 (S.D.N.Y. 1998).

89. *See, e.g.*, Ets–Hokin v. Skyy Spirits, Inc., 225 F.3d 1068 (9th Cir. 2000)(photograph of vodka bottle not a derivative work because the bottle is not a "work")

90. *See, e.g.*, Nichols v. Universal Pictures Corp., 45 F.2d 119, 121 (2d Cir.1930) (motion picture borrowed from play only its general theme and broad character types).

the first author's right to control the creation of derivative works (discussed in Chapter 6) extend to her "ideas" and other non-copyrightable contributions. Where the second-comer has merely drawn inspiration from the first author, the new creation will be a "work" (assuming sufficient originality), but it will not be a *"derivative* work."

When the putative derivative work does rework a prior work's expression, the issue becomes whether the adaptation or transformation manifests sufficient original authorship. Principles derived from *Feist* suggest that modest but discernible variations on the underlying work should sustain a copyright. The principles are particularly put to the test in cases in which the variations on the underlying work result primarily from the transformation of the work from one medium to another. The medium change standing alone, might, in order to avoid anticompetitive outcomes, be deemed an unprotectible "idea";[91] the question thus becomes whether the alleged derivative work manifests alterations that do not of necessity flow from the choice of the new medium. For example, in *L. Batlin & Son, Inc. v. Snyder,*[92] the Court of Appeals for the Second Circuit, sitting en banc, held that a plastic "Uncle Sam Bank" modeled on a cast-iron public domain bank from the late nineteenth century lacked sufficient elements of originality to warrant copyright protection. The copier had used Snyder's plastic bank as a model for its own, and had not copied directly from the public domain bank. Although there were some purposeful design variations in Snyder's plastic bank, the court found them to be trivial, not readily discernible, and largely dictated by the mechanical needs of the plastic-molding process.[93]

Some courts however, have applied the "original authorship" requirement to derivative works in a way that arguably departs from these basic principles. They have read the *Batlin* case as endorsing a standard of "originality" for authorized derivative works that is arguably stiffer than that which obtains for copyrightable works generally. It cannot, however, be said with confidence that this reading of *Batlin* is the prevailing one regarding derivative works. On the one hand, the Court of Appeals for the Seventh Circuit, in *Gracen v. Bradford Exchange,*[94]

91. *See, e.g.,* Oriental Art Printing, Inc. v. Goldstar Printing Corp., 175 F.Supp.2d 542 (S.D.N.Y.2001) (ruling that photographs of familiar Chinese foods, and their placement on restaurant menu, lack creativity appears to be motivated by concern that photographer might lay claim to any menu photographs because most menu photos, depicting the same dishes, are bound to look alike).

92. 536 F.2d 486 (2d Cir. 1976) (en banc).

93. *See also* Sherry Mfg. Co. v. Towel King of Fla., Inc., 753 F.2d 1565 (11th Cir. 1985) (variations in graphic design on towels were trivial, and improperly motivated). *But see* Eden Toys, Inc. v. Florelee Undergarment Co., 697 F.2d 27 (2d Cir. 1982) (depicting Paddington Bear image as "smoother" and "cleaner" than underlying drawing is nontrivial variation and thus copyrightable).

94. 698 F.2d 300 (7th Cir. 1983).

exalted the concern of the *Batlin* court regarding potential harassment by claimants of derivative-work copyrights into the very rationale for a heightened originality requirement. There, an authorized drawing of the Dorothy (Judy Garland) character from the motion picture film *The Wizard of Oz* was found to lack sufficient creativity, even though it had been chosen as a contest winner. The court held that "originality" with respect to derivative works "is not to guide aesthetic judgments but to assure a sufficiently gross difference between the underlying and the derivative work to avoid entangling subsequent artists depicting the underlying work in copyright problems."[95] That is, the creator of a nearly exact derivative work, if given a copyright, could threaten litigation that would chill legitimate recourse by others to the underlying work.

On the other hand, the same court of appeals has since largely repudiated (through restatement) *Gracen*'s requirement of a higher standard of originality for derivative works. In *Schrock v. Learning Curve*,[96] the plaintiff photographer alleged that the producer of the Thomas the Tank Engine toys had exceeded its license to reproduce and distribute plaintiff's photographs of the toys. Learning Curve, invoking *Gracen*, rejoined that Schrock had no copyright to infringe because the photographs lacked sufficient originality.

> Our review of Schrock's photographs convinces us that they do not fall into the narrow category of photographs that can be classified as "slavish copies," lacking any independently created expression. To be sure, the photographs are accurate depictions of the three-dimensional "Thomas & Friends" toys, but Schrock's artistic and technical choices combine to create a two-dimensional image that is subtly but nonetheless sufficiently his own ... The original expression in the representative sample is not particularly great (it was not meant to be), but it is enough under the applicable standard to warrant the limited copyright protection accorded derivative works under § 103(b).

Schrock's evocation of section 103(b) is a reminder of an important limiting principle: the copyright in a derivative work (or a compilation) extends only to the "new matter" introduced by the second author. That author cannot "bootstrap" the underlying work to her variations on it. Nor, under the "idea/expression dichotomy" now codified in section 102(b), can the derivative-work author prevent others from exploiting the "idea" that animates her variations. For example, Marcel Duchamp's addition of a moustache and a goatee to a postcard of the Mona Lisa would not have entitled him to prevent others from acquiring postcards

---

95. *Id.* at 305.   **96.** 586 F.3d 513 (7th Cir. 2009).

of the Mona Lisa and superimposing different combinations or depictions of facial hair or coiffure.

IV. Other Categories of Works: Particular Problems

A. *Pictorial, Graphic, and Sculptural Works*

One of the categories of copyrightable works in section 102(a) of the Act is "pictorial, graphic, and sculptural works" (PGS works). The same requirement of original authorship obtains for artistic works as for literary works, and in neither case does it import any standard of aesthetic merit or appeal—only noncopying and a minimal measure of creativity. The latter element has been reflected for many years in section 202.1(a) of the Copyright Office regulations, which excludes from copyright "familiar symbols or designs" and "mere variations of typographic ornamentation, lettering or coloring." Even before the Supreme Court in *Feist* definitively announced the requirement of minimal creativity, courts had denied copyright to a cardboard display-stand in the shape of a circle within a five-pointed star,[97] to a handful of overlapping angular lines (evoking arrowheads) in a sports-team logo,[98] and to variations in color choices for map territories.[99]

On the other hand, "colorized" versions of motion picture films originally made in black and white have been declared by the Copyright Office generally to contain enough original authorship in color selection as to constitute separately copyrightable derivative works.[100] Copyright has also been sustained in a realistic color drawing of a slice of chocolate cake, designed for use on a cake wrapper;[101] and the same court of appeals, much more recently, overturned a summary judgment of noncopyrightability of the Barbie Doll's nose, lips and eyes.[102]

Photographs may test the boundaries of copyrightable expression precisely because of their apparent capacity faithfully to represent "reality." We have seen that the Supreme Court rejected such a challenge to the protectability of Napoleon Sarony's photographic portrait of Oscar Wilde, but Sarony there effectively "staged" his portrait to create an "artistic" effect through the selection of costume, props, camera angle and lighting. Nonetheless, even when the image partakes more of the "ordinary production of a photograph," such as a common snapshot or home motion picture film, these have been held eligible for copyright,

---

97. Bailie v. Fisher, 258 F.2d 425 (D.C. Cir. 1958).

98. John Muller & Co. v. New York Arrows Soccer Team, 802 F.2d 989 (8th Cir. 1986).

99. United States v. Hamilton, 583 F.2d 448 (9th Cir. 1978).

100. 52 Fed. Reg. 23,442 (1987).

101. Kitchens of Sara Lee, Inc. v. Nifty Foods Corp., 266 F.2d 541 (2d Cir. 1959).

102. Mattel, Inc. v. Goldberger Doll Mfg. Co., 365 F.3d 133 (2d Cir. 2004).

given the photographer's judgment regarding angle, placement, shading, timing and the like.[103] This approach was extended by the Court of Appeals for the Ninth Circuit to protect a head-on product photograph of a bottle of vodka[104]—although the court ultimately concluded that the "merger" of idea and expression justified only a "thin" copyright and held that a nearly identical photograph did not infringe.[105]

The court in *Mannion v. Coors Brewing Co.*,[106] grappled with the nature of a photograph's original authorship. In that case, the defendant did not directly copy the photograph, but rather reconstituted its elements by photographing from a similar angle a similar-appearing model wearing similar dress and ostentatious jewelry. Arguably, then, the defendant had simply gone back to the noncopyrightable source elements and independently produced its own image. In finding that the plaintiff's expression extended to his composition of those elements, the court articulated three kinds of originality. First, "originality in the rendition" resulting from "angle of shot, light and shade, exposure, effects achieved by means of filters, developing techniques etc." "[T]o the extent a photograph is original in this way, copyright protects not what is depicted, but rather how it is depicted." Second, "originality in timing," consisting of the selection of the moment in which to capture the animate elements and/or natural lighting effects of the scene. The court offered the example of "Alfred Eisenstaedt's photograph of a sailor kissing a young woman on VJ Day in Times Square, the memorability of which is attributable in significant part to the timing of its creation." With respect to these kinds of original authorship, the copyright does not extend to the subject matter depicted in the photograph. By contrast, the third kind of originality, of which Mannion's photograph was an example, lies in the "creation of the subject," in which, in addition to manipulating effects of angle or lighting, the photographer "orchestrates the scene" through the selection and arrangement of its components. Thus, at least for some photographs, the "pictorial, graphic or sculptural work" consists of the image as distinguished from the particularities of the photographic medium. The "orchestrated" image that Napoleon Sarony created would have been equally protectable had it been created as a photograph or as a painting.[107]

103. Time, Inc. v. Bernard Geis Assocs., 293 F. Supp. 130 (S.D.N.Y. 1968).

104. Ets–Hokin v. Skyy Spirits, Inc., 225 F.3d 1068 (9th Cir. 2000).

105. Ets–Hokin v. Skyy Spirits, Inc., 323 F.3d 763 (9th Cir. 2003).

106. 377 F. Supp. 2d 444 (S.D.N.Y. 2005).

107. In fact, in the *Sarony* case, the defendant's work was not a photographic copy of the photograph, but a lithograph closely based on the photograph.

1. Useful articles

Perhaps the most difficult issue that arises regarding the copyright-ability of pictorial, graphic, and sculptural works concerns those works, typically "sculptural," that serve useful functions, such as furniture, flatware, appliances, garments, and automobiles. The pertinent law begins with an important Supreme Court decision, moves through some not altogether clear provisions of the 1976 Act, and continues today in a number of court decisions applying the statute in an inconsistent and uncertain manner.

Until 1954, when the Supreme Court decided *Mazer v. Stein*,[108] it was widely assumed that protection for the design of useful articles had to be secured through the design-patent law—which requires that the design be "novel" and "nonobvious"—and that copyright protection was not available. In *Mazer*, the Court held that copyright protection could be extended to sculptural figures that were used as bases for lamps. The Court stated that, so long as the statues embodied originality, copyright was not displaced by virtue of the potential availability of design-patent protection or by the fact that the design was embodied in a useful article that was mass-produced and merchandised commercially. Since the *Mazer* decision, the Copyright Office has registered many ornamentally shaped useful articles. Section 113(a) of the Copyright Act now provides that the copyright in a PGS work "includes the right to reproduce the work in or on any kind of article, whether useful or otherwise."

A perplexing problem that remained after *Mazer* was whether copyright could extend not simply to a separate and independent artistic drawing or sculpture that was incorporated as part of a useful article (such as the statuette lamp base in that case), but also to attractively shaped useful articles in themselves. To permit the copyright owner to prevent the manufacture of a useful article would create the risk that copyright—quick and easy to secure, and long in duration—could be used to obtain a patent-like monopoly over articles of manufacture without complying with the more exacting prerequisites for a product patent or a design patent. This concern induced several courts to hold under the 1909 Act that copyright in a two-dimensional drawing of a useful article would not carry with it the exclusive right to manufacture the article itself, and that copyright was not appropriate for the overall three-dimensional shape of such an article.[109] Congress, in section 113(b) of the 1976 Act, approved these earlier precedents, simply by incorporating by reference the law as it had existed on December 31, 1977—in effect withholding from the copyright owner the exclusive right to finish or to build the object portrayed.

---

108. 347 U.S. 201 (1954).

109. *E.g.*, Muller v. Triborough Bridge Auth., 43 F. Supp. 298 (S.D.N.Y. 1942) (plan for cloverleaf bridge approach).

Congress attempted a formulation of the scope of protection for useful articles by its definitions in section 101. A "useful article" is defined as "an article having an intrinsic utilitarian function that is not merely to portray the appearance of the article or to convey information." (A dress or an automobile is thus a "useful article" but a designer's rendering in a drawing or photograph is not because it would "portray the appearance of the article."[110]) The "not merely to portray" language indicates that articles which both portray and perform some other function are "useful articles." For example, Halloween costumes have (perhaps unconvincingly) been deemed "useful articles" because, in addition to depicting animals real and fanciful, they can be used to clothe the body.[111] Nonetheless the inference to be drawn from "not merely" is not absolute: courts have recognized that when the "utility" is intellectual, the article is not "useful." Thus, as the Third Circuit held in *Masquerade Novelty v. Unique Indus.*,[112] in a controversy concerning animal nose masks:

> When hung on a wall, a painting may evoke a myriad of human emotions, but we would not say that the painting is not copyrightable because its artistic elements could not be separated from the emotional effect its creator hoped it would have on persons viewing it. The utilitarian nature of an animal nose mask or a painting of the crucifixion of Jesus Christ inheres solely in its appearance, regardless of the fact that the nose mask's appearance is intended to evoke mirth and the painting's appearance a feeling of religious reverence.

2. Separability

If the alleged "pictorial, graphic, and sculptural work" is a "useful article," then the Copyright Act requires the separation of beauty from utility.

Pictorial, graphic, and sculptural works include two-dimensional and three-dimensional works of fine, graphic, and applied art,

---

110. Courts have disagreed on the question whether mannequins are "useful articles," with the line apparently being drawn—somewhat unconvincingly—between human mannequins (yes), *Carol Barnhart Inc. v. Economy Cover Corp.*, 773 F.2d 411 (2d Cir. 1985), and animal mannequins (no), *Hart v. Dan Chase Taxidermy Supply Co.*, 86 F.3d 320 (2d Cir. 1996). *See also* Pivot Point Int'l, Inc. v. Charlene Prods., Inc., 372 F.3d 913 (7th Cir. 2004) (mannequin head used in training hairdressers and makeup artists).

111. *See, e.g.*, Whimsicality, Inc. v. Maison Joseph Battat, 27 F. Supp. 2d 456 (S.D.N.Y.1998). *See also* Copyright Office Policy Decision on the Registrability of Costume Designs, 56 FR 56530 (November 5, 1991): "Costumes serve a dual purpose of clothing the body and portraying their appearance. Since clothing the body serves as a useful function, costumes fall within the literal definition of useful article."

112. 912 F.2d 663 (3d Cir. 1990). *Accord*, Celebration Int'l, Inc. v. Chosun Int'l, Inc., 234 F. Supp. 2d 905 (S.D. Ind. 2002).

photographs, prints and art reproductions, maps, globes, charts, diagrams, models, and technical drawings, including architectural plans. Such works shall include works of artistic craftsmanship insofar as their form but not their mechanical or utilitarian aspects are concerned; the design of a useful article, as defined in this section, shall be considered a pictorial, graphic, or sculptural work only if, and only to the extent that, such design incorporates pictorial, graphic, or sculptural features that can be identified separately from, and are capable of existing independently of, the utilitarian aspects of the article.[113]

If, for example, a corkscrew is composed of a small plastic sculptured human head and a pointed spiral-shaped piece of metal, it is a PGS work, but copyright extends only to the sculptured head and not to the shape of the spiraling metal.

In the words of the House Report, the statutory definitions attempt to distinguish between "works of applied art protectible under the bill and industrial designs not subject to copyright protection."[114] The Report continues:

A two-dimensional painting, drawing, or graphic work is still capable of being identified as such when it is printed on or applied to utilitarian articles such as textile fabrics, wallpaper, containers, and the like. The same is true when a statue or carving is used to embellish an industrial product or, as in the *Mazer* case, is incorporated into a product without losing its ability to exist independently as a work of art. On the other hand, although the shape of an industrial product may be aesthetically satisfying and valuable, the Committee's intention is not to offer it copyright protection under the bill. Unless the shape of an automobile, airplane, ladies' dress, food processor, television set, or any other industrial product contains some element that, physically or conceptually, can be identified as separable from the utilitarian aspects of that article, the design would not be copyrighted under the bill.[115]

As to the attractive shape of useful articles in themselves, Congress had, during the copyright revision process, formulated a separate body of legislation that would have extended a special 10–year term of copyright to "the design of a useful article" including its "two-dimensional or three-dimensional features of shape and surface, which make up the appearance of the article"; but this legislation was never enacted. Repeated efforts since to enact such design-protection legislation have

---

113. 17 U.S.C. § 101.

114. H.R. Rep. No. 94–1476, at 55 (1976).

115. *Id.*

been unsuccessful, except for the rather curious and particularistic protection accorded to the shape of vessel hulls.[116] Legislation is currently pending that would extend limited protection to fashion design.[117]

The key to copyright protection of the features of useful articles thus depends on whether the feature is—in the words of the House Report—physically or conceptually separable from the utilitarian features. Examples given in the Report include a carving on the back of a chair or a floral relief design on silver flatware. Although copyrightability might be clear at that extreme, and noncopyrightability clear at the other extreme of a flat rectangular table top resting on four cylindrical legs at each corner, it is of course the intermediate cases that reach the courts, sometimes after a refusal by the Copyright Office to register the work.

It is important to appreciate that the "separability" threshold will in most cases set a higher bar than the idea/expression "merger" doctrine. The latter inquires whether the "idea" is susceptible to multiple forms of expression, or whether instead, as exemplified by the sweepstakes rules and jeweled bee-pin cases evoked earlier,[118] plaintiff's work represents the only way, or one of only a few ways, of presenting the idea. By contrast, that the overall shape of a table or chair may be expressed through multiple different designs does not itself suffice to make any one of those designs "separable" in whole or in part.

The effort to apply the "separability" standard has not resulted in a clear or consistent pattern of decisions. In noteworthy decisions of the Court of Appeals for the Second Circuit, copyright protection has been upheld for an attractively contoured belt buckle (in part, no doubt, because many persons wore the buckle separately as pinned-on jewelry),[119] but has been denied for the shape of mannequin torsos used for the draping of shirts in clothing stores (despite the allusion to the sculptures of ancient Greece and Rome)[120] and for the undulating "sine-curve" design of a bicycle rack.[121] The Seventh Circuit, now followed by the Fourth Circuit, has more recently drawn upon those decisions to develop a "separability" test focusing on the causal relationship between the useful purpose of the article and its design.[122] Where the article's appearance results from "artistic judgment exercised independently of functional influences," these courts have found the test satisfied. Such a

116. 17 U.S.C. §§ 1301–1332.

117. S. 3728, 111th Cong. (2010).

118. *See* Chapter 2, *supra*, at p. 31.

119. Kieselstein–Cord v. Accessories by Pearl, Inc., 632 F.2d 989 (2d Cir. 1980).

120. Carol Barnhart Inc. v. Economy Cover Corp., 773 F.2d 411 (2d Cir. 1985).

121. Brandir Int'l v. Cascade Pac. Lumber Co., 834 F.2d 1142 (2d Cir. 1987).

122. Pivot Point Int'l, Inc. v. Charlene Prods., Inc., 372 F.3d 913 (7th Cir. 2004) (2–1 decision)(beauty school manikin heads); *see also* Universal Furniture Int'l., Inc. v. Collezione Europa USA, Inc., 618 F.3d 417 (4th Cir. 2010)(furniture designs).

test may, however, risk inviting self-serving testimony. Given the overall uncertainty across the Circuits, all that can be said with any confidence is that the more flamboyant the shape, and the less the shape is dictated by the function of the article (however that causal element is assessed), the more readily copyright will protect the overall shape of useful articles. For example, the Fourth Circuit described the items of furniture there at issue as "an ornamentation explosion"—"highly ornate collections of furniture adorned with three-dimensional shells, acanthus leaves, columns, finials, rosettes, and other carvings."

B. *Architectural works*

Another example of a useful article—one that has given rise to some difficulties in determining the proper scope of copyright protection—is architecture. Both under the 1909 Act and the 1976 Act as originally enacted, courts generally held that although architectural plans and three-dimensional models were copyrightable, that protection would not afford the copyright owner the exclusive right to build the structure depicted therein. By virtue of analysis stemming from *Baker v. Selden*,[123] courts were reluctant to permit copyright—rather easily secured and of long duration—to be used to prevent the construction of houses and office buildings; there was also, no doubt, reluctance to uphold copyright in architectural "styles" manifested in standard design elements. Under the "pre–1978 saving clause" in section 113(b) of the 1976 Act and the "separability" requirement in the definition of PGS works, these earlier precedents had been applied so that the unauthorized construction of a building would not constitute copyright infringement.[124]

This body of law was significantly altered when, in October 1990, Congress amended the Copyright Act so as to extend its protection to the overall shape of three-dimensional works of architecture. The Architectural Works Copyright Protection Act, among other things, amended section 101 to define "architectural work" as "the design of a building as embodied in any tangible medium of expression, including a building, architectural plans, or drawings. The work includes the overall form and elements in the design, but does not include individual standard features." By protecting the "overall form" of buildings, and by defining "architectural work" separately from all other PGS works so that the "separability" requirement does not obtain for this particular category of useful article, the amended statute now makes it an infringement to construct a building that copies from another's protectible two- or three-dimensional design. The purpose of the 1990 statutory changes was to

123. 101 U.S. 99 (1879).

124. Demetriades v. Kaufmann, 680 F. Supp. 658 (S.D.N.Y. 1988).

bring U.S. law more into harmony with the architectural-protection provisions of the Berne Convention.

The protection for building designs is subject to certain statutory limitations found principally in section 120: it is not an infringement to draw or photograph a building that is "located in or ordinarily visible from a public space," and the owner of a building embodying a copyrighted design does not infringe by making alterations to the building or by destroying it. Moreover, the extended copyright protection described here does not apply to buildings that were completed or "substantially constructed" before December 1, 1990.[125]

C. Works of visual art

In what is perhaps an even more dramatic change in the Copyright Act than the inclusion of architectural works, the October 1990 amendments expressly accorded visual artists for the first time as a matter of federal law the rights of "attribution and integrity." These are the two principal components of what is known in civil-law nations as "moral rights." These rights, during the life of the artist, to have a work attributed to the artist, and to prevent mutilation or destruction of the work—were granted by the Visual Artists Rights Act (VARA) of 1990 and are now set forth in section 106A of the Copyright Act (to be discussed more fully *infra* Chapter 6).

These two newly created statutory rights are given only to authors of what is defined as a "work of visual art" and not to authors of all pictorial, graphic, or sculptural works. The definition of a "work of visual art" (particularly the exclusions) is elaborate. It covers a painting, a sculpture, and a "still photographic image produced for exhibition purposes only," in their embodiment as a single copy or in numbered and signed limited editions not in excess of 200. Excluded are works made for hire and a broad range of graphic works such as posters, technical drawings, applied art, motion pictures and other audiovisual works, art in books, newspapers and periodicals, and advertising[126] and packaging materials.

These excluded categories of works remain within the definition of "pictorial, graphic, and sculptural works," and they are accorded protection against unauthorized reproduction and unauthorized preparation of derivative works. They are not, however, protected against non-attribution or physical mutilation or destruction.

VARA therefore contemplates three sets of rights in art works—the copyright owner of a PGS work can assert the basic right of reproduction

125. Zitz v. Pereira, 232 F.3d 290 (2d Cir. 2000).

126. Pollara v. Seymour, 344 F.3d 265 (2d Cir. 2003).

set forth in section 106; the artist who has created "a work of visual art" can assert the moral rights set forth in section 106A; and the owner of the physical canvas or sculpture can assert chattel ownership rights under state law. Section 106A(e)(2) expressly provides for this fragmentation of rights.

A dozen states have enacted similar "moral rights" statutes for the protection of artists; most of these laws are broader in both subject-matter coverage and substantive rights than the federal Act. Section 301(f) of the Copyright Act preempts the enforcement of state-law rights equivalent to those conferred by section 106A upon "works of visual art," but this would allow states to grant rights of attribution and integrity to works that fall outside that federally defined phrase (such as motion pictures) and to grant perhaps more expansive substantive rights even to "works of visual art." In any event, section 301(f) expressly preserves state rights that extend beyond the life of the artist.

D. *Pictorial and Literary Characters*

Owners of copyright in literary or pictorial stories have on occasion attempted to assert an exclusive right to the characters depicted therein. The right to continue certain characters in television series, or in novelistic and motion picture sequels, or video games, is of great economic value, as is the right to "merchandise" these characters on shirts, bed linens, dolls and other such paraphernalia.

Pictorial characters drawn for comic books or film cartoons are readily protected by copyright, as pictorial and graphic works, provided they meet the minimal requirements for "original authorship."[127] The copyrightable elements of an animated character have been said to "extend not merely to the physical appearance of the animated figure, but also to the manner in which it moves, acts and portrays a combination of characteristics."[128]

Far less likely to be protected by copyright are characters who are delineated by words in literary works. Most such literary characters are "types" with a limited number of not uncommon personality attributes; their "character" is more a reflection of a story line or plot than of any intrinsic detailed nature. Literary characters as such are thus commonly regarded as falling on the "idea" side of the dichotomy between unprotectible idea and protectible expression. Frequently cited are the memorable lines penned by Learned Hand in 1930:

127. Gaiman v. McFarlane, 360 F.3d 644 (7th Cir. 2004); Walt Disney Prods. v. Air Pirates, 581 F.2d 751 (9th Cir. 1978) (Mickey Mouse parodied in defendant's risqué comic books).

128. DeCarlo v. Archie Comic Publ'ns, Inc., 127 F. Supp. 2d 497 (S.D.N.Y.), aff'd, 11 Fed. Appx. 26 (2d Cir. 2001) (unpublished).

If Twelfth Night were copyrighted, it is quite possible that a second comer might so closely imitate Sir Toby Belch or Malvolio as to infringe, but it would not be enough that for one of his characters he cast a riotous knight who kept wassail to the discomfort of the household, or a vain and foppish steward who became amorous of his mistress. These would be no more than Shakespeare's "ideas" in the play, as little capable of monopoly as Einstein's Doctrine of Relativity, or Darwin's theory of the Origin of Species. It follows that the less developed the characters, the less they can be copyrighted; that is the penalty an author must bear for marking them too indistinctly.[129]

No court appears to have held that a strictly literary character (i.e., one described only in words intended for reading) that was the subject of litigation meets the standard of copyrightability, so that it would infringe to depict such a character (particularly without his or her name) in an altogether different tale. The Court of Appeals for the Second Circuit has however intimated, without elaboration, that the Hopalong Cassidy and Amos & Andy characters, in their textual description, pass Judge Hand's test.[130]

Characters that are delineated through human actors on the motion-picture or television screen fall somewhere between cartoon or animated characters on the one hand and literary characters on the other.[131] Although the decided cases are few, courts appear to be inclined to grant copyright to those film characters—perhaps indeed to an extent that affords copyright to stock character "types" and thus to literary "ideas." Thus, a televised automobile commercial depicting a fast-driving debonair and handsome tuxedoed man, saving himself and his attractive female partner from the clutches of a high-tech villain, was held to infringe the James Bond character (even though that name was not used).[132] And another district court held: "This Court has no difficulty ruling as a matter of law that the Rocky characters are delineated so extensively that they are protected from bodily appropriation when taken as a group and transposed into a sequel by another author."[133] This conclusion—resting on the Learned Hand test of detailed "delinea-

---

129. Nichols v. Universal Pictures Corp., 45 F.2d 119, 121 (2d Cir. 1930) (holding play, *Abie's Irish Rose*, and its characters not infringed by motion picture, *The Cohens and the Kellys*).

130. Filmvideo Releasing Corp. v. Hastings, 668 F.2d 91 (2d Cir. 1981); Silverman v. CBS, Inc., 870 F.2d 40 (2d Cir. 1989). *See also* Anderson v. Stallone, 11 U.S.P.Q.2D 1161 (C.D Cal. 1989) (holding characters in *Rocky* motion pictures copyrightable).

131. *See* Gaiman, 360 F.3d at 660, 661 ("The description of a character in prose leaves much to the imagination, even when the description is detailed. . . . [O]ne hardly knows what Sam Spade looked like. But everyone knows what Humphrey Bogart looked like.").

132. Metro–Goldwyn–Mayer, Inc. v. American Honda Motor Co., 900 F. Supp. 1287 (C.D. Cal. 1995).

133. Anderson v. Stallone, 11 U.S.P.Q.2d 1161 (C.D. Cal. 1989).

tion"—was no doubt reinforced by the previous appearances and development of Rocky, Adrian, Apollo, Clubber and Paulie in three motion pictures, and the adoption of their names in the screenplay of the alleged infringer.

E.   Sound Recordings

U.S. copyright law, unlike most other countries' copyright laws, includes sound recordings within the subject matter of copyright (rather than a "neighboring rights" regime), though, as we shall see in Chapter 6, the exclusive rights of the sound recording copyright owner are somewhat truncated compared to the rights of the copyright holder of the musical or literary works that may be incorporated in a sound recording. While sound recordings necessarily result from a mechanical (or now, digital) process, the intervention of a machine in these works' creation does not deprive them of originality, any more than does the participation of a machine in the creation of a photograph. The House Report recognizes two different kinds of originality manifested in a sound recording:

The copyrightable elements in a sound recording will usually, though not always, involve "authorship" both on the part of the performers whose performance is captured and on the part of the record producer responsible for setting up the recording session, capturing and electronically processing the sounds, and compiling and editing them to make the final sound recording. There may, however, be cases where the record producer's contribution is so minimal that the performance is the only copyrightable element in the work, and there may be cases (for example, recordings of bird calls, sounds of racing cars, et cetera) where only the record producer's contribution is copyrightable.[134]

Sound recordings typically incorporate copyrighted works, most often musical compositions. Indeed, a sound recording may serve as the medium of first fixation of a musical composition—imagine a recording of a performance of a spontaneous jazz composition: once the work is recorded, it meets the fixation threshold for federal copyright protection. The musical composition now comes within federal copyright regardless of any subsequent reduction of the composition to sheet music form. Whether recorded in an audible format or in notation, the musical composition exists as a copyrighted work apart from its medium of fixation. Sound recordings, by contrast, are defined in section 101 as "works that result from the fixation of a series of musical, spoken or other sounds." In addition, because section 114(b) makes clear that the scope of protection extends only to "the actual sounds fixed in the

---

134. H.R. Rep. No. 94–1476, 94th Cong., 2d Sess. 55–56 (1976).

recording," the copyrighted work does not exist apart from its fixation. Thus, creation of another recording that imitates the first recording's recorded sounds (imagine a "sound alike" rendition of a singer's performance) cannot infringe the copyright in the sound recording. By way of comparison, consider a photograph: the fixation, that is, the image as imprinted on some medium, may sometimes constitute the entire "work," but as the *Mannion* court recognized, the "work" may also comprehend the photographer's construction of the elements of the photographed image; as a result, reconstruction and rephotographing of those elements may infringe the copyright in the photograph, even though the second photographer has not copied the first photographer's fixation of the image.[135]

It is important not to conflate the categories of a sound recording and the work it records. The sound recording evidences the composition, but in copyright terms it is also a work in its own right, assuming the performance or process of recording it demonstrates sufficient originality. Hence, copyright will protect a sound recording of Dvorak's Symphony *From the New World*, not on account of the musical composition (which is in the public domain), but because of the authorship manifested in the playing of the orchestra and the engineering of the recording. By the same token, as we have seen regarding the relationship of derivative and underlying works, a copyrighted sound recording of a public domain musical composition will not restore the recorded composition to copyright protection: any one else remains free to make his or her own performance and/or recording of the *New World* symphony (and even to approximate the way in which the first orchestra performed the work).

F. Government Works

It is obviously in the public interest that persons be able freely to quote from—and indeed to reproduce in full—federal statutes, regulations, court opinions, legislative and commission reports, and the like. Section 105 of the Copyright Act provides: "Copyright protection under this title is not available for any work of the United States Government, but the United States Government is not precluded from receiving and holding copyrights transferred to it by assignment, bequest, or otherwise." In section 101, a "work of the United States Government" is defined as "a work prepared by an officer or employee of the United States Government as part of that person's official duties." The House Report states that the intention is to apply this definition in the same

---

135. Mannion v. Coors Brewing, 377 F. Supp. 2d 444 (S.D.N.Y. 2005), discussed *supra*, p. 46.

manner as the definition of "works made for hire" by employees in the scope of their employment.[136] Not swept within the exclusion under section 105 would be a work commissioned by a branch of the U.S. Government and authored by an "independent contractor" or a free-lance writer or artist.

As an example of the operation of these statutory provisions, consider a work of public art, a war memorial commissioned by the Federal Government.[137] The sculptor is not an "employee" of the U.S. Government, and so the work cannot be prepared as part of any "official duties" with the Government. Accordingly, the sculpture is eligible for copyright protection in the name of the author. The sculptor can, however, agree voluntarily to transfer the copyright to the relevant Federal entity, say, the National Parks Service, which would then hold a valid copyright as transferee pursuant to section 105. Suppose the National Parks service prepared a brochure about the sculpture, and assigned one of its employee photographers to create images of the monument as part of his or her job responsibilities. The photographs (but not the sculpture) would be treated as a work of the U.S. Government and would thus be ineligible for copyright protection. (But a third party's reproduction of the photographs would infringe the copyright in the underlying sculpture. The Parks Service thus might bring an action, not for the copying of the photograph, but for the reproduction of the sculpture depicted in the photo.)

No express provision of the Copyright Act similarly consigns to the public domain works prepared by employees of state and local governments. In 1888, however, the Supreme Court in *Banks v. Manchester*[138] held that state judicial opinions are ineligible for federal copyright protection because state judges are paid with public funds (the implication being that the public is therefore the owner), and because, as a matter of policy, the public interest is served by free access to the law by persons expected to conform their conduct to it (a "due process" rationale). The same rationales were without much dispute extended to state legislation and administrative regulations. After an uncontentious century, the issue of copyrightability of official state materials has come to the fore in two contexts.

The first is the nature and range of state materials that are to be analogized to legislation and court decisions, which are denied copyright.

---

136. H.R. Rep. No. 94–1476, at 58 (1976).

137. This example is loosely inspired by *Gaylord v. United States*, 595 F.3d 1364 (Fed. Cir. 2010). Frank Gaylord, a sculptor, was commissioned to create a monument for the Korean War memorial. A freelance photographer created images of the memo-

rial and sold reproduction rights to the U.S. Postal Service for use as a stamp. Gaylord sued the U.S. government for unauthorized reproductions, through the stamp, in violation of his copyright in the sculpture.

138. 128 U.S. 244 (1888).

The Court of Appeals for the Second Circuit has held[139] that official county "tax maps"—showing the ownership, size, and location of real property parcels in each of the political subdivisions of Suffolk County in New York—are not automatically stripped of copyright simply because they are authored by county officials and because they are used as a basis for the assessment of property taxes. The court held that the taxing statute affords the public adequate notice of their obligations, so that state ownership of the maps would create no problems of due process, and it remanded so that further evidence could be presented on the issue of the county's need for copyright as a financial incentive for its mapmaking activity.

The second issue of current importance is whether privately authored codes—such as building codes and fire codes, or even model laws—that are written by expert groups lose their copyright when they are adopted (often simply by reference) by a legislative body, say in a county or town. The few cases addressing this question have provided a less-than-definitive answer. However, the Court of Appeals for the Fifth Circuit, sitting en banc, concluded in 2002 in a sharply divided decision[140] that, although such privately drafted codes are protected by copyright at the outset, they are thrust into the public domain when they are adopted by a town as its authoritative legal text, at least when such adoption is actively sought by the drafting body. The principles of *Banks v. Manchester* were held to be controlling, although the dissent concluded that a denial of copyright would pose a threat to the useful provision of such codes to busy and underfunded municipal entities. The majority distinguished the situation from the several cases involving the mere "reference" by a city or state to some copyrighted material, privately authored and already in private commercial use; in those cases, involving for example a state's reference for insurance purposes to automobile values contained in the well-known *Red Book* (of the National Automobile Dealers' Association), the courts have concluded that copyright is not lost.[141]

139. County of Suffolk, N.Y. v. First Am. Real Estate Solutions, 261 F.3d 179 (2d Cir. 2001).

140. Veeck v. Southern Bldg. Code Cong. Int'l, Inc., 293 F.3d 791 (5th Cir. 2002) (en banc).

141. Practice Mgmt. Info. Corp. v. American Med. Ass'n, 121 F.3d 516 (9th Cir. 1997) (AMA coding system to identify medical procedures); CCC Info. Servs., Inc. v. Maclean Hunter Mkt. Reports, 44 F.3d 61 (2d Cir. 1994) (NADA *Red Book* auto values).

Chapter 3

OWNERSHIP OF COPYRIGHT

The provisions of the Copyright Act that deal with the ownership of copyright are for the most part straightforward. They declare that the author of a work is the initial copyright owner; that joint authors are co-owners of copyright; that the employer in the case of a work made for hire is considered the author and is presumed to be the copyright owner; that copyright ownership of a contribution to a collective work is different from the copyright ownership of the collective work itself; that copyright ownership is distinct from ownership of the physical object in which the copyrighted work is embodied (a distinction discussed *supra* Chapter 1);[1] and that copyright may be transferred in whole or in part. The relationship between federal copyright rules regarding transfers of rights and state contract law makes these issues somewhat more complex, particularly regarding the interpretation of the scope of the grant. Even more complex are the provisions regarding authors' rights to terminate transfers of copyright. Because these reversion rights derive from the prior two-term structure of the duration of copyright, we will consider them at the end of the next chapter, which addresses the copyright term.

I. Initial Ownership of Copyright

Under section 201(a) of the Copyright Act, copyright ownership of a work vests initially in the author. Who is an "author" under the Copyright Act? The statute does not define the term. The Supreme Court has stated, "As a general rule, the author is the party who actually creates the work, that is, the person who translates an idea into a fixed, tangible expression entitled to copyright protection."[2] The "general rule" requires some nuance, however, because it appears to elide the difference between a "work" and the "tangible medium" in which it is embodied; one person can be an author of a literary or musical work, without writing it down himself, by dictating to another who, or to a machine which, "fixes" the words or notes. The former is the "author;" the act of fixation no more converts the amanuensis into an "author" than it elevates the machine to that status. The copyright law elects between two competing concepts of authorship: one based on conception, the other based on execution. The dominant view today prefers the intellectual to the muscular contribution to creation. But it would be an

---

1. 17 U.S.C. §§ 201, 202.

2. CCNV v. Reid, 490 U.S. 730, 737 (1989).

59

overstatement to claim that U.S. copyright today rests entirely on an intellectual characterization of authorship. The statute enshrines yet another concept of authorship in our copyright law, an economic one. Under this conception, the "author" is the person or entity who finances the work's creation and dissemination, including covering the cost of the persons actually creating the work. This person's or entity's assumption of all economic risks entitles it to be treated as the "author." This is the concept sustaining the "works made for hire" provision of the U.S. Copyright Act, which endows employers and certain commissioning parties with the statutory status of "author."[3]

The economic characterization of authorship nonetheless may be in some tension with the Constitutional direction that exclusive rights be "secur[ed] to authors." Does "author" in the constitutional sense mean anyone Congress says it is? The close parallels between the Constitutional copyright clause and the English Statute of Anne, the latter of which leaves no doubt that the "authors" it addresses are the actual creators,[4] suggest that the Framers also envisioned the creators, and not their hiring parties.[5] As we will see, the universe of works made for hire under the 1976 Act is narrower than under the judicial interpretation of the 1909 Act, but the question remains whether Congress in fact has power to vest copyright initially in a person or entity other than the work's creator(s).[6]

A. Works made for hire

However shaky its constitutional foundation, the "work made for hire" is in fact a widely endorsed and a most important concept in the area of copyright ownership. If a biochemist employed by a pharmaceutical company prepares as part of her duties a technical manual on the company's research and development procedures, the manual would be a clear example of a "work made for hire." In such a case, section 201(b) of the Copyright Act declares that the employer rather than the creative human employee is considered the "author" for all purposes under the Act. Moreover, the employer is deemed to be the *owner* of the copyright unless the employer and employee agree otherwise in a signed writing.

---

3. For a comprehensive recounting of the historical development of the work for hire doctrine in the United States, *see* Catherine L. Fisk, *Authors at Work: The Origins of the Work-for-Hire Doctrine*, 15 YALE J.L. & HUMAN. 1 (2003).

4. An Act For the Encouragement of Learning by Vesting the Copies of Printed Books in the Authors or Purchasers of such Copies, 8 Anne ch. 19 (1709–1710).

5. *See* Catherine L. Fisk, WORKING KNOWLEDGE, EMPLOYEE INNOVATION AND THE RISE OF CORPORATE INTELLECTUAL PROPERTY, 1800–1930, pp. 31—33 (2009).

6. *Cf.* Childress v. Taylor, 945 F.2d 500, 506 n.5 (2d Cir. 1991) (in dicta, presuming constitutionality of work for hire).

Because characterizing a work as one "made for hire" has implications not only for ownership of copyright, but also for duration (as discussed in the following chapter, the "life-plus–70" formula does not apply) and other important aspects of the statute, it is useful to set out the statutory definition in section 101:

> A "work made for hire" is—(1) a work prepared by an employee within the scope of his or her employment; or (2) a work specially ordered or commissioned for use as a contribution to a collective work, as a part of a motion picture or other audiovisual work, as a translation, as a supplementary work, as a compilation, as an instructional text, as a test, as answer material for a test, or as an atlas, if the parties expressly agree in a written instrument signed by them that the work shall be considered a work made for hire.

This elaborate provision is a congressional reaction to the failure of the 1909 Act to define the phrase and to the confusion in much of the case law that had developed under that Act.[7]

1. Employee-created works

Despite the 1976 Act's detail, the definition of "work made for hire" proved soon after 1978 to be a source of disagreement among a number of courts of appeals. In particular, there was confusion as to whether a commissioned work could become the equivalent of a work prepared by an employee when the commissioning party closely supervised the execution of the work by the independent contractor. A unanimous Supreme Court dispelled such a misconception in its 1989 decision in *Community for Creative Non–Violence v. Reid*,[8] which involved conflicting ownership claims in a statue that was prepared by a sculptor at the request of a group devoted to advocacy of the rights of the homeless. The Court examined the 1976 Act's structure, its purpose, and the underlying legislative and judicial history, and concluded that—absent compliance with the strict requirements in the second part of the definition of "work made for hire"—a work will be "made for hire" only if it is created within the scope of employment by a person found to be an "employee" under the rules of agency commonly applied in tort cases. There is to be essentially an airtight differentiation of works by employees and works by independent contractors, and the latter must fall within both the subject-category and writing requirements to be works made for hire.

---

7. For works created before 1978, the work-for-hire precedents under the 1909 Act will still govern. *See* Twentieth Century Fox Film Corp. v. Entertainment Distrib., 429 F.3d 869 (9th Cir. 2005); Martha Gra- ham Sch. & Dance Found., Inc. v. Martha Graham Ctr. of Contemporary Dance, Inc., 380 F.3d 624 (2d Cir. 2004).

8. 490 U.S. 730 (1989).

The Court held that whether the "employee" standard is satisfied is a factual determination to be made on a case-by-case basis by examining a number of circumstances:

> In determining whether a hired party is an employee under the general common law of agency, we consider the hiring party's right to control the manner and means by which the product is accomplished. Among the other factors relevant to this inquiry are the skill required; the source of the instrumentalities and tools; the location of the work; the duration of the relationship between the parties; whether the hiring party has the right to assign additional projects to the hired party; the extent of the hired party's discretion over when and how long to work; the method of payment; the hired party's role in hiring and paying assistants; whether the work is part of the regular business of the hiring party; whether the hiring party is in business; the provision of employee benefits; and the tax treatment of the hired party. See Restatement [of Agency, Second] § 220(2) (setting forth a nonexhaustive list of factors relevant to determining whether a hired party is an employee). No one of these factors is determinative.[9]

The outcome in *Reid* is of great significance to many freelance writers and artists whose works do not fall within the "independent contractor" subject-matter categories of the statutory definition, or who have not stipulated in writing that their work has been made for hire. Because under *Reid* their works will be found *not* to be works made for hire, the freelancers (or their surviving family members) are given the power, as will be seen in the next Chapter, after a substantial number of years to recapture the copyright from the putative "employer" and to assert all the rights of ownership. The power to terminate copyright transfers does not apply to works made for hire.[10]

Although the Supreme Court, in *Reid*, stressed the importance of advance predictability in resolving questions of ownership, the multi-factor definition of "employee" that it borrowed from the Restatement of Agency is of course among the most elusive definitions in the law. Accordingly, courts of appeals have gradually come to identify those fewer elements that are the most important in applying the first part of the "work made for hire" definition: the hiring party's right to control the manner and means of creation; the skill required; whether the hiring party has the right to assign additional projects; the provision of employ-

---

9. *Id.* at 751–52 (citations and footnotes omitted).

10. Nor are the artist-protective provisions of the Visual Artists Rights Act (section 106A of the Copyright Act) applicable to works made for hire. *See* Carter v. Helmsley–Spear, Inc., 71 F.3d 77 (2d Cir. 1995).

ee benefits; and the tax treatment of the hired party.[11] Moreover, under the statutory definition, even an "employee's" creative work will not be a work for hire if it is prepared otherwise than "within the scope of employment," and here too the pertinent definition is provided by the Restatement of Agency.[12]

The 1976 Copyright Act denominates all employee-created work (within the scope of employment) as "for hire"; it does not distinguish among employees. But caselaw under the 1909 Act and English copyright law recognized a "teacher exception" for the lectures and articles and books of university professors, even though academics are hired to teach and to publish. While there is no specific caselaw under the 1976 Copyright Act, Judge Posner, himself a noted academic, has suggested that the "teacher exception" persists because section 201(b) vests work for hire copyright in the "employer or other person *for whom the work was prepared*" (emphasis supplied), and notwithstanding "publish or perish," the tradition of academic freedom insulates professors from preparing work "for" their employers.[13] Arguably, this rationale extends beyond teachers to any employed author who enjoys creative autonomy in her work. Nonetheless, courts have declined to forge a general "genius exception" to the work for hire doctrine in favor of especially creative employees. Thus, the Second Circuit held that Martha Graham, as the employee of her dance company, created much of her choreography as work for hire; the company, rather than Graham's legatee, therefore owned her dances.[14]

2. Certain commissioned works

If the work is not prepared by an employee in the scope of her employment, but rather is commissioned, then it cannot be a "work made for hire" unless the work falls into one of the list of nine statutory categories of "specially ordered or commissioned works," *and* unless the creator and the commissioning party both sign an agreement stating that the work will be for hire. Both the subject-matter and the signed-writing prerequisites have given rise to questions. Regarding the nine

---

11. Aymes v. Bonelli, 980 F.2d 857 (2d Cir. 1992) (emphasizing in particular the latter two factors).

12. *See* Shaul v. Cherry Valley–Springfield Cent. Sch. Dist., 363 F.3d 177, 185–86 (2d Cir. 2004); Avtec Sys., Inc. v. Peiffer, 21 F.3d 568 (4th Cir. 1994); Molinelli–Freytes v. University of P.R., 792 F.Supp.2d 150 (D.P.R. 2010). *See also* Warren Freedenfeld Associates, Inc. v. McTigue, 531 F.3d 38, 48 (1st Cir. 2008) (without applying Restatement, upholds the general application of agency law to the concept of the "scope of employment").

13. Hays v. Sony Corp. of Am., 847 F.2d 412 (7th Cir. 1988); *accord*, Weinstein v. University of Illinois, 811 F.2d 1091 (7th Cir. 1987) (Easterbrook, J.—also an academic).

14. Martha Graham School & Dance Foundation, Inc. v. Martha Graham Center of Contemporary Dance, Inc., 380 F.3d 624 (2d Cir.2004).

statutory categories, the list is limitative and should be read restrictive-ly. While many of the listed works may involve multiple authors, so that vesting ownership in a single person or entity can considerably reduce subsequent transactions costs, the categories themselves defy synthesis into an overall principle, probably because they reflect the lobbying of the interested industries. The specificity of these categories, as well as the traditional approach that exceptions to the general statutory rule of creator-ownership should be narrowly construed, together counsel against analogizing from the statutory categories in order to include additional multiple-authored works.

For example, the category of compilations may cover many works, but because, as we saw in Chapter 2, the copyright in a compilation is distinct from, and does not affect the ownership of, the compiled compo-nents, the compilation's work-for-hire status will not make the commis-sioning party the "author" and owner of the works of which the compilation is comprised. Thus, if a publisher commissions an anthology of poetry, and both the publisher and the editor sign a work-for-hire agreement, the publisher will be the "author" only of the selection and arrangement of the poems, but not of the poems themselves. (And, in order to include the poems, the publisher will require agreements from the individual poets.) By contrast, the category of "contributions to a collective work" would appear to cover the components of the collective work, as well as the collection. Thus, a newspaper is a "collective work," and a commissioned contribution to the newspaper, such as an article or a photograph, could be a work-for-hire, if the signed writing condition is also fulfilled.

Falling within a statutory category is a necessary but not sufficient condition to work-for-hire status. The second condition is a signed agreement between the commissioning party and all the creators specify-ing that the commissioned work will be "for hire." Although courts have enforced the writing requirement, and thus denied work-for-hire status to insufficiently documented agreements, they have disagreed as to the timing of the writing. That is, some have required that the writing be executed before the work is created, while others have permitted a subsequent writing to confirm an oral agreement reached before the work's creation.[15] The better view, we believe, would require execution of the writing before creation, lest leaving the formalization of the alleged oral agreement till after the work is completed afford commissioning parties an opportunity to refuse payment unless the creators sign the agreement.

---

15. *Compare* Schiller & Schmidt, Inc. v. Nordisco, 969 F.2d 410 (7th Cir. 1992), *with* Playboy Enters. v. Dumas, 53 F.3d 549 (2d Cir. 1995). For the same proposition as *Schiller, see* Gladwell Gov't Servs., Inc. v. County of Marin, 265 Fed. Appx. 624 (9th Cir. 2008). To date, no other Circuits ap-pear to follow the *Playboy* approach.

It is important to recognize that not all multiple-authored commissioned works are "for hire." On the contrary, the statutory default position is to classify these as "joint works" whose copyrights are shared among the creators. The further requirement of a writing signed by the commissioning party and all co-creators in effect reinforces the default position. Noncompliance with this condition prevents the default from shifting, and the copyright will vest in the creators.

B.   *Joint works*

If the work is a "joint work," the authors are co-owners of the copyright. The term "joint work" is defined in section 101 to mean "a work prepared by two or more authors with the intention that their contributions be merged into inseparable or interdependent parts of a unitary whole." The statutory specification of "interdependent" parts makes clear that contributions which could be freestanding, if created to go together, will generate a joint work.[16] For example, if a popular song is created collaboratively by composer and lyricist, they are both regarded as co-owners of the copyright, even though the composer's melody and the lyricist's words could have constituted separate works. If, however, the tune is written initially as a purely instrumental work without lyrics, is marketed that way, and the lyrics are added at a later date by a lyricist at the composer's invitation, the work is not a "joint work" within the statutory definition.

A work may be treated as a joint work under the Copyright Act even though the contributions of the collaborating authors are by no means equal, whether measured by quantity, quality, or commercial value. Even though, for example, the musical public may be enthralled by a song's catchy melody and may have only the faintest recollection of the accompanying lyrics, both composer and lyricist will be treated as joint authors provided the statutory definition is satisfied. Courts generally hold, however, that to be a joint author one's contribution must be more than *de minimis* and must manifest original authorship. Therefore a homebuyer who makes suggestions or provides fragmentary sketches to an architect cannot claim joint authorship of the final and detailed architectural plans;[17] an explanation by a business person to a computer programmer regarding the operations of the business and the desired functions to be performed through the program does not make the

---

16. *Compare* UK Copyright Designs and Patents Act 1988 s. 10(1): "In this Part a 'work of joint authorship' means a work produced by the collaboration of two or more authors *in which the contribution of each author is not distinct from that of the other author or authors.*" (emphasis supplied)

17. Meltzer v. Zoller, 520 F. Supp. 847 (D.N.J. 1981).

business person a joint author of the program;[18] and a person does not become a joint author of a play merely by contributing factual research and general character suggestions.[19] Courts thus have interpolated into the statutory requirement that the co-authors merge their "contributions" the further condition that these contributions be "copyrightable."[20] Arguably, this additional requirement derives implicitly from the statute, which defines a joint work as "prepared by two or more *authors*" (emphasis supplied); if one contributes only noncopyrightable material, perhaps one is not an "author."[21]

More likely, the genesis of the requirement is a practical one. In these situations, where there is a stark imbalance between the contributions of each of the two (or multiple) authors, the courts are concerned that a finding of joint authorship will result in an equal sharing of the proceeds derived from the exploitation of the copyrighted work; before the "subordinate" author can make a convincing claim to such equal financial rewards, he or she must do more than contribute general ideas, suggestions or the like, and should bear the burden of protecting his or her financial interests through a negotiated contract.[22] There is also an apparent concern that a less demanding rule will too readily invite claims of joint authorship on the part of any number of persons who are involved in a collaborative creative enterprise (such as putting the final touches to the text of a play or screenplay), and who make minor suggestions that are adopted by the playwright or director.[23] To rationalize these safeguards, courts have come to adopt the approach that—in addition to the statutory requirement of a mutual subjective intention to merge contributions into a unitary work—it is also necessary, to create a joint work, that there be a mutual intention to share authorship (especially including the ownership consequences of joint authorship), as

---

18. Whelan Assocs., Inc. v. Jaslow Dental Lab., Inc., 609 F. Supp. 1307 (E.D. Pa. 1985), *aff'd on other grounds*, 797 F.2d 1222 (3d Cir. 1986).

19. Childress v. Taylor, 945 F.2d 500 (2d Cir. 1991). There is some question whether, to be a joint author, one's creative contribution—no matter how detailed and substantial—must be fixed in a tangible medium of expression. *Meltzer*, 520 F. Supp. 847 (homeowner did not "fix" specific suggestions).

20. *See, e.g.*, Gaylord v. United States, 595 F.3d 1364 (Fed. Cir. 2010); Brown v. Flowers, 196 Fed. Appx. 178 (4th Cir. 2006); Aalmuhammed v. Lee, 202 F.3d 1227 (9th Cir. 2000); Thomson v. Larson, 147 F.3d 195 (2d Cir. 1998); *Childress*, 945 F.2d 500.

21. *But see* Gaiman v. McFarlane, 360 F.3d 644 (7th Cir. 2004) (Posner, J.): "Here is a typical case from academe. One professor has brilliant ideas but can't write; another is an excellent writer, but his ideas are commonplace. So they collaborate on an academic article, one contributing the ideas, which are not copyrightable, and the other the prose envelope, and . . . they sign as co-authors. Their intent to be the joint owners of the copyright in the article would be plain, and that should be enough to constitute them joint authors within the meaning of 17 U.S.C. § 201(a)."

22. *See Childress*, 945 F.2d 500.

23. Erickson v. Trinity Theatre, Inc., 13 F.3d 1061 (7th Cir. 1994).

manifested by shared credit or billing and by shared approval over revisions, promotion and the like.[24]

Although the copyright law has never expressly defined the nature of the co-ownership held by joint authors, courts through the years have treated joint copyright owners as tenants in common, each owning an undivided interest in the whole of the copyright. Each co-owner is therefore entitled to exercise all of the exclusive rights set forth in section 106 of the Act herself, or to license other persons to exercise those rights—on a nonexclusive basis—even without obtaining the other co-author(s)' approval; but there is a duty to account to all other co-owners for their respective shares of the proceeds of the co-author's own or her licensees' authorized exploitations.[25] To grant exclusive rights, however, all co-authors must agree.[26] Upon the death of a co-owner of copyright, his or her share passes pursuant to will or through the usual intestate channels; it is not automatically vested in the surviving co-owners.

Thus, if Composer and Lyricist together write a popular song, either one of them may license the public performance of the song or its recording onto a motion picture soundtrack, subject to a duty to account to the other for half of the proceeds (and subject to any contractual agreement to share in some other proportion, and/or to condition any third-party grants on all co-authors' approval). If Composer dies, her half interest in the copyright will pass to her surviving spouse if he is named as legatee in the will, and not to Lyricist by way of survivorship.

If, however, the song was not created as a "joint work" within the statutory definition—for example, because the melody is written one year and the lyrics are added years later—then Composer would own the copyright only in the tune, and Lyricist would own the copyright only in the words. Neither could exploit the entire song, or license a third person to do so, without securing the consent of the other—and the duration of copyright protection would be calculated separately for each of the two components.

C. *Collective works*

Another area of confusion under prior law had been the respective rights of, on one side, persons contributing articles to journals, magazines, encyclopedias, and other "collective works" and, on the other side, the person who owns copyright in the collective work. Section 101 of the 1976 Act defines "collective work" as "a work, such as a periodical issue,

---

24. Thomson v. Larson, 147 F.3d 195 (2d Cir. 1998). *See also* Aalmuhammed v. Lee, 202 F.3d 1227 (9th Cir. 2000).

25. *Larson,* 147 F.3d 195.

26. *Id.* at 200.

anthology, or encyclopedia, in which a number of contributions, constituting separate and independent works in themselves, are assembled into a collective whole." Collective works are thus a species of "compilation," and as with all compilations,[27] a copyright in a collective work embraces only those elements of original authorship manifested therein, which may be no more than the choice of contributions and the sequence in which those contributions are published.

Section 201(c) makes clear that copyright in an individual contribution vests initially in the author of that contribution and is distinct from copyright in the collective work as a whole. Absent an express written transfer from that author, the owner of copyright in the collective work (e.g., the magazine) does not own the copyright in the individual contribution, but is presumed to have acquired "only the privilege of reproducing and distributing the contribution as part of that particular collective work, any revision of that collective work, and any later collective work in the same series." The publisher cannot, therefore, revise the contribution itself or publish it in an altogether different magazine.

A significant question was decided in 2001 by the Supreme Court, interpreting the statutory language just quoted. In *New York Times Co. v. Tasini*,[28] freelance authors had contributed articles to (and been paid therefor by) newspapers and magazines, which had published those articles in hardcopy form. Nothing was said, orally or in writing, about the electronic publication rights because in many cases the Internet and the CD–ROM were not yet on the scene when the freelancers authorized publication. When, at a later date, the newspapers and magazines licensed the distribution of those articles online (in Lexis–Nexis, among other places) and on disks, the authors complained that they had never initially conveyed those rights and that they were thus entitled to new and separate compensation therefor. The respective rights of the publishers (the owners of copyright in the hardcopy collective works) and the authors turned upon whether the statutory presumption that the former may make "any revision of that collective work" embraced the incorporation of the articles in digital compilations. The Supreme Court held for the authors. The Court found that the articles were individually searchable from among the thousands of articles in the electronic databases and could be retrieved by the user altogether out of the context of the hardcopy collective work, so that it was a distortion of language to find that the latter had merely been "revised."

Applying the Supreme Court's direction that the section 201(c) privilege applies only if the "revision" maintains the individual articles in their original context, courts of appeals have concluded that there is

---

27. *See supra* pp. 37–41.   **28.** 533 U.S. 483 (2001).

an allowable "revision" under section 201(c) when the electronic version visually reproduces the totality of the pages and journal issues as they appeared in the print version, including photographs, advertisements and the like.[29]

II. Transfer of Copyright Ownership

Copyright, like other forms of tangible and intangible property, can be transferred *inter vivos* or upon death from the author, or a subsequent copyright owner, and transferred again. This basic principle is affirmed in section 201(d)(1) of the 1976 Act, which provides: "The ownership of a copyright may be transferred in whole or in part by any means of conveyance or by operation of law, and may be bequeathed by will or pass as personal property by the applicable laws of intestate succession."

A. *Divisibility*

Under prior law, courts developed an important distinction between an "assignment" of copyright, which carried the entire copyright to a person who then was known as the "proprietor" or owner of copyright, and a "license," which carried to another less than the entire copyright, for example, only the right to dramatize a novel or to publicly perform a musical composition. Copyright was generally said to be "indivisible," in the sense that only one person at any given time could validly claim to "own" it. The concept of indivisibility and the distinction between an assignment and a license were important under the 1909 Act, because only the name of the "proprietor" could properly be placed in the copyright notice (the insertion of the wrong name could thrust the work into the public domain), and only the "proprietor" could bring an action for copyright infringement.

The 1976 Act made a significant break with the past when it abandoned the concept of indivisibility of copyright ownership along with its more dubious ramifications. Section 201(d)(2) provides:

> Any of the exclusive rights comprised in a copyright, including any subdivision of any of the rights specified by section 106, may be transferred as provided by clause (1) and owned separately. The owner of any particular exclusive right is entitled, to the extent of that right, to all of the protection and remedies accorded to the copyright owner by this title.

Thus, a person who owns no more than an exclusive license to perform publicly a dramatic work or to broadcast a motion picture (but

---

29. *See, e.g.,* Greenberg v. National Geographic Soc'y, 533 F.3d 1244 (11th Cir. 2008); Faulkner v. National Geographic Enters. Inc., 409 F.3d 26 (2d Cir. 2005).

not to make or sell copies) is nonetheless regarded as the "owner" of that right. It is that person who can properly bring an action for infringement of that particular exclusive right.[30] The Copyright Act refers to the conveyance of either all rights or less than all rights as a "transfer," and it eliminates the significance of characterizing a transfer as either an assignment or a license.

B. Formal requirements

Under current law, what is important in connection with copyright transfers is whether the transfer is exclusive or nonexclusive.[31] Section 204(a) provides that "a transfer of copyright ownership, other than by operation of law, is not valid unless an instrument of conveyance, or a note or memorandum of the transfer, is in writing and signed by the owner of the rights conveyed or such owner's duly authorized agent." Because section 101 defines "transfer of copyright ownership" to include both assignments and exclusive licenses, a grant of an exclusive license of any of the rights or subdivisions of rights in section 106 must be manifested in a signed writing if it is to be effective, by virtue of the copyright statute of frauds set forth in section 204(a).

The 1976 Act, however, sets out no rules regarding the conditions for a valid grant of *non*-exclusive rights—for example, separate grants to several production companies to perform a dramatic work. Such licenses will be valid even without a signed written memorial (although, of course, the practicing attorney will routinely give or take such a license by written agreement). Courts have held that non-exclusive licenses may be oral or inferred from conduct.[32] On the other hand, relevant state statutes of frauds, such as those applicable to agreements whose value exceeds $500,[33] might nonetheless require certain grants of non-exclusive rights to be in writing. Given the author-protective policy of section

---

30. Section 501(b). Note, however, that even after the author has transferred exclusive rights, she still may have standing to sue in the event of their infringement, if she qualifies as a "beneficial owner," which the House Report defines as "an author who had parted with legal title to the copyright in exchange for percentage royalties based on sales or license fees." H.R. Rep. No. 94–1476 at 114 (1976). Section 501(b) provides: "The legal or beneficial owner of an exclusive right under a copyright is entitled ... to institute an action for any infringement of that particular right committed while he or she is the owner of it."

31. The influence of the old law, however, is still felt. For example, the Court of Appeals for the Ninth Circuit, incorporating doctrine developed under the 1909 Act, has held that the transferee of an exclusive right must, in order to make a valid retransfer of that right to a third party, give notice to and secure the assent of its own initial transferor. Gardner v. Nike, Inc., 279 F.3d 774 (9th Cir. 2002). *Compare* Traicoff v. Digital Media, Inc., 439 F. Supp. 2d 872 (S.D. Ind. 2006) (holding that exclusive licensee may sublicense without approval of copyright owner).

32. Effects Assocs., Inc. v. Cohen, 908 F.2d 555 (9th Cir. 1990).

33. *See, e.g.,* N.Y. U.C.C. § 2–201 (McKinney 2001); Cal. Com. Code § 2201 (West 2002).

204(a),[34] to interpret the 1976 Act's silence on non-exclusive grants as preempting a state-law requirement of a writing seems unwarranted. Where the Copyright Act articulates no specific rules regarding copyright contracts, the general contract norms of the State whose law governs the contract, including the statute of frauds, would apply.

In the interest of maintaining intelligible records relating to copyright ownership, the Copyright Office not only *registers* initial (and renewal) claims of copyright but also *records* "any transfer of copyright ownership or other document pertaining to a copyright," under section 205(a) of the Copyright Act. Recordation of a transfer of copyright in a registered work will provide constructive notice of the facts stated in the recorded document; and, much like a recording system for real estate, copyright recordation will protect the transferee of the copyright against subsequent conflicting transfers even to good-faith purchasers.[35]

C. *Scope of the grant*

Even when there is a valid transfer of an exclusive right—properly documented by a signed writing—there are many cases in which, after the passing of years and the development of a commercially remunerative new technology, the parties dispute whether the grant was meant to embrace the new technology. This first became an issue when dramatization rights were granted prior to the advent of motion pictures, and when film rights were granted prior to the advent of television. More recently, there have been disputes about whether the grant of film rights includes the right to make and distribute videocassettes and DVDs of the film, and whether magazine or book publishing rights embrace digital versions (online and in CD–ROM form). The principal complicating factor is that in most such cases the contract was made before the new technology was even known, let alone commercially widespread, so that it is something of a fiction to describe contract interpretation as a search for the parties' "intentions."

The court decisions (placing weight more on contract analysis than analysis of the Copyright Act, and therefore generally applying state law rules of contract interpretation) do not form a consistent pattern: some courts emphasize the lack of awareness of the new technology and the obligation of the drafter (usually the large media company) to make its intentions clear;[36] other courts emphasize that new technologies will

---

34. *See* Konigsberg Int'l, Inc. v. Rice, 16 F.3d 355, 357 (9th Cir. 1994) ("Section 204's writing requirement not only protects authors from fraudulent claims, but also enhances predictability and certainty of ownership—Congress's paramount goal when it revised the Act in 1976." (quoting *Effects Assocs.*, 908 F.2d at 557) (internal quotation marks omitted)).

35. Sections 205(c), (e), (f).

36. *E.g.*, Cohen v. Paramount Pictures Corp., 845 F.2d 851 (9th Cir. 1988) (music

ordinarily be facilitated through a contract presumption favoring transfer of rights.[37] Most recently, book publishers have been found not to have taken transfers of the right to publish in the form of electronic books, so that several major authors were held to have acted lawfully when conveying "e-Book" rights to digital publishers.[38] And a similar result was reached (as explained immediately above) by the Supreme Court in *New York Times Co. v. Tasini*,[39] when the Court interpreted section 201(c) of the Copyright Act to give to a freelance author, rather than to his or her newspaper or magazine publisher, the right to distribute articles online and on CD–ROM, in the absence of an express contract to the contrary.

Most of the "old license/new media" caselaw to date has concerned grants of rights made before the effective date of the 1976 Copyright Act, and questions going to the scope of the grant were thought not to "arise under" the 1909 Act, because they did not go to the construction of that Act's provisions.[40] The combination of the 1976 Act's provisions for divisibility and signed writings (as well as the provisions on termination of transfers, as we will see in the next chapter) may, by contrast, form the elements of a federal law of copyright transfers. The scope of the grant might then be a matter of federal, rather than state law, and the combined provisions of the 1976 Act may justify a presumption that, when the author assigns something less than all her rights, the scope of a grant made in or after 1978 should be interpreted narrowly.[41] Because Congress has now clarified that "any of the exclusive rights comprised in a copyright, including any subdivision of any of the rights specified by section 106, may be transferred ... and owned separately", it should follow that the grant of any of the exclusive rights, for example, the right to reproduce the work in copies, does not, absent express statement in the signed writing, carry with it the right to perform the work publicly. By the same token, given the statute's specification that "subdivisions" of exclusive rights can be the object of a transfer, it should follow that the grant of the exclusive right to perform a work through one medium of communication, such as broadcasting, does not extend to other media, such as webcasting. The author may, of course, authorize exploitation in

incorporated in motion picture, later distributed in videocassettes).

37. *E.g.*, Boosey & Hawkes Music Publishers, Ltd. v. Walt Disney Co., 145 F.3d 481 (2d Cir. 1998) (Stravinsky's transfer of music rights for Disney film *Fantasia*, later distributed in videocassettes) (relying on Bartsch v. Metro–Goldwyn–Mayer, Inc., 391 F.2d 150 (2d Cir. 1968)).

38. Random House, Inc. v. Rosetta Books, L.L.C., 150 F. Supp. 2d 613 (S.D.N.Y. 2001).

39. 533 U.S. 483 (2001).

40. *See, e.g.*, T.B. Harms Co. v. Eliscu, 339 F.2d 823 (2d Cir.1964).

41. We are not aware that any court has yet so held, but neither are we aware that the issue has yet been presented in these terms. For grants made before 1978, state contract law continues to govern the interpretation of their scope.

multiple media, but if the contract does not clearly cover the exploitation at issue, the proposed presumption would exclude it from the scope of the transfer.

Chapter 4

DURATION AND RENEWAL AND AUTHORS' REVERSION RIGHTS

The Copyright Clause of the Constitution empowers Congress to grant exclusive rights to authors "for limited times." The first United States Copyright Act, enacted in 1790, was patterned on the Statute of Anne of 1710 and gave authors a 14-year period of protection running from the date of first publication, and a right to renew the copyright for 14 more years if the author was alive at the end of the first term. The renewal format, with two rather short terms of protection, was a feature of U.S. copyright law through 1977. The 1909 Copyright Act granted an initial term of protection for 28 years starting from first publication, and a renewal term of another 28 years upon timely registration by the author or by certain designated statutory successors. Under the 1909 Act, an author of an unpublished work could invoke state common-law copyright protection indefinitely until the work was "published" (a term of art to be discussed in the next chapter); for most unpublished works, the author had the option to secure federal copyright protection by registering the work with the Copyright Office. For published works, common-law copyright was preempted and protection could be secured only by complying with the formalities of the federal act.

With the 1976 Copyright Act, effective January 1, 1978, both the starting point and ending point of federal copyright protection were changed. As already noted, copyright attaches as soon as a work is "created," i.e., as soon as it is "fixed" in a tangible medium of expression. This is true even for works that were created before the effective date of that Act, whether those preexisting works were at the time published or unpublished. State common-law copyright for "fixed" works was from that date displaced by federal copyright.[1]

The 1976 Act also dramatically altered the period during which copyright protection lasts, most notably by abandoning the renewal format for works created (or first published) after January 1, 1978, and substituting a term of protection for such works of the author's life plus 50 years. The 1998 "Sonny Bono Copyright Term Extension Act" (CTEA) (named for the late popular singer and congressman) prolonged the term to life plus 70 years. The renewal provisions of the 1909 Act remain important, however, if only because disputes concerning renewal rights (who owns them? were they properly secured?) that accrued with

---

1. 17 U.S.C. §§ 301(a), (b).

respect to works published in 1977 or earlier will no doubt continue to be presented in future litigation. Moreover, Congress in the 1976 Act preserved the renewal format, with some modifications to be explored immediately below, for works first published between 1950 and 1977 (during the life of the 1909 Act) so that they still have come within that format as they have reached the twenty-eighth year thereafter (between 1978 and 2005). In other words, many features of the 1909 Act's intertwining of duration and copyright ownership will remain with us until the copyrights in the last of the works published under the aegis of the 1909 Act expires—that is, until 2072!

A discussion of the renewal format is followed by a discussion of the term of copyright under the 1976 Act and the 1998 CTEA, as well as an analysis of the 1994 Uruguay Round Amendments Act's restoration of copyright in certain non-U.S. works previously in the public domain. The chapter concludes with the 1976 Act's reprise of authors' reversion rights; while the 1976 Act, in implementing a unitary term of copyright, abandoned the renewal format that had triggered reversion rights, the Act also carried forward the policy of the reversion right by introducing new provisions on termination of grants of copyright.

I. The Renewal Format

A. *Under the 1909 Act*

Under section 24 of the 1909 Copyright Act, the author or a person claiming copyright (for example, by way of an assignment) was entitled to a 28–year initial term of copyright protection. Although such protection was available for most unpublished works, the typical work protected by the statute was a work that had been "published," i.e., distributed in copies to the public, with proper notice of copyright. Copyright protection continued for 28 years from the date of publication, and could be prolonged for another 28–year term upon timely application by the person designated in the statute:

> [T]he author of such work, if still living, or the widow, widower, or children of the author, if the author be not living, or if such author, widow, widower, or children be not living, then the author's executors, or in the absence of a will, his next of kin shall be entitled to a renewal and extension of the copyright in such work for a further term of twenty-eight years when application for such renewal and extension shall have been made to the Copyright Office and duly registered therein within one year prior to the expiration of the original term of copyright.

The renewal term, in effect, granted a statutory reversion of interest. Congress's purpose was principally to afford to the author or the author's family an opportunity to claim ownership and to make new transfers for a new remuneration, free and clear of any transfers of or encumbrances on the initial copyright term. An author who had conveyed copyright before or shortly after the publication of his or her work, at a time when its economic value was unknown or speculative, was given by Congress an opportunity to market the copyright a second time, when its economic value was more readily determinable.

If the author were not alive in the twenty-eighth year of the initial copyright term, the right to apply for and to claim the renewal copyright fell to the next available statutory successor. If the author left a widow, widower or children, such person(s) would become the owner(s) of the copyright for the renewal term. Despite the precise statutory language, the Supreme Court held that, in a case in which the author was outlived by a widow or widower *and* one or more children, all of those survivors would take ownership as a class, and the surviving spouse would not take all.[2] The Court, however, did not have to determine whether the spouse takes half and the children divide the other half or whether all of the surviving family members share the copyright equally. Indeed, no lower federal court was called upon for a holding on this issue for nearly a century (after 1909), when in 2005 two different courts of appeals did decide the matter. The First and Sixth Circuit Courts of Appeals both held that the surviving spouse takes 50% of the renewal interest and the children share equally in the other 50%.[3]

If the author left no widow, widower or children, then section 24 of the 1909 Act provided that the renewal copyright could be claimed by the "author's executors." As interpreted, this provision gave ownership of the renewal term to the executors as trustees for the persons named in the author's will as legatees; the executor was not to hold the renewal copyright on behalf of the author's estate, which would be subject to the claims of creditors. In default of any persons in the first three statutory categories, the author's "next of kin" could validly claim the renewal term of copyright.

An example will demonstrate the operation of the statutory renewal provision of the 1909 Act. If an author during his lifetime licensed a publisher to print and distribute his book in paperback form, and the author died unmarried and without children prior to the twenty-eighth year from the date of publication, the renewal term could be claimed by the author's executors holding on behalf of the persons designated in his

---

2. De Sylva v. Ballentine, 351 U.S. 570 (1956).

3. Venegas–Hernandez v. Asociacion de Compositores, Editores De Musica Latinoamericana, 424 F.3d 50 (1st Cir. 2005); Broadcast Music, Inc. v. Roger Miller Mu-

sic, Inc., 396 F.3d 762 (6th Cir. 2005). Both courts drew upon the *per stirpes* ownership principle found in the termination-of-transfer provisions of 17 U.S.C. §§ 203 and 304(c).

will. The publisher's license would be terminated at the end of 28 years, and the legatees could bargain for a new license with the same or a different publisher, for new compensation, free and clear of the earlier transfer. (As noted above, effective in 1978, 19 years were added to existing 28–year renewal terms, and another 20 years were added to those terms in 1998, for 67 total renewal years—and a possible 95 overall years of protection for such older works.)

It became common under the 1909 Act for a transferee of copyright to negotiate with an author for the ownership of both the initial and the renewal terms of copyright. Most conspicuously, in the case of popular musical compositions the popularity of which might well span beyond the initial 28–year term, the publisher wanted to ensure that it would have the right to derive income from sheet music and public perform-ances into the renewal term. The statute made it clear that an author's transfer of the renewal copyright during the initial term of copyright could not deprive the statutory successor—such as the widow—of her ownership of the renewal term in the event the author–husband was not alive in the twenty-eighth year. The statute did not make it quite so clear whether, in the event the author lived through the initial term, the renewal term to which the author was entitled would immediately be owned by the transferee. In other words, the statute left open the question whether an initial-term transfer of the renewal copyright would be valid and enforceable (if the author survived into the renewal term).

In a controversial 1943 decision, *Fred Fisher Music Co. v. M. Witmark & Sons*,[4] a divided Supreme Court held—despite the obvious author-protective purpose of the renewal format—that an early assign-ment of the renewal term was binding and valid. But all that can be transferred is the author's contingent interest in that term, dependent upon his survival through the initial term. If, despite such a purported transfer, the author dies before expiration of the initial term, then the assignee's contingent interest in the renewal term is terminated and the widow or children, or subsequent statutory successors, can assert superi-or claims to the renewal term.[5] Of course, under *Fisher v. Witmark*, there would be nothing to prevent the assignee from securing from the widow or children valid transfers of *their* contingent interests in the renewal term, and grantees regularly demanded that the author's statu-tory heirs also execute transfers of their contingent interests.

The four-tiered succession to the renewal term, as outlined above, applies for most copyrighted works. Section 24 of the 1909 Act, however, listed a number of exceptions, the most important of which are works made for hire and "posthumous works"; both excluded categories were

---

4. 318 U.S. 643 (1943).

5. Miller Music Corp. v. Charles N. Dan-iels, Inc., 362 U.S. 373 (1960).

left undefined by the 1909 Act. In such cases, section 24 provided that "the proprietor of such copyright shall be entitled to a renewal and extension of the copyright" for the 28–year term upon timely registration. In other words, the person who was the owner of the copyright at the end of the initial term of copyright was the valid claimant of the renewal term as well—and family members were not given the sort of priority they had in the generality of copyrighted works as described above. This allocation of ownership of the renewal term was preserved in the 1976 Act, with "work made for hire" being defined and with the House Report endorsing a narrow view of the still undefined phrase "posthumous work."[6]

B.   Subsequent amendments to the renewal scheme

Although a feature of the U.S. Copyright Act for more than two centuries, the renewal format was almost unique in the world's copyright jurisprudence and became subject to increasing criticism as many individuals (and even corporations) neglected, by oversight, to comply with the renewal technicalities, which required a timely filing of an application with the Copyright Office. For that reason, the 1976 Act provided that for works created or published thereafter, there would be a single term of protection measured from the death of the author. Works already in copyright under the 1909 Act were not disturbed, however, with respect to the renewal framework, and timely renewal still had to be secured in order to extend the term beyond the first 28 years. With inadvertent failures to renew continuing even after 1978, Congress decided in 1992 to provide for the *automatic* renewal of pre–1978 works then in their first term of copyright. The law thus substituted the equivalent of a single 75–year term for the prior dual terms, by making the second term (extended by 19 years) vest without filing for renewal.[7] Then, in 1998, the Sonny Bono Copyright Term Extension Act added another 20 years, for a total of 95. This means that pre–1978 works then in their first term of copyright, i.e., works first published between 1964 and 1977 (inclusive), will enjoy the full 95–year copyright term, without having to register initially and then to renew the registration during the twenty-eighth year following publication.

However, Congress in 1994 coupled the new automatic-renewal arrangements with certain incentives to renew "voluntarily." These are set forth in the rather elaborate provisions of section 304(a) of the

---

6. *See* H.R. Rep. No. 94–1476, at 139–40, expressly approving the construction given in *Bartok v. Boosey & Hawkes, Inc.*, 523 F.2d 941 (2d Cir. 1975).

7. *See* Kahle v. Ashcroft, 72 U.S.P.Q.2d 1888 (N.D. Cal. 2004), *aff'd. sub nom.* Kahle

v. Gonzales, 487 F.3d 697 (9th Cir. 2007) (sustaining constitutionality of automatic-renewal statute against Copyright Clause and First Amendment challenges).

Copyright Act. One such incentive, for example, is that with a voluntary renewal application the certificate of registration that is issued by the Copyright Office is to constitute prima facie evidence of the validity of the copyright and of the facts stated in the certificate (such as those relating to the author, date of publication, and the like). Another incentive is explained in the next subsection.

C. Derivative works prepared during the initial term

A difficult and important question that arises from the renewal provisions of the 1909 Act as carried forward in the 1976 Act relates to the utilization, during the renewal term of copyright, of derivative works that had been validly prepared by others during the initial term of copyright in the underlying work. For example, the author and copyright owner of a novel might, during the initial copyright term, license another to prepare a motion picture based on that novel; the motion picture, which will typically involve substantial creative contributions by the film producer and those it employs (actors, director, cinematographer, composer), will itself be a copyrightable work. If the license expressly included the right to exhibit and distribute the derivative film during the renewal term of the novel, and if the author of the novel survived into the renewal term, the film producer could lawfully continue to utilize the film during the renewal term of the novel.

If, however, the license did not expressly cover the renewal term, or if it did but the novelist died during the initial term of copyright in the novel and another person succeeded to the renewal copyright, then the question arises whether the film can continue to be exploited by its copyright owner during the renewal term of the underlying novel.

A strict application of the principles of the renewal format would suggest that once the renewal copyright in the underlying novel "springs back" to the author or to the author's statutory successor, it does so free and clear of any licenses given during the initial term. Thus the continued exhibition or distribution of the film—which contains copyrightable elements from the novel—would constitute an infringement of copyright in the novel. Under this approach, not only would the novelist during the renewal term be able undeniably to license some other motion picture producer to base a new film on the novel, but he would also be entitled to renegotiate with the copyright owner of the first film for the right to continue its exploitation. This would, of course, deprive the producer or copyright owner of the first film of the fruits of its own copyrightable contributions, which may as a practical matter account far more for the film's success than do its borrowed elements from the novel.

An arguably more equitable view would be that the creative and copyrighted derivative work, the motion picture film produced pursuant to a license from the novelist, should be treated as "taking on a life of its own" such that it can continue to be exhibited and distributed even after the beginning of the renewal term of copyright in the underlying novel. The film producer could not, however, produce a *new* film based on the underlying novel without the consent of the owner of the renewal copyright in the latter work.

The courts of appeals were unable to make a clear and consistent choice between these two theories.[8] The Supreme Court ultimately resolved the uncertainties when, in 1990, it decided *Stewart v. Abend*.[9] There, the Court held that the continued exhibition and distribution of the well-known Hitchcock film *Rear Window*, as well as the marketing of videocassettes of the film, constituted an infringement of the renewal copyright in the short story on which the film was based. The Court relied on the terms and legislative histories of the 1909 and 1976 Copyright Acts, and its own precedents, in holding that an author seeking to convey a license to create a derivative motion picture can transfer only the contingent interest that he has in the renewal term; if the author dies before the end of the initial term of the underlying story (as occurred in *Stewart*), the interest of his statutory successor to the renewal term cannot be diluted by the continued unauthorized exploitation of the derivative work.

In 1992, in addition to providing for the future automatic renewal of works originally published beginning in 1964, Congress sought to encourage "voluntary" renewals; one such incentive concerns the continued exploitation of derivative works. A person who voluntarily renews gets the benefits of the rule in *Stewart* that cuts off continued exploitation by others of derivative works they may have created during the initial term of an underlying work, while in the case of an automatic renewal section 304(a)(4)(A) now provides that "a derivative work prepared under authority of a grant of a transfer or license of the copyright that is made before the expiration of the original term of copyright may continue to be used under the terms of the grant during the renewed and extended term of copyright without infringing the copyright."

Automatic renewal reduces the likelihood that the copyright in a derivative work will expire before the copyright in the underlying work. This scenario most often transpired when the rightholder renewed the

---

8. *Compare* G. Ricordi & Co. v. Paramount Pictures, Inc., 189 F.2d 469 (2d Cir. 1951) (the opera *Madame Butterfly* cannot be converted by initial licensee into a motion picture after renewal of the underlying novel), *with* Rohauer v. Killiam Shows, Inc., 551 F.2d 484 (2d Cir. 1977) (Valentino film, *Son of the Sheik*, may be shown on television during the renewal term of the underlying novel).

9. 495 U.S. 207 (1990).

pre–1976 copyright in an underlying work, such as a novel or a play, but the copyright holder of a derivative work, such as a motion picture, failed to renew the copyright in the derivative work. As a result, the motion picture would have fallen into the public domain, but the holder of the copyright in the underlying literary work could nonetheless bar third parties' exploitation of the film because "a derivative copyright protects only the new material contained in the derivative work, not the matter derived from the underlying work."[10] Thus, expiration of the derivative work's copyright could not diminish the force of the copyright in the underlying work;[11] accordingly, the exhibition or transmission of the motion picture violated the public performance rights in the underlying literary work.

The single term of copyright for 1976 Act works does not eliminate the possibility that the copyright in an underlying work could survive the expiration of copyright in a derivative work, thus effectively blocking third-party exploitation of the derivative work despite its public domain status. Because duration now is calculated based on the death of the author, such will be the case if the author of the derivative work predeceases the author of the underlying work. This result will also obtain if the derivative work is "for hire," as many audiovisual works are, and if the author of the underlying work is still alive more than twenty-five years after the publication of the film. (The film's copyright will endure for ninety-five years from publication; the copyright in the novel or play will endure seventy years from the death of its author.)

II. Duration of Copyright Under the 1976 Act

A. *Works created after 1977*

Perhaps the most significant step taken by Congress in the 1976 Act, as originally written, with regard to duration was to provide in section 302(a) that "Copyright in a work created on or after January 1, 1978, subsists from its creation and, except as provided by the following subsections, endures for a term consisting of the life of the author and fifty years after the author's death." The drafters of the law had concluded early in the revision process that the "28 plus 28" copyright

---

10. *See, e.g.,* Russell v. Price, 612 F.2d 1123, 1128 (9th Cir. 1979) (unauthorized televising of motion picture *Pygmalion*, whose copyright had not been renewed, violated rights in George Bernard Shaw's eponymous play, which was still in its second term of U.S. copyright).

11. *Accord*, Stewart v. Abend, 495 U.S. 207, 222–224, 230 (1990) ("Absent an ex-

plicit statement of congressional intent that the rights in the renewal term of an owner of a pre-existing work are extinguished upon incorporation of his work into [a derivative] work, it is not our role to alter the delicate balance Congress has labored to achieve.").

term was inadequate and should be discarded. Authors were living longer than in 1909, and many were seeing their works fall into the public domain during their lifetimes. The growth of communications media was lengthening the commercial life of many works. The renewal format, placing a premium on the definition of the elusive term "publication" as well as on timely renewal applications, resulted in unfairly shortened copyright protection in many cases. Finally, in the words of the House Report, "a very large majority of the world's countries have adopted a copyright term of the life of the author and fifty years after the author's death."[12]

The move to the formula of "life plus 50" (and after enactment of the 1998 Copyright Term Extension Act, "life plus 70") also provided a clear measuring rod for the period of copyright protection and had the convenient byproduct of sending all of an author's post–1977 works into the public domain at the same time, rather than on varying dates depending upon the date of initial publication.

Having decided in the 1976 Act to measure copyright protection from the death of the author, Congress had to deal with certain instances where such a measure might lead to uncertainty in calculating the term. In the case of a jointly authored work—defined in section 101 as a "work prepared by two or more authors with the intention that their contributions be merged into inseparable or interdependent parts of a unitary whole"—section 302(b) provides (as amended by the CTEA) that "copyright endures for a term consisting of the life of the last surviving author and 70 years after such last surviving author's death." In the case of works made for hire, section 302(c) provides that copyright endures "for a term of 95 years from the year of its first publication, or a term of 120 years from the year of its creation, whichever expires first." This term applies whether the "employer–author" of a work made for hire is a human or a corporate person. The 95-from-publication/120-from-creation measuring period also applies to anonymous and pseudonymous works.

B. The Transition from the 1909 Act: the Duration of Works First Published, or Created but not yet Published, before the 1976 Act's Effective Date

The duration of copyright protection under the 1909 Act, which was in effect through the end of 1977, was as noted 28 years from the date of publication, with the possibility of renewal for an additional 28 years upon application to the Copyright Office in the twenty-eighth year of the initial term. This term of protection was significantly modified by the

12. H.R. Rep. No. 94–1476, at 133–36 (1976).

1976 Act and again by the 1998 "Sonny Bono Copyright Term Extension Act" (CTEA). Under the current law, the term of copyright protection depends principally upon what the copyright status of the work was on the effective date of the 1976 Act, January 1, 1978.

1. Transitional rules

The 1976 Act provides a transition regime for five different categories of works:

(1) *Created but unpublished before 1978*: If the work was created prior to January 1, 1978, but unpublished as of that date, it is made subject to the now "life-plus–70" period of protection. Because this cap on the works' duration would have the effect of throwing many works immediately into the public domain—for example, unpublished letters or manuscripts of eighteenth and nineteenth century authors—section 303 currently provides: "In no case . . . shall the term of copyright in such a work expire before December 31, 2002; and, if the work is published on or before December 31, 2002, the term of copyright shall not expire before December 31, 2047." The provision thus afforded such unpublished works 25 years of protection under the federal act, in lieu of the potentially perpetual protection previously afforded by common-law copyright. If at the end of those 25 years the work remained unpublished, it fell into the public domain. Accordingly, at the outset of 2003, a vast number of unpublished works whose authors had died in 1932 or earlier went into the public domain.[13] The 1976 Act also provided the copyright owner of an unpublished work with an incentive to publish it during that 25–year period, by offering yet another 45 years of federal protection in the event of such publication. Thus, a nineteenth-century manuscript published before the end of 2002 now will remain in copyright until the end of 2047.

(2) *Sound recordings first fixed before 1972*: Congress did not bring sound recordings within the scope of federal copyright protection until February 15, 1972. Pre–1972 sound recordings thus were protected under State copyright, unfair competition or record piracy laws, and the 1972 incorporation of sound recordings did not affect sound recordings fixed before the Act's effective date. The 1976 Act preserves state law protection until February 15, 2067. States may provide a shorter term, but in the one case to date posing the issue, the New York Court of Appeals applied the maximum term allowable.[14]

---

13. *See* R. Anthony Reese, *Public But Private: Copyright's New Unpublished Public Domain*, 85 TEX. L. REV. 585, 586 (2007).

14. Capitol Records v. Naxos of America, 4 N.Y.3d 540, 797 N.Y.S.2d 352, 830 N.E.2d 250 (2005). The Copyright Office has recommended extending federal copyright protection to pre–1972 sound recordings, see *Federal Copyright Protection for pre–1972 Sound recordings: A Report of the*

(3) *Works already in the Public Domain*: If on the 1976 Act's effective date, a published work was already in the public domain under the 1909 Act or earlier laws, the work remains in the public domain and no copyright protection is available.[15]

(4) *Works in their first term of copyright in 1978*: If on January 1, 1978, a work was in its *initial* 28–year copyright term under the 1909 Act, the copyright expires at the end of that term, unless the copyright is renewed by timely application. (Renewal was made automatic for works published between 1964 and 1977.) If it is renewed, the renewal term will last not for 28 years but rather for 67 years (with 19 years having been added by the 1976 Act and another 20 years by the CTEA). Section 304(a) so provides, for what is thus effectively a 95–year term of copyright. Although Congress was interested in extending the period of statutory copyright protection and discarding the renewal format, it nevertheless chose to retain that format for works then under federal copyright in order to avoid the undue disruption of expectations and transactions.

(5) *Works in their renewal term in 1978*: Under section 304(b) of the 1976 Act, works in their *renewal* term of copyright as of January 1, 1978, are to be automatically accorded an extended term of protection lasting for a total of 95 years from the date copyright was originally secured. In effect, the renewal term of such works is extended from 28 years to 67 years. Because Congress, as early as 1962, anticipated major imminent changes in the copyright law and particularly an extension of the period of copyright protection, it granted what are known as "interim extensions" of protection for works the renewal term of which was about to expire; these works were thus still in their renewal term when the 1976 Act became effective and had their copyright extended to the full 75–year term. For example, a work published and copyrighted in 1925, and renewed in 1953, would in due course (under the 1909 Act) have fallen into the public domain after 1981; by virtue of the 47–year renewal term as so extended in 1976 and the 20–year extension of 1998, section 304(b) now keeps the copyright in existence through the year 2020.

2. General rule for calculation of term

Under the 1909 Act, the 28– and 56–year periods of protection were measured from the precise date of publication, resulting in often inconvenient calculations. Under section 305 of the 1976 Act, "all terms of copyright provided by sections 302 through 304 run to the end of the

Register of Copyrights (December 2011), http://www.copyright.gov/docs/sound/pre-72–report.pdf

15. Transitional and supplementary provisions, section 103. *But see* 17 U.S.C. § 104A, discussed *infra*.

calendar year in which they would otherwise expire." The key date, therefore, for such matters as applying for renewal copyright, the end of the renewal term, and the end of the "life-plus–70" term, will be December 31 of the pertinent year.

C. The 1998 "Sonny Bono Copyright Term Extension Act"

The earliest works to benefit from the 1998 Term Extension Act were published in 1923 (works published in 1923 being in their final— 75th—year under the 1976 Act; the 1998 term extension did not affect the public domain status of any works whose copyrights had already expired). Works first published in 1923 will thus fall into the public domain not at the end of 1998 but rather at the end of 2018. Works such as those from the 1920s and 1930s—motion pictures, songs (by Gershwin, Kern, Berlin and Porter), and novels (by Fitzgerald and Hemingway)—whose copyrights would otherwise have begun to expire after 1998, are among the principal beneficiaries of the term extension.

Congress's purposes in adding 20 years to the copyright term were to provide for authors' heirs at a time when individuals are living longer, to give them the benefit of the new technological and entertainment media, and, most importantly, to move the duration of U.S. works into closer conformity to the norm prevailing in Europe (where the long-prevailing term of life-plus-50-years was moved to life-plus-70-years in the course of the 1990s). Because the European Union would grant the extra 20 years of protection to non-EU works only on condition of reciprocity, U.S. works would not have benefitted from a major export market's longer term unless the U.S. provided EU works with the same term in the U.S. as they enjoyed in the EU.[16]

The 20–year extension granted by the CTEA, and its underlying rationales, were the targets of considerable criticism—particularly with respect to its retroactive application to works already created and published—and ultimately of a challenge that reached the Supreme Court. In *Eldred v. Ashcroft*,[17] decided in 2003, the Court, with two Justices dissenting, sustained the CTEA against claims that the recurrent extensions of copyright violated the "limited times" restriction in the Copyright and Patent Clause of the Constitution; that the retroactive application of the CTEA could not "promote the progress of science" by stimulating the creation of new works, as that constitutional clause required; and that the CTEA inhibited creative speech in violation of the

---

16. Sonny Bono Copyright Term Extension Act, Sec. 102(b)(1)–2, Pub. L. No. 105–298, 112 Stat. 2827 (1998) (codified at 17 U.S.C. 302(a)–(b)). See also 144 Cong. Rec. H9946–01, H9950 (daily ed. Oct. 7, 1998) (statement of Rep. McCollum) (discussing "extreme economic disadvantage" to American copyright interests).

17. 537 U.S. 186 (2003).

First Amendment. The Court concluded that the preambular phrase did not confine Congress's power to legislation that establishes a direct quid pro quo for new creations; that Congress's reasons for the 20–year extension were principally a legislative matter and were in any event rational; and that retroactive application to existing works was a feature of the several congressional term extensions throughout our copyright history stretching back to the early nineteenth century (and even to the first Copyright Act of 1790). With regard to the First Amendment, the court ruled that, given "a copyright scheme that incorporates its own speech-protective purposes and safeguards"[18] which the CTEA did not alter, no heightened scrutiny was appropriate for assessing the validity of the CTEA.

D.   *Restoration of copyrights in foreign works*

Among the world's copyright regimes, the 1909 Act's 28–year term was peculiarly short. As discussed, *infra*, in Chapter 5, another peculiarity of U.S. copyright, the notice requirement, also could cause a work's early demise into the public domain. As a result, pressure had been brought from time to time to revive the copyrights in foreign works that fell prey to the draconian features of the U.S. copyright system. When the U.S. joined the Berne Convention on the Protection of Literary and Artistic Works in 1988, the U.S. did not implement that treaty's provisions on restoration of copyrights of foreign works prematurely in the new Member State's public domain.[19] The U.S.'s subsequent adherence to the agreement on Trade Related Aspects of Intellectual Property (TRIPs), which established sanctions for non-compliance with the Berne Convention, finally obliged Congress in 1994 to enact detailed provisions restoring copyright protection to (non-U.S.) works from qualifying countries.

1.   Implementation of copyright restoration

The resulting provision, section 104A(h) defines a "restored work" as one not first published in the U.S. (nor published in the U.S. within 30 days of first publication), and at least one of whose authors was, at the time of the work's creation, not a U.S. citizen or domiciliary. Under section 104A, works still protected in their source countries that had been denied protection in the U.S. as a result, for example, of failure to

---

18.   *Id.* at 219.

19.   Berne Convention art. 18 sets out member States' obligation to restore the copyrights in works from other Union members whose copyrights have not yet expired in their countries of origin. For the U.S. failure to implement art. 18, *see* FINAL RE-PORT OF THE AD HOC WORKING GROUP ON U.S. ADHERENCE TO THE BERNE CONVENTION *reprinted in* 10 COLUM. J.L. & ARTS 513 (1986).

comply with notice or renewal formalities, or because the work was first published in a country with which the U.S. then had no copyright relations, retrieved U.S. copyright protection as of January 1, 1996. Protection attached automatically, and copyright may be enforced without formalities against all exploiters other than "reliance parties."

A reliance party is defined as "any person who with respect to a particular work, engages in acts which, before the source country of that work becomes an eligible country, would have violated section 106 if the restored work had been subject to copyright protection, and who, after the source country becomes an eligible country, continues to engage in such acts."[20] A reliance party can, for example, be one who distributes the foreign work in its original form or who has used it as the basis for a new derivative work. Section 104A(h)(3) defines an "eligible country" as one which, on the date of "enactment [of the Uruguay Round Amendments Act (URAA), December 8, 1994,] is, or after such date of enactment becomes, a nation adhering to the Berne Convention." Courts have interpreted "continues to engage" to require continuous conduct going back to December 1994 (or the relevant eligibility date); an alleged infringer who exploited the work before December 1994, and then ceases its exploitation, may not later start up again and still qualify as a "reliance party."[21]

Reliance parties receive a grace period of 12 months to continue to exploit the work following notification by the owner of the restored copyright. The owner of the restored copyright may notify the reliance party either directly, or constructively by filing within 24 months of the effective date of the restoration a notice of intent with the Copyright Office. In the case of constructive notification, the 12–month grace period runs from publication of the notice by the Copyright Office in the Federal Register. The owner of the restored copyright is defined as the author "as determined by the law of the source country of the work." A reliance party who has created a derivative work based on the restored work before the restoration of copyright may continue to exploit the derivative work during the copyright term of the restored work, but must pay a royalty to the restored copyright owner. In the event of the parties' inability to agree, a court will set the royalty rate.[22]

---

20. 17 U.S.C. § 104A(h)(4).

21. *See, e.g.,* Troll Co. v. Uneeda Doll Co., 483 F.3d 150 (2d Cir. 2007).

22. 17 U.S.C. § 104A(d)(3).

2. Constitutionality of copyright restoration

While neither the 1976 Copyright Act nor the 1998 CTEA removed any works from the public domain (but, by extending the terms of extant copyrights, simply delayed a work's falling into the public domain), section 104A expressly covers non-U.S. works which never enjoyed U.S. copyright, either for failure to comply with the notice formality or because the U.S. did not protect a particular source country's works. An example of the latter would be the former Soviet Union, which did not join an international copyright agreement to which the U.S. was also party until 1973. Section 104A also revives copyrights which expired for failure to renew the registration of a non-U.S. work. The question therefore arises whether Congress has power, given the constitutional restriction of copyright to "limited Times," to reanimate dead copyrights. A related question, akin to one posed in *Eldred v. Ashcroft*, is whether the removal of a work from the public domain, and thus from unhindered reutilization by the public, violates the First Amendment's guarantees of free expression.

It bears emphasis that section 104A revives only copyrights in eligible *foreign* works. The United States' obligations under the Berne Convention and under the TRIPs agreement do not apply to a member State's own works.[23] U.S. works which fell into the public domain for non-compliance with formalities remain in the public domain. Nonetheless, even as to foreign works, and notwithstanding the U.S.'s international agreements, is Congress absolutely barred either by the copyright clause or by the First Amendment from removing a work from the public domain?

In *Golan v. Holder*,[24] decided in 2012, the Supreme Court rejected the contention that once a work is for whatever reason in the public domain, the "limited Times" provision denies Congress the power to bestow copyright protection either anew or for the first time. Petitioners, musicians who had performed and others who had exploited pre–1973 Soviet works (such as Prokoffiev's *Peter and the Wolf*) without authorization or payment, contended that, pursuant to a strict interpretation of "limited Times," an immutable public domain was necessary to ensure the free circulation of knowledge from public domain works and from

---

23. *See* Berne Convention, art 18 (obligation of new Berne member to restore copyrights of works from other member States if those works are still protected in their countries of origin); art. 5(3) (protection within the country of origin is a matter of domestic law).

24. 132 S.Ct. 873 (2012).

derivative works created in good faith reliance on their public domain status. Petitioners also urged that removing a work from the public domain fails to conform to the constitutional requirement that copyright legislation promote science, because the work has already been created, and retroactive conferral of copyright cannot serve as an incentive to create.

A majority of the Supreme Court rejected the petitioners' absolutist articulation, holding that the Constitution can be interpreted to allow both extension of extant terms (as the court had recognized in *Eldred*), and restoration commensurate with the terms the works would have enjoyed had they not fallen into the public domain due to premature (by international standards) expiration of protection, or to the lack of copyright relations with the country of origin at the time of the work's first publication.[25] At the least, the term "limited Times" implies that the work enjoyed some period of protection; yet in the case of failure to comply with certain formalities, or the absence of copyright relations, the "term" of U.S. protection was zero.[26] In emphasizing the legislation's focus on compliance with the U.S.'s international obligations, the Court dismissed petitioners' warning that without an "immutable" public domain, Congress could perpetually extend copyright in installments:

> [T]he hypothetical legislative misbehavior petitioners posit is far afield from the case before us. In aligning the United States with other nations bound by the Berne Convention, and thereby according equitable treatment to once disfavored foreign authors, Congress can hardly be charged with a design to move stealthily toward a regime of perpetual copyrights.[27]

The Court also revisited and again rejected the contention earlier advanced in *Eldred* that Congress lacks power to enact laws that do not provide an incentive to create new works:

> Nothing in the text of the Copyright Clause confines the "Progress of Science" exclusively to "incentives for creation." Evidence from the founding, moreover, suggests that inducing *dissemination*—as opposed to creation—was viewed as an appropriate means to promote science. Until 1976, in fact, Congress made "federal copyright contingent on publication[,] [thereby] providing incentives not primarily for creation," but for dissemination. Our decisions correspondingly recognize that "copyright supplies the economic incentive to create *and disseminate* ideas."[28]

---

25. *Id.* at 885–88.

26. *Id.* at 885 ("surely a 'limited time' of exclusivity must begin before it may end.")

27. *Id.*

28. *Id.* at 888–89 (citations omitted). The Court later pointed out that protecting foreign authors to an extent commensurate

Turning to the First Amendment challenge, the Court reiterated its view that copyright both furthers First Amendment goals and incorporates limiting doctrines that avoid conflicts with free speech norms. In restoring certain foreign copyrights, Congress left undisturbed the "traditional contours" of copyright—the idea/expression dichotomy and the fair use defense—therefore, the legislation provided no call for heightened scrutiny.[29] The Court rejected the contention that the public's prior "unfettered access" to the previously public domain works meant that "Congress impermissibly revoked [petitioners'] right to exploit foreign works that "belonged to them" once the works were in the public domain." Suggesting that petitioners' rhetorical construction of a vested public property right in copyright-expired works "might sound exactly backwards," the Court corrected, "Anyone has free access to the public domain, but no one, after the copyright term has expired, acquires ownership rights in the once-protected works."[30]

Justice Breyer's dissent, joined by Justice Alito, principally took strong issue with the majority's determination that Congress may legislate consistently with the Copyright Clause even if it cannot be shown that the law will "encourage anyone to produce a single new work."[31] For the dissent, only utilitarian goals, untainted by Continental European notions of natural rights, justify the limited monopoly, and, lacking the required "quid pro quo," Congress' restoration of foreign copyrights "does not serve copyright's traditional public ends."[32]

---

with American authors results in a copyright system more fair to American authors (and, implicitly, more likely to incentivize them) because market "distortions . . . occurred . . .—to the detriment of both foreign and domestic authors—when, before 1891, foreign works were excluded entirely from U.S. copyright protection. *See* Kampelman, *The United States and International Copyright*, 41 Am. J. Int'l L. 406, 413 (1947) ('American readers were less inclined to read the novels of Cooper or Hawthorne for a dollar when they could buy a novel of Scott or Dickens for a quarter.')."

29. *Id.* at 890. The Court emphasized that the "traditional contours" of copyright, a phrase coined in *Eldred*, meant only the idea/expression dichotomy and the fair use defense; the Tenth Circuit's "unconfined reading" to encompass other longstanding limitations on copyright, in that case the public domain, "was incorrect, as we here clarify." *Id.* at 890 n.29.

30. *Id.* at 892.

31. *Id.* at 900 (Breyer, J., dissenting).

32. *Id.* at 908. *Cf.* majority opinion at n. 28 ("see Austin, Does the Copyright Clause Mandate Isolationism? 26 Colum. J. L. & Arts 17, 59 (2002) (cautioning against 'an isolationist reading of the Copyright Clause that is in tension with . . . America's international copyright relations over the last hundred or so years').")

Duration and Renewal: The Transition from the 1909 Act to the 1976 Act

Date of Work	When Protection Attaches	First Term	Renewal Term
Created in 1978 or later	Upon being fixed in a tangible medium	Unitary term of life + 70 (or, if anonymous or pseudonymous work, or work for hire, 95 years from publication, or 120 years from creation, whichever is shorter)	
Published 1964–1977	Upon publication with notice	28 years	67 years, second term commenced automatically; renewal registration optional
Published between 1923 and 1963, inclusive	Upon publication with notice	28 years	67 years, if renewal was sought (for works whose first terms expired after 1977, renewal registration remained necessary); otherwise in the public domain (unless the work is a foreign work in which copyright has been restored)
Published before 1923	The work is now in the public domain		
Created, but not published, before 1978	On Jan. 1, 1978, when federal copyright displaced state copyright	Unitary term of at least life + 70 (or, if anonymous or pseudonymous work, or work for hire, 95 years from publication, or 120 years from creation, whichever is shorter), but no expiration before 12/31/2002 (if work remained unpublished) or 12/31/2047 (if work was published by the end of 2002)	
Sound recordings Fixed before Feb. 15, 1972	Governed by state common law or statute, limited to Feb. 15, 2067		

III. Termination of Transfers

A. Contracts concluded after 1977

1. In general

An unusual and important feature of the 1976 Copyright Act is its grant to the author or to the author's survivors of the power to terminate transfers of copyright. It will be recalled that the principal purpose of the renewal provisions of earlier U.S. copyright statutes was to give to authors the power at the end of the initial term of copyright to reclaim the copyright for a second term free and clear of any earlier transfers or encumbrances, and to afford authors an opportunity to renegotiate assignments and licenses with a better knowledge of the economic value of their works. It will also be recalled that the renewal right has been abolished for works created or first published on or after January 1, 1978, the term of copyright protection of which is now the life of the author plus 70 years. If, for example, a work is created in 1979 and the author transfers copyright in 1980, that copyright might continue—depending on when the author dies—for another 75 or 125 years (or more), without any renewal term that can restore an unencumbered copyright to the author.

Congress therefore decided to grant to authors and their survivors a power to recapture the copyright, similar to the right to claim the renewal copyright provided under the 1909 Act and its predecessors. The termination right applies only to the grant of rights under U.S. copyright; any revocation of rights under other countries' laws would result either from a contractual agreement to rescind a grant, or from recapture provisions (if any) of the relevant foreign copyright laws. On the other hand, the author of a foreign work protected under U.S. copyright is assimilated to a U.S. author and therefore is entitled to terminate grants of rights made for the U.S.

The very elaborate provisions for the termination of U.S. transfers of copyright are set forth in section 203. Given the background just recounted, the power to terminate under section 203 applies only to copyright transfers (and licenses), whether exclusive or nonexclusive, executed by the author on or after January 1, 1978. By serving a timely notice of termination, the author may effect such a termination—and recapture an unencumbered copyright—"at any time during a period of five years beginning at the end of thirty-five years from the date of execution of the grant." Mindful of the controversial Supreme Court decision that held that under the 1909 Act the author could, during the initial term of copyright, validly transfer his interest in the renewal term,[1] Congress provided to the contrary in section 203(a)(5) with regard to the power to terminate transfers: "Termination of the grant may be effected notwithstanding any agreement to the contrary, including an agreement to make a will or to make any future grant."[2] Although the

---

1. Fred Fisher Music Co. v. M. Witmark & Sons, 318 U.S. 643, 651 (1943)

2. The Court of Appeals for the Second Circuit held that, when an agreement settling a dispute about copyright ownership stipulated that the work had been "made

for hire" many years before, this constituted an "agreement to the contrary" (because the termination power does not apply at all to works made for hire) and thus did not validly extinguish the author's termination power. Marvel Characters, Inc. v. Simon,

termination power is inalienable, it must be exercised in a timely manner, through the proper procedures, and by the proper persons announced in the statute; the transfer is not terminated automatically when 35 years have passed.

Section 203 is detailed and complex, but its main points can be summarized here. The termination power does not apply to works made for hire, and it applies only to grants made by the author during the author's lifetime (not by the author's will, and not by the author's surviving spouse or children). If the notice of termination is to be served after the author's death, then the author's surviving family members may terminate the author's earlier grant, provided they can amass more than one half of the author's termination interest as calculated pursuant to a statutory formula (e.g., the author's surviving spouse would own one half of such termination interest, and each of three surviving children one sixth).

2. Derivative works exception

Particularly significant is the provision, in section 203(b)(1), that

A derivative work prepared under authority of the grant before its termination may continue to be utilized under the terms of the grant after its termination, but this privilege does not extend to the preparation after the termination of other derivative works based upon the copyrighted work covered by the terminated grant.

Thus, the copyright is not necessarily returned to the author or family altogether unencumbered. For example, assume that our hypothetical novelist transferred in 1980 an exclusive license to base a motion picture on his novel, the motion picture is released in 1985, and the author terminates his transfer effective 2015. The motion picture producer (or its successor as copyright owner in 2015) may continue to exhibit and distribute the film thereafter, pursuant to the terms of the 1980 license. But the film producer may not after 2015 remake the film with a new cast; that would be an infringement of the author's recaptured copyright.

A related issue concerns the interpretation of the phrase "a derivative work *prepared* under authority of the grant before its termination"[3] (emphasis supplied): must the derivative work have been fully created before termination, or will the derivative work escape termination so long as its creation has been undertaken before the effective date of termination? If "prepared" encompassed derivative works begun but

---

310 F.3d 280 (2d Cir. 2002). *But compare* Milne ex rel. Coyne v. Stephen Slesinger, Inc., 430 F.3d 1036 (9th Cir. 2005) (1983 renegotiation by author's heir revokes 1930 grant of Winnie the Pooh merchandising rights, and so deprives later heir of termi-nation right under section 304(d) governing pre–1978 transfers). To similar effect, *see* Penguin Group (USA) Inc. v. Steinbeck, 537 F.3d 193 (2d Cir. 2008). *See* discussion *infra.*

3. 17 U.S.C. § 304(c)(6)(A).

not yet completed, then one might anticipate that grantees would rush to initiate the creation of the maximum number of derivative works during the minimum two-year period between the notification and the effective date of termination. While the notice period may well have been intended to allow grantees the opportunity to wind down their exploitation in anticipation of termination,[4] the termination right would be considerably compromised if the notice period also enabled grantees to gear up to engage in further development of derivative works. No decisions yet appear to confront this issue.[5]

3. "Gap works"—terminability of pre–1978 agreements to transfer copyright in works not created until 1978 or later

As the deadline approached for filing notice to terminate contracts executed in 1978, the earliest year of works to which the termination power applied—for a termination to become effective 35 years later in 2013, notice must have been filed by 2011—a question arose regarding works created in 1978 or later, but for which a contract for transfer of rights had been entered into before 1978. As to these works, there could be no reversion of renewal rights nor a Section 304(c) termination right because, having not yet been created, they could not have been published before 1978. But if the transfer was agreed-to before 1978, then the contract might not come within the scope of Section 203, and the transfers would fall between the cracks of the 1909 and 1976 Acts. The Copyright Office initiated a rulemaking procedure to determine whether these "Gap Grants" were subject to termination, and concluded

> that the better interpretation of the law is that Gap Grants *are* terminable under section 203, as currently codified, because as a matter of copyright law, a transfer that predates the existence of the copyrighted work cannot be effective (and therefore cannot be "executed") until the work of authorship (and the copyright) come into existence. In arriving at this conclusion, the Copyright Office looked at the plain meaning of Title 17, including section 203, as well as the legislative history of the termination provisions.[6]

---

4. *See, e.g.*, SUPPLEMENTARY REPORT OF THE REGISTER OF COPYRIGHTS ON THE GENERAL REVISION OF THE US COPYRIGHT LAW: 1965 REVISION BILL 75 (May 1965) ("The thought behind the 2–to–10–year limitation on the time for serving a notice was to establish a definite period for filing the notice toward the end of the 35– or 40–year term, thus avoiding earlier, indiscriminate terminations, and to provide a fair period of advance notice to the grantee that his rights are to be terminated.").

5. *Cf.* 2 Melville B. Nimmer & David Nimmer, NIMMER ON COPYRIGHT, § 11.02[C][1] n.65 (2011) (suggesting that

as much of a derivative work as had been created by the date of termination may continue to be exploited, and if the remainder of the derivative work is not based upon the underlying work—e.g., a soundtrack for a film based on a terminated novel—then the whole derivative work may continue to be exploited. By the same token, one may infer from this suggestion that the termination would preclude further additions to the derivative work-in-progress if those additions derive from the underlying terminated work.).

6. 76 Fed. Reg. 32316 (June 6, 2011) (emphasis in original).

The Copyright Office accordingly announced a new subsection (f) (5) to 37 C.F.R. § 201.10 "Notice of termination of transfers and licenses"

(5) In any case where an author agreed, prior to January 1, 1978, to a grant of a transfer of a license of rights in a work that was not created until on or after January 1, 1978, a notice of termination of a grant under section 203 of title 18 may be recorded if it recites, as the date of execution, the date on which the work was created.

The Copyright Office's position that a contract to transfer rights in future works is not "executed" until the works are created and fixed, i.e., until the copyright which is the object of the transfer comes into being, carries implications beyond the issue of "Gap Grants." This interpretation of "executed" indicates that the termination time clock starts running not from the date of the agreement, but from the date of creation. This date may, however, pose practical problems. The date the contract was signed provides a readily ascertainable starting point for calculating when to send a notice of termination. The date of creation of the work may prove more elusive. The statute offers evidence of Congress's expectation that the author should be able to identify the *year* date of creation: section 409(7) requires that the application for registration "shall include" "the year in which creation of the work was completed". By contrast, the Section 203 termination-of-transfer clock starts ticking on the *actual date* of execution of the grant. Many authors may be unable to recall or document the month and day on which they completed creating a work. But this objection could equally well apply to oral or inferred-from-conduct nonexclusive licenses: the date of their "execution" may be equally if not more unsusceptible to reliable documentation, yet the statute clearly provides for the termination of such licenses.

B. Termination of transfers of copyright executed before 1978

[handwritten: Before 1978 — termination ~ 56 years]

1. In general

It is appropriate at this point to mention that the statute contains a different provision for termination of transfers of copyright that were made *prior to* January 1, 1978. Recall that Congress, in enacting the 1976 Copyright Act, provided that works then in statutory copyright would have their term of renewal automatically extended from 28 years to 47 years (resulting in a total of 75 years of protection). Prior to the effective date of the statute, many persons had already transferred their renewal interests to third persons, with both parties believing that the renewal term would last for only 28 years. When Congress added 19 years to the renewal term, effective January 1, 1978, it also decided that persons who had previously transferred their renewal interests should be allowed to recapture those transfers at the end of 56 years from the initial date of copyright, so that the statutory "windfall" of the additional 19 years could be enjoyed by the author or the author's survivors, rather than by the then current owner of the renewal term.

Section 304(c) therefore provides that "in the case of any copyright subsisting in either its first or renewal term on January 1, 1978, other than a copyright in a work made for hire, the exclusive or nonexclusive grant of a transfer or license of the renewal copyright or any right under it, executed before January 1, 1978"—by the author or by any of the statutory successors to the renewal term under the 1909 Act, otherwise than by will—is subject to termination, effective 56 years from the date copyright was originally secured. The details regarding the serving of notice, the persons entitled to do so, the inalienable but non-automatic nature of the termination right, and the like are essentially identical to those provided in section 203 for transfers made *after* January 1, 1978.

When Congress in 1998 added 20 years to the various copyright terms, it once again decided to address the issue of persons who had transferred renewal interests prior to January 1, 1978, because neither such a transferor nor his or her transferee could have at that time foreseen the extension of the renewal term from 28 years to what is now 67 years. Accordingly, section 304(d) provides that such a renewal-term transfer may be terminated (provided there has been no earlier termination and recapture of the 19–year addition) in the same manner, by the same class of persons, and with the same consequences as under section 304(c), effective during the five-year period beginning at the end of 75 years from the beginning of the copyright term.[7]

2.   Caselaw

Controversies under section 304(c), governing the termination of the extended renewal term, began to arise with the effective date of the 1976 Act, and are likely to continue for as long as the right to reclaim the section 304(c) or (d) extended renewal term remains enforceable, that is, until 2055.[8] The cases calling for interpretation of section 304(c) have fallen into three general categories: adequacy of notice given to grantees; scope of the derivative-works-right exception to termination; and evasion of the inalienability principle embodied in the "notwithstanding any agreement to the contrary" proviso.

---

7. *See Milne*, 430 F.3d 1036 (1983 agreement with author's heir displaced author's 1930 transfer, so that neither could be terminated under section 304(d)).

8. The last works under the aegis of the 1909 Act were published in 1977; the sec-ond extended renewal term will vest seventy-five years later, 2052. The author (or heir) has five years in which to effect termination (2057), but must give at least two years advance notice, hence 2055.

a. Adequacy of notice to grantees

The notice provisions of section 304(c) are not author-friendly. As the court in *Siegel v. Warner Bros.*, concerning the recapture of rights in *Superman,* lamented, section 304(c)'s "intricate provisions oftentimes create unexpected pitfalls that thwart or blunt the effort of the terminating party to reclaim the full measure of the copyright in a work of authorship."[9] The caselaw confirms this sobering assessment. In *Burroughs v. MGM*,[10] Edgar Rice Burroughs' heirs sought to recapture film rights in the *Tarzan* books. While the derivative-works exception insulated the grantees of rights in previously-created motion pictures, the Burroughs heirs aimed to exercise control over future films incorporating the *Tarzan* characters. The Second Circuit held that the termination notice's "undoubtedly inadvertent" failure to include five of fourteen "Tarzan" book titles rendered the termination ineffective even though the five omitted titles did not include the first appearances of the various *Tarzan* characters. In theory, any rights conveyed in the five remaining titles should have been limited to the new matter contributed by those titles, the basic character attributes and adventures having been set out in the earlier books covered by the notice of termination.[11] As a result, the terminated grantee seeking to make a new film should not have been entitled to rely on its remaining rights in the later works because any new film would inevitably incorporate character traits and plot elements contained in the earlier works in which the grantee no longer had rights.

The Second Circuit, however, citing no authority, proclaimed "when an author grants the rights to a work that contains material protected by the author's copyright in an earlier work, the grant implicitly authorizes the use of all material contained in the licensed work, including material that may be covered by the author's other copyrights." The decision is especially devastating for authors of works in which the same characters appear in multiple sequels. The court's reasoning has the effect of nullifying the limitation on the derivative-works exception to already-created derivative works: Section 304(c)(6)(A) specifies that the "privilege [to continue to exploit previously prepared derivative works] does not extend to the preparation after the termination of other derivative works based upon the copyrighted work covered by the

9. Siegel v. Warner Bros. Ent., Inc., 542 F. Supp. 2d 1098, 1117 (C.D. Cal. 2008).

10. Burroughs v. Metro–Goldwyn–Mayer, Inc., 683 F.2d 610 (2d Cir. 1982).

11. *Cf.* 17 U.S.C. § 103(b) (2006) (copyright in a derivative work "extends only to the material contributed by the author of such work, as distinguished from the preexisting material employed in the work, and does not imply any exclusive right in the preexisting material. The copyright in such work is independent of, and does not affect or enlarge the scope, duration, ownership, or subsistence of, any copyright protection in the preexisting material.").

terminated grant." If derivative-works rights granted in later works in the series may continue to be exploited based on an "implicit" grant of rights in earlier works, then the character rights will not be retrieved until fifty-six years following the publication of the last pre–1978 sequel, or thirty-five years following a post–1978 grant of rights in the last sequel.

In *Siegel v. Warner Bros.* the termination notice served by the heirs of Jerome Siegel, one of the two creators of *Superman*, specified an effective date that failed, by a few days, to encompass the first published appearance of the *Superman* character in promotional announcements for the forthcoming first comic book featuring the character. Though the timing of the notice did encompass the comic book, Warner Bros. claimed that the subsistence of its rights in the earlier advertisements preserved its rights in the essential visual and story elements of the character. The court agreed that as much of the character as was depicted in the announcements remained unaffected by the termination. However, the court emphasized that only those elements of the Superman persona or story depicted in the advertisement escaped the effect of termination. "What remains of the Siegel and Shuster's Superman copyright that is still subject to termination (and, of course, what defendants truly seek) is the entire storyline from *Action Comics*, Vol. 1, Superman's distinctive blue leotard (complete with its inverted triangular crest across the chest with a red 'S' on a yellow background), a red cape and boots, and his superhuman ability to leap tall buildings, repel bullets, and run faster than a locomotive, none of which is apparent from the announcement."[12]

The *Siegel* court correctly construed the relationship between the copyright in a work containing a character's first appearance and the copyright in each subsequent work containing additional iterations of the character. *Superman* may be unusual in that the first published works (the promotional announcements) did not convey all the essential elements of the character's appearance and story. The heirs' recapture, while incomplete, was nonetheless sufficiently substantial to oblige Warner Bros. to account to the heirs for profits generated by at least some of the exploitations of the Superman copyright.[13]

b. *Scope of the derivative-works exception to termination*

In 1985 a divided Supreme Court rendered a controversial decision regarding the language in sections 203 and 304 that provides that when

---

12. *Siegel*, 542 F. Supp. 2d at 1126.

13. The court does not appear to have considered whether Warner Bros.' rights in later iterations of *Superman* derived from subsequent, unterminated (or untermina-ble, if later iterations were work for hire) grants which "implicitly" incorporated grants of rights in the earliest versions of the character.

a copyright transfer is terminated, derivative works lawfully prepared under the contract prior to termination may continue to be utilized after termination. In *Mills Music, Inc. v. Snyder*,[14] simplifying the facts slightly, a songwriter conveyed his interest in the initial and renewal terms of copyright to a music publisher, prior to January 1, 1978; the publisher in turn entered into licenses for the manufacture of phonograph records and tapes of the song, with the license fees to be paid half to the publishing company and half to the songwriter. When the songwriter's widow validly terminated the transfer of the latter part of the copyright renewal term, effective 56 years from the date of initial copyright, there was no doubt that the recording company could lawfully continue to manufacture and distribute recordings of the song. The question that remained was whether the termination entitled the widow to 100% of the recording royalties or whether the publishing company (no longer the copyright owner) remained entitled to 50% of those royalties. The Court majority held that the publishing company could continue to collect 50% of the recording royalties "under the terms of the grant after its termination," in the language of the statute. While the derivative-works licenses in *Mills Music* split the royalties evenly, so that the author continued to be remunerated, the Court's reasoning would seem to apply even when the licensing intermediary keeps most or all of the royalties.[15] The decision has been widely criticized as inconsistent with legislative intent;[16] subsequent decisions of lower courts appear to endeavor to limit the potential damage.

In *Woods v. Bourne*, the Second Circuit considered the post-termination distribution of royalties in arrangements of the song "When the Red Red Robin Comes Bob Bob Bobbin' Along" as sold in sheet music.[17] The Court faced the question of what constituted the underlying musical composition (the subject of the now-terminated grant of rights), and what constituted a derivative work within the scope of the exception. The composer's heirs had identified the underlying musical composition as the piano-vocal version, from which subsequent arrangements were

14. 469 U.S. 153 (1985).

15. *See id.* at 177 ("no support . . . for the proposition that Congress expected the author to be able to collect an increased royalty for the use of a derivative work").

16. *See, e.g.*, PAUL GOLDSTEIN, COPYRIGHT § 5:132–34.; Howard B. Abrams, *Who's Sorry Now? Termination Rights and the Derivative Works Exception*, 62 U. DETROIT L. REV. 181, 224–32, 238–39 (1985); Jessica D. Litman, *Copyright, Compromise, and Legislative History*, 72 CORNELL L. REV. 857, 901–02 (1987) ("With this interpretation, the [*Mills Music*] Court did to the right of termination essentially the same thing as it had done to

the 1909 Act's renewal provision 42 years earlier. With termination, as with renewal, the author's recapture expectancy is essentially alienable. In industries such as music publishing where authors and composers typically assign to the publisher the right to license any further uses, the statutory right to terminate will have little value. As with the renewal term, the author will have assigned most of what is valuable in her work to people from whom she will be unable to recapture it.").

17. Woods v. Bourne Co., 60 F.3d 978 (2d Cir. 1995).

adapted. The publisher had argued that the initial iteration of the song in the "lead sheet" constituted the "work" that was the subject of the "grant." The lead sheet was "a very simple, hand-written rendering of the lyrics and melody of the composition without harmonies or other embellishments. [The publisher argued that it] modified the lead sheet by adding harmonies and other elements to create a commercially exploitable piano-vocal arrangement that qualifies as a derivative work." In that event, if all the commercially exploited versions of the song were derivative works, then none would be terminable, and under *Mills Music*, the publisher would keep its share of the royalties from the continued sale of the sheet music. Distinguishing *Mills Music*, the court affirmed the district court's ruling that the "work" was the piano-vocal version, and, moreover, that most of the arrangements derived from the piano-vocal version lacked sufficient originality to constitute derivative works. If the works for which the royalties were owed were not derivative works, then the derivative works exception would be irrelevant. The disqualification of the alleged derivative works meant not only that the terminated intermediary publisher would not receive royalties for the continued exploitation of the arrangements, but that the terminating author (or his subsequent grantee) would determine whether and when the arrangements might henceforth be exploited.

In *Fred Ahlert Music Corp. v. Warner–Chappell Music*, the Second Circuit adapted *Mills Music*'s interpretation of "under the terms of the grant" in the author's favor.[18] The writers of the song "Bye–Bye Blackbird" had assigned their copyright in the song to defendant Warner's predecessor, who in turn licensed A & M Records to make and distribute a sound recording of Joe Cocker performing the song. The court ruled that the derivative works exception did not entitle Warner to license the derivative recording for the soundtrack and soundtrack album of the film "Sleepless in Seattle" once the songwriter reclaimed his rights for the extended renewal term. The Second Circuit emphasized that in *Mills Music*, the Supreme Court interpreted "the grant" as "*the entire set of documents* that created and defined each licensee's right to prepare and distribute [the] derivative work[ ]." Thus, the court determined that "the grant" at issue combined the songwriter's original grant to the music publisher with the publisher's subsequent grant to the record producer. Because the music publisher had not, pre-termination, authorized additional uses of the licensed derivative work, it was now too late to engage in new exploitations, and the rights to license and receive

18. Fred Ahlert Music Corp. v. Warner/Chappell Music, Inc., 155 F.3d 17 (2d Cir. 1998).

100

royalties from those exploitations reverted to the author (or his statutory heirs).

Whether *Fred Ahlert* effectively cabins *Mills Music* may turn on whether, during the minimum two-year period between service of the notice of termination and the effective date of the termination,[19] the grantee engages in a flurry of downstream licensing to cover the exploitations the grantee did not previously authorize. If "[t]he effect of *Mills Music* . . . is to preserve during the post-termination period the panoply of contractual obligations that governed pre-termination uses of derivative works by derivative work owners or their licensees,"[20] then perhaps intermediary grantees may elude the effect of *Fred Ahlert* by expanding the "panoply" before the effective date of the termination.[21]

c. Inalienability: "any agreement to the contrary"

The termination right remains available to the author or her heirs "notwithstanding any agreement to the contrary, including an agreement to make a will or to make any future grant."[22] The Second Circuit has held that a subsequent agreement to recharacterize as a "work for hire" an author's creation of "Captain America" for a series of comic books was an impermissible "agreement to the contrary" because grants of rights in works made for hire are not terminable.[23] The determination long after the work's creation that it was "for hire" thus constituted an impermissible agreement that the creator would have no termination rights. But it appears that not every agreement whose effect is to deprive the author or the statutory heir of the opportunity to terminate a grant is an "agreement to the contrary" within the meaning of section 304(c)(5). The Second and Ninth Circuits have issued conflicting decisions when the parties to an initial pre–1978 grant (or their successors) agreed post–1978 to rescind the grant and enter into a new agreement. Because the initial agreement would have been terminable under section 304(c), but the new agreement would not (nor would it be under section 203), the question arose whether the new agreement was "contrary" to section 304(c).

Milne ex. rel. Coyne v. Stephen Slesinger, Inc., concerned transfers of renewal rights in A.A. Milne's *Winnie the Pooh* works.[24] Milne wrote and published several *Winnie the Pooh* stories between 1924 and 1929. Beginning in 1930 a series of agreements involving Milne, and later his

---

19. *See* 17 U.S.C. § 304(c)(4)(A) (2006).

20. Woods v. Bourne Co., 60 F.3d 978, 987 (2d Cir. 1995).

21. Section 304(c)(6)(B) provides that the "future rights that will revert upon termination of the grant become vested on the date the notice of termination has been served," but it seems doubtful that the

vesting cuts off the grantee's present rights during the notice period.

22. 17 U.S.C. §§ 203(a)(5), 304(c)(5) (2006).

23. Marvel Characters, Inc. v. Simon, 310 F.3d 280 (2d Cir. 2002).

24. Milne *ex rel.* Coyne v. Stephen Slesinger, Inc., 430 F.3d 1036 (9th Cir. 2005).

widow, granted to Walt Disney Productions an exclusive license of merchandising and other rights to the Pooh character in the U.S., for the initial and renewal copyright terms, in exchange for royalties. In 1983, after Mrs. Milne's death, her only child—Christopher Robin Milne—contracted not to exercise his statutory termination rights in return for an increase in royalties from the Pooh properties. The 1983 agreement revoked the prior agreements and re-granted the rights in the Pooh works ultimately to Disney. In 2002, Clare Milne, Christopher Robin's sole surviving child, attempted to terminate her grandfather's original 1930 grant under Section 304(d).

The Ninth Circuit concluded that the execution of the 1983 agreement revoked the 1930 grant, so that when Clare Milne served her termination notice, there was no longer any pre–1978 agreement to be terminated. The court did not view the 1983 agreement as one inconsistent with the statutory goal of protecting authors or their families against unremunerative transfers, apparently because the 1983 agreement achieved the same objective as termination: obtaining a better deal for the author's heir (in this case the son, rather than the granddaughter).

The Ninth Circuit reached the opposite result, however, in *Classic Media, Inc. v. Mewborn*,[25] which involved Eric Knight's 1938 story "Lassie Come Home," as well as Knight's 1940 novel based on the short story. Knight granted the predecessor to Classic Media the right to make a television series based on the works. Knight died in 1943, and his widow and three daughters later renewed the copyrights. In July 1976, Ms. Mewborn, one of Knight's daughters, assigned her share of the film, TV, and radio rights in the Lassie works to Classic's predecessor. In March 1978, Classic's predecessor paid Mewborn $3,000 to sign a new agreement that conformed with assignment agreements signed by her sisters, except that it referred to the 1976 agreement, specifying that Mewborn was granting the identified rights "to the extent such rights are owned by me" and that the rights granted "are in addition to" the rights granted in the 1976 agreement. In April 1996, Mewborn served a notice of termination on Classic's predecessor, seeking to terminate her 1976 grant of film, TV, and radio rights effective May 1, 1998.

The court ruled that Mewborn's 1976 assignment had transferred all of her film, TV, and radio rights in the Lassie works, so that in 1978 she had nothing left to transfer. The court concluded that the 1978 agreement left the 1976 agreement intact and explicitly affirmed it. Thus, the 1976 agreement was properly subject to termination by her 1996 notice.[26]

25. Classic Media, Inc. v. Mewborn, 532 F.3d 978 (9th Cir. 2008).

26. Because the *Classic Media* court found that the 1978 agreement did not pre-

One might distinguish the "Lassie" case from "Pooh" on the ground that where Christopher Robin knew that the agreement bargained away future termination rights for a substantial sum, it does not appear that Mewborn understood that Classic's predecessor had devised the agreement to divest her of a later termination opportunity. The Ninth Circuit appears to distinguish a successful revocation and novation from one that violates the "any agreement to the contrary" proscription based on its evaluation of the extent to which the author or her heirs benefit from the new arrangement and are aware that the conclusion of a new agreement will deprive them of a future termination opportunity.

Finally, *Penguin Group (USA) Inc. v. Steinbeck*[27] concerned a 1938 grant by John Steinbeck to Penguin's predecessor in title of the exclusive right to publish in the United States and Canada some of his best known works, in which he held the copyright, in return for royalty payments. Steinbeck died in 1968; his will left his interest in his copyrights to his widow Elaine. The section 304(c) termination window for the earliest work covered by the 1938 agreement opened in 1985; the termination window for the latest work closed in 2000. In 1994 Elaine and Penguin signed a new contract covering all works included in the 1938 agreement, and increasing royalty payments; the 1994 agreement expressly provided that it canceled and superseded the 1938 agreement. Elaine died in 2003, leaving her interest in Steinbeck's copyrights to her children and grandchildren from a previous marriage, and excluding Steinback's two sons from a previous marriage, Thomas and John IV. In 2004, Steinbeck's son Thomas and granddaughter (the only surviving child of the now-deceased John IV) served notice on Penguin seeking to terminate Steinbeck's 1938 grants under section 304(d). Each party sought a declaration as to ownership of the rights in question.

As in *Milne*, the *Steinbeck* court found the subsequent agreement superseded the original agreements, leaving no subsisting agreement to be terminated under section 304(c). According to the Second Circuit, the parties' intention to terminate the 1938 contract was clear from the language of the 1994 agreement. The court noted that, under applicable New York law, "parties to an agreement can mutually agree to terminate it by expressly assenting to its rescission while simultaneously entering into a new agreement dealing with the same subject matter." The court therefore concluded that the 1938 contract had been extin-

---

vent Mewborn from terminating the 1976 grant, it did not need to decide whether the later contract was an "agreement to the contrary." (It did indicate, however, that interpreting the 1978 agreement as conveying film, TV, and radio rights to Classic would make that assignment void as an "agreement to the contrary.")

27. Penguin Group (USA) Inc. v. Steinbeck, 537 F.3d 193 (2d Cir. 2008).

guished, and thus the 1994 agreement left no pre–1978 grants in effect that could be subject to termination under section 304.

The Second Circuit similarly concluded that the 1994 agreement was not an "agreement to the contrary," notwithstanding which the termination could be effected. Steinbeck's son and granddaughter argued that the effect of that agreement, as interpreted by the court, was to eliminate their opportunity to exercise their section 304 termination interest. The court explained that not every agreement which effectively eliminates an author's or heir's statutory termination right was "an agreement to the contrary."[28] Like the *Milne* court, the Second Circuit viewed Elaine's actions in 1994 as consistent with the statutory purpose because she obtained an increased return on Steinbeck's works.[29] Ultimately, The Second and Ninth Circuits thus may understand "agreement to the contrary" not to mean contrary to the *exercise* of the termination right, but contrary to the *policy underlying* the termination right.

Some questions might nonetheless be raised regarding the rescission-and-rollover technique employed in *Milne* and *Steinbeck*, because it not only postpones exercise of the termination right by another thirty-five years, but as to post–1977 re-grants made by heirs, will prevent effecting the termination altogether.[30] While the thirty-five-year accrual date for the statutory termination right does not prevent the parties from *ending* their relationship before thirty-five years have elapsed,[31] a *new agreement between the same parties* (or their successors in title) that follows the rescission might attract suspicion.[32]

---

28. The court noted, for example, that, in instances in which multiple parties share the right to terminate a particular agreement, the holders of a majority of the interest might agree among themselves not to terminate, which would effectively eliminate the minority parties' right to terminate the grant, but that the agreement among the majority would not be an invalid "agreement to the contrary."

29. The Second Circuit explained that under its interpretation of an "agreement to the contrary," authors or their heirs are not "entitled to more than one opportunity, between them, to use termination rights to enhance their bargaining power or to exercise them." *Steinbeck*, 537 F.3d at 204.

30. 17 U.S.C. § 203(a) (stating that "the exclusive or nonexclusive grant of a transfer or license of copyright or of any right under a copyright, executed by the author on or after January 1, 1978, otherwise than by will, is subject to termination"). Thus, only those made by the author are terminable; heirs who re-grant

rights in lieu of termination thereby lose their statutory termination rights.

31. *Compare* Rano v. Sipa Press, Inc., 987 F.2d 580 (9th Cir. 1993) (holding thirty-five year termination period preempted earlier terminations), *with* Walthal v. Rusk, 172 F.3d 481 (7th Cir. 1999) (rejecting *Rano*), *and* Korman v. HBC Florida, Inc., 182 F.3d 1291 (11th Cir. 1999) (same). *See also* Latin Am. Music Co. v. American Soc'y of Composers Authors & Publishers, 593 F.3d 95 (1st Cir. 2010) (section 203 requirements do not apply to terminations under state contract law); Foley v. Luster, 249 F.3d 1281 (11th Cir. 2001) (referring to caselaw upholding right under state contract law to terminate agreement before 35 years).

32. The statute casts some doubt on these arrangements, for both sections 203(b)(4) and 304(c)(6)(D) bar agreements to make a further grant of any right covered by a terminated grant unless made after the effective date of termination;

C. *Termination Time Line*

Given the complexity of the termination provisions in sections 203 and 304(c), the following chart may afford a useful summary:

Work published before 1978

Reversion of renewal-term rights

For works published before 1964: renewal-term reversion of rights vested automatically (upon proper application and registration): in the author, if the author did not grant renewal term rights; in the author's surviving spouse or children if the author granted renewal term rights but died before the renewal term vested. No deadline was imposed on the renewal term rights holder's exercise of the reverted rights.[33]

For works published between 1964 and 1977, inclusive: if the author did not grant the renewal term, or if the author died before the renewal term vested, then renewal-term rights will revert *if the renewal is effected during the 28th year of copyright.* (If the author, or survivor, does not renew, then the term of copyright will be automatically renewed, *but* the transferee may continue to use already-created derivative works.)

Reversion of extended-renewal-term rights

Termination becomes effective in the five-year period beginning at the end of 56 years from publication (with a minimum of two years, and a maximum of 10 years, advance notice; but the transferee may continue to use already-created derivative works).

Termination becomes effective in the five-year period beginning at the end of 75 years from publication (with a minimum of two years, and a maximum of 10 years, advance notice), *if* the author or the author's heirs did not terminate at the end of 56 years; the transferee may continue to use already-created derivative works.

Grant of exclusive or non-exclusive rights executed by the author after 1977 (regardless of the work's date of publication)

Termination may be effected during the five-year period beginning 35 years from execution of the grant (or, if a grant of publication rights, 35 years from publication or 40 years from execution, whichever is

---

while the statute allows the terminating author or heir to make an agreement with the original grantee, she may do so only after the termination notice has been served. See 17 U.S.C. §§ 203(a)(4), 304(c)(4) (2006).

33. *See, e.g.,* Rohauer v. Killiam Shows, 551 F.2d 484 (2d Cir.1977) (author's surviving daughter effected the renewal in 1952, but did not assign the rights to Rohauer until 1965).

earlier), with a minimum of two years, and a maximum of 10 years, advance notice; the transferee may continue to use already-created derivative works.

Chapter 5

COPYRIGHT FORMALITIES

Copyright formalities have performed (or are thought to have performed) a variety of functions in U.S. copyright history. Formalities that condition the existence or enforcement of copyright on supplying information about works of authorship should enable effective title searching, thus furthering the economic interests both of copyright owners and of potential exploiters. Copyright-constitutive formalities, principally notice of copyright, but also at various times deposit of copies, registration and renewal, erect a barrier to the existence of protection, concomitantly casting into the public domain published works that fail to comply. These formalities thus (at least in theory) have divided works of perceived economic significance worth the effort of compliance from the mass of other creations, leaving the latter free for others to exploit. When failure to comply with formalities results in forfeiture of the copyright, this extreme sanction arguably protects exploiters who, in the absence of notice, might not otherwise have known that its author has claimed copyright in the work. Authors might have exclusive rights to print, reprint and vend, but they first would be put to the burden of making their claims clear.

The extent to which the U.S. system of formalities in fact achieved all or any of the above objectives is open to question, as the ensuing discussion will indicate. In any event, over time, the draconian features of the formalities system set the U.S. apart from most other nations and for many years prevented the U.S. from joining the principal multilateral copyright treaty, the Berne Convention for the Protection of Literary and Artistic Works. As a result, in the slightly more than a decade between 1977 and 1989, no feature of U.S. copyright law was more dramatically changed than the law relating to the formalities of notice, registration and deposit. Most notably, Congress, effective March 1, 1989, as part of the legislation designed to conform U.S. copyright law to the Berne Convention, eliminated the requirement that the copyright owner give public notice of his or her claim of copyright, a requirement that had been a central feature of our law since 1790.

I. Formalities Under the 1909 Copyright Act

Because the drafters of the 1976 Copyright Act did not intend to restore to copyright works that had previously fallen into the public domain,[1] it is imperative to understand the somewhat Byzantine rules that had developed under the 1909 Act for purposes of determining when a work had been "published" so as to precipitate the requirement to place proper notice on copies of the work. Litigation taking place even in the twenty-first century will no doubt continue to bring before the federal courts claims that the plaintiff's copyright on a work created prior to January 1, 1978, was lost by failure to comply with the notice requirements of the 1909 Act.

Under the 1909 Act, a work that was kept unpublished could be protected by state law against unauthorized copying, performance or other exploitation. State common-law copyright afforded to the author (or the author's assignee) the right to publish a work for the first time. Once the work was published, state copyright protection was ousted, by virtue both of state law and of the federal statute. If such publication was accompanied by compliance with the federal statutory formalities—in particular the placement of proper notice on all copies distributed to the public—federal copyright protection was afforded. Section 10 of the 1909 Act provided that

> Any person entitled thereto by this title may secure copyright for his work by publication thereof with the notice of copyright required by this title; and such notice shall be affixed to each copy thereof published or offered for sale in the United States by authority of the copyright proprietor.

Once federal copyright attached, it would last for 28 years from the date of publication, subject to renewal for another 28 years.

If, however, the owner of common-law copyright published the work but failed to place a proper copyright notice on the distributed copies, this was generally regarded as fatal to the copyright. If the wrong name was placed in the notice (i.e., the name of someone other than the "proprietor" of copyright), or if the year of publication was materially inaccurate, or if either of those elements was omitted or the notice was omitted altogether, the work would be thrust irretrievably into the public domain. Moreover, if the notice—even though accurate in form and conspicuous—was placed on the work in a location other than that dictated by the statute, it could be expected that a court would hold that this too was a fatal error and that the work had fallen into the public domain.[2]

---

1. Transitional and supplementary provisions, section 103.

2. *See* Robert A. Gorman, Jane C. Ginsburg & R. Anthony Reese, Copyright: Cases and Materials, Chapter 5A (8th ed. 2011).

A. "Publication"

Determining when a work was "published" was thus crucial under the 1909 Act, for it served to determine three important features of copyright protection: the demarcation between state and federal protection, the loss of all protection for failure to comply with federal formalities, and the beginning point from which the 28– or 56–year term of federal copyright was measured.

As was the case with almost all such crucial language, the 1909 Act did not define "publication." It was therefore left to the courts to define, and the courts—sometimes federal and sometimes state—generated a number of important interpretive rules. Perhaps most important was the rule that only a "general publication" would divest a work of copyright protection, while a "limited publication" would not.[3] The courts found a limited publication when a work was disseminated only to a limited group of persons for a limited purpose.

A striking application of the doctrine was that of the Court of Appeals for the Ninth Circuit in *Academy of Motion Picture Arts & Sciences v. Creative House Promotions, Inc.*[4] In that 1991 decision, the court addressed the question whether the distribution of 159 Oscar statuettes by the Academy between 1929 and 1941—without notices of copyright—constituted a divestive general publication that thrust the familiar sculptural figure into the public domain. The court held that the distribution did not result in a loss of copyright. It found that the Oscar was awarded only to a select group of persons, that the purpose was limited (to advance the art of motion-picture making), and that no recipient had the right of sale or further distribution. And in 1999, in *Estate of Martin Luther King, Jr., Inc. v. CBS, Inc.*,[5] the Court of Appeals for the Eleventh Circuit, confronted with the question whether Reverend King lost the copyright on his epochal "I Have a Dream" speech, concluded that even Dr. King's distribution of copies (without a copyright notice) to the news media was merely a "limited publication" because that was for the purpose of enabling the reporting of a newsworthy event and not a distribution directly to the general public. These cases clearly demonstrate that the limited-publication doctrine is, as the court stated in *Academy of Motion Picture Arts & Sciences*, "an attempt by courts to mitigate the harsh forfeiture effects of a divesting general publication."[6]

---

3. Estate of Martin Luther King, Jr., Inc. v. CBS, Inc., 194 F.3d 1211 (11th Cir. 1999); Academy of Motion Picture Arts & Sciences v. Creative House Promotions, Inc., 944 F.2d 1446 (9th Cir. 1991).

4. 944 F.2d 1446 (9th Cir. 1991).

5. 194 F.3d 1211 (11th Cir. 1999).

6. *Academy of Motion Picture Arts & Sciences*, 944 F.2d at 1452 (citing American Vitagraph, Inc. v. Levy, 659 F.2d 1023, 1027 (9th Cir. 1981)).

Other examples of limited publications that would not, in all likelihood, have required the use of a copyright notice (there were no squarely authoritative judicial decisions) are the distribution of a manuscript to several magazine or book publishers for the purpose of soliciting expressions of interest, and the distribution of the professor's own teaching materials to students in a university course.

Another important aspect of the definition of "publication" that evolved under the 1909 Act was the prevailing view that the performance of a work, no matter how many times to no matter how large an audience, would not constitute a publication that would divest the author of common-law copyright protection.[7] The performance of a play, for example, every night to a packed house in a large theater would not be regarded as a divestive publication. The rule was also applied in the *King* case so as to preserve common-law copyright in the speech given by Dr. King to the 200,000 people in attendance and over radio and television broadcasts.[8]

It therefore came to be understood that, in order for a work to be "published" for copyright purposes, tangible copies had to be distributed, essentially indiscriminately, to any interested member of the public. If a work was thus distributed, the copies had to bear a proper notice, or else the work would fall into the public domain. It was therefore generally understood that the exhibition of a painting or sculpture was not a divestive general publication, at least if the artist or gallery did not permit members of the public to photograph or make copies of the work.[9] It was also held that the public distribution of phonograph records of a song did not constitute a divestive general publication, because the records were not eye-readable copies.[10] This focus on eye-readability characterized the judicial interpretation of the 1909 Act in several important respects, though it has been essentially abandoned under the present Copyright Act. A few cases also raised the question whether the public exhibition of a motion picture or television film was to be regarded as a divestive general publication, and it was usually held that such exhibition (like a performance) was not.[11]

7. Ferris v. Frohman, 223 U.S. 424 (1912).

8. *King*, 194 F.3d 1211.

9. Letter Edged in Black Press, Inc. v. Public Bldg. Comm'n of Chicago, 320 F. Supp. 1303 (N.D. Ill. 1970).

10. Rosette v. Rainbo Record Mfg. Corp., 354 F. Supp. 1183 (S.D.N.Y. 1973), *aff'd per curiam*, 546 F.2d 461 (2d Cir. 1976). In a striking departure, the Court of Appeals for the Ninth Circuit held in 1995

that the distribution of phonorecords did constitute a divestive publication under the 1909 Act. La Cienega Music Co. v. ZZ Top, 53 F.3d 950 (9th Cir. 1995). Congress within two years overruled that decision by adding section 303(b) to the Copyright Act: "The distribution before January 1, 1978, of a phonorecord shall not for any purpose constitute a publication of the musical work embodied therein."

11. *See, e.g.,* Burke v. NBC, 598 F.2d 688 (1st Cir. 1979).

B. *Registration*

It has been a widespread misconception that copyright attaches to a work only when registration of the copyright is secured with the Copyright Office. Registration was not, under the 1909 Act (and is not today), a prerequisite of a valid copyright. All that was necessary to secure copyright in a published work under the 1909 Act was that a proper notice be placed on all publicly distributed copies. At that point, federal protection attached and the copyright owner could validly enter into transactions involving the copyright, such as assignments and licenses. Registration was, however, a prerequisite for the commencement of an action for copyright infringement,[12] and registration for an initial copyright term was a prerequisite for a valid renewal application.

II. Formalities Under the 1976 Act

Upon the effective date of the 1976 Copyright Act, January 1, 1978, the drastic consequences of failing to place a copyright notice on published works were initially ameliorated and ultimately eliminated altogether. From January 1978 through February 1989, notice was still required, but neither mistakes in nor complete omission of notice thrust the work into the public domain, and reasonable steps could be taken within five years by the copyright owner to preserve the copyright. Since March 1, 1989, when the Copyright Act was further amended in order to permit United States adherence to the Berne Convention, the notice requirement has been eliminated completely for works published on or after that date.

Under the 1976 Act, federal copyright attaches to a work immediately upon its "creation," i.e., its manifestation in a tangible medium of expression; common-law copyright is preempted and "publication" no longer serves as the dividing line between state and federal protection. Nonetheless, until March 1989, the federal protection that attaches once a work was fixed could—under the 1976 Act as originally enacted—be forfeited if proper copyright notice was omitted when the work was later "published." Both the act of "publication" and the requirement of notice thus continued to be significant under the 1976 Act.

A. *"Publication"*

Unlike the 1909 Copyright Act, the 1976 Act defines "publication":

"Publication" is the distribution of copies or phonorecords of a work to the public by sale or other transfer of ownership, or by rental, lease, or lending. The offering to distribute copies or

---

12. *See* Washingtonian Publ'g Co. v. Pearson, 306 U.S. 30 (1939).

phonorecords to a group of persons for purposes of further distribution, public performance, or public display, constitutes publication. A public performance or display of a work does not of itself constitute publication.

"Publication" still requires an authorized distribution to the public, but the work may be distributed either in the form of "copies" that appeal to the eye or of "phonorecords" that appeal to the ear. Morever, as was the case under the 1909 Act, neither public performance nor public display in itself constitutes the kind of publication that requires the use of a copyright notice. The statute also defines a "public" display or performance, a definition that can provide some guidance in determining whether a "distribution" of copies or phonorecords is "to the public"; this would contemplate a distribution to members of the public generally or to a substantial number of persons "outside of a normal circle of a family and its social acquaintances." In that context, the status of a distribution of teaching materials (constituting for example, a draft of a casebook) to a large class might be somewhat unclear. Common sense suggests that the distributed draft should not be deemed "published," but, if the "public" for purposes of the public performance right is the same as for purposes of "publication," then arguably the distribution to a large class could effect a "publication" (while a distribution of the same material to a small seminar would not).

The meaning of the "offering to distribute" language introduced in the 1976 Act is not entirely clear. The distribution of a manuscript to a number of magazines for the purpose of generating an offer to print, or to a number of theater producers for the purpose of generating an offer to perform the play would most likely not be a publication, but the offering of a film to a group of theaters for public exhibition. probably would be.[13] As we will see in the next chapter, concerning the distribution right, this language has been interpreted in a context unforeseen by the drafters of the 1976 Act: the distribution of works over the Internet, particularly in the context of peer-to-peer file sharing.

B. *The notice requirement*

1. In general

In any event, given an authorized distribution of a work to the public in the form of copies, section 401 of the 1976 Act as originally enacted required that copyright notice be placed on each copy in order to preserve the copyright. Section 401(a) provided:

---

13. *See* H.R. Rep. No. 1476, 94th Cong., 2d Sess. 138 (1976) ("[T]he definition ... makes clear that, when copies or phonorecords are offered to a group of wholesalers, broadcasters, motion picture theaters, etc., publication takes place if the purpose is 'further distribution, public performance, or display.' ").

Whenever a work protected under this title is published in the United States or elsewhere by authority of the copyright owner, a notice of copyright as provided by this section shall be placed on all publicly distributed copies from which the work can be visually perceived, either directly or with the aid of a machine or device.

Section 401(b) prescribes the form of notice; it is the familiar © or the word "Copyright" (or "Copr.") plus the year of first publication and the name of the copyright owner. Section 401(c) announces a far more flexible set of rules than under the 1909 Act for the placement of the notice: it "shall be affixed to the copies in such manner and location as to give reasonable notice of the claim of copyright."

Section 403 addresses works "consisting predominantly of one or more works of the United States government" and encourages the placement of a statement identifying the copyrighted material, as distinguished from the public domain U.S. government works. For example, reports of decisions of U.S. courts may contain both the unprotectible text of the decisions and such value-added as headnotes and summaries prepared by the editor of the reports. Query whether the notice "no claim to U.S. government works" which frequently appears in connection with such reports meets the statutory standard.[14]

Section 402 announces comparable rules for what is known as a "P notice" (℗), which is to be affixed to phonorecords that are distributed to the public, as a way of signaling that there is a claim of copyright in the sound recording as distinguished from the musical or literary work that is performed on the recording.

Before discussing the potential adverse effects of failure to comply with the notice provisions of sections 401 and 402, it is essential to point out that the mandated notice applies only to copies and phonorecords distributed to the public between January 1, 1978, and February 28, 1989. On March 1, 1989, the Berne Convention Implementation Act of 1988 went into effect. In order to make our law compatible with the Berne Convention, which forbids making compliance with formalities a condition of enjoying copyright protection, Congress for the first time eliminated the mandatory notice provisions of our law.[15] This was

---

14. 17 U.S.C. § 403 provides that "Sections 401(d) and 402(d) shall not apply to a work published in copies or phonorecords consisting predominantly of one or more works of the United States Government unless the notice of copyright appearing on the published copies or phonorecords to which a defendant in the copyright infringement suit had access includes a statement identifying, either affirmatively or negatively, those portions of the copies or phonorec-ords embodying any work or works protected under this title."

15. *See* Kahle v. Ashcroft, 72 U.S.P.Q.2d 1888 (N.D. Cal. 2004) (rejecting constitutional challenge to elimination of notice requirement). But the elimination of this formality is not retroactive. The rules relating to copyright notice for the 11–year period under discussion are preserved. *See* 17 U.S.C. §§ 405(a) & 406(a).

accomplished by replacing the phrase "shall be placed" in sections 401 and 402 with the phrase "may be placed." The amended statute gives the copyright owner only one explicit incentive to place a copyright notice on copies and phonorecords distributed after March 1, 1989: a defendant copying such a work will be unable to claim that it is an "innocent infringer" entitled thereby to reduced liability for statutory damages.

2.   Effect of noncompliance with the notice requirement (for works published between 1978–1989)

An omission of copyright notice on works distributed prior to January 1, 1978, was generally fatal to the copyright, whereas an omission on or after March 1, 1989, is of very limited significance. Only for copies distributed in the intervening 11 years are the mandatory-notice provisions of the 1976 Act important.

The consequences of noncompliance with those provisions are set forth in sections 405 and 406. Under section 405, a complete omission of notice from copies or phonorecords distributed by authority of the copyright owner does not invalidate the copyright if "the notice has been omitted from no more than a relatively small number" of such copies or phonorecords, or if the notice was omitted in violation of an express written agreement by which the copyright owner made the use of the notice a condition of the authority to distribute. Most significantly, section 405(a)(2) permits a copyright owner to "cure" the omission of notice from more than a "relatively small" number of copies or phono-records, provided two steps are taken: (1) registration for the work is made prior to, or within five years after, publication without notice; and (2) "a reasonable effort is made to add notice to all copies or phonorec-ords that are distributed to the public in the United States after the omission has been discovered." If, after the distribution without notice, registration is not secured within five years *or* reasonable efforts are not made to add notice to later-distributed copies or phonorecords, the copyright is invalidated and the work falls into the public domain.

For instances in which the copyright owner's omission of notice was not fatal, Congress saw a need (during the period January 1, 1978, to February 28, 1989) to protect a person innocently relying on that omission of notice in copying or otherwise exploiting the work in question. Under section 405(b), such an innocent infringer is sheltered against an award of damages resulting from infringing acts committed before receiving actual notice that the copyright has been timely regis-tered; however, even such an innocent infringer may be required to disgorge all or part of its profits and is subject to an injunction for the future.

On occasion, a copyright owner will attempt to comply with the notice provisions of the 1976 Act but will make an error or omission with regard to one component. Section 406 deals with the implications of such an error or omission in the name or date alone. The general framework is to protect a person who acts innocently in reliance upon the mistaken name; to use an erroneously early date as the measuring rod for copyright where the publication date is pertinent; and to treat an erroneously late date (by more than one year) as equivalent to a total omission of copyright notice—which will be fatal to the copyright unless cured within five years, a rather harsh sanction for an error that is typically of negligible significance in the administration of the copyright system.

3.   Effect of omission of notice after February 1989

After Berne adherence, the amended 1976 Act provided that, for works first published on or after March 1, 1989—and also for copies or phonorecords distributed after that date of works that had been published previously—§§ 401(a) and 402(a) no longer require placement of notice on publicly distributed copies and phonorecords, but instead provide that the © notice "may" be placed on copies and the P-in-a-circle notice "may" be placed on phonorecords of sound recordings.[16] The form and placement of the optional notice are the same as they were when the notice was mandated.[17] The elimination of the notice requirement thus imposes a responsibility on putative copyists to investigate in the Copyright Office—or to inquire of author or publisher—to determine the status of recently published works that lack copyright notice. Despite this highly significant, and author-favorable, change in the law concerning copyright formalities, publishers have continued since 1989 to use copyright notices in any event, both because of human and institutional inertia and because the notice inexpensively serves the useful function of signaling that the work is in copyright and that copyists should beware (or secure a license).

---

16.   17 U.S.C. §§ 401(a), 402(a) (2006).

17.   Under § 404(a), a notice of copyright applicable to a collective work as a whole suffices as notice for the separately-owned contents of the collective work, although the authors or copyright owners of these contributions may also affix separate notices. Section 404 carries over the practice of "blanket notice" which courts have held preserved the copyrights in contributions to collective works published under the 1909 Copyright Act. *See, e.g.,* Abend v. MCA, Inc., 863 F.2d 1465, 1469 (9th Cir. 1988) (holding that blanket notice "is sufficient to obtain a valid copyright on behalf of the beneficial owner, the author or proprietor" under the 1909 Act (quoting Goodis v. United Artists Television, Inc., 425 F.2d 397, 399 (2d Cir. 1970)), *aff'd sub nom.* Stewart v. Abend, 495 U.S. 207 (1990).

In addition, a new subsection (d) to §§ 401 and 402 sets forth an incentive for use of the notice; these provisions disallow an innocent-infringement defense if the requisite notice "appears on the published copy [or phonorecord] or copies [or phonorecords] to which a defendant in a copyright infringement suit had access."[18] The incentive is rather weak, however, because the innocent-infringer defense applies only to the calculus of statutory damages; it affects neither actual damages nor the existence of liability.[19]

On the other hand, as we will see in Chapter 9, *infra*, statutory damages can both be substantial and afford the most meaningful remedy for infringement. Because omission of notice can trigger an "innocent infringer" defense, and the defense may affect the award of statutory damages, the question has arisen whether the copy "to which a defendant ... had access" means the source copy for the infringing act, or generally available copies, whether or not such a copy was the one from which the defendant copied. In *BMG Music v. Gonzalez*, the defendant downloaded numerous recorded songs from the Internet.[20] She sought a diminution of statutory damages on the ground that the copies from which she copied did not bear a copyright notice. Recognizing that unauthorized source copies may often lack copyright notice or other copyright-owner-identifying indicia (which the source infringer may deliberately have removed), the court rejected the defendant's contention: "the statutory question is whether 'access' to legitimate works was available rather than whether infringers earlier in the chain attached copyright notices to the pirated works. Gonzalez readily could have learned, had she inquired, that the music was under copyright."

The court's interpretation may be in tension with the text of the statute: Section 402(d) provides: "If a notice of copyright in the form and the position specified by this section appears on *the* published phonorecord or phonorecords to which a defendant in a copyright infringement suit had access ..." (emphasis supplied) (the equivalent provision for copies is § 401(d)). The *Gonzalez* court interpreted the text to mean "if a notice of copyright ... appears on *a* copy [or phonorecord] to which a defendant ... *could have* had access ..." On the other hand, a literal interpretation would provide the participants in peer-to-peer or other infringement arrangements a perverse incentive to circulate copies or

---

18. 17 U.S.C. §§ 401(d), 402(d) (2006). As to whether continued use of the notice may be expected once no meaningful sanctions attach to its omission, *see* H.R. REP. No. 100–609, at 26–27 (1988) ("It is entirely possible that elimination of the notice formality may not in the end curtail its use. Old habits die hard; it remains useful under the Universal Copyright Convention; and, it is, in all probability, the cheapest deterrent to infringement which a copyright holder may take.").

19. *See* 17 U.S.C. §§ 401(d), 504(c)(2) (2006).

20. 430 F.3d 888 (7th Cir. 2005).

phonorecords lacking the notice, even though the copyright owner will have affixed the notice at the outset.

It is important to remember that the Berne Implementation amendments concerning notice do not apply retroactively. Thus, as to copies or phonorecords first distributed before the amendments' effective date of March 1, 1989, one must still ascertain whether notice was properly affixed. With respect to copies distributed without notice between 1978 and February 1989 (inclusive), it is necessary to determine whether the omission was discovered and cured within five years of initial publication, and whether the copyright owner made reasonable efforts to add notice to subsequently-distributed copies.[21]

C.   Deposit and Registration

The other two elements of formalities that have been a fixture of our copyright law since the beginning of the twentieth century are deposit and registration. In the interest of maintaining a full collection in the Library of Congress, section 407 of the 1976 Copyright Act—unaffected by the 1988 Berne Implementation Act—requires the copyright owner to deposit with the Copyright Office, within three months after publication of a work, two copies or phonorecords of the "best edition" (subject to some exemptions). If no deposit is made, the Register of Copyrights may make a written demand for such deposit, and continued failure of the copyright owner to comply may result in a fine. Failure to make the required deposit will not, however, invalidate the copyright. There is, in any event, no requirement to deposit copies of unpublished works.

As distinguished from the requirement of *deposit* of copies of a published work, there is no requirement that the copyright owner *register* the copyright in the Copyright Office; registration is optional. Under section 408, a registration application may be filed with respect to either a published or unpublished work by "the owner of copyright or of any exclusive right in the work," and is to be accompanied by the application fee (currently $65 for most works, and $35 if the application for registration is made online) and the deposit of copies or phonorecords of the work. A deposit made in compliance with the statutory requirement of section 407 also satisfies the deposit provision of section 408 relating to registration. The deposit copy must in fact be a copy of the work in which copyright is claimed.[22] For certain types of works, howev-

---

21. *See, e.g.,* Garnier v. Andin Int'l, Inc., 36 F.3d 1214 (1st Cir. 1994). By virtue of § 104A, however, the copyrights in foreign works published without notice before 1989 were restored, effective January 1, 1996.

22. *Compare* Nova Design Build, Inc. v. Grace Hotels, LLC, 652 F.3d 814 (7th Cir. 2011) (validating deposit copies of designs of architectural work regenerated from printouts and computer-aided design files, when final copies of design were lost with

er, it is permissible to deposit "identifying material" in lieu of a copy of the work.[23]

Section 409 lists the information that an application for registration "shall" include. Among the required items are the name(s) of the author(s). This apparently banal item is noteworthy because the U.S. copyright does not include a general author's right to be recognized as the creator of the work. As we will see in the next chapter, it is not an infringement of the copyrights in most works to leave off the author's name when making an otherwise lawful copy or communication to the public. When it comes to the establishment of a public record of the work through the Copyright Office registry, however, authors (other than creators of works made for hire) are entitled to be identified as such. As a result, one court has recently invalidated a Copyright Office regulation, developed for group registrations of automated databases, serials, and photographs, that permits the applicant to forgo listing all the names of all the authors of the collectively registered works if there is only one copyright claimant.[24]

Section 410(b) of the 1976 Copyright Act expressly authorizes the Register of Copyrights to refuse to register a work, provided the applicant is notified of the reasons therefor. Although no intensive scrutiny of the "prior art" is carried out in the Examining Division of the Copyright Office—in contrast to the search undertaken in connection with patent applications—the Register will on occasion refuse to issue a certificate of copyright. For example, he or she may determine that the work lacks original authorship (such as in the case of blank forms or slogans) or that it comprises solely uncopyrightable subject matter (such as useful articles having no separable decorative elements). Section 411(a) of the 1976 Act allows a person making an application for registration to institute an infringement action despite the Register's refusal, provided that the applicant gives notice thereof to the Register, who may then intervene to challenge the validity of the copyright.

1. Registration as a prerequisite to suit

Although registration is not a condition of a valid copyright, it has been a prerequisite for the commencement of an infringement action,

theft of computers in whose memories designs were stored), *with* Coles v. Wonder, 283 F.3d 798 (6th Cir. 2002) (1990 registration of 1982 song was invalid when the deposited copy was a "reconstruction" of the song from memory and without direct reference to the original).

23. 37 C.F.R. §§ 202.20–202.21 (2009).

24. *See* 37 CFR 202.3(b)(5)(6); Muench Photography v. Houghton Mifflin Harcourt

Publishing Co., 712 F. Supp. 2d 84 (S.D.N.Y. 2010), *decision on rehearing pending.* Ironically, in that case, the beneficiaries of the regulation were photographers who developed a practice of assigning their copyrights to photography "stock houses" for purposes of group registration, after which the stock house would transfer the copyrights back to the various authors.

under both the 1909 Act and the 1976 Act.[25] Courts will, moreover, verify that the work allegedly infringed corresponds to the work identified in the registration. Thus, the Court of Appeals for the Eleventh Circuit has rejected a claim of violation of the copyright in an architectural work when the registration was made in the category of pictorial, graphic and sculptural works.[26] The Second Circuit has held the registration of a journal will not permit suit for infringement of an article that was included therein when the copyright in the journal is owned by another person.[27]

The Berne Convention Implementation Act (BCIA),[28] effective March 1, 1989, made a significant change in the pre-suit registration provisions of the Copyright Act. Because there was serious doubt that making registration a condition of an infringement action was consistent with the declaration in article 5(2) of the Berne Convention that "the enjoyment and the exercise of [copyright] shall not be subject to any formality," Congress decided to eliminate such a condition with respect to "Berne Convention works whose country of origin is not the United States," i.e., for works initially published in some other nation that adheres to the Berne Convention. Because the Berne Convention does not require any adhering nation to abolish formalities (as a condition on the enjoyment or exercise of copyright) for works published *domestically*,[29] the 1976 Act as amended by the BCIA still requires, in section 411(a), that registration be made as a condition of an infringement action relating to a "United States work."

That term is defined in the Copyright Act, and principally targets first publication in the U.S.[30] New technology has, however, complicated

---

25. *See* Washingtonian Publ'g Co. v. Pearson, 306 U.S. 30 (1939); 17 U.S.C. § 411(a).

26. Oravec v. Sunny Isles Luxury Ventures L.C., 527 F.3d 1218 (11th Cir. 2008). *See also* Well–Made Toy Mfg. Corp. v. Goffa Int'l Corp., 354 F.3d 112 (2d Cir. 2003) (dismissing action when plaintiff registered its 20–inch doll but alleged copying of its 48–inch version, which was not registered); Xoom, Inc. v. Imageline, Inc., 323 F.3d 279 (4th Cir.2003) (after registering a compilation of clip-art images, plaintiff sues for infringement of certain individual images and of the underlying computer program that generated the images; court upholds jurisdiction concerning former but not latter).

27. Morris v. Business Concepts, Inc., 283 F.3d 502 (2d Cir. 2002).

28. Pub. L. No. 100–568, 102 Stat. 2853 (1988).

29. *See* Berne Convention, art. 5(3): "Protection in the country of origin is governed by domestic law ..."

30. *See* 17 U.S.C. § 101: For purposes of section 411, a work is a "United States work" only if—

(1) in the case of a published work, the work is first published—

(A) in the United States;

(B) simultaneously in the United States and another treaty party or parties, whose law grants a term of copyright protection that is the same as or longer than the term provided in the United States;

(C) simultaneously in the United States and a foreign nation that is not a treaty party; or

(D) in a foreign nation that is not a treaty party, and all of the authors of the work are nationals, domiciliaries, or habitual resi-

the ascertaining of the country of first publication, because the first disclosure of a work over the Internet potentially "publishes" the work in every country from which users may access copies of the work. (Whether the website thus "distributes copies" tantamount to publication is a topic we will consider in Chapter 6.) The U.S. Copyright Act's definition of a U.S. work as any work "first published ... simultaneously in the United States and a foreign nation that is not a treaty party," could lead to the surprising (appalling?) result that all works first disclosed on publicly accessible websites, wherever located, may be "United States works" because the work will be simultaneously accessible all over the world, including in at least one of the few remaining countries that do not have treaty relations with the U.S.[31] If making a work available over the Internet has the effect of designating the work a "United States work" for purposes of the pre-suit registration requirement, no matter what the nationality of the author or of the source website, then the authors or copyright owners of all such works would be obliged to comply with the U.S. registration formality if they wished to enforce their copyrights in the U.S. It is very doubtful that this outcome is consistent with the U.S.'s obligations under the Berne Convention.

2. 1976 Act incentives to registration

Whatever the country in which a work is first published, prompt registration—even though permissive—will continue to provide significant advantages for copyright owners, particularly with respect to proof and remedies in infringement actions:

(1) if registration is made within five years after first publication of the work, the certificate issued by the Copyright Office shall, in an infringement action, "constitute *prima facie* evidence of the validity of the copyright and of the facts stated in the certificate";[32] and

(2) in an infringement action, prompt registration is a condition to an award of attorneys' fees and, even more significantly, of statutory

---

dents of, or in the case of an audiovisual work legal entities with headquarters in, the United States;

(2) in the case of an unpublished work, all the authors of the work are nationals, domiciliaries, or habitual residents of the United States, or, in the case of an unpublished audiovisual work, all the authors are legal entities with headquarters in the United States; or

(3) in the case of a pictorial, graphic, or sculptural work incorporated in a building or structure, the building or structure is located in the United States.

31. *See* Kernal Records Oy v. Mosley, 794 F. Supp. 2d 1355 (S.D. Fla. 2011) (holding that work of a Norwegian composer first publicly disclosed on an Australian website was a "United States work," and that Congress intended this result). *Contra*, Moberg v. 33T LLC, 666 F. Supp. 2d 415 (D. Del. 2009) (display on German gallery's website of photos by Swedish photographer did not constitute simultaneous first publication in the U.S.)

32. 17 U.S.C. § 410(c).

damages, which can be as high as $30,000 (and as high as $150,000 for willful infringement) for each work infringed even in the absence of specific proof of actual damages or profits.[33]

Given the high costs of litigation, this second incentive is crucial, and indeed, for smaller litigants, may determine whether bringing an infringement action is financially feasible. It is important to emphasize that these incentives apply to all works regardless of their countries of origin. As a practical matter, then, copyright registration promptly upon publication remains key to effective enforcement of copyright, even for non-U.S. works for which registration is not a prerequisite to suit.

3. Other issues regarding registration under the 1976 Act

Although section 411(a) requires registration for a U.S.-origin work as a prerequisite to an infringement suit, the Supreme Court ruled in *Reed Elsevier v. Muchnick* that this requirement is not jurisdictional, and failure to register does not absolutely deprive a court of subject-matter jurisdiction to hear an infringement claim.[34] While the Court decided that courts have jurisdiction to hear infringement claims even where the plaintiff has not satisfied the statutorily required precondition, the justices declined to address "whether § 411(a)'s registration requirement is a mandatory precondition to suit that ... district courts may or should enforce *sua sponte* by dismissing copyright infringement claims involving unregistered works."[35]

But when is a work "registered"? Section 410(d) sets as the effective date of registration the date on which the application was "received in the Copyright Office." Does this date also suffice for the § 411(a) prerequisite? Courts have divided over what the Ninth Circuit[36] has called an "application approach," whereby a copyright is registered when the Copyright Office receives the copyright holder's application.[37] Other circuits used a "registration approach," under which a copyright is registered only at the time the Copyright Office acts on the application.[38]

---

33. *Id.* §§ 412, 504(c).

34. Reed Elsevier, Inc. v. Muchnick, 559 U.S. ___, 130 S.Ct. 1237 (2010).

35. At least one district court, in the wake of *Muchnick*, has held that the Supreme Court "did not conclude ... that 17 U.S.C. § 411(a) was to be ignored," and dismissed a plaintiff's copyright claim in an unregistered work. Marketing Technology Solutions, Inc. v. Medizine LLC, 2010 WL 2034404 (S.D.N.Y. May 18, 2010), at *5–*6. *See also Kernal Records*, 794 F. Supp. 2d 1355 (denying leave to amend complaint after registration effected during pendency of litigation, and dismissing complaint).

36. Cosmetic Ideas v. IAC/Interactive Corp., 606 F.3d 612 (9th Cir. 2010).

37. *See, e.g.*, Apple Barrel Prods., Inc. v. Beard, 730 F.2d 384, 386–87 (5th Cir. 1984); Chicago Bd. of Educ. v. Substance, Inc., 354 F.3d 624, 631 (7th Cir. 2003).

38. *See, e.g.*, La Resolana Architects, PA v. Clay Realtors Angel Fire, 416 F.3d 1195, 1202–04 (10th Cir. 2005); M.G.B. Homes, Inc. v. Ameron Homes, Inc., 903 F.2d 1486, 1489 (11th Cir. 1990).

There may be some tension between the text of the statute and its sensible interpretation. As the Ninth Circuit acknowledged, some statutory provisions favor the "registration approach." For example, § 410(a) "places an active burden of examination and registration upon the Register, suggesting that registration is not accomplished by application alone." Additionally, in § 411(a), registration "is juxtaposed with the separate act of delivering the necessary application materials to the Copyright Office," implying that "Congress intended registration to require acceptance or refusal by the Register, not mere delivery." However, § 408(a) implies that "the sole requirement for obtaining registration is delivery of the appropriate documents and fee."

Looking to the overall statutory purpose and to common sense, the "application approach" should prevail. Under the "registration approach," an author who promptly *filed* an application for registration, but the determination of whose application falls prey to backlogs in the Copyright Office, may not have her claims adjudicated until the Copyright Office acts on the application.[39] Where the author has in fact sought to make the requisite public record of her claim, an approach that requires actual registration or rejection of the application "amounts to little more than just the type of needless formality Congress generally worked to eliminate in the 1976 Act." By contrast, the Ninth Circuit concluded, the "application approach" "fully accomplishes the central purpose of registration—the compilation of a robust national register of existing copyrights—and at the same time avoids unfairness and waste of judicial resources."[40] Whether the pre-suit registration formality and other statutory incentives to registration in fact significantly contribute to a "robust national register of existing copyrights," the registration incentives do achieve a gatekeeper function, forestalling the claims of litigants, many of whom are likely to be individual authors.[41]

---

39. In 2005, Congress amended the registration provisions to add § 408(f), Pub. L. No. 109–9, § 408(f), 119 Stat. 218, 221 (2005), allowing for "Preregistration of works being prepared for commercial distribution." The provision assists enforcement of copyright in a "class of works that the Register determines has had a history of infringement prior to authorized commercial distribution." *Id.* This class consists of motion pictures, sound recordings, musical compositions, literary works being prepared for publication in book form, computer programs (including videogames), or advertising or marketing photographs. *See* 37 C.F.R. § 202.16(b) (2008). The fee is $115 per work. 37 C.F.R § 201.3(c)(7) (2009).

While it is possible to obtain rapid resolution of an application for registration, the expedited procedure involves substantial additional expense: where the standard fee is sixty-five dollars (or thirty-five dollars for an online filing), the fee for "special handling" is $760. 37 C.F.R. §§ 201.3(c)(2), 201.3(d). Where the registration claim has been pending for at least six months, however, the Copyright Office will waive the additional fee for "special handling." Fees for Special Handling of Registration Claims, 74 Fed. Reg. 39899, 39901 (Aug. 10, 2009) (to be codified at 37 C.F.R. pt. 201).

40. *Cosmetic Ideas*, 606 F.3d at 621.

41. As one study observes:

The prompt registration requirement for statutory damages has not become a meaningful inducement to registration for all authors who value copyright pro-

D. *"Orphan Works"*

As elucidated at the outset of this Chapter, formalities should assist potential exploiters of works in finding the rightholders from whom to obtain licenses. With the relaxation of formalities, on the one hand, and the extension of the copyright term on the other, however, reliable title-searching information may be difficult to obtain, The relaxation of formalities has led to the existence, or persistence, of copyright in works which formerly would never have been protected in the first instance, or whose 1909 Act copyrights would have lapsed after 28 years. If these works have not been registered, or their registrations renewed, or transfers of title in them not recorded, the title-searching task becomes correspondingly more daunting. The extension of the copyright term compounds the problem, as the ownership of older works may become progressively more difficult to trace over time. Moreover, even where a transferee can be found, it may not be clear whether it in fact owns the rights the title-searcher seeks, as the "old license/new media" controversies addressed in Chapter 3 illustrate.[42] Even if the author did grant a broad scope of rights, the rights may have reverted to her by operation of contractual "out of print" clauses, or through the statutory renewal or termination rights. Works with unlocatable rightholders have come colloquially to be known as "orphan works."

Would-be users who are unable to locate the copyright owner, but whose use or exploitation would not qualify for a copyright limitation or exception (such as fair use), thus must decide whether to renounce their projects or to incur the risk that the copyright owner will reappear once the exploitation is underway, and will demand both injunctive and substantial monetary relief in an ensuing infringement action. Potentially frustrated users range widely, from commercial entities who seek to reissue out-of-print works or to create new works based on "orphan"

---

tection, but rather a substantial boon to major copyright industry players—the commercial exploiters of copyrighted works whose rights largely derive from the Act's work for hire rules or assignments from authors.... "Little guy" authors thus, in theory, have the same strong legal rights as major copyright industry players, but effectively no way to get relief when their rights are infringed.

Pamela Samuelson & Tara Wheatland, *Statutory Damages in Copyright Law: A Remedy in Need of Reform*, 51 Wm. & Mary L. Rev. 439, 454–55 (2009).

42. In addition, one consequence of "divisible" copyright, introduced in the 1976 Copyright Act, is to proliferate the number of potential rightholders, as "Any of the exclusive rights comprised in a copyright, including any subdivision of any of the rights specified by section 106, may be transferred as provided by clause (1) and owned separately." 17 USC § 201(d)(2). *See* Jessica Litman, Sharing and Stealing, 26 COMM/ENT 1, 18–21 (2004) ("largely because of the adoption of divisibility of copyright, in many if not most cases, it can be difficult and sometimes impossible to discover who the copyright owners of all of those rights are.").

works, to cultural institutions, notably museums and libraries, who seek to digitize works for preservation and educational purposes, to individuals who seek to incorporate an "orphan" work in their webpage or blog. The U.S. Register of Copyrights has deemed the orphan-works problem "pervasive."[43]

The intensity of the problem varies with the nature of the work. Chains of title may be more reliable and prevalent in some sectors, for example musical compositions and commercially published print works, than in others, particularly photographs.[44] Moreover, the problem of identifying the right owner, while perhaps exacerbated by the age of the work, is not confined to older works; at least some of the potentially "orphaned" works may be of recent vintage. Pictorial and graphic works, particularly photographs and illustrations in digital form, may be at risk of "imposed orphanage," because third parties can digitize the works without identifying information, or if the works are already in digital form, their identifying information can be removed and the works recirculated without apparent attribution.[45]

An orphan-works regime must therefore aim to make works more widely available by reducing the exploiter's risk with respect to truly "orphaned" works while avoiding the other extreme of thrusting "orphanage" upon works whose rightholders can in fact be found. The solution adopted must also be consistent with international obligations under the Berne Convention and the TRIPs Accord. For the United States, this means that orphan-works legislation should not occasion back-door reimposition of formalities that condition the "enjoyment or exercise" of copyright.[46] In theory, a bill could "two-tier" reimposition of formalities, to limit the obligations to U.S. works,[47] but in practice this solution may not significantly lessen exploiters' burden, because in many

43. *See* Statement of Marybeth Peters, Register of Copyrights, before the Subcommittee on Courts, the Internet, and Intellectual Property, Committee on the Judiciary, United States House of Representatives, 110th Congress, 2nd Session, March 13, 2008, available at http://www.copyright.gov/docs/regstat031308.html

44. *See, e.g.,* Comments of the American Society of Authors, Composers and Publishers Regarding Orphan Works, OW0628–AS-CAP.pdf (25 March 2005)(asserting no orphanage of nondramatic public performance rights in musical compositions); College Art Association, Comments on Orphan Works Notice of Inquiry, OW0647–CAA.pdf, pp. 7, 9–13 (25 March 2005) (emphasizing difficulty of identifying copyright owner of photographs).

45. *See, e.g.,* Brad Holland & Cynthia Turner, Comments on Orphan Works Notice of Inquiry, OW0660–Holland-Turner.pdf (24 March 2005); Stephen Morris, Professional Photographers of America, Comments on Orphan Works Notice of Inquiry, OW0642–PPA.pdf (25 March 2005).

46. *See* Berne Convention for the Protection of Literary and Artistic Works, art. 5.2., Sept. 9, 1886 *as revised* July 24, 1971, 828 U.N.T.S. 221.

47. *Id.*, art. 5.4 (application of local law in country of origin). *See, e.g.,* 17 USC § 411 (requiring copyright registration of U.S. works as a prerequisite to initiation of an infringement action).

cases exploiters will have to spend resources in order to determine whether or not the work was of U.S. origin.

The U.S. has not yet enacted orphan-works legislation though bills were proposed in 2006[48] and 2008.[49] The approach favored by the Copyright Office and adopted by the bills sought to alleviate the risk of exploiting a work whose rightholder is unlocatable by limiting the remedies available against the user in the event the rightholder reappears and initiates an infringement action. In particular, the bills would have disallowed statutory damages, limited actual damages to "reasonable compensation," and would have substituted "reasonable compensation" for injunctive relief in the case of derivative works created in reliance on the underlying work's "orphan" status. Only users who had performed a diligent search for the rightholder would have qualified for the limitations on liability.

An appropriately rigorous search is crucial to any "orphan works" scheme, for it should ensure that specious "orphans" do not end up in the pool of parentless works whose unauthorized exploitation the scheme seeks to encourage.[50] Making sure that the "orphan" category is accurately circumscribed is essential to the proposal's fairness and to its consistency with international norms. In this respect, it is important to appreciate that the legislation should not be designed to short-cut title searching. An "orphan work" is not one whose author or rightholder is costly or onerous to find; it is one whose rightholder, despite the user's expenditure of effort and resources, remains unlocatable. That said, a side benefit of an orphan-works regime may be to make rights-clearance easier, and, one may hope, cheaper, for all users of all works, whether or not "orphaned," by publicizing and systematizing the information a would-be user should be gathering with respect to any work whose rightholders are not already known to the user, and by encouraging the development of professional title-searching businesses, as well as of rightholder databases and rights-clearance guidelines of interested associations and organizations.

It is important to appreciate, nonetheless, that an "orphan works" regime, precisely because it is anchored (and legitimated) by the requirement of a diligent search, does not address the problems of rights-clearance in the context of mass digitization. The "diligent search" approach essentially substitutes for rights clearance on a retail scale; mass-digitization may require wholesale responses, akin to those devel-

---

48. Orphan Works Act of 2006, HR 5439, 109 Cong., 2d sess. (2006).

49. H.R. 5889, S. 2913, 110th Cong, 2d sess. (2008).

50. *Cf.* European Commission, Proposal for a Directive of the European Parliament and of the Council on Certain Permitted Uses of Orphan Works, COM (2011) 289 final (24 May 2011), art. 3 (requiring "diligent search" as part of process establishing a work as an orphan work).

oped by collective licensing societies for music performance rights, to be discussed in the next Chapter.

Formalities Under the 1909 Act and Under the 1976 Act Before and After Berne Convention Implementation Act

	Work published before 1978	1978–Feb. 1989	After Feb. 1989
Notice*	Federal copyright arose upon publication with notice; if no notice, work fell into public domain.*	Affixation of notice perfected protection; five years to cure omissions, otherwise work fell into public domain.*	Optional: incentive—unavailability of innocent infringer defense.
Registration*	Optional until last year of first term; mandatory for renewal of works first published before 1964*; prerequisite to initiation of infringement suit during *both* terms of copyright.	Optional, *but* prerequisite to initiation of suit. Incentives: statutory damages and attorney's fees not available unless work was registered before infringement commenced.	Optional for non-U.S. Berne and WTO works; remains prerequisite to suit for U.S. and other foreign works. Same incentives apply.
Deposit	Prerequisite to suit; in addition, fines may be imposed for failure to deposit copies with Library of Congress.	Same.	No longer a prerequisite to suit for non-U.S. Berne works; *but* fines may still be imposed.
Recordation of Transfers	Unrecorded transfer void against subsequent good faith purchaser for value.	Same, plus a prerequisite to suit.	No longer a prerequisite to suit; unrecorded transfers still void against subsequent good faith purchasers for value.

* As of Jan. 1, 1996, the Uruguay Round Amendment Act of 1994 restored to the full 1976 Act copyright term the copyrights in qualifying non-U.S. works which had fallen into the public domain for failure to comply with U.S. formalities.

Chapter 6

EXCLUSIVE RIGHTS OF THE COPYRIGHT OWNER

Perhaps the most significant provisions of the Copyright Act are found in section 106, which sets forth the exclusive rights of the copyright owner. Anyone who violates any of those rights is (by virtue of section 501) "an infringer of the copyright." Section 106 gives the owner of copyright

> the exclusive rights to do and to authorize any of the following:
>
> (1) to reproduce the copyrighted work in copies or phonorecords;
>
> (2) to prepare derivative works based upon the copyrighted work;
>
> (3) to distribute copies or phonorecords of the copyrighted work to the public by sale or other transfer of ownership, or by rental, lease, or lending;
>
> (4) in the case of literary, musical, dramatic, and choreographic works, pantomimes, and motion pictures and other audiovisual works, to perform the copyrighted work publicly;
>
> (5) in the case of literary, musical, dramatic, and choreographic works, pantomimes, and pictorial, graphic, or sculptural works, including the individual images of a motion picture or other audiovisual work, to display the copyrighted work publicly; and
>
> (6) in the case of sound recordings, to perform the copyrighted work publicly by means of a digital audio transmission.

It should be noted that the copyright owner has the exclusive right not only to do the listed acts but also to authorize others to do them. Thus, if *A* owns the copyright in a novel, which is published by *B,* and *B* (without *A*'s consent) authorizes producer *C* to make a motion picture based upon the novel, when *C*'s film is later released *A* can bring infringement actions against both *B* and *C.* The Supreme Court has, in effect, concluded that this "authorize" language furnishes the basis for incorporating into copyright law the principle of contributory infringement.[1] Note also that although a work to be eligible for copyright

---

1. Sony Corp. of Am. v. Universal City Studios, Inc., 464 U.S. 417, 435 & n.17 (1984) (manufacturer-seller of videotape recorder is not contributorily liable for home taping of copyrighted television programs, which is fair use under the circumstances).

protection must be fixed in tangible form, unauthorized conduct can infringe even though it does not involve a fixing of the work by the defendant—for it may be by public sale, performance or display. Most obviously, for example, a copyrighted song or play can be infringed by an unauthorized (and "unfixed") public performance in a theater.

The first three listed exclusive rights—reproduction, preparation of derivative works, and public distribution—are applicable to all forms of copyrightable works listed in section 102(a). The next two listed rights—public performance and public display—apply only to certain categories of copyrightable works, and those categories are expressly set forth in sections 106(4) and (5). For example, the general right of public performance attaches to musical works but not to sound recordings; that means that an unauthorized public playing by a disk jockey in a nightclub of a recording of a copyrighted song will constitute an infringement of the song but not of the sound recording, so that the songwriter-author will have legal redress but the record manufacturer and performer will not. If, however, the public playing of the recorded song is "by means of a digital audio transmission," such as from a website on the Internet, then this is among the exclusive rights of the sound-recording copyright owner, by virtue of a 1995 amendment that added section 106(6) ("Digital public performance right in sound recordings") to the Copyright Act.

All of the exclusive rights in section 106 are subject to the provisions in sections 107 through 122. Those latter provisions exempt from liability a wide range of reproductions, derivative works, and the like that would otherwise constitute infringements, particularly for nonprofit, charitable or educational purposes. These exemption provisions will be discussed in some detail in Chapter 7.

I. The Right of Reproduction

The first U.S. Copyright Act, enacted in 1790, forbade unauthorized printing of copyrighted works. Today, the equivalent right, afforded by section 106(1) of the 1976 Act, is the right "to reproduce the copyrighted work in copies or phonorecords."

A. *Reproduction in copies or phonorecords*

Copies and phonorecords are the tangible forms in which reproductions of a work can be made; copies communicate to the eye while phonorecords communicate to the ear. More precisely, "phonorecords" are defined in section 101 as "material objects in which sounds ... are

See Columbia Pictures Indus. v. Aveco, Inc., 800 F.2d 59 (3d Cir. 1986). For more recent developments concerning secondary infringement, see *infra* Chapter 8.

fixed by any method now known or later developed, and from which the sounds can be perceived, reproduced, or otherwise communicated, either directly or with the aid of a machine or device." "Copies" are defined as "material objects, other than phonorecords, in which a work is fixed by any method now known or later developed, and from which the work can be perceived, reproduced, or otherwise communicated, either directly or with the aid of a machine or device." The owner of copyright in a musical composition has the exclusive right, therefore, to make "copies" in the form of music notations intended for piano or for orchestra, as well as to make "phonorecords" that can be activated by a playback device such as a compact disk or MP3 player. A significant reason for distinguishing copies and phonorecords relates to the proper form of optional copyright notice—with the © notice on copies, and the ℗ notice (for the sound recording) on phonorecords.

1. What is a "copy"?

The application of the word "copy" as used in section 106(1) has kept up with the advent of new technologies. Thus, if a copyrighted photograph is scanned, without permission, from a magazine into a computer for storage in a hard-drive or on a website, that will generate a copy and an infringement;[2] as we will see in a later subsection, the unauthorized transmission of that digitized photograph to others is treated as a distribution of copies that has been held unlawful under section 106(3).[3] In 2005, the Supreme Court decided *Metro-Goldwyn–Mayer Studios Inc. v. Grokster, Ltd.*,[4] which involved so-called peer-to-peer file-sharing of music recordings through the Internet. The court assumed—as did even the defendants who made available the file-sharing software—that the private users of computers for downloading were making illicit copies. (This was directly so held, soon after, by the Court of Appeals for the Seventh Circuit.)[5]

As these decisions indicate, although the definitions of "copy" and "phonorecord" refer to "material objects," the "Copyright Act does not use materiality in its most obvious sense—to mean a tangible object with

---

2. *See* Advance Magazine Pub. Inc. v. Leach, 466 F. Supp. 2d 628 (D. Md. 2006); *see also* Pasha Publ'ns, Inc. v. Enmark Gas Corp., 22 U.S.P.Q.2d 1076 (N.D. Tex. 1992) (copies generated by a fax machine).

3. Playboy Enters., Inc. v. Webbworld, Inc., 991 F. Supp. 543 (N.D. Tex. 1997); Phillips v. Kidsoft, L.L.C., 52 U.S.P.Q.2d 1102 (D. Md. 1999).

4. 545 U.S. 913 (2005). The idea that unauthorized downloading constitutes infringement was established well before

Grokster. See, e.g., Playboy Enters. Inc. v. Sanfilippo, 46 U.S.P.Q.2d 1350 (S.D. Cal. 1998); Playboy Enters., Inc. v. Webbworld, Inc., 991 F. Supp. 543 (N.D. Tex. 1997).

5. BMG Music v. Gonzalez, 430 F.3d 888 (7th Cir. 2005) (finding infringement in unauthorized downloading of more than 1,300 songs, despite defendant's claim of fair use). *See also* A & M Records, Inc. v. Napster, Inc., 239 F.3d 1004 (9th Cir. 2001).

a certain heft, like a book or compact disc. Rather, it refers to materiality as a medium in which a copyrighted work can be 'fixed.' "[A]ny object in which a sound recording can be fixed is a 'material object.' That includes ... electronic files ... magnetically encoded on a segment of [a computer] hard disk (or likewise written on other media.) ... The electronic file (or, perhaps more accurately, the appropriate segment of the hard disk) is therefore a ['copy' or] 'phonorecord' within the meaning of the statute."[6]

The statutory reference to "fixed in a *tangible* medium of expression" (emphasis added) certainly embraces traditional media such as books, CDs or video tape which are free-standing and designed to be handled. A "digital file" may seem too elusive to be "tangible": one cannot put one's hands on a collection of ones-and-zeros. But one can put one's hands on a digital recording medium, such as a CD or a DVD, or for that matter on an external digital hard drive, in which a digital instantiation of a work may be stored and from which it can be "perceived, reproduced, or otherwise communicated." Presumably, if one took a computer apart, one could also handle the internal hard drive or circuits in which the digital file is "magnetically encoded." The Copyright Act elsewhere specifies that "tangible media of expression" include those "now known or later developed;"[7] Congress's direction to encompass unanticipated storage media would be undermined by an interpretation which limited "tangible medium" to conventional free-standing formats.

Finally, there is the vexed question of the temporal persistence of the "copy." Specifically, is the temporary digital copy of a program that resides on a computer's random access memory (RAM) considered "fixed," even though the copy remains more or less briefly in the RAM and is lost when the computer is shut down? Is there a difference between a copy temporarily resident in RAM (which could remain there for days until the user turns the computer off), and a copy transiting through a computer network? Both types of copy appear to meet the statutory prerequisite of capacity to be "perceived, reproduced or otherwise communicated ... with the aid of a machine or device." But the statute also requires that this capacity endure for "a period of more than transitory duration." The 1976 House Report states that "transient reproductions ... captured momentarily in the 'memory' of a computer" should not be deemed "fixed." But it is not clear how fleeting Congress expected a "transient reproduction" to be. The subsequent report of the congressionally created Commission on New Technological Uses of Copyrighted Works (CONTU) led to amendments of section 117 of the

6. London-Sire Records v. Doe 1, 542 F.   **7.** 17 U.S.C. § 102(a).
Supp. 2d 153, 171 (D. Mass. 2008).

Copyright Act exempting a temporary reproduction of a computer program that is made simply by turning on the computer (sections 117(a)(1) and 117(c). (Those provisions accorded exemptions for such copying when unauthorized, if for the expected use of purchased programs or in connection with the "maintenance or repair" of the computer.[8]) This legislation appears to adopt the principle, expressed in the CONTU report, that entry of a work into the memory of a computer makes a "copy" of the work, apparently without distinction as to the duration of the copy. Congress's provision of narrow exemptions for RAM copying in section 117 of the Copyright Act points toward a congressional understanding that such copying would otherwise be infringing under section 106.[9]

But neither CONTU nor the section 117 amendments explicitly addressed fleeting reproductions in transit from one computer to another. Is there a point at which a reproduction is too fleeting to be a "copy" within the scope of the exclusive right of reproduction? The Second Circuit, in *Cartoon Network v. CSC Holdings*,[10] emphasizing what it called the "duration requirement" in the definition of "fixed," held that reproductions made in a computer's "buffer" and lasting 1.2 seconds, were insufficiently "fixed" to be "copies." The ruling may be in some tension with decisions from other Circuits and a study by the Copyright Office interpreting the reproduction right to encompass a broad temporal range of "RAM copies."[11]

The court distinguished the caselaw authorities for failure explicitly to address the duration requirement. It also criticized the Copyright Office report, which had confronted the duration issue, but had reached a different conclusion: "According to the Copyright Office, if the work is capable of being copied from that medium *for any amount of time*, the answer to both questions [embodiment and duration] is 'yes.' The

---

8. 17 U.S.C. § 117(c) responds to the Ninth Circuit's decision in MAI Sys. Corp. v. Peak Computer, Inc., 991 F.2d 511 (9th Cir. 1993), which had found the repair service's creation of a temporary copy to infringe.

9. *But see* R. Anthony Reese, *The Public Display Right: The Copyright Act's Neglected Solution to the Controversy Over RAM "Copies,"* 2001 U. ILL. L. REV. 83 (2001), contending that applying reproduction analysis to RAM copying disputes creates an overbroad "RAM copy doctrine" that "may allow a copyright owner not only to use copyright to control activities by third parties ... that would not otherwise infringe [and] allow copyright owners ... [but] to control other people's access to, and use of,

noncopyrightable elements contained in a copyrighted work." *Id.* at 145.

10. 536 F.3d 121 (2d Cir. 2008).

11. *See, e.g.,* MAI Systems Corp. v. Peak Computer, Inc., 991 F.2d 511 (9th Cir. 1993); Stenograph L.L.C. v. Bossard Assocs., Inc., 144 F.3d 96, 101–02 (D.C. Cir. 1998); U.S. Copyright Office, DMCA Section 104 Report (Aug. 2001) [hereinafter Copyright Office Section 104 Report], available at http://www.copyright.gov/reports/studies/dmca/sec–104–report–vol–1.pdf, pp. 107–23. Of these authorities, however, only the Copyright Office report specifically addresses reproductions as transient as "buffer copies." The Ninth and D.C. Circuit decisions involved software loaded into RAM and apparently retained for some minutes.

problem with this interpretation is that it reads the 'transitory duration' language out of the statute.'"[12] Inquiring, therefore, "Does any such embodiment [in Cablevision's buffer] last 'for a period of more than transitory duration'?'"[13] the court answered no. While ruling that 1.2 seconds were not "more than transitory," the court did not indicate what period of embodiment would suffice, although it did imply that "at least several minutes" would meet the duration requirement.[14] Nor did the court suggest how to characterize durations falling between those two limits.[15]

2. Who makes the copy?

The *Cartoon Network* court also confronted the question whether the (clearly "fixed") copies stored on Cablevision's servers for subsequent transmission to subscribers were "made" by Cablevision, or instead by the subscribers whose request for subsequent viewing of the designated programs initiated the copying and storage. The Second Circuit Court of Appeals ruled that because Cablevision's actions were entirely automated they lacked the "volitional" character required of one who "actually 'makes' a copy.'"[16] The court distinguished prior cases holding photocopy shops liable for copies made at the request of users, on the ground that the human element of the shop employees supplied the necessary volitional conduct. Instead, the court likened Cablevision's system to a copyshop in which the customers themselves made photocopies on store premises on machines supplied by the shop.

The court's principal authority for a volition requirement, *Religious Technology Center v. Netcom On-Line Communications Services,*[17] concerned an online service provider who simply conveyed copies of works from one subscriber to another. By contrast, Cablevision's own transmis-

---

12. 536 F.3d at 129.

13. *Id.*

14. *Id.* at 128.

15. *See* Copyright Office, Compulsory License for Making and Distributing Phonorecords, Including Digital Phonorecord Deliveries, Interim rule and request for comments, Fed. Reg. Vol. 73, No. 217 (November 7, 2008) 66173, 66177 ("The [*Cablevision*] court's reasoning leaves at least something to be desired and offers no guidance as to when a copy might be considered to be 'embodied' for 'a period of more than transitory duration.' ... Indeed, it leaves open the possibility that a buffer copy that exists for several seconds might have sufficient duration to satisfy the fixation requirement. We can glean no principle from

the Second Circuit's opinion which offers any guidance as to where the line is to be drawn.")

16. 536 F.3d at 131.

17. 907 F. Supp. 1361 (N.D. Cal. 1995). Another district court in the Ninth Circuit has more recently remarked, however, "no Ninth Circuit case has adopted this volitional conduct requirement," and "in light of the fact that copyright infringement is a strict liability offense, the Court is not inclined to adopt a volitional conduct requirement without clear instruction from the Ninth Circuit, and so declines to apply the so-called volitional conduct requirement." Warner Bros. Ent. v. WTV Sys., 2011 WL 4001121, at *10 n. 7 (E.D.Cal. 2011).

sions were the *source* of the copies the subscribers requested. This difference also demonstrates the inaptness of the copyshop analogy, which neither tracked the conduct at issue nor conveyed the extent of the entrepreneur's volition: one would have to imagine a copyshop that also provided the works to be copied, automatically printed out the document, charged the customer's account, and retained the copies for the customers' later retrieval. A more pertinent analogy may be to document-delivery services. In the analog world, the customer would request a document, which the service would obtain and copy and then send to the customer. Although the customer initiated the transaction and selected the work, the status of the service as the copy's "maker" would have been clear.[18] The change in the medium of the delivery from analog to digital does not diminish the active agency of the service. Like Cablevision, services such as Lexis "sell[ ] access to a system that automatically produces copies on command."[19] But, in *New York Times v. Tasini*,[20] the Supreme Court appears to have assumed that, when a customer requests a particular article that was published in the New York Times, Lexis itself creates that copy from its database containing the full contents of the collective work: the *Tasini* Court declared, "the databases reproduce and distribute articles..."[21] Thus, even supposing that only those who so intend can be the "makers" of copies, "volition" on the part of the online service providers may be found in the structuring of the service. To require specific intent at the moment of delivery, particularly in a technological environment in which pervasive automation is increasingly foreseeable, risks overlooking the role of the principal economic actors in the scheme.

3.   Proving copying and infringement

The exclusive right to "reproduce" the copyrighted work—which involves *copying*—is more confined than the patent right, which can be infringed even by a product or process that has been developed wholly independent of, and has not been copied from, the patented invention. Perhaps the best-known discussion of proof of copyright infringement is found in *Arnstein v. Porter*,[22] decided by the Court of Appeals for the Second Circuit in 1946. Judge Frank there stated, "[I]t is important to avoid confusing two separate elements essential to a plaintiff's case in such a suit: (a) that defendant copied from plaintiff's copyrighted work and (b) that the copying (assuming it to be proved) went so far as to constitute improper appropriation."[23] Proof of copying can be found, said

---

18. *See* Ryan v. CARL Corp., 23 F. Supp. 2d 1146 (N.D.Cal. 1998).

19. *Cartoon Network*, 536 F.3d at 132.

20. 533 U.S. 483 (2001).

21. *Id.* at 488.

22. 154 F.2d 464 (2d Cir. 1946).

23. *Id.* at 468.

the court, either in defendant's admission or, far more commonly, by circumstantial evidence—usually evidence of access and similarity—from which the trier of fact may reasonably infer copying. Of course, if there are no similarities, no amount of evidence of access will suffice to prove copying. If there is evidence of access and similarities exist, then the trier of fact must determine whether the similarities are sufficient to prove copying. On this issue, analysis ("dissection") is relevant, and the testimony of experts may be received to aid the trier of fact.

Although "similarity" is an element of both stages of the *Arnstein* test for infringement, the purposes and scope are different. At the first stage, similarity is used for the purpose of determining whether there has been copying. The similarities between the two works need not be extensive, so long as they are "probative" of copying: for example, the Rural Company planted four fictitious directory entries in its white-page telephone directory, and these entries then showed up in the Feist directory, which obviously negated independent creation.[24] On the other hand, the similarities that are necessary to make out an illicit taking, at the second stage, must be "substantial" as measured either qualitatively or quantitatively.

In proving copying through the use of circumstantial evidence, there is sometimes said to be an inverse proportion between the weight of proof of access and of similarity: the less likely it is that the defendant had access to the plaintiff's work, the more convincing must be proof of similarities in the two works; the fewer the similarities, the more compelling must be the proof of access. An inference of copying can be drawn even in the absence of specific evidence of access if the similarities between the plaintiff's and defendant's works are found to be "striking." As the Court of Appeals for the Seventh Circuit has stated: "A similarity that is so close as to be highly unlikely to have been an accident of independent creation *is* evidence of access. . . . Access (and copying) may be inferred when two works are so similar to each other and not to anything in the public domain that it is likely that the creator of the second work copied the first, but the inference can be rebutted by disproving access or otherwise showing independent creation."[25]

In any event, proof of copying is not sufficient to make out a case of infringement. The plaintiff must also prove that what has been copied is substantial in degree; only then, in the words of the *Arnstein* decision, is the copying illicit and the appropriation unlawful. Although *Arnstein* acknowledged that expert witnesses, through dissection of the two com-

---

24. Feist Publ'ns, Inc. v. Rural Tel. Serv., 499 U.S. 340 (1991). *See generally* Positive Black Talk Inc. v. Cash Money Records Inc., 394 F.3d 357 (5th Cir. 2004), and Laureyssens v. Idea Group, Inc., 964 F.2d 131 (2d Cir. 1992), for thoughtful discussions of "probative similarity" and its implications.

25. Ty, Inc. v. GMA Accessories, Inc., 132 F.3d 1167 (7th Cir. 1997).

pared works, may usefully contribute to an understanding by the trier of fact as to the similarities for the purpose of determining copying, such expert dissection is essentially regarded as irrelevant on the second issue, as to which "the test is the response of the ordinary lay hearer."[26] In a later case involving claimed infringement of a fabric pattern, Learned Hand stated that the perspective in determining whether the alleged infringing work is "substantially similar" to the copyrighted work must be that of "the ordinary observer."[27] If the parties' works are intended for purchase or appreciation by a particular audience—such as choir directors or even very young children—the question of substantial similarity is to be addressed with those persons in mind.[28]

Under this universally accepted two-step approach to proof of infringement,[29] it might be found that although the defendant did copy from the plaintiff's copyrighted novel, song or fabric design, proof of substantial similarity of copyrightable expression is lacking, so that there is no infringement. This would occur, for example, if the defendant copied only isolated and minor elements that did not create an appearance of similarity when viewed or heard by a typical member of the audience to whom the two works are addressed. In these cases, the doctrine of *de minimis* would apply.[30] An example would be a case in which a short, perhaps even copyrightable, pattern in a recorded song is digitally duplicated, or "sampled," on another recording.[31]

Relatedly, even if the defendant has recognizably copied from the plaintiff's copyrighted work, there is no infringement if he or she has

26. *Arnstein*, 154 F.2d at 468.

27. Peter Pan Fabrics, Inc. v. Martin Weiner Corp., 274 F.2d 487 (2d Cir. 1960). *See also* Steinberg v. Columbia Pictures Indus., Inc., 663 F. Supp. 706 (S.D.N.Y. 1987).

28. Kohus v. Mariol, 328 F.3d 848 (6th Cir. 2003) (technical drawings); Lyons P'ship, L.P. v. Morris Costumes, Inc., 243 F.3d 789 (4th Cir. 2001) (animal costumes purchased by adults for the entertainment of children); Dawson v. Hinshaw Music, Inc., 905 F.2d 731 (4th Cir. 1990) (religious musical arrangement). *But see* Williams v. Crichton, 84 F.3d 581, 590 (2d Cir. 1996) (stating "copyright law is to be uniformly applied across a variety of media and audiences," and judging substantial similarity of children's books from perspective of ordinary, adult observer).

29. Other courts have sometimes utilized a different form of two-step infringement analysis, involving the application of so-called extrinsic and intrinsic tests. The source of that approach is *Sid & Marty*

Krofft Television Productions, Inc. v. McDonald's Corp., 562 F.2d 1157 (9th Cir. 1977). This test is rather confusing and misleading, has been applied inconsistently, and in any event largely reduces itself to an analysis very much like that in *Arnstein*.

30. *See* Ringgold v. Black Entertainment Television, Inc., 126 F.3d 70 (2d Cir. 1997), for a thorough discussion of the variant uses of the *de minimis* doctrine in copyright, but rejecting the doctrine's application in that case. *See also* Gottlieb Development v. Paramount Pictures Corp., 590 F. Supp. 2d 625 (S.D.N.Y. 2008) (holding *de minimis* the fleeting incorporation into the set of the Mel Gibson film *What Women Want* of plaintiff's "Silver Slugger" pinball machine that depicted copyrighted designs on its front and sides).

31. Newton v. Diamond, 349 F.3d 591 (9th Cir. 2003). *But see* Bridgeport Music, Inc. v. Dimension Films, 410 F.3d 792 (6th Cir. 2005) (*de minimis* doctrine inapplicable to sampling of music recordings).

copied only elements that are themselves unprotected by copyright. Thus, anyone is free to copy facts, concepts, methods, and systems described in the plaintiff's work, and to express them in his or her own words, for such facts, concepts, methods, and systems fall outside the protection of copyright by virtue of section 102(b) of the Copyright Act. The same is true when the defendant copies such unprotectible elements as commonplace phrases, or language that is in the public domain. As the Supreme Court observed in a case involving copyright protection for fact-based directories,[32] copyright may protect the original pattern in which the facts are organized but the facts themselves are in the public domain and free for all to use. The Court stated:

> As applied to a factual compilation, assuming the absence of original [prose] expression, only the compiler's selection and arrangement may be protected; the raw facts may be copied at will. This result is neither unfair nor unfortunate. It is the means by which copyright advances the progress of science and art.[33]

If protectible expression has been substantially copied, it is not a defense that the copying was done unknowingly; like trespass in the law of real property, even unintended encroaching upon another's copyright is unlawful. This principle takes two forms. First, if *B* takes to publisher *C* a work actually written by copyright owner *A*, and *B* represents to publisher *C* that *B* is the author and copyright owner, *C*'s publication of the work will infringe *A*'s copyright, no matter how honestly *C* may have believed that *B* was the true copyright owner.[34] Obviously, *C* is in a better position than *A* to protect its rights, either through a copyright search, insurance, or contractual indemnity arrangements with *B*. Second, one may infringe even through "unconscious" copying. In a well-known case,[35] former Beatle George Harrison was found to have written a song essentially identical to a popular song written by another, through assimilation of the earlier song in Harrison's subconscious. Although the court found the copying was not deliberate, it concluded that infringement "is no less so even though subconsciously accomplished."[36]

---

32. *See* Feist Publ'ns, Inc. v. Rural Tel. Serv., 499 U.S. 340 (1991).

33. *Id.* at 350.

34. De Acosta v. Brown, 146 F.2d 408 (2d Cir. 1944). *See also* Well–Made Toy Mfg. Corp. v. Goffa Int'l Corp., 210 F. Supp. 2d 147, 165 (E.D.N.Y. 2002).

35. Bright Tunes Music Corp. v. Harrisongs Music, Ltd., 420 F. Supp. 177 (S.D.N.Y. 1976).

36. *Id.* at 181. *See also* Three Boys Music Corp. v. Bolton, 212 F.3d 477 (9th Cir. 2000). The principle of "subconscious infringement" was endorsed by Learned Hand in *Sheldon v. Metro–Goldwyn Pictures Corp.*, 81 F.2d 49 (2d Cir. 1936), perhaps as a means of avoiding a finding that the defendant's executives had been less than truthful when denying copying.

4. Idea versus expression

Recall that there is no infringement when one copies unprotectible ideas from another—as distinguished from protectible "expression." The distinction between idea and expression is perhaps the most elusive of all lines in copyright jurisprudence. As Learned Hand has stated: "Obviously, no principle can be stated as to when an imitator has gone beyond copying the 'idea,' and has borrowed its 'expression.' Decisions must therefore inevitably be ad hoc."[37]

In cases involving literary works, copyright protection would, of course, be trivialized were it limited to no more than the precise sequence of the author's words, or were it even extended to embrace no more than very close paraphrase. It is undisputed that copyright also protects the details and sequences of plot, story line, and character development, but that it does not protect the author's more general themes. Hand is once again the source of eloquent insight:

> [W]hen the plagiarist does not take out a block in situ, but an abstract of the whole, decision is more troublesome. Upon any work, and especially upon a play, a great number of patterns of increasing generality will fit equally well, as more and more of the incident is left out. The last may perhaps be no more than the most general statement of what the play is about, and at times might consist only of its title; but there is a point in this series of abstractions where they are no longer protected, since otherwise the playwright could prevent the use of his "ideas," to which, apart from their expression, his property is never extended. Nobody has ever been able to fix that boundary, and nobody ever can.[38]

In the case from which this observation is taken, *Nichols v. Universal Pictures Corp.*, Judge Hand concluded that a very popular copyrighted play, *Abie's Irish Rose*, was not infringed by the defendant's motion picture *The Cohens and the Kellys.* The only story elements that were similar (and that were, for purposes of decision, assumed to have been original with the plaintiff and copied by the defendant) were a conflict between Irish and Jewish fathers, the marriage of their children, the birth of a grandchild, and the reconciliation of the elders. The court characterized these elements as "too generalized an abstraction . . . only a part of [the playwright's] 'ideas.' "[39] The plaintiff also failed in her claim that her characters, isolated from the story line, were infringed;

37. Peter Pan Fabrics, Inc. v. Martin Weiner Corp., 274 F.2d 487 (2d Cir. 1960).

38. Nichols v. Universal Pictures Corp., 45 F.2d 119, 121 (2d Cir. 1930).

39. *Id.* at 122.

137

the court found them to be stock characters, too vaguely drawn for protection.

A court's determination that a plot or a character is an unprotectible "idea" reflects its conclusion that the plot or character is so skeletal or fundamental that to protect it by copyright would "fence off" too great a preserve for the plaintiff and would inhibit the creative use and embellishment of such plot or character by other authors. For the same reason, copyright does not extend to simply recorded facts, to commonplace phrases, or to what are known as *scènes à faire*, i.e., plot incidents that are commonplace or stock or that are necessarily dictated by a story's general themes (such as soldiers nervously partying on the eve of battle, or the exchange of salutes between military personnel).[40]

The same approach to the idea-expression dichotomy is found in cases involving pictorial, graphic, or sculptural works.[41] Copyright does not extend to commonplace designs, lest others be forbidden—potentially for more than a century—to borrow these "building blocks" on which to base other creative works. In ruling that a jewelry designer could not preclude another from copying his jeweled pin in the shape of a bee, a court stated:

> The guiding consideration in drawing the line is the preservation of the balance between competition and protection reflected in the patent and copyright laws.
>
> What is basically at stake is the extent of the copyright owner's monopoly—from how large an area of activity did Congress intend to allow the copyright owner to exclude others? We think the production of jeweled bee pins is a larger private preserve than Congress intended to be set aside in the public market without a patent. A jeweled bee pin is therefore an "idea" that defendants were free to copy.[42]

A contrary outcome was reached by Judge Learned Hand, in a decision usually contrasted with his decision in *Nichols*. He found infringement in *Sheldon v. Metro–Goldwyn Pictures Corp.*,[43] because the defendant's motion picture had copied too many detailed plot incidents and scenes from the plaintiff's play. Whether or not those incidents or scenes were protectible "expression" when each was considered separately, their sequential grouping—and thus the detailed storytelling—was deemed protectible by copyright.

---

40. Narell v. Freeman, 872 F.2d 907 (9th Cir. 1989); Hoehling v. Universal City Studios, Inc., 618 F.2d 972 (2d Cir. 1980).

41. *But see* Mannion v. Coors Brewing Co., 377 F. Supp. 2d 444 (S.D.N.Y. 2005) (finding the dichotomy inapplicable to photographic works).

42. Herbert Rosenthal Jewelry Corp. v. Kalpakian, 446 F.2d 738, 742 (9th Cir. 1971).

43. 81 F.2d 49 (2d Cir. 1936).

Similar tests for distinguishing idea and expression have been applied to all varieties of copyrighted works, including computer programs. The tasks to be accomplished by a computer program, either in driving the computer hardware or in effecting a particular external result (such as creating the sights and sounds of a video game, or accomplishing word-processing tasks) are not subject to copyright protection; they are methods or systems that can be protected, if at all, only by satisfying the more rigorous demands of the patent system. On the other hand, the exact or very close copying of computer-program code—whether in human-readable source code or in object code (a string of ones and zeroes) intended to be "read" by and to operate the computer—will constitute an infringement of copyright.[44] As is true in literature, music and art, difficult questions can arise in drawing the line for infringement at various places in between a program's overall purpose and its literal code; there is no question, however, that the fact that computer code is shaped by uniquely functional objectives justifies a "thinner" copyright for programs than for art as broadly understood.

Perhaps the most influential formulation for determining what "nonliteral" elements of computer code warrant copyright protection is found in *Computer Associates International, Inc. v. Altai, Inc.*[45] There, the Court of Appeals for the Second Circuit articulated a three-step process of analysis. At the first, or "abstraction" step, very much like the "patterns" analysis of Learned Hand in the *Nichols* and *Sheldon* drama cases,

> a court should dissect the allegedly copied program's structure and isolate each level of abstraction contained within it. This process begins with the code and ends with an articulation of the program's ultimate function.... A program has structure at every level of abstraction at which it is viewed. At low levels of abstraction, a program's structure may be quite complex; at the highest level it is trivial.[46]

At the second, or "filtration," step, nonprotectible materials are removed from the plaintiff's computer program.

This process entails examining the structural components at each level of abstraction to determine whether their particular inclusion at that level was "idea" or was dictated by considerations of efficiency, so as to be necessarily incidental to that idea; required by factors external to the program itself; or taken from the public domain and hence is non-

---

44. *See* Sega Enters., Ltd. v. Accolade, Inc., 977 F.2d 1510 (9th Cir. 1992) (decompiling computer code creates a copy that technically infringes, even though only an "intermediate" copy, but under the circumstances of the case was privileged as a "fair use").

45. 982 F.2d 693 (2d Cir. 1992).

46. *Id.* at 707.

protectable expression.... By applying well developed doctrines of copyright law, it may ultimately leave behind a "core of protectable material."[47]

At the third, or "comparison," step, the court compares what is left (the "golden nugget") of protectible material in the plaintiff's work and "focuses on whether the defendant copied any aspect of this protected expression, as well as an assessment of the copied portion's relative importance with respect to the plaintiff's overall program."[48] Despite the influence of the court's analysis—and indeed its importation into cases involving motion pictures[49]—it is arguably too focused upon the deletion of uncopyrightable elements and insufficiently attentive to the possible creative ways in which those elements can be selected, coordinated, or arranged so as to generate a protectible work in the nature of a compilation.[50]

B. *Reproduction of Music and Sound Recordings*

The exclusive right to reproduce the copyrighted work, afforded by section 106(1), applies not only when the work is reproduced in "copies," i.e., material objects that are perceivable by the human eye, but also when the work is embodied in "phonorecords." A copyright-protected dramatic or nondramatic literary work (a short story, poem and lecture are examples of the latter) is infringed by an unauthorized taping or recording of the text of that work.

1. Reproducing musical works in phonorecords

The same is true of musical compositions, subject to an important exception known as the compulsory license. Section 115(a)(1) of the Copyright Act provides:

> When phonorecords of a nondramatic musical work have been distributed to the public in the United States under the authority of the copyright owner, any other person may, by complying with the provisions of this section, obtain a compulsory license to make and distribute phonorecords of the work.

In substance, once the copyright owner of a musical composition permits one person to manufacture and distribute recordings in the United

---

47. *Id.*

48. *Id.* at 710.

49. Stromback v. New Line Cinema, 384 F.3d 283 (6th Cir. 2004) (applying *Altai* test and holding that there was no substantial similarity between poem and motion picture).

50. *Compare* Apple Computer, Inc. v. Microsoft Corp., 779 F. Supp. 133 (N.D. Cal. 1991). *Cf.* Lotus Dev. Corp. v. Borland Int'l, Inc., 49 F.3d 807, 814–815 (1st Cir. 1995) (stating *Altai* test might be "misleading" in cases of literal infringement).

States, any other person may record the composition (with its own performers) and distribute its own recordings, provided that person complies with the provisions of section 115—most significantly by paying to the copyright owner a royalty provided by statute "for every phono-record made and distributed in accordance with the license."[51]

The compulsory license for musical recordings (known as "mechanical" royalties, based on the early statutory language) can be traced back to the 1909 Copyright Act, enacted when the recording industry was in its infancy and when Congress was concerned that a single record manufacturer (the Aeolian Company) would secure a monopoly by buying up all recording rights from popular songwriters. By "compelling" the copyright owner to license such rights to all record companies, after the initial recording and distribution, Congress facilitated the development of many smaller record companies. The statutory royalty rate in the 1909 Act was 2 cents per record of the copyrighted song. In 1976, Congress increased that rate only to 2.75 cents. Realizing that economic conditions might warrant a change in the statutory rate, and that it would be inconvenient to achieve such change through statutory amendment, Congress in the 1976 Act created an administrative agency called the Copyright Royalty Tribunal and empowered it periodically to reconsider the royalty rate under section 115 and to promulgate new rates. In 1993 Congress transferred the functions of the Tribunal to ad hoc arbitration panels convened by the Librarian of Congress; and in 2004 the Act was amended to give such authority instead to three Copyright Royalty Judges, also appointed by the Librarian of Congress, with decisions of the Copyright Royalty Judges being appealable to the District of Columbia Circuit.

Section 801(b)(1) of the Copyright Act directs the Copyright Royalty Judges, in their rate-setting under the compulsory-license provisions for recorded music, to achieve the following objectives:

(A) To maximize the availability of creative works to the public.

(B) To afford the copyright owner a fair return for his or her creative work and the copyright user a fair income under existing economic conditions.

(C) To reflect the relative roles of the copyright owner and the copyright user in the product made available to the public with respect to relative creative contribution, technological contribution, capital investment, cost, risk, and contribution to the opening of new markets for creative expression and media for their communication.

---

51.   17 U.S.C. § 115(c)(2).

(D) To minimize any disruptive impact on the structure of the industries involved and on generally prevailing industry practices.

After formal hearings, the Copyright Royalty Tribunal in 1980 increased the statutory rate from 2.75 cents per record to 4 cents per record, and between then and the year 2000, the royalty rate mounted gradually through formal linkage to the Consumer Price Index. Beginning on January 1, 2000, Copyright Office regulations endorsed an agreement reached by representatives of music copyright owners (songwriters and publishers) and of the recording companies, providing for biannual rate increases beginning at 7.55 cents per song; the rate for 2004–2005 was 8.5 cents (or 1.65 cents per minute), and beginning January 1, 2006, the rate has become 9.1 cents per song (or 1.75 cents per minute). These compulsory-license royalty rates are set forth in Copyright Office regulations at 37 C.F.R. § 255.3. This royalty figure is for each recording made of each copyrighted composition embodied in the phonorecord; it is not a single amount covering the aggregate of all of the music on a multiple-track compact disk or audiotape.

To avail itself of the compulsory license, a record manufacturer must file a timely "notice of intention" with the copyright owner, file regular accounting statements, and make monthly royalty payments to the copyright owner. Failure to comply with these requirements entitles the copyright owner to terminate the license and sue for infringement. The monitoring of the compulsory license system, and particularly the scrutiny of accounting statements and the collection of royalties from the recording companies, is a major administrative task; most musical-work copyright owners have turned over that task to an organization (based in New York City) known as the Harry Fox Agency.

Congress, of course, contemplated that persons making music recordings (known in the industry as "covers") pursuant to the statutory compulsory license under section 115 would use the services of recording artists selected by them and make arrangements of the music suitable to the artists' performing style. Section 115(a)(2) provides, however, that such "arrangement shall not change the basic melody or fundamental character of the work, and shall not be subject to protection as a derivative work under this title, except with the express consent of the copyright owner." While it is not clear that the first proviso has significantly constrained arrangements,[52] the second entails meaningful practical consequences. Section 115 requires composers and copyright owners of musical compositions to tolerate "covers," but it confers no

---

52. Indeed, the prohibited changes might produce a parody, which might enjoy immunity as a "fair use," see *infra* Chapter 7. Ironically, a respectful arranger is obliged to pay the compulsory license fee, while the sardonic parodist may pillory the musical composition for free.

copyright on the arrangements. Unless the arranger obtains the agreement of the owner of the underlying composition, she will have no copyright to enforce against unauthorized reproductions or public performances.

The statute places three other important limitations upon the availability of the compulsory license. It does not apply to works other than "nondramatic musical works" (that is, it does not authorize the making of recordings of literary works or of operas); it comes into operation only after the first authorized recording; and it authorizes only the making of recordings that are intended primarily for distribution to the public for private use (i.e., it does not apply to recordings for music subscription services, such as Muzak, or the incorporation of the music in a motion-picture soundtrack).

Until recently, the compulsory license for the recording of copyright-protected music resulted in phonorecords—whether vinyl records, audiotapes, or compact disks—that reached the public through sales in retail record stores. With the advent of the Internet, retail-store purchases are being displaced by the online sale of downloads of music recordings (when the purchases are not displaced by outright end-user infringements, for example over peer-to-peer networks). When the computer user downloads recorded music, say for 99 cents per recorded song, this is what the Copyright Act refers to in section 115(c)(3) as a "digital phonorecord delivery." Because of their functional equivalence, the compulsory royalty rate to be paid to the music copyright owner by the recording company for such digital phonorecord deliveries is the same as for phonorecords sold in retail stores.

2. Reproducing sound recordings in phonorecords

The right under section 106(1) to reproduce a copyrighted work in the form of phonorecords applies to all copyrighted works (other than visual works), including not only musical works but also sound recordings. "Sound recordings" are defined in section 101 of the Copyright Act as "works that result from the fixation of a series of musical, spoken, or other sounds, but not including the sounds accompanying a motion picture or other audiovisual work, regardless of the nature of the material objects, such as disks, tapes, or other phonorecords, in which they are embodied." (As we have seen earlier, this embodiment can be in the memory of a computer.) Thus, a work recorded onto (in the trade, "synchronized" with) a motion picture as its soundtrack is not a "sound recording," but the same soundtrack separated from the accompanying images and purveyed solely in audio form is a "sound recording." Sound recordings are copyrightable works distinct from the musical or literary works that are performed on those recordings.[53] There can, for example, be a copyrightable sound recording of a public domain classical musical composition.

Section 114 of the Copyright Act limits the exclusive right to reproduce a sound recording to "the right to duplicate the sound recording in the form of phonorecords that directly or indirectly recapture the actual sounds fixed in the recording." Infringement of this right involves the dubbing of the sounds of the copyrighted sound recording onto another sound medium—for example, from a pre-recorded compact disk onto a blank audiotape (the then-prevailing technique) or from a computer hard-drive onto a blank CD (i.e., "burning"). Copyright in a sound recording is therefore not infringed by the "independent fixation of other sounds, even though such sounds imitate or simulate those in the copyrighted sound recording," as expressly stated in section 114(b).

Thus, when a commercial recording incorporates a "digital sample" taken directly from another recording, without permission, there is technically a violation of section 106(1), because the first "sound recording" (as well as the thread of musical notes) is being "reproduced in phonorecords." These samples, although usually of only a small bit of recorded music, are often "catchy" and thus of qualitative significance and possible commercial value, as the development of the "ringtones" market attests. Courts take differing views on whether the sampling, under particular circumstances, is nonetheless privileged, typically by invoking (or not) the *de minimis* principle[54] or the principle of fair use. In the recording industry, it is common practice to pay royalties for such samples (on the theory that today's borrower may find himself or herself sampled tomorrow and will wish to be compensated). [55]

3. Private copying

A major issue under section 106(1) is the "home recording" of copyright-protected music and sound recordings. Again, this is technically a violation of section 106(1). However, at the time of enactment of the 1976 Act, it was generally understood that the "taping" of music from radio broadcasts or from recordings, for personal use and without commercial objective, was allowable. This was at a time when the analog

53. *See* Newton v. Diamond, 349 F.3d 591 (9th Cir. 2003).

54. *Compare* Williams v. Broadus, 60 U.S.P.Q.2d 1051 (S.D.N.Y. 2001) (question of fact whether sampling 2 of 54 musical measures, consisting of opening 10 notes, is substantial copying), *with* Bridgeport Music, Inc. v. Dimension Films, 410 F.3d 792 (6th Cir. 2005) (announcing a "bright line" test making all sampling unlawful, and *de minimis* standard inapplicable).

55. *See* Kembrew McLeod & Peter DiCola, Creative License: The Law and Culture of Digital Sampling 121–24 (2011). *But see id.* at 110 ("Those who sample—and those who have been sampled—hold varying opinions about the subject.").

technology was such that multiple and serial copying was inherently limited. This legal conclusion was essentially confirmed by the Supreme Court in the somewhat different context of home videotaping for "time-shifting" purposes (rather than for permanent retention).[56]

Subsequently, for the first time in U.S. statutory copyright law, Congress in 1992 enacted legislation specifically addressing the problem of private copying: the Audio Home Recording Act (AHRA).[57] The AHRA, enacted in response to the advent of digital audiotape (which ultimately proved to have only limited commercial success), in section 1008 barred, *inter alia*, infringement actions "based on the noncommercial use by a consumer of a [digital audio recording device or an analog recording] device or medium for making digital or analog musical recordings." In other words, home reproduction for noncommercial purposes, by *analog* means, is exempted from the reach of the section 106(1) reproduction right held by owners of copyright in musical works and in sound recordings.

The provision does not, however, preclude all infringement actions respecting *digital* private copying of musical recordings, but only those actions addressing "a digital audio recording device" or a "digital audio recording medium." Section 1001 defines those terms very narrowly to cover only those devices "the digital recording function of which is designed or marketed *for the primary purpose of* ... making a digital audio copied recording for private use" and only those recording media that are "*primarily marketed or most commonly used* by consumers for the purpose of making digital audio copied recordings *by use of a digital audio recording device*" (emphases added). Thus the section 1008 exemption does *not* apply to the use of general-purpose computers to make private copies of musical recordings (much less to "share" copies or phonorecords over a peer-to-peer network). As a result, the practical impact of the AHRA is now almost negligible.

To the extent the AHRA does apply, it compensates copyright owners and performers through the payment of a royalty on the sales of digital audio recording machines and blank digital audio recording media.[58] The provisions on royalty distribution pre-sage those in Section 114(g) respecting the compulsory license for certain digital transmissions

---

56. Sony Corp. of Am. v. Universal City Studios, Inc., 464 U.S. 417 (1984).

57. 17 U.S.C. §§ 1001–1010.

58. *Id.* §§ 1003–1007. *See also* Recording Indus. Ass'n of Am. v. Diamond Multimedia Sys., Inc., 180 F.3d 1072 (9th Cir. 1999) (holding that hand-held digital devices that store music recordings transferred from computer hard-drives are not the sort of devices ("digital audio recording device") for which royalties must be paid).

As of 2008, the amount of royalties in the digital audio recording fund pool was about 1.5 million dollars. *See, e.g.,* Geoffrey P. Hull, Thomas Hutchinson & Richard Strasser, The Music Business and Recording Industry: Delivering Music in the 21st Century 100–02 (3rd ed. 2011).

of sound recordings (discussed *infra* Chapter 7). The AHRA creates two "funds," and explicitly allocates defined percentages of the "sound recordings fund" to featured (40%) and non-featured (collectively 4%) performing artists, and 50% of the "musical works fund" to composers and lyricists. (The other 50% of each fund goes to the producers.) The AHRA thus marks the Copyright Act's first endeavor to guarantee performers a proportional participation in the exploitation of their works. Admittedly, the guaranteed royalties pertain only to government-imposed licenses, rather than to privately-ordered contracts, where one-time, lump-sum payments remain lawful (and in some sectors, prevalent), but even this faint statutory nod to creators deserves to be signaled.

II.   The Right to Prepare Derivative Works

Among the most valuable rights given by the Copyright Act is the right under section 106(2) "to prepare derivative works based upon the copyrighted work." As defined in section 101, a derivative work

> is a work based upon one or more preexisting works, such as a translation, musical arrangement, dramatization, fictionalization, motion picture version, sound recording, art reproduction, abridgment, condensation, or any other form in which a work may be recast, transformed, or adapted. A work consisting of editorial revisions, annotations, elaborations, or other modifications which, as a whole, represent an original work of authorship, is a "derivative work."

The copyright owner thus has the exclusive right to convert her novel into a motion picture, to translate her play into a foreign language, to make an orchestral arrangement of her piano piece, or to make photographic reproductions of her painting or sculpture—or to license third persons to do so. In the cases already discussed—infringing motion pictures based on copyrighted plays or novels—the courts have traditionally analyzed them as involving "copies" under the 1909 Act or "reproductions" under the 1976 Act. The courts could just as well have analyzed these cases as allegedly infringing derivative works under what is today section 106(2). The elements of proof are the same: the plaintiff must show that the defendant copied protectible elements from the copyrighted work and that as a result the infringing work is "substantially similar."

The derivative work need not be "fixed in a tangible medium" in order to make out a case of infringement.[59] The live performance of an

---

59. *But see* Lewis Galoob Toys, Inc. v. Nintendo of Am., Inc., 964 F.2d 965 (9th Cir.1992) (statutory definition's reference to "any other *form* in which the work may be recast, transformed or adapted"—emphasis supplied—implies that the alleged arrangement of a copyrighted song, without the authorization of the copyright owner, will infringe section 106(2).[60] (The performance, if public, will constitute a separate infringement under section 106(4).) Nor need any words be borrowed from the copyrighted work. In a classic copyright case, Justice Holmes spoke for the Supreme Court in finding that a silent motion picture adaptation of the novel *Ben Hur* constituted copyright infringement.[61] In a later treatment of a similar issue, the Court of Appeals for the Second Circuit held that a book containing a series of still photographs of performers dancing a copyrighted choreographic work (Balanchine's *Nutcracker* ballet) can be an infringing derivative work if there is "substantial similarity," even though it is not possible to reconstruct the ballet from the photographs alone, and even if permission for the book was secured from the ballet company, the set and costume designers, and the dancers—but not from the choreographer–copyright owner.[62]

As the statutory examples of "abridgment" and "condensation" indicate, an infringing derivative work may take the form of deletion, abbreviation, and abridgment as well as elaboration and embellishment. The Court of Appeals for the Second Circuit, in the well-known case *Gilliam v. American Broadcasting Companies*,[63] thus held that the heavy editing of television programs without the consent of the Monty Python comedy group, which held the copyrights in the underlying scripts, constituted copyright infringement.

Questions remain, however, regarding the meaning of "any other form in which the work may be recast, transformed or adapted." The statutory phrase enlarges the range of derivative works beyond the specific examples that precede it, but still assumes that the "derivative work" will in some way incorporate the expression of the underlying work. Thus, not every work that is "inspired by" or "goes with" the underlying work, or, more broadly, that capitalizes on the economic value of the underlying work, is necessarily a "derivative work." For example, a playwright who, having seen "West Side Story" (or to use a famous copyright example, "Abie's Irish Rose,"[64]) is inspired to pen her own ethnic variation on "Romeo and Juliet," has not created an infringing derivative work. Her work may be "derivative" as a matter of literary criticism, and she may be capitalizing on a market the first author created for ethnic transpositions, but if she has embroidered only

---

derivative work must exist in a "concrete or permanent form").

60. *See* H.R. Rep.No. 1476, 94th Cong. 2d. Sess. at 62 (1976) ("the preparation of a derivative work, such as a ballet, pantomime, or improvised performance, may be an infringement even though nothing is ever fixed in tangible form").

61. Kalem Co. v. Harper Bros., 222 U.S. 55 (1911).

62. Horgan v. MacMillan, Inc., 789 F.2d 157 (2d Cir. 1986).

63. 538 F.2d 14 (2d Cir. 1976).

64. *Supra*, p. 137.

on the prior author's ideas, she has not incorporated the prior work's expression, and so cannot be deemed to have infringed. Similarly, a work, such as a bibliography or abstract, that recapitulates only factual information from or about a prior work, has not copied or adapted its "expression," and so does not infringe.

But, as in controversies involving the reproduction right, the idea/expression or fact/expression distinction may be elusive. Detailed plot summaries of a television series arguably recount only the "facts" of what occurred in each episode, but those "facts" are created by the writers and producers, and are properly classed among the work's expressive elements; the resulting summaries should be considered a — "condensation" or similar derivative work.[65] Congress's 1870 enactment of translation and dramatization rights[66]—in response to the court decision that an unauthorized German translation of *Uncle Tom's Cabin* did not infringe Harriet Beecher Stowe's copyright because it took only the novel's "ideas"[67] —further underscores the inappropriateness of treating developed plots and characters as freely appropriable "facts" or "ideas." Hence, after Congress enacted the dramatization right, Justice Holmes squarely rejected the "idea" defense in the *Ben Hur* decision referred to earlier.

Nonetheless, mere reference to a prior work does not create an infringing derivative work, even if the association of the two works economically benefits the second. For example, if an entrepreneur markets a sound recording of 1920s popular music as a perfect audio background for reading *The Great Gatsby*, the suggestion that one freestanding work makes an ideal accompaniment to another does not convert the complementary work into a "derivative work." (By contrast, an audiobook that included the music in the soundtrack of a recorded reading of the book would, by virtue of the incorporation of the two works into one, probably constitute a recasting, transforming or adapting of the novel, as would the audiobook without accompanying music.)[68]

65. *See, e.g.,* Twin Peaks Prods., Inc. v. Publications Int'l Ltd., 996 F.2d 1366 (2d Cir. 1993) (holding television show's plots are not uncopyrightable facts); Castle Rock Entm't, Inc. v. Carol Publ'g Group, Inc., 150 F.3d 132 (2d Cir. 1998) (rejecting characterization of plot and character elements from the *Seinfeld* television series as "facts"); *see also* Warner Bros. v. RDR Books, 575 F. Supp. 2d 513, 544 (S.D.N.Y. 2008) (discussing "Harry Potter Encyclopedia" and drawing distinction between writing *about* a prior work, and copying work's expression).

66. Copyright Act of 1870, sec. 86, 41st Cong., 2d Sess. Ch 230, 16 Stat. 198.

67. *Stowe v. Thomas,* 23 F. Cas. 201 (C.C.E.D.Pa. 1853).

68. The above analysis suggests that the "Teddy Ruxpin" case, Worlds of Wonder, Inc. v. Veritel Learning Systems, Inc., 658 F. Supp. 351 (N.D. Tex. 1986), involving unauthorized third-party audio cassettes designed to be played in talking teddy bears, and Addison–Wesley Publ'g Co. v. Brown, 223 F. Supp. 219 (E.D.N.Y. 1963), holding an answer key to a high school science text book infringing even though the key did not reproduce the questions, were wrongly decided.

Although no derivative work is created unless the underlying work is in some way comprised within the alleged derivative work, and most derivative-work infringement claims concern works that reproduce expression from the underlying work, the derivative work right may be infringed even though the underlying work is not copied. Thus, for example, in *Clean Flicks v. Soderbergh*,[69] the declaratory-judgment plaintiff purchased copies of motion pictures, and then deleted from each copy foul language and scenes of sex or violence. Although Clean Flicks made no further copies, and it obliged customers to prove they had purchased their own copies, the court found that the alterations to the films made by Clean Flicks' edits resulted in the creation of unauthorized derivative works.

In other instances, however, it may be less clear whether courts will deem a "repurposed" copy of a work an infringing derivative work. The courts are split on the question whether an infringing derivative work is created when one lawfully acquires a lawfully made pictorial work (say, a color photograph from a magazine, or a drawing on the face of a greeting card) and affixes it to a hard substance, thus creating a border around the work, and applies some transparent sealing substance. As will be seen immediately below, under the "first sale doctrine," the purchase and resale of the artwork is not a copyright infringement, but the copyright owner of the photograph or greeting card has claimed that an infringing derivative work has been created. The Court of Appeals for the Ninth Circuit has held that, absent consent, a new bordered work has been unlawfully created; while the Seventh Circuit held that there has been no "recasting" or "transforming" of the underlying artwork but simply what is equivalent to framing, and so no derivative work at all.[70] In a case involving an Internet analogy—the unauthorized "framing" by one website owner of images from another (complaining) website that are called forward through a linking process—a district court in the Ninth Circuit has found an unauthorized derivative work.[71]

The pasting and framing cases point to a broader confusion regarding the scope of the derivative-work right. Infringement of the derivative-work right arises out of the creation of a work that "transforms, recasts or adapts" the underlying work. If the changes are made to a

---

69. 433 F. Supp. 2d 1236 (D. Colo. 2006).

70. *Compare* Mirage Editions, Inc. v. Albuquerque A.R.T. Co., 856 F.2d 1341 (9th Cir. 1988), *with* Lee v. A.R.T. Co., 125 F.3d 580 (7th Cir. 1997). A district court within the Ninth Circuit has indeed held that what is essentially mere framing of an artwork constitutes the unlawful creation of a deriv-

ative work. Greenwich Workshop, Inc. v. Timber Creations, Inc., 932 F. Supp. 1210 (C.D. Cal. 1996). *See also* Munoz v. Albuquerque A.R.T. Co., 829 F. Supp. 309 (D. Alaska 1993) (holding that affixing a notecard to a ceramic tile created a derivative work).

71. Futuredontics, Inc. v. Applied Anagramics, Inc., 45 U.S.P.Q.2d 2005 (C.D. Cal. 1997).

lawfully acquired copy of a work, no new copy is made, so analysis trains on the nature of the changes. If these do not "transform" the work, no derivative work results, and, in the absence of a copy or of certain public communications of the altered work, no exclusive rights are infringed. In considering whether the alterations "recast, transform or adapt" the underlying work, some courts have assumed that there can be no infringing derivative work unless the alterations encompassed in the accused work manifested sufficient originality to constitute a work in its own right (had it not infringed). This equation of originality and infringement is in fact a fallacy, as the following hypothetical demonstrates. It is generally recognized that a translation is a kind of derivative work.[72] Today, computer programs can generate automated translations even of idiomatic expressions, thus yielding serviceable, if not elegant, language-transformed texts. But a computer program is not an "author," and the automated translation would therefore likely be deemed to lack originality.

If the derivative-work right is infringed only by adaptations that manifest original authorship, does it then follow that the derivative-work right is ineffective with respect to automated adaptations, and that any third party therefore may commercialize a computer-generated translation free of the author's copyright? The same question might also be raised concerning other computer-generated interventions which noticeably alter the work, for example, colorization of motion pictures, or deletion of films' vulgar, violent, or erotic scenes, but which may lack sufficient human intervention to yield an "original work of authorship."[73]

Arguably, rejection of the derivative-work claim in such situations does not leave the author remediless if she also owns the reproduction right, for the unoriginal adaptation, assuming it remains substantially similar to the underlying work, and if "fixed," would infringe that right. But, particularly in a world of "divisible copyright" (see *supra* Chapter 3), the principal value of the distinct articulation of a derivative-work right becomes apparent if one thinks about copyright from the point of view of licensing rather than of infringement. The derivative-work right adds to the author's management of the economic value of her work by reserving to her (absent a contract to the contrary) the exclusive rights to exploit the work not only in its original form and format, but also in a wide panoply of alterations and rearrangements of her work, whether in

---

72. *See* 17 U.S.C § 101 ("A 'derivative work' is a work based upon one or more preexisting works, such as a translation. . . ."); Society of the Holy Transfiguration Monastery, Inc. v. Archbishop Gregory, 685 F. Supp. 2d 217, 225–26 (D. Mass. 2010); International Film Exchange v. Corinth Films, Inc., 621 F. Supp. 631 (S.D.N.Y. 1985).

73. *Cf.* Family Movie Act of 2005, 17 U.S.C. § 110(11) (exempting certain bowdlerizing technologies).

sequels, prequels, re-orchestrations, medium transformations, and so on. Thus, to return to translations, if the author licenses the right to publish her book in English, she still owns the rights to publish the book in an infinity of other languages. An unauthorized translation into Spanish or Hindi will not violate any rights of the licensee of the reproduction right, but it will infringe the author's retained rights for other languages. The derivative-work right, viewed from a licensing perspective, thus produces important "investment effects," as Professor Paul Goldstein has observed:

> Derivative rights affect the *level* of investment in copyrighted works by enabling the copyright owner to proportion its investment to the level of expected returns from all markets, not just the market in which the work first appears, as is generally the case with reproduction rights. The publisher who knows that it can license, and obtain payment for, the translation, serialization, condensation and motion picture rights for a novel will invest more in purchasing, producing and marketing the novel than it would if its returns were limited to revenues from book sales in the English language.
>
> Derivative rights also affect the *direction* of investment in copyrighted works. By spreading the duty to pay over different markets, section 106(2) tends to perfect the information available to the copyright owner respecting the value of its works to different groups of users.... [B]y securing exclusive rights to all derivative markets, the statute enables the copyright proprietor to select those toward which it will direct investment.[74]

III. The Right of Public Distribution

Section 106(3) of the Copyright Act gives the copyright owner the exclusive right "to distribute copies or phonorecords of the copyrighted work to the public by sale or other transfer of ownership, or by rental, lease, or lending." Thus, if *A* owns the copyright in a novel, and *B* prints unauthorized copies and supplies them to *C*, who sells them to the public, both *B* and *C* are copyright infringers—*B* violates section 106(1) and *C* violates section 106(3).[75] *C* will be liable, under the general rule of copyright that recognizes even "innocent" infringement, regardless whether he sells the books in the belief *B* was their lawful author. While the distribution right often seems an adjunct to the reproduction right— for example the first U.S. copyright statute of 1790 provided for the

---

74. Paul Goldstein, Derivative Rights and Derivative Works in Copyright, 30 J.Copyr. Soc. 209, 227 (1983).

75. Columbia Pictures Indus., Inc. v. Garcia, 996 F. Supp. 770 (N.D. Ill. 1998).

rights to "print, publish and vend"[76]—there are instances in which only the distribution right is at issue. Examples include copies made unlawfully abroad but distributed here[77] (the reproduction abroad may violate the copyright law of the country of manufacture), and copies unlawfully made in the U.S. and sold by a third party, where the copyright owner seeks relief only against the distributor ("C" above).[78]

A. *Digital distribution*

If it is clear that there is a public distribution when a bookseller distributes copies throughout the United States, is it equally true when the "distributed" copies are in digital rather than analog formats? The caselaw on unauthorized availability of works via the Internet has brought the scope of the distribution right to the fore.[79] When a person, without authorization, places copyrighted material on a website or in her "sharing" file and makes it available for all interested persons to download into their computer hard-drives (or even simply to view on their computer monitors) has she publicly distributed that material, and thus infringed the section 106(3) right?

We have seen, in connection with the reproduction right, that the 1976 Copyright Act encompasses digital as well as analog copies (and phonorecords);[80] it would follow, then, that the distribution right extends to the provision of digital copies to end-users (or, for that matter, to intermediaries). But the nature of digital copies may at first blush clash with the text of section 106(3), which grants the exclusive right "to distribute copies or phonorecords of the copyrighted work to the public *by sale or other transfer of ownership*, or by rental, lease or lending" (emphasis supplied). This text prompts the initial question whether the "by sale or other transfer of ownership . . ." clause offers examples of

---

76. Act of May 31, 1790 ch. 15, 1 Stat. 124, *reprinted in* COPYRIGHT ENACTMENTS OF THE UNITED STATES 1783–1906, at 32 (T. Solberg, ed. 1906).

77. *See, e.g.*, Psihoyos v. Liberation, Inc., 42 U.S.P.Q.2d 1947 (S.D.N.Y. 1997) (photographs reproduced in Austrian magazine in Austria, but magazine sold in U.S.).

78. *See, e.g.*, Ortiz–Gonzalez v. Fonovisa, 277 F.3d 59 (1st Cir. 2002); Columbia Pictures Indus., Inc. v. Garcia, 996 F. Supp. 770 (N.D. Ill. 1998).

79. *Compare* Playboy Enters., Inc. v. Frena, 839 F. Supp. 1552 (M.D. Fla. 1993) (BBS "distributes" photographs posted to it for users' access); Playboy Enters., Inc. v. Webbworld, Inc., 991 F. Supp. 543 (N.D. Tex. 1997) (website operator "distributes" copyright-protected works "by allowing its users to download and print copies of electronic image files"); London–Sire Records v. Doe 1, 542 F. Supp. 2d 153 (D. Mass. 2008) (placing sound recordings in "sharing" file in P2P network gives rise to presumption that copies were distributed to other participants in the network), *with* Atlantic Recording Corp. v. Brennan 534 F. Supp. 2d 278, 282 (D. Conn. 2008) ("making available" does not constitute distribution); Capitol Records v. Thomas, 579 F. Supp. 2d 1210 (D. Minn. 2008) (same).

80. *See, e.g.*, Sec. 102(a) ("Fixed in any tangible medium of expression now known *or later developed*") (emphasis supplied).

kinds of distribution, or should be read as a *limitation* so that *only* those distributions which constitute sales, etc. count under section 106(3).

It might seem odd for a statute which endeavored to be forward-looking[81] to leave a vacuum for forms of distribution that might not have been contemplated in 1976. In 1976, however, the list probably covered the means of distribution then envisioned; specifying that the right reached transfers both of ownership and of possession (rental, lease or lending) appears designed to reinforce the right's comprehensiveness.[82] It is therefore unlikely that Congress in 1976 intended "transfer of ownership" to have a limiting effect on the scope of the distribution right. Congress did indeed establish limitations on the right's scope, but it did so in a separate section announcing an explicit exception removing copies "lawfully made under this title" from the copyright owner's control over their subsequent disposition by the owner of the copy.[83] The structure of the statute, articulating broad rights in section 106, and specific exceptions in the following sections,[84] therefore argues against giving "transfer of ownership" a constraining interpretation. In any event, the question whether the "by" clause should be read as a limitation becomes moot if digital distribution effects a "transfer of ownership."

This is the point at which the particularity of digital copies as compared with analog copies enters the analysis. A transfer of ownership of an analog copy implicitly involves the transferor's divestiture of her copy so that the transferee may take possession. A book sold by a bookstore leaves the store with the customer; there is one fewer copy in the store's inventory. With digital copies, by contrast, one typically "sends" a copy, but retains one's "original" or "own" copy in one's computer memory. There is no divestiture; rather at least two people now own copies where before there was only one owner. Under these circumstances, is there a "transfer of ownership"?

In *London-Sire Records, Inc. v. Doe*,[85] the district court focused on the creation of a new copy in the computer of the recipient, a copy which

---

81. Supplementary Report of the Register of Copyrights on the General Revision of the U.S. Copyright Law: 1965 Revision Bill, 89th Cong., 1st Sess. 13–14 (1965).

82. Compare the 1909 Copyright Act, whose section 1 did not express a general right of distribution covering transfers of possession as well as of ownership:

Any person entitled thereto, upon complying with the provisions of this title, shall have the exclusive right:

(a) To print, reprint, publish, copy, and vend the copyrighted work; . . .

(f) To reproduce and distribute to the public by sale or other transfer of ownership, or by rental, lease, or lending, reproductions of the copyrighted work if it be a sound recording

83. 17 U.S.C. § 109(a) (codifying the "first sale doctrine" see discussion *infra*).

84. Section 106 states: "Subject to sections 107 through 122, the owner of copyright under this title has the exclusive rights to do and to authorize any of the following: . . ."

85. 542 F. Supp. 2d 153 (D. Mass. 2008)

the recipient now owns: "What matters in the marketplace is not whether a material object 'changes hands,' but whether, when the transaction is completed, the distributee has a material object."[86] The concept of "transfer" in the digital world does not imply the disappearance of the transferor's copy, yet the term appears as a matter of course, for example the phrase "file transfer" (as in "file transfer protocol" or "FTP") is widely used to denote sending a digital file without necessarily (or ever) deleting the file from the sender's computer.[87] Moreover, on further examination, a "distribution" need not always result in a loss of possession, even in the analog world. For one very old technological example, consider the biblical loaves and fishes. English versions of the gospels recount that Jesus ordered his disciples to "distribute" the loaves and fishes to the public. Though the supply seemed inadequate, all the public were served, yet at the end, the same number of loaves and fishes remained in the baskets as at the outset.[88]

Legislation subsequent to the 1976 enactment endorses the characterization of a transfer of a digital file as a form of "distribution." Congress in 1995 amended the section 115 "compulsory license for making and distributing phonorecords" to include among the beneficiaries of the license "those who make phonorecords or digital phonorecord deliveries," and further specifying, "A person may obtain a compulsory license only if his or her primary purpose in making phonorecords is to distribute them to the public for private use, including by means of a digital phonorecord delivery."[89] The definition of "digital phonorecord delivery" confirms that the constitution of the copy in the recipient's computer is the key activity: "A 'digital phonorecord delivery' is each individual delivery of a phonorecord by digital transmission of a sound recording which *results in a specifically identifiable reproduction by or for any transmission recipient* of a phonorecord of that sound recording

---

86. Taken out of context, the court's end-up-with-a-copy test could be overbroad. For example, if a home viewer records a television broadcast, thus creating a copy, has the broadcaster "distributed" the "copy" the viewer ended up with? Indeed, with contemporary recording media, any performance or display could result in "copies," though, as a matter of common sense, it is doubtful that many of them would constitute "distributions." For example, if passers-by photograph the wearer of a t-shirt emblazoned with copyrightable text or image, copies will result, but the wearer cannot reasonably be said to have distributed them. For a distribution to take place, the exchange (or new creation) of a copy should be the object of the transaction.

87. Other common uses of "transfer" that do not imply divestiture include Hypertext Transfer Protocol (HTTP), and Simple Mail Transfer Protocol (SMTP). See "What is file transfer protocol," http://searchnet working.techtarget.com/sDefinition/0,,sid7_gci213976,00.html A Google search reveals "about 20,500,000" results for "file transfer."

88. Matthew 14:20 (King James); Mark 6:41 (King James); Luke 9:16 (King James); John 6:11 (King James).

89. *Id.* § 115(a)(1), as amended by the Digital Performance Right in Sound Recordings Act of 1995, Pub. L. No. 104–39, 109 Stat. 336.

...'"[90] It is reasonable to assume that by 1995 Congress was aware that digital deliveries create new copies without divesting the sender's copy; if Congress nonetheless equated "digital phonorecord delivery" with distribution, then "transfer of ownership" cannot, at least with respect to the distribution rights in musical works and sound recordings,[91] have been understood to require dispossession of the transferor's copy.

1. "Making available" as "distribution"

If "distribution" encompasses the creation of new copies in the computers of the recipients, does it follow that absent actual receipt, there is no "distribution"? Is simply making a work available so that third parties may make copies of it, but without demonstrating that any potential recipients did in fact acquire copies, also a "distribution of copies"? So far the caselaw has provided inconsistent responses. While early decisions generally considered (without extended analysis) that making a work available for end-user access and copying "distributed" copies of the work,[92] later rulings are more tormented. Some require a showing of actual receipt, but disagree whether the court may presume receipt if the making available has set in motion all the other elements of distribution.[93] At least one other court, emphasizing the definition of "publication," which covers both distribution of copies and the offering to distribute copies, has concluded that making copies available for download is akin to offering to distribute, which constitutes a "publication," which is synonymous with distribution.[94]

Whether "making available" constitutes distribution, or it must also be shown that new copies resulted in users' computers or other devices, in either event an intent to deliver copies to end users (or to enable end users to create those copies) appears to be a key element of the conduct that violates the right. If, however, the alleged infringer is merely an online service provider that plays a passive role in allowing access to an infringing website, without creating or controlling the content of the information available to its subscribers, it will generally be found not to have made an unlawful public distribution.[95]

90. *Id.* § 115(d) (emphasis supplied).

91. *See* S. Rep. No. 104–128 at 17 (1995) (legislative history of 1995 Act: adverting to uncertainty whether a "transmission can constitute a distribution of copies" and "express[ing] no [general] view on current law in this regard" but wanting to remove uncertainty "as to digital transmissions of recorded music").

92. *See, e.g.,* Playboy Enters., Inc. v. Webbworld, Inc., 991 F. Supp. 543 (N.D.Tex. 1997); Playboy Enters., Inc. v. Frena, 839 F. Supp. 1552 (M.D.Fla.1993).

93. *Compare* London–Sire Records, Inc. v. Doe 1, 542 F. Supp. 2d 153 (D. Mass. 2008), *with* Capitol Records, Inc. v. Thomas 579 F. Supp. 2d 1210 (D. Minn. 2008).

94. Elektra Entertainment Group, Inc. v. Barker, 551 F. Supp. 2d 234 (S.D.N.Y. 2008).

95. Religious Tech. Ctr. v. Netcom On–Line Communication Servs., Inc., 907 F. Supp. 1361 (N.D. Cal. 1995). The liability of internet service providers for contributory and vicarious liability is a matter of detailed

B.   *First-sale doctrine*

1.   In general

If read literally, section 106(3) would make it an infringement for a book dealer to sell used books, or for a library to lend a book in its collection to students or other patrons. This anomaly is quickly dispelled by virtue of section 109(a), which provides:

> Notwithstanding the provisions of section 106(3), the owner of a particular copy or phonorecord lawfully made under this title, or any person authorized by such owner, is entitled, without the authority of the copyright owner, to sell or otherwise dispose of the possession of that copy or phonorecord.

This provision articulates what has been a fundamental part of our copyright jurisprudence for a century: the "first-sale doctrine." The Supreme Court in its 1908 decision in *Bobbs-Merrill Co. v. Straus* stated: "[O]ne who has sold a copyrighted article, without restriction, has parted with all right to control the sale of it. The purchaser of a book, once sold by authority of the owner of the copyright, may sell it again, although he could not publish a new edition of it."[96]

Conceptually, however, the basis of the first-sale doctrine long precedes *Bobbs-Merrill*. The first-sale doctrine may be seen as the consequence of the essential distinction, articulated by Lord Chancellor Hardwicke in 1741 in *Pope v. Curll*,[97] between the "property of the paper" on which Alexander Pope wrote his letters, and Pope's exclusive right to publish their words. The English law, followed by American decisions, recognized two distinct property rights: a chattel right in the physical medium in which the words were embodied, and the incorporeal copyright in the words themselves.[98] Just as ownership of the paper on which a letter is written, or of the tangible medium in which a pictorial work appears, confers of itself no right to copy and publicly distribute the letter's expressive content or to reproduce or alter the image,[99] so the author's incorporeal rights to make and vend copies do not import any right to dispose of the chattel owner's physical object once she has acquired lawful ownership of it. The copyright owner's rights stop where the chattel-owner's rights begin. (And vice-versa.)

The exclusive right to distribute the copyrighted work to the public thus embraces only the first sale, and purchasers of copies or phonorec-

---

regulation under section 512 of the Copyright Act, added in 1998.

96.   210 U.S. 339, 350 (1908).

97.   2 Atk. 341.

98.   For a detailed listing and description of the eighteenth and nineteenth-century English and American authorities, *see generally* Baker v. Libbie, 97 N.E. 109 (1912).

99.   The 1976 Copyright Act codifies this principle in section 202.

ords are free to transfer them to others by sale, gift, or otherwise. The first sale "exhausts" the right of the copyright owner under section 106(3), and he or she must exact whatever royalty can be negotiated from the initial publisher-distributor, knowing that that will have to provide recompense for all subsequent transfers as well.

Thus it is lawful, for example, for a person to purchase second-hand copies of copyrighted works, to remove the covers or to bind them in new covers, and to resell them to the public.[100] If, however, the reseller goes a step farther and makes some alteration in or compilation of the lawfully purchased works, he or she may be found liable for creating an unlawful *derivative work* even if not for unlawful *public distribution*. A court so held when the defendant purchased old copies of *National Geographic* magazine, tore out articles, and bound together for sale articles relating to a common subject matter.[101] The creation of the derivative work invades the author's exclusive right to create new versions of her works, and thus exceeds the prerogatives of the owner of the physical paper on which the reshuffled pages of the magazines were printed.

The chattel-owner's exercise of her property rights in her physical copy traditionally did not significantly compete with the author's exploitation of her copyright. While the revenue from the second-hand book market remained outside the copyright owner's control, those sales traditionally did not systematically compete with the sales of new (copyright owner-controlled) copies. Similarly, the first-sale doctrine also shields library-lending of books (assuming libraries own the copies they lend), but that lending is not thought to result in significant lost sales to copyright owners. While recent developments in online information aggregation make it possible to organize the used book market to compete more closely with the sale of new copies (consider, for example, Amazon.com's listings that make it as easy for a book shopper seeking a given title to "buy it used" as to acquire a new copy), the first-sale doctrine nonetheless shields this business model. That result is consistent with the chattel rationale for the doctrine.

Used books and library lending recirculate particular tangible copies; they exploit the individual physical object, they do not reproduce or publicly perform or display its incorporeal content. Where the first-sale doctrine has impinged on the incorporeal rights, however, Congress has devised exceptions to the rule. There are two such exceptions. They relate to the rental for profit of either a phonorecord embodying a copyrighted sound recording of music or a copy of a copyrighted computer program. Congress concluded in 1984 that the newly emerging "rec-

---

100. Fawcett Publ'ns, Inc. v. Elliot Publ'g Co., 46 F. Supp. 717 (S.D.N.Y. 1942).

101. National Geographic Soc'y v. Classified Geographic, Inc., 27 F. Supp. 655 (D. Mass. 1939).

ord rental store" was being used by consumers as an inexpensive supplier of musical sound recordings that could be taped at home, thus substituting for a purchase of the recording. Comparable conclusions were reached in 1990 with respect to the rental of computer software, which was also susceptible to reproduction for nonprofit personal use, by individuals on their home computers. In other words, in both cases, the "rentals" were a smokescreen for the unauthorized production of copies; the business model was not based in the circulation of a particular physical copy, but rather in the copying that the circulation would enable.

In the Record Rental Amendment of 1984 and the Computer Software Rental Amendments Act of 1990, Congress forbade the owner of a phonorecord or the possessor of a copy of a computer program "for the purposes of direct or indirect commercial advantage, [to] dispose of, or authorize the disposal of, the possession of that phonorecord or computer program . . . by rental, lease, or lending, or by any other act or practice in the nature of rental, lease, or lending." These exceptions to the first-sale doctrine are codified in section 109(b) of the Copyright Act. Explicitly excluded from the ban is the not-for-profit rental, lease, or lending of phonorecords or computer software by most nonprofit libraries and educational institutions. These amendments do not affect the application of the first-sale doctrine to video rentals.

2.   Contractual avoidance of the first-sale doctrine?

As we have seen, the sale (or other transfer of ownership) of a copy triggers the first-sale doctrine. By contrast, if the copyright owner alienates possession of a copy without in fact selling it, and thus engages in "rental, lease or lending," the copyright owner can control secondary markets for the recirculation of the copy because the only beneficiaries of section 109(a) are "owners" of copies; lawfully possessing a copy does not suffice without ownership. Not surprisingly, then, some copyright owners, particularly in certain industries, prefer to "lease" rather than to "sell" copies of their works. If copyright owners could simply recharacterize any "sale" as a "lease," however, there would be little left to the first-sale doctrine, because, if the apparent sale is in fact only a "lease," the copyright owner may prevent the possessor-lessee from reselling the copy. The caselaw addressing the question whether a purported "lease" should be deemed a "sale" appears to turn on whether the work has traditionally been distributed with restrictive license conditions so that the possessor would not have expected to be able freely to dispose of her copy.

In *Vernor v. Autodesk*,[102] the Ninth Circuit Court of Appeals upheld a software producer's claim that it distributed copies of its computer-aided-design (CAD) software by means of a lease. The license terms, consistent with long-standing practice in the industry, entitled the licensee to updated versions of the CAD software, but prohibited reselling the older versions; the terms included a variety of other restrictions as well. The court ruled that "because Autodesk reserved title to Release 14 copies and imposed significant transfer and use restrictions, we conclude that its customers are licensees of their copies of Release 14 rather than owners."

By contrast, in *UMG Recordings, Inc. v. Augusto*,[103] the same court ruled insufficient to create a license the distribution to music critics and radio programmers of promotional CDs bearing the following legend: "This CD is the property of the record company and is licensed to the intended recipient for personal use only. Acceptance of this CD shall constitute an agreement to comply with the terms of the license. Resale or transfer of possession is not allowed and may be punishable under federal and state laws." Unlike software, music CDs traditionally are distributed to the public through unencumbered sales. Moreover, "mere labeling" does not create a license when "under all the circumstances of the CDs' distribution, the recipients were entitled to use or dispose of them in any manner they saw fit." The sound recording producer's lack of control over the CDs proved fatal to the copyright owner's claim to have leased rather than sold them.

The nature of the work may determine whether saying a distribution is a license makes it so. Software producers may succeed in imposing restrictive conditions on their customers because the customers depend on updates and other services; the customers therefore remain in contact with the producer even after they have acquired copies of the work. By contrast, it is neither typical nor practical to "tether" the consumer of a recorded song. Stand-alone works thus are unlikely candidates for lease transactions, at least under current patterns of consumer behavior. One may anticipate, however, forms of entertainment product, for example videogames, where remaining in contact with the producer for updates, or for participating in multi-player sessions, contributes important value-added to the enjoyment of the work.

3.   Digital first-sale?

As more works are distributed online, the question arises whether the first-sale doctrine applies not only to digital hardcopies, such as CDs and DVDs, but also to the copies stored in computer memory. The short

---

102.   621 F.3d 1102 (9th Cir. 2010).   **103.**   628 F.3d 1175 (9th Cir. 2011).

answer is "no" because "sending" someone a copy inevitably creates additional copies. Moreover, the doctrine's grounding in the rights of the owner of the physical object ill adapts it to dematerialized transactions. Nonetheless, one might imagine a digital equivalent, if the sender of the copy simultaneously deleted her copy from her files. Although proponents of a digital first-sale exemption claimed that such a forwarding and deleting is the digital equivalent of giving away a book—an activity squarely covered by the current first-sale doctrine—the Copyright Office, in rejecting the proposal, articulated some pragmatic distinctions. The Office first noted that the urged doctrine in fact involved creating a new exception to the *reproduction* right, rather than a new application of the exhaustion doctrine which centers on physical objects. It then stressed that software currently in use does not include a forward-and-delete function, and that one cannot expect that senders will systematically delete their copies themselves.[104]

One may also wonder whether, even were the first-sale doctrine to extend to digital transfers, the exemption would much matter in the evolving markets for digital distribution. Recall that the doctrine turns on "ownership" of a copy, whatever its format. But with the increased devising of business models premised on offering access to works, rather than ownership of copies, consumers may forgo "having" copies to resell or give away.[105]

4. First-sale and the importation right

Section 602(a)(1) of the 1976 Copyright Act accords copyright owners the right to control importation of copies into the U.S.:

> Importation into the United States, without the authority of the owner of copyright under this title, of copies or phonorecords of a work that have been acquired outside the United States is an infringement of the exclusive right to distribute copies or phonorecords under section 106, actionable under section 501.

This provision does not distinguish between copies that were made in violation of the copyright law of the country of manufacture and those that were lawfully produced there, for example under license from the copyright owner. Compare section 602(a)(2), which addresses unlawfully made copies, and subjects their importer to criminal as well as civil liability. Because section 602(a)(1) on its face applies to lawfully made copies, it may be in tension with section 109(a). Reference to section

---

104. *See* http://www.loc.gov/copyright/reports/studies/dmca/sec_104_report-vol_1.pdf.

105. *See, e.g.,* Jane C. Ginsburg, Essay, *From Having Copies to Experiencing Works:*

The Development of an Access Right in U.S. Copyright Law, 50 J. Copyr. Soc. 113 (2003).

109(a)'s specification of copies "lawfully made under this title" may reconcile the two provisions. A foreign-made copy may have been produced lawfully, but not "under this title," that is, not under U.S. law, because U.S. law does not govern the foreign manufacture of copies. Arguably "under this title" could mean "lawfully made, had this title applied," but the presence of that phrase in section 601(a)(2) in the context of unlawfully made copies ("the making of which either constituted an infringement of copyright, or which would have constituted an infringement of copyright if this title had been applicable") suggests that section 109(a)'s "lawfully made under this title" is territorially restricted to the U.S.

In 1998, in *Quality King Distributors, Inc. v. L'anza Research International, Inc.,*[106] the Supreme Court confronted the question whether the first-sale doctrine applies not only to copies and phonorecords manufactured in the United States and subsequently sold here, but also when those subsequent sales follow purchases made abroad. The central issue was whether the first-sale limitation set forth in section 109(a) applied to imported goods, or whether section 602(a) afforded a freestanding right not subject to the various exemptions (including fair use and first sale) in the Copyright Act. The Court concluded that the importation right under section 602(a) is a species of the public-distribution right under section 106(3), so that the copyright owner exercises that right subject to the first-sale doctrine. But the copies there at issue (labels on shampoo bottles)[107] had been made in the U.S.; their subsequent export, repurchase and import did not efface the exhaustion of the distribution right that attached to their first sale. Section 109(a) requires only that the copies have been lawfully made under title 17, not that they have been sold under the aegis of U.S. law.[108] *Quality King* therefore did not resolve the question whether sale of *foreign-made* grey goods or parallel imports, at unauthorized discounted prices, escaped the control of U.S. copyright owners.

Courts of appeals have since emphasized the distinction between *Quality King*'s "round-trip" copies,[109] and importation of copies lawfully made abroad. In *Omega S.A. v. Costco Wholesale Corp.,*[110] a case involv-

---

106. 523 U.S. 135 (1998).

107. The nature of the work may have influenced the analysis of section 602 because it was obvious that the producer was using the copyright on the labels to bootstrap a prohibition on the brand-name shampoo, a result it could not have obtained under the Trademarks law, *see* K Mart Corp. v. Cartier, Inc., 485 U.S. 176 (1988).

108. Section 109(a)'s failure to specify that *sale* of copies in the U.S., whatever the place of their manufacture, exhausts the distribution right creates other problems, see *infra*.

109. Quality King, 523 U.S. at 153 (Ginsburg, J. concurring).

110. 541 F.3d 982 (9th Cir. 2008), *aff'd. by an equally divided court,* 562 S. ___, 131 S.Ct. 565, 178 L.Ed.2d 470 (2010).

ing a (minimally) copyrighted design engraved on the back of watch casings, the Ninth Circuit determined that *Quality King* did not disturb that circuit's prior rulings that section 109(a) did not apply to "foreign-made, nonpiratical copies of a U.S.-copyrighted work ... unless those same copies have already been sold in the United States with the copyright owner's authority." In *Wiley v. Kirtsaeng*,[111] an unauthorized-importation case for once concerning core copyright material—textbooks printed abroad by the plaintiff's Asian subsidiary in lower quality editions for foreign markets—the Second Circuit, while finding no authority outside the Ninth Circuit for that court's application of the first sale doctrine to foreign-made copies once they have been sold in the US, held that "the phrase 'lawfully made under this Title' in § 109(a) refers specifically and exclusively to copies that are made in territories in which the Copyright Act is law, and not to foreign-manufactured copies."

While the Second Circuit is correct that the Ninth Circuit's application of the first-sale doctrine to U.S. sales as well as U.S. manufacture lacks textual basis, it avoids the anomaly that copyright owners could control secondary markets for foreign-made copies even after they have lawfully been sold here. Such a disparity in treatment of U.S.-made and foreign-made copies could enhance the incentive to manufacture copies abroad already implicit in a reading that declines to subjugate section 602(a)(1) to section 109(a). But the policy arguments cut both ways: while section 602(a)(1) could allow some copyright owners to end-run the first sale doctrine, it also allows copyright owners to price discriminate, offering cheaper copies to third-world countries, secure in the knowledge that they may prevent initial U.S. distribution of those copies in competition with the U.S. editions.

5. *Droit de suite*

The "*droit de suite*," or artists' resale royalty right, qualifies the freedom to resell at the core of the first sale doctrine: the right requires that, for the duration of the copyright term, the creator receive a specified percentage of the price of every subsequent resale. Because there may be no market for reproduction (or public display by transmission) of many works of art, exploitations of incorporeal copyright rights may not benefit many artists; the *droit de suite* therefore seeks to ensure that artists share in the subsequent profitable disposition of lawfully owned copies of their works. Although the *droit de suite* exists in the European Union, California is the only U.S. state that has enacted a resale-royalties statute. It provides that:

> Whenever a work of fine art is sold and the seller resides in
> California or the sale takes place in California, the seller or his

111. 654 F.3d 210 (2d Cir. 2011).

agent shall pay to the artist of such work of fine art or to such artist's agent 5 percent of the amount of such sale.[112]

The artist's right is nonwaivable and may be enforced by an action for damages with a three-year period of limitations; moneys payable to the artist will be paid to the state Arts Council if the seller cannot locate the artist within 90 days, and all moneys due the artist are exempt from attachment or execution of judgment by creditors of the seller. Among those sales exempted from the statute are resales for a gross price of less than $1,000, resales made more than 20 years after the death of the artist, and resales for a gross sales price less than the purchase price paid by the seller. Two federal courts have held that the federal copyright law does not preempt the state resale-royalty law.[113]

On the federal level, proponents of the *droit de suite* have made several attempts to incorporate the concept into the Copyright Act, including as a provision in the Visual Artists Rights Act of 1990. Though the 1990 provision was ultimately deleted from the final bill, the effort was more successful than its predecessors: Congress did direct the Register of Copyrights to conduct a study examining the feasibility of adopting a resale rights program in the United States.

In response, the Register reported that, based on the record developed through the inquiry, there was insufficient justification for the adoption of the system in the U.S. copyright law.[114] However, the Register's negative assessment was explicitly qualified by both the lack of conclusive data and the possibility that a harmonization of policy within the European Community countries might dictate a different conclusion. The EU subsequently adopted a Directive on the resale royalty; its terms deny royalties to foreign artists whose work is resold in an EU member State, unless the State of the artist's nationality offers European artists reciprocal protection.[115] Federal bills are currently pending. The "Equity for Visual Artists Act of 2011,"[116] would set aside 7% of the price for works resold at auction for more than $10,000, with the proceeds divided equally between the artists and non-profit art museums.

112. Cal. Civ. Code, § 986(a).

113. *See* Morseburg v. Balyon, 621 F.2d 972 (9th Cir. 1980); Baby Moose Drawings, Inc. v. Valentine, No. 2:11–cv–00697, 2011 WL 1258529 (N.D. Cal. April 1, 2011) (citing House Judiciary Committee Report to 1990 Visual Artists Rights Act explicitly preserving state resale-royalty laws).

114. *See generally* U.S. Copyright Office, Droit de Suite: The Artists Resale Royalty (1992). *But see* Shira Perlmutter, *Resale Royalties for Artists: An Analysis of the Register of Copyrights' Report,* 16 Colum.-VLA J. L. & Arts 395 (1993) (criticizing Register's report).

115. Directive 2001/84/EC of the European Parliaments and of the Council of 27 September 2001 on the resale right for the benefit of the author of an original work of art, art. 7.1.

116. H.R. 3688, 112th Cong. (1st Sess. 2011); S. 2000 112th Cong. (1st Sess. 2011).

IV. The Right of Public Performance

Another exclusive right under section 106 of the Copyright Act is the right "to perform the copyrighted work publicly." The public-performance right is a particularly significant right for dramatic works, motion pictures, and musical works. But it is accorded to all categories of copyright-protected works except for pictorial, graphic, and sculptural works (for obvious reasons) and sound recordings (sound-engineered performances captured on phonorecords). The exclusion of sound recordings from section 106(4) is largely for historical reasons; although musical compositions have had public-performance rights in the U.S. since the turn of the twentieth century, our copyright law was slow to recognize original authorship in recorded performances and gave no protection to sound recordings at all until 1972 and then only against direct "dubbing" or piracy of the recorded sounds. Thus, even today, when a recorded song is broadcast over the air on the radio, or is played by a disk jockey in a nightclub, that is potentially a copyright infringement of the musical composition, but it is not an infringement of the sound recording; the songwriter (or other copyright owner in the song) can claim a royalty, but neither the record company nor the recording artist can. As will be discussed below, however, Congress in 1995 added section 106(6) to the Copyright Act, which accords to the copyright owner of a sound recording (typically the recording company) the exclusive right "to perform the work publicly by means of a digital audio transmission"; this is a right that has become highly important in the age of the Internet.

Section 101 sets forth broad definitions of "perform" and "publicly."

> To "perform" a work means to recite, render, play, dance, or act it, either directly or by means of any device or process or, in the case of a motion picture or other audiovisual work, to show its images in any sequence or to make the sounds accompanying it audible.

> To perform or display a work "publicly" means—

> (1) to perform or display it at a place open to the public or at any place where a substantial number of persons outside of a normal circle of a family and its social acquaintances is gathered;

> (2) to transmit or otherwise communicate a performance or display of the work to a place specified by clause (1) or to the public, by means of any device or process, whether the members of the public capable of receiving the performance or display

receive it in the same place or in separate places and at the same time or at different times.

A. *Performance*

The definition of "perform" embraces not only live face-to-face performances but also "rendering" a work by any device or process, such as a compact disk or MP3 player for music and a DVD player or laptop or tablet for motion pictures, as well as by radio or television transmission. The definitive House Committee Report states that a performance can be effected through "all kinds of equipment for reproducing or amplifying sounds or visual images, any sort of transmitting apparatus, any type of electronic retrieval system, and any other techniques and systems not yet in use or even invented."[117] Just as a live dramatic production constitutes a "performance" of the work, as does its broadcast on television, the theater exhibition of a motion picture (which "shows its images in . . . sequence") also constitutes a "performance" that if unauthorized (and made "publicly," see *infra*) will infringe the copyright.

Because of the breadth of the definition of "perform," the television broadcast (or other transmissions) of a singer's rendition of a copyrighted song will give rise to a multiple series of "performances." As is stated in the House Report:

> [A] singer is performing when he or she sings a song; a broadcasting network is performing when it transmits his or her performance (whether simultaneously or from records); a local broadcaster is performing when it transmits the network broadcast; a cable television system is performing when it retransmits the broadcast to its subscribers; and any individual is performing whenever he or she plays a phonorecord embodying the performance or communicates the performance by turning on a receiving set.[118]

The private owner of the "receiving set," however, although a "performer" of the broadcast song, would not normally be liable for infringement, because his or her performance would not be "public" (see discussion *infra*).

New technologies have called into question the meaning of "perform." The problem has arisen in the context of digital deliveries of musical recordings, but could equally apply to the online communication of a digital file of any work capable of being "performed," notably, audiovisual works. If a digital file is sent to an end-user, who later opens

---

117. H.R. Rep. No. 94–1476, at 63 (1976).

118. *Id.*

and plays it, the post-receipt conduct is a "performance," but it is not "public," and therefore does not implicate the right of public performance. But is the delivery of the file itself a "performance" by "transmission"? There is a "transmission," to the members of the public who request the file, but does that delivery transmit a "performance?" In *U.S. v. American Society of Composers, Authors and Publishers (Applications of RealNetworks, Inc., Yahoo! Inc.),*[119] the Second Circuit held that a download of a musical file that was not simultaneously played (streamed) to the listener was not a "performance": "The downloads at issue in this appeal are not musical performances that are contemporaneously perceived by the listener. They are simply transfers of electronic files containing digital copies from an on-line server to a local hard drive. The downloaded songs are not performed in any perceptible manner during the transfers; the user must take some further action to play the songs after they are downloaded. Because the electronic download itself involves no recitation, rendering, or playing of the musical work encoded in the digital transmission, we hold that such a download is not a performance of that work, as defined by § 101."

The requirement that, to be "performed" by transmission, the work must be "contemporaneously perceived" is consistent with the statutory definition of "to perform."[120] Nonetheless, the distinction between transmissions "that are contemporaneously perceived" and those that enable subsequent perception may not fully correspond to the spectrum of online communications of works that are performed or displayed. The distinction does reflect the extremes of the spectrum: downloads of songs, for example, from iTunes (reproduction), and webcasting, in which songs are "playing" on a website to which users can connect (public performance). The "contemporaneous perception" characterization also seems to fit audio and video on demand that the user receives in "real time." But "real time" can in fact be elusive. Suppose, for example, that the user connects to an online music service in order to listen immediately to the songs she selects. The music starts to play, but then the user chooses to "pause" the performance for a few minutes, or perhaps hours. When she hits "play" again, the music resumes, but, depending on how the service works, the music might be "coming from" the server of the online service, or it may be emanating from the user's own computer, having been "sent" to her computer when she requested to hear the song. If one takes "contemporaneous perception" at face

119. 627 F.3d 64 (2d Cir. 2010)

120. *Accord,* INTELLECTUAL PROPERTY AND THE NATIONAL INFORMATION INFRASTRUCTURE: THE REPORT OF THE WORKING GROUP ON INTELLECTUAL PROPERTY RIGHTS 226, note 536 (1995) (emphasis added).: "If a copy of a motion picture is transmitted to a computer's memory, for instance, *and in the process, the sounds are capable of being heard and the images viewed as they are received in memory,* then the public performance right may well be implicated as well. See 17 U.S.C. § 101 (1988) (definition of "perform")."

value, perhaps only the first transmission is a "performance" of the music. But it is problematic for the characterization of the exploitation to turn on what happens once the user pushes the pause button. Moreover, such a limited concept of perform seems inconsistent with Congress's intent, expressed in the House Report, to embrace new modes of performance enabled by "any type of electronic retrieval system, and any other techniques and systems not yet in use or even invented." The Second Circuit appears to have anticipated this concern, because it acknowledged in footnote: "Our opinion does not foreclose the possibility, under certain circumstances not presented in this case, that a transmission could constitute both a stream and a download, each of which implicates a different right of the copyright holder."[121]

The court's reservation of the possibility that some transmissions may be hybrids calling into play *both* the reproduction and public-performance rights may be pertinent to some other exploitations on the spectrum between "downloads" and "streams." If there is no "performance" unless the work is "played" either at the point of origin, or at the moment of receipt, then similar communications may be classified as performances (or not) solely on the basis of the technology of the transmission. For example, suppose on the one hand, a conditional download-on-demand scheme that sends the file during low traffic hours, and allows the consumer to listen once to the work at the time chosen by her. The transmission will "feel" like a "stream" (or a radio broadcast), but it is technically a "download" because the music file will have been sitting inertly in the computer during the time between the actual transmission, say 4:00 AM, and the time the user told the service she wanted to hear the song, say, 4:00 PM. Suppose on the other hand that the work is being both broadcast and simultaneously streamed to the user's set-top box, which records the work as it is being transmitted; the consumer views the recorded transmission at a later date. Under the "contemporaneous perception" test, the streaming is a performance because the streaming was capable of contemporaneous perception, even though only the set-top box was home to perceive it. The consumer's subsequent private viewing, albeit consciously not contemporaneous with the initial communication, does not detract from the characterization of the initial communication as a performance. Because the court stopped short of imposing an "either/or" characterization of the exploitation, it left room for future adjudications to interpret the scope of the rights flexibly to address the full range of economic interests at stake.

---

121.   627 F.3d at 74 n.10.

B.   Public performance

Section 106(4) provides that the exclusive right covers only those performances that are "public." Public performances arise in two ways: (1) directly to the audience at a place open to the public, or (2) by transmission to members of the public, whether separated in space or in time. The definition of "publicly" in section 101 is designed to dispel the confusion that had arisen under the 1909 Act, which had left the word undefined. As stated in the House Report: "[P]erformances in 'semipublic' places such as clubs, lodges, factories, summer camps, and schools are 'public performances' subject to copyright control.... Routine meetings of businesses and governmental personnel would be excluded because they do not represent the gathering of a 'substantial number of persons.' "[122] Performances that take place at any of the former venues are, in the words of the statute, "at any place where a substantial number of persons outside of a normal circle of a family and its social acquaintances is gathered."

Notwithstanding the text and its legislative history, courts have disagreed over the meaning of "a place open to the public." The Court of Appeals for the Third Circuit has held that the public-performance right in motion pictures was infringed by a business that invited members of the public to rent videotapes (lawfully made and purchased) and then to view them in rooms provided under the same roof for very small groups of family or friends.[123] The court concluded that the showings in even the small rooms were "public" because access to the rooms was open to the public,[124] and that the defendant store had "authorized" those public performances and thus infringed. A different outcome was reached, however, by the Court of Appeals for the Ninth Circuit in the case of a motel that rented videocassettes for viewing in private guest rooms; the motel was deemed to be facilitating a number of discrete private performances.[125]

The definition in section 101 also makes it clear that a *transmitted* performance is "public" even though the recipients are themselves

---

122. H.R. Rep. No. 94–1476, at 64.

123. Columbia Pictures Indus., Inc. v. Aveco, Inc., 800 F.2d 59 (3d Cir. 1986). In 2011, major motion picture studios won a preliminary injunction against Zediva, a company that played physical DVDs at a central location and then streamed the results into viewer's homes. Warner Bros. Entm't v. WTV Sys. Inc, No. CV 11–2817–JFW, 2011 WL 4001121 (C.D. Cal. Aug. 1, 2011) (issuing injunction on grounds that Zediva service violated copyright owners' exclusive public-performance right).

124. The court pointed out that a place "open to the public" might nonetheless ac-

commodate very few people or only one person at a given time, such as a "pay toilet." *Aveco*, 800 F.2d at 63.

125. Columbia Pictures Indus., Inc. v. Professional Real Estate Investors, Inc., 866 F.2d 278 (9th Cir. 1989). *But see* On Command Video Corp. v. Columbia Pictures Indus., 777 F. Supp. 787 (N.D.Cal.1991) (transmission from central point in hotel of individualized performances to private guest rooms effects a public performance by transmission because hotel guests are "members of the public").

located in private settings, such as their own homes or hotel rooms. (Under another definition in section 101, to "transmit" a performance is "to communicate it by any device or process whereby images or sounds are received beyond the place from which they are sent.") A public performance thus takes place when a work is transmitted to the public by radio or television, or to a computer over the Internet.

The right of public performance is more broadly written than had been the case under the 1909 Copyright Act. Under the earlier statute, the exclusive right to perform music had been limited to public performances "for profit." Accordingly, performances of copyrighted music in schools, in public parks, at charitable events, and the like were not infringements and generated no royalties for the copyright owner. Performances of copyrighted dramatic works would infringe, if in public, regardless whether or not they were "for profit." This distinction between dramatic and musical works was abandoned in the definition of exclusive rights under the 1976 Copyright Act; section 106(4) eliminates the "for profit" limitation upon the music performance right. Nonetheless, the present statute provides certain specific exemptions for public performances of music that do not obtain for public performances of dramatic works; these exemptions will be explored in the next Chapter.

While the 1976 Act embraces a broader range of public performances than its predecessor, and sought to ensure that new and even then-unknown modes of exploitation would be covered (see *supra*), technology entrepreneurs have developed new business models that call into question the "public" characterization of certain transmissions of performances. In *Cartoon Network LP v. CSC Holdings, Inc.*,[126] the defendant cable television service offered subscribers a remote playback system. Cablevision stored copies of television programming in virtual storage boxes dedicated to individual subscribers. When the subscriber chose to view the program, Cablevision would transmit it to her, using the copy in the subscriber's storage box as the source of the transmission. Cablevision therefore asserted that the transmission was not "to the public" because there was no centralized copy from which multiple transmissions emanated, rather each subscriber had a dedicated copy that was transmitted only to the particular subscriber.

The Second Circuit agreed, focusing on "who precisely is 'capable of receiving' a particular transmission of a performance.... [The definition] speaks of people capable of receiving a particular 'transmission' or 'performance,' and not of the potential audience of a particular 'work.' "[127] Because Cablevision had set up the playback system so that only one person (or her family or circle of social acquaintance—the

126.   536 F.3d 121 (2d Cir. 2008).   127.   536 F.3d at 135.

statutory non-"public"[128]) would be "capable" of receiving the transmission that originates from her storage box, the performance was not "public," the court ruled.

The court's parsing of the text of the Copyright Act is very problematic. The key phrase in the definition is "to the public." "The public" in the case of a television transmission is the intended audience, or, in the case of a cable service, the subscribers. The phrase "members of the public capable of receiving the performance" is not intended to *narrow* the universe of "the public." On the contrary, its role is to clarify that a transmission is still "to the public" even if its receipt is individualized.[129] The "members of the public capable of receiving the performance" do not stop being "members of the public" just because they are "capable of receiving the performance" one at a time. By the same token, it should not matter whether "the performance" originates from a single source copy repeatedly transmitted to individual members of the public "in different places at different times,"[130] or from multiple copies each corresponding to a particular place and/or time.

The court's construction clashes with the text of the Act in another important way: it is not possible to transmit a performance "created by *the* act of transmission" to members of the public "at different times." While such a "performance" could be transmitted simultaneously to differently located recipients, recipients differently situated in time cannot receive the same transmission. The court's interpretation thus appears to read nonsimultaneous receipt out of the statute. As a result, *Cablevision*'s potential impact on the scope of the public-performance right could place beyond the reach of the exclusive right of public performance the many emerging "cloud" services in which the transmission entity stores individual copies for subsequent individual transmission from its server to subscribers. Moreover, if the "performance" does not occur "publicly" because its transmission is individualized (only one member of the public is "capable of receiving" the particular transmission that she requests), then the decision's rationale would reach even conventional on-demand streaming operations. Such a result would disregard the statute's explicit coverage of performances that are transmitted to members of the public who are separated in time.

---

128. *See* 17 U.S.C. § 101 (first part of the definition of public performance: in a "place open to the public or at any place where a substantial number of persons outside of a normal circle of a family and its social acquaintances is gathered").

129. 1976 House Report, at 64–65.

130. *See* On Command Video Corp. v. Columbia Pictures Industries, 777 F. Supp. 787 (N.D. Cal. 1991)(videocassette machine transmitted individualized showings of the same cassette to different hotel guestrooms at different times: held a public performance)

C. *Public Performance Right in Sound Recordings*

Conspicuously not accorded the section 106(4) exclusive right of public performance is the "sound recording," which is the work created through the combined creative efforts of performing artists and recording company—as distinguished from the "musical composition," which does get the benefit of the public-performance right. Thus, when a musical recording is played on the radio, licenses must be secured from and royalties paid to the owner of copyright in the song, but not to the owner of copyright in the sound recording. This differentiation is primarily a matter of historical development (and lobbying, notably by the National Association of Broadcasters), but has also been justified on the ground that public performances of sound recordings were a kind of free advertising for sales; the justification assumes that sales of copies (phonorecords) constitute the "real" market for sound recordings, and that any revenue from public performance would have been ancillary at most.

But in the 1990s, with the widespread development of digital media for storing and transmitting music, Congress concluded that recording artists and companies should be compensated for online performances that would likely displace the purchase of conventional recordings. In 1995, Congress thus added to the Copyright Act section 106(6), which gives the exclusive right "in the case of sound recordings, to perform the copyrighted work publicly by means of a digital audio transmission." Initially, this provided compensation for the playing of recordings on digital home subscription services akin to cable-television services, but an even greater potential source of revenue became evident as home computers, powered by the Internet, came more widely to be used to listen to music (and potentially to substitute for record purchases). Congress in 1998, as part of the Digital Millennium Copyright Act, saw the need for further articulation of policy concerning the digital transmission of music on the Internet ("nonsubscription transmission"), and many of these transmissions are allowed subject to a compulsory license, spelled out in complex detail in section 114.

Compulsory licenses are discussed in Chapter 7. For present purposes, it suffices to point out that the conditions on eligibility of the transmission for the compulsory license primarily endeavor to ensure that the transmitting organization does not facilitate a user's substitution of the recorded performance for a purchase of a copy. Hence, for example, the amendments retain the "sound recording performance complement," which, during any three-hour period, limits the number of selections from a particular album or the number of recorded performances by a particular artist; they bar the transmitting entity from advance announcement of the content of the programs; they oblige the entity to accommodate technological measures imposed by the sound

171

recording copyright owner to protect the works, and to cooperate with the sound recording copyright owner to prevent users or other third parties from scanning the transmissions to select particular transmissions.[131] The last-mentioned requirement addresses the copyright owners' concern that third parties will develop search engines that will identify and download particular sound recordings from a variety of webcasting sites. Copyright owners apparently feared that a user might employ such a search engine to find and reproduce, for example, any Grateful Dead song transmitted by any webcaster, thus enabling the user to avoid purchasing authorized Grateful Dead recordings.[132]

If the 1995 amendments produced a hybrid public-performance reproduction-right regime for sound recordings, the 1998 amendments more closely approached a full fledged performance right, albeit one in which statutory licensing may outweigh a right to prohibit. Fear of unauthorized copying still pervades the text, but the text more fully enables copyright owners to benefit from the public-performance right as an independent source of revenue. This marks an important shift in the sales-based economics of sound recordings. In the digital environment, sales of phonorecords may well persist (at least via the Internet), but performances of recorded music, whether by on-demand interactive services or by webcasting, are likely to displace acquisition of retention copies. This is because having the recorded performance is likely to matter less to consumers than hearing it, and the digital environment may well make it as easy for the user to hear the desired performance via transmission as to play her own copy of it. This observation applies to many kinds of copyrighted works beyond sound recordings. The easier it becomes to access and experience works of authorship by means of digital transmission, the less necessary, and perhaps also the less desirable, it becomes to possess retention copies. The evolution of the scope of the sound-recording copyright thus is just one manifestation of an overall change in the exploitation of works of authorship.

D. *Performing rights organizations*

It is obvious that the owners of copyright in, say, a popular song cannot personally monitor, license, and collect royalties from the potentially vast number of public performances of their music—in live nightclub and restaurant performances, in radio and television broadcasts, in background music subscription services for supermarkets, elevators and

---

131. *See* 17 U.S.C. sec. 114(d)(2)(A).

132. For a discussion of the "sound recording performance complement" and the difference between on-demand services subject to an exclusive digital public perform-ance right, and a webcasting service that tracks a user's preferences but remains within the scope of the compulsory license, see Arista Records, LLC v. Launch Media, Inc., 578 F.3d 148 (2d Cir. 2009).

production plants, on college campuses, in "streamed" music programs on the Internet, in motion picture theaters from film soundtracks, and the like. The owners of musical copyright (songwriters and their assignees, music publishers) have formed so-called performing rights societies (now generally called "performing rights organizations") to do so. The first such organization in the United States, ASCAP (American Society of Composers, Authors and Publishers), was formed in 1914 by eminent American composers including Victor Herbert and John Philip Sousa. The other major performing rights organizations are BMI (Broadcast Music, Inc.), formed in 1939, and SESAC (formerly, Society of European Stage Authors and Composers). Technically, these organizations serve as nonexclusive licensees, which in turn license others (principally entertainment venues and broadcasters) pursuant to standard royalty arrangements the terms of which are regulated by antitrust decrees. Suits for infringement, brought in the name of the copyright owner, are typically managed by representatives of the performing rights organizations. Public-performance royalties collected by these societies total about $1.5 billion per year and are distributed to their members according to elaborate formulas.[133]

V. The Right of Public Display

Under the 1909 Act, it was unclear how to treat the public display of copyrighted works (e.g., the showing of a painting, sculpture, or literary manuscript on television). This form of exploitation did not fit comfortably within the statutory terms "copy" and "performance." Congress dispelled the uncertainty by providing in section 106(5) of the 1976 Copyright Act for the exclusive right "to display the copyrighted work publicly." This right applies to all copyrighted works except for sound recordings (for obvious reasons); the showing of a motion picture or other audiovisual work is treated as a "performance," but the showing of "individual images of a motion picture or other audiovisual work" falls within the display right.

Section 101 defines the "display" of a work as the showing of "a copy of it, either directly or by means of a film, slide, television image, or any other device or process or, in the case of a motion picture or other audiovisual work, to show individual images nonsequentially." The "public" display of a work is defined in precisely the same manner as the public performance of a work. Thus, to show a painting or sculpture on a television broadcast, or via an Internet transmission from a website, is a public display of the work, which (in the absence of an applicable exemption) must be authorized in order to avoid infringement.

---

133. *See* Matthew S. DelNero, *Long Overdue: An Exploration of the Status and Merit of a General Public Performance* *Right in Sound Recordings*, 51 J. COPYR. Soc. 473 (2004).

Were the language of section 106(5) not conditioned in any way, the owner of a copyrighted work of art would infringe by displaying the work in a place open to the public, such as a gallery, museum, restaurant or retail space. But, just as Congress's accommodation of the private property right in the owner's material object has counterbalanced the right of "public distribution" through the first-sale doctrine, so too has Congress decided to limit the public-display right by a specific exemption for the owner of the physical object in which the copyrighted work is embodied. Section 109(c) provides:

> Notwithstanding the provisions of section 106(5), the owner of a particular copy lawfully made under this title, or any person authorized by such owner, is entitled, without the authority of the copyright owner, to display that copy publicly, either directly or by the projection of no more than one image at a time, to viewers present at the place where the copy is located.

Thus, a face-to-face display by the owner of a copy of a copyrighted work to a public gathering will not infringe; nor will the use of a projection device to throw an image of the work onto a screen. If, however, the display is by closed-circuit television with the work in one location and the viewers in another, or if the display is by multiple television screens or computer screen to facilitate closer audience viewing, the exemption in section 109(c) will not obtain, and the unauthorized display will constitute an infringement. This fine line reflects Congress's desire to protect the copyright interest of the artist against the incursion of new technological developments that may threaten to displace the artist's market for individual copies (with attendant dilution of royalty rights).

The public-display right of the copyright owner has taken on added significance with the development of the Internet. If, for example, a copyright-protected work of art is incorporated on a website, so that the accessing of that site by any Internet user produces an image of that artwork on a computer screen, this constitutes a public display, which, if unauthorized by the rightholder or by an applicable exception, will infringe. (The same is true for the text of a literary work.) A number of courts have held that the unauthorized scanning of a copyrighted picture from a magazine, and its resulting conversion into digital form for storage on a computer hard-drive—an infringing "reproduction"—will generate an infringing public display when that image is made available by "uploading" over the Internet (on a website or bulletin board) to persons who can then view the image on their computer (whether or not they make an additional analog or digital retention copy at the receiving end).[134]

---

134. Playboy Enters., Inc. v. Webbworld, Inc., 991 F. Supp. 543 (N.D. Tex. 1997); Playboy Enters., Inc. v. Frena, 839 F. Supp. 1552 (M.D. Fla. 1993). *But see*

On the other hand, it has also been held that a search engine which "frames" a webpage that shows the copyrighted work, is not "displaying" the depicted work. In *Perfect 10 v. Amazon.com*,[135] the plaintiff publisher of "adult" print and online magazines, claimed that Google violated its exclusive right to publicly display its copyrighted photographs. When a user employs the Google search engine to locate photographs, Google will display thumbnail images that respond to the search query. If the user clicks on one of those images, he will be directed to the website on which the photograph is stored, but will perceive the full-size image (in the context of the webpage on which it appears) through the frame of the Google website. As a result of this "in-line framing" the user will experience the display as if it were emanating from Google, but in fact the image will be residing on a third party computer. The Ninth Circuit, endorsing the "server theory" of public display, held that Google publicly displayed the thumbnails, which were stored on Google's servers, but not the full-size images, which were stored on other computers.[136]

VI. Visual Artists' Rights

In the Visual Artists Rights Act (VARA) of 1990, Congress amended the Copyright Act to give to an "author of a work of visual art" rights that are different from those given to a copyright owner. These are the rights of "attribution and integrity" and are equivalent to those "moral rights" traditionally recognized in most civil-law nations as well as in the Berne Convention.

CoStar Group v. LoopNet Inc., 373 F.3d 544 (4th Cir. 2004) (holding ISP not liable for uploaded infringing images despite ISP's control of upload process).

135. 508 F.3d 1146 (9th Cir. 2007). *See also* Righthaven LLC v. Choudhry, No. 2:10–CV–2155 JCM(PAL), 2011 WL 1743839 at*2 (D. Nevada May 3, 2011) ("[T]he process of 'linking' may not constitute direct copyright infringement under *Perfect 10*."). *But see* Flava Works v. Gunter, No. 10 C 6517, 2011 WL 3876910 at *4 (N.D. Ill. Sept. 1, 2011) ("To the extent *Perfect 10* can be read to stand for the proposition that inline linking can never cause a display of images or videos that would give rise to a claim of direct copyright infringement, we respectfully disagree.").

136. By endorsing the "server theory," the Ninth Circuit arguably ignored the specificity of the display right, conflating it with the reproduction right. For an analysis of the application of the display right to the Internet, *see* R. Anthony Reese, *The Public Display Right: The Copyright Act's Neglected Solution to the Controversy Over RAM "Copies,"* 2001 U. ILL. L. REV. 83 (2001), contending that the legislative history of section 106 makes clear that the display right "fundamentally gives copyright owners control over the transmission of their images or texts from one place to another" and that "transmitted displays of work over computer networks . . . raise precisely the concern that the display right was intended to address." *Id.* at 86–92, 114. Applying the display right in lieu of the reproduction right, particularly regarding RAM copies, ensures that "specific rights implicated by . . . transmitting images over the World Wide Web[ ] be properly identified" and limits copyright owners to asserting only those rights which are properly under their control. *Id.* at 115.

These statutory rights are accorded by section 106A to persons who, under the definition of "work of visual art"[137] in section 101 of the Copyright Act, create singular paintings, sculptures, or photographs produced for exhibition only, or such works in a signed and numbered series of no more than 200.

The "right of attribution" entitles a visual artist to "claim authorship" of a work of visual art, and to prevent the use of his or her name as author of a work created by another or as author of his or her own work in distorted or mutilated form. The artist could, for example, secure an injunction directing a museum to identify a displayed work as her own (rather than misattributing it to another artist), or seek money damages for harm to her reputation that results from attributing to her a physically mangled canvas or sculpture.

The "right of integrity" entitles the visual artist "to prevent any intentional distortion, mutilation, or other modification of that work which would be prejudicial to his or her honor or reputation." If, for example, an artist produces a three-segment painting, and a purchaser of that painting separates the three segments in an effort to maximize the proceeds of resale (or simply for display in three separate locations), the artist has a claim for copyright infringement provided she can prove that there has been prejudice to her reputation. Section 106A—as part of the right of integrity—also bars the intentional or grossly negligent "destruction of a work of recognized stature." (The latter term—a departure from the fundamental copyright principle that proof of artistic merit is not a prerequisite to copyright protection[138]—is not defined, although its content was delineated in earlier versions of the legislation.)

The 1990 amendments also added a new section 113(d) to deal with the removal of works of visual art that are incorporated into buildings, such as murals or fixed statuary. But courts have held that VARA does not protect "site-specific" artwork, thus rejecting a sculptor's VARA claim against the transfer of his sculptures from a park for whose landscape they had been created.[139]

VARA excludes from infringement the modification or distortion of a work that results from the "passage of time or the inherent nature of the materials" or that results from conservation efforts (unless grossly negligent) or from the lighting or placement of the work in a public exhibition. Perhaps most important, the statute expressly excludes from

---

137. The definition is narrowly drawn, and excludes *inter alia* "advertising." *See* Pollara v. Seymour, 344 F.3d 265 (2d Cir. 2003).

138. *See supra* Chapter 1; Burrow–Giles Lithographic Co. v. Sarony, 111 U.S. 53 (1884).

139. Phillips v. Pembroke Real Estate, Inc., 459 F.3d 128 (1st Cir. 2006). *But see* Kelley v. Chicago Park District, 635 F.3d 290, 307 (7th Cir. 2011) (discussing reasons *"Phillips'*s all or nothing approach to site-specific art may be unwarranted").

its ban alleged distortions or mutilations that take the form of "any reproduction, depiction, portrayal, or other use of a work" in books, magazines, newspapers, posters, advertising material, motion pictures and other forms set forth in sections 101 and 106A(c)(3). In other words, it is the physical integrity of the singular work of art that is protected, and not its use in discolored or badly cropped reproductions. (Such reproductions might, however, be barred by the copyright owner as unauthorized derivative works prepared in violation of section 106(2).)

Because a "work of visual art" is a category that fits within the larger category of "pictorial, graphic and sculptural work," a case could arise in which an artist's right of integrity conflicts with the rights of a copyright owner to create a derivative work under section 106(2). Thus, if in the hypothetical set forth above, the artist of a three-segment painting were to transfer both the physical property and the copyright in that painting to another, the copyright owner's claim to separate the segments—and thus to create "derivative works"—could presumably be defeated by the artist's claim under section 106A that such action constitutes an infringing distortion, mutilation, or modification. The 1990 amendments provide for the independence of section 106 exclusive rights and the VARA integrity right: neither transfer of the physical copy of the work nor of its copyright transfers the visual artist's rights,[140] but they do not expressly address this possible clash of statutory rights. A solution may nonetheless be inferred from the "transfer and waiver" provision of VARA,[141] which provides that the artist's rights, including the right to prevent prejudicial modifications to the work, may be expressly waived. The required signed writing must "specifically identify the work, and the uses of that work, to which the waiver applies ..." Because the acquirer of the derivative works right may seek a waiver from the artist to permit a particular modification of the work, in the absence of such a waiver one should conclude that that artist's VARA rights limit that particular exercise of the derivative works right.

Under section 106A(d)(2), the protections of VARA are not afforded to works created (i.e., fixed in a tangible medium) before the effective date of that Act, June 1, 1991, unless the title to such work was not as of that date transferred from the artist.[142]

---

140. 17 U.S.C. sec. 106A(e)(2); *see also* 106A(a) ("Subject to section 107 and independent of the exclusive rights provided in section 106 ...")

141. *Id.* sec. 106A(e)(1).

142. *See* Pavia v. 1120 Ave. of the Americas Assocs., 901 F. Supp. 620 (S.D.N.Y. 1995) (work was created, title was transferred, and work was dismantled without authorization, all before June 1991; its continued display in that condition after June 1991 was held not to violate VARA).

Chapter 7

FAIR USE AND OTHER EXEMPTIONS FROM THE EXCLUSIVE RIGHTS OF THE COPYRIGHT OWNER

All of the rights set forth in section 106 of the Copyright Act are expressly granted "subject to sections 107 through 122." The latter sections impose a variety of limits on the rights of the copyright owner, in the form of compulsory licenses, complete exemptions from liability, and other privileges such as fair use. A discussion of the jurisprudence that has developed under section 107 dealing with fair use is followed by an overview of sections 108 through 122.

I. Fair Use

The fair use doctrine constitutes perhaps the most significant limitation on the exclusive rights held by a copyright owner. The doctrine was developed by courts in the mid-nineteenth century. Ironically, the first case to articulate factors that Congress subsequently adapted into section 107 of the 1976 Copyright Act, Justice Story's decision in *Folsom v. Marsh*,[1] rendered in the Massachusetts federal circuit court in 1841, adduced these considerations in order to *expand* the scope of copyright to reach certain kinds of derivative works.[2] Justice Story focused on the impact of the defendant's work upon the market for the plaintiff's. He opined that quoting copyrighted material in the course of preparing a biography or a critical commentary might be excusable, but not "if so much is taken, that the value of the original is sensibly diminished, or the labors of the original author are substantially to an injurious extent appropriated by another."[3] He thought it proper to consider "the nature and objects of the selections made" and "the quantity and value of the materials used."[4] Later courts also placed weight on whether unauthorized quotation of copyrighted material "would serve the public interest in the free dissemination of information" and whether the preparation of the defendant's work "requires some use of prior materials dealing with the same subject matter."[5] Although some courts and scholars anchored

---

1. 9 F. Cas. 342 (C.C.D. Mass. 1841) (No. 4,901).

2. *See* R. Anthony Reese, *The Story of Folsom v. Marsh: Distinguishing Between Infringing and Legitimate Uses, in* INTELLECTUAL PROPERTY STORIES 259 (Jane C. Gins-

burg & Rochelle Cooper Dreyfuss eds., 2005).

3. *Id.* at 348.

4. *Id.*

5. Rosemont Enters. v. Random House, Inc., 366 F.2d 303 (2d Cir. 1966).

"fair use" in the plaintiff's implied consent to quotation, as when excerpts are used in literary criticism or comment, this consent proved to be fictive more often than not.

The more soundly based rationale for the fair use doctrine is the very purpose articulated in the constitutional copyright clause: "to promote the progress of science."[6] The fair use doctrine comes into play when a too literal enforcement of the copyright owner's rights would operate to the detriment of the public interest in access to and dissemination of knowledge and culture, and unauthorized copying can be tolerated without significant economic injury to the copyright owner.[7] These two prongs, promotion of learning and lack of economic injury, underlie the two principal currents of fair use cases under the 1976 Copyright Act: copying in order to create a new work that advances the progress of knowledge, and copying in order to exploit new, usually technologically-driven, forms of dissemination. The first line of cases confronts two (or more) different creators: the author of the copied work, and the author of the work that copies from it. The fair use doctrine in appropriate circumstances frees second authors from the constraints of the first authors' copyrights. In these instances, fair use advances First Amendment goals.[8] In the second line of cases, any First Amendment claims derive from the public's interest in receiving "information," rather than from a new creator's interest in speaking (and hence may seem comparatively less compelling[9]), but the absence of market harm, or the failure of a relevant market to emerge, may justify the exception.[10]

The 1976 House Report set forth a number of examples of possible fair uses, as generally understood under the 1909 Act:

> quotation of excerpts in a review or criticism for purposes of illustration or comment; quotation of short passages in a scholarly or technical work, for illustration or clarification of the author's observations; use in a parody of some of the content of the work parodied; summary of an address or article, with brief quotations, in a news report; reproduction by a library of a portion of a work to replace part of a damaged copy; reproduction by a teacher or student of a small part of a work to

---

6. U.S. Const. Art. I, § 8, cl. 8.

7. *See generally* Campbell v. Acuff–Rose Music, Inc., 510 U.S. 569 (1994).

8. Harper & Row Publishers, Inc. v. Nation Enters., 471 U.S. 539, 559–60 (1985); *see also* Eldred v. Ashcroft, 537 U.S. 186, 219–20 (2003).

9. *See, e.g., Harper & Row,* 471 U.S. at 555; *Eldred,* 537 U.S. at 221 ("The First Amendment securely protects the freedom to make—or decline to make—one's own

speech; it bears less heavily when speakers assert the right to make other people's speeches.").

10. *See* Wendy J. Gordon, *Fair Use as Market Failure: A Structural and Economic Analysis of the Betamax Case and Its Predecessors,* 82 Colum. L. Rev. 1600 (1982); *see also* Robert P. Merges, *Intellectual Property and the Costs of Commercial Exchange: A Review Essay,* 93 Mich. L. Rev. 1570 (1995).

illustrate a lesson; reproduction of a work in legislative or judicial proceedings or reports; incidental and fortuitous reproduction, in a newsreel or broadcast, of a work located in the scene of an event being reported.[11]

Although it was easy enough to give a variety of readily accepted examples of fair use, it was not so easy to articulate any clear standards or a "litmus test." "Indeed, since the doctrine is an equitable rule of reason, no generally applicable definition is possible, and each case raising the question must be decided on its own facts."[12]

A. *Statutory uses and factors*

In the 1976 Copyright Act, Congress took the bold steps of incorporating the fair use doctrine into the statute, of setting forth a number of illustrative potential fair uses and, most important, of delineating four factors that courts are to consider (possibly along with other factors) when passing upon a fair use defense. Section 107 provides:

> Notwithstanding the provisions of section 106, the fair use of a copyrighted work, including such use by reproduction in copies or phonorecords or by any other means specified by that section, for purposes such as criticism, comment, news reporting, teaching (including multiple copies for classroom use), scholarship, or research, is not an infringement of copyright. In determining whether the use made of a work in any particular case is a fair use the factors to be considered shall include—
>
> (1) the purpose and character of the use, including whether such use is of a commercial nature or is for nonprofit educational purposes;
>
> (2) the nature of the copyrighted work;
>
> (3) the amount and substantiality of the portion used in relation to the copyrighted work as a whole; and
>
> (4) the effect of the use upon the potential market for or value of the copyrighted work.
>
> The fact that a work is unpublished shall not of itself bar a finding of fair use if such finding is made upon consideration of all the above factors.[13]

The drafters of section 107 regarded it as endorsing

11. H.R. Rep. No. 94–1476, at 65 (1976).

12. *Id.*

13. This final sentence was added in 1992, to deal with the issue raised in several then-recent court of appeals decisions involving biographers' and historians' use of unpublished letters, diaries and the like.

the purpose and general scope of the judicial doctrine of fair use, but there is no disposition to freeze the doctrine in the statute, especially during a period of rapid technological change.... [T]he courts must be free to adapt the doctrine to particular situations on a case-by-case basis. Section 107 is intended to restate the present judicial doctrine of fair use, not to change, narrow, or enlarge it in any way.[14]

The Supreme Court has held that "fair use is a mixed question of law and fact."[15] If a district court has found facts sufficient to evaluate each of the statutory factors, the court of appeals may determine, without remand, whether the defendant has made a fair use of copyrighted material as a matter of law.

1. The Preamble

The opening paragraph of section 107 sets forth a number of illustrative uses that may fall within the fair use privilege. The listed uses are indicative of the kinds of uses that have traditionally been held to be fair, but the presence of defendant's use on the list, or for that matter, its absence from the list, is by no means determinative, as the first two Supreme Court decisions that construed section 107 illustrate. In *Sony Corp. of America v. Universal City Studios, Inc.,*[16] the Court sustained a claim of fair use for home videotaping of copyrighted free broadcast television programs (for more convenient viewing)—a use rather clearly falling outside the enumerated categories. In *Harper & Row Publishers, Inc. v. Nation Enterprises,*[17] involving a news magazine's quotations from the soon-to-be-published memoirs of President Ford relating to his pardon of President Nixon—a use falling rather clearly within the enumerated category of news reporting—the Court rejected the defendant's claim of fair use. In explaining the weight to be given to the listing of uses in the first sentence of section 107, the Court in *Harper & Row* stated that the enumeration "give[s] some idea of the sort of activities the courts might regard as fair use under the circumstances.... This listing was not intended to be exhaustive, ... or to single out any particular use as presumptively a 'fair' use."[18] The Court made clear that whether a use is fair in particular circumstances "will depend upon the application of the determinative factors, including those mentioned in the second sentence."[19] Even though the enumerated uses

---

14. H.R. Rep. No. 94–1476, at 66 (1976).

15. Harper & Row Publishers, Inc. v. Nation Enters., 471 U.S. 539, 560 (1985).

16. 464 U.S. 417 (1984).

17. 471 U.S. 539 (1985).

18. *Id.* at 561 (citations omitted).

19. *Id.* (citing S. Rep. No. 94–473, at 62 (1975)). A court of appeals had concluded, shortly before, that consideration of at least the four factors in the second sentence was a mandated part of the fair use analysis, by pointing out Congress's use of the phrase "shall include" in that sentence. Pacific &

in the first sentence are not dispositive and not even presumptive, they have nonetheless come to play an important role in application of the first of the four factors in the second sentence ("purpose and character of the use"), as later elaborated by the Supreme Court in *Campbell v. Acuff–Rose Music, Inc.*, discussed below.

2.   The four factors: Supreme Court fair use jurisprudence

The Supreme Court has decided several cases involving the application of the fair use doctrine and section 107 of the Copyright Act. In *Sony Corp. of America v. Universal City Studios, Inc.*,[20] decided in 1984, the Court, dividing 5 to 4, reviewed the statutory factors somewhat hurriedly and found that home videotaping of free broadcast television programs, for more convenient time-shifting purposes, constituted a fair use. The Court held that the first factor supported fair use because the home viewer taped the program for personal and noncommercial use. The Court majority in fact announced that "every commercial use of copyrighted material is presumptively an unfair [use]" and also presumptively demonstrates a likelihood of economic harm to the copyright owner (the fourth statutory factor); "but if [the copying] is for a noncommercial purpose, the likelihood must be demonstrated."[21] The Court acknowledged that, even though typically the entire program was taped (the third factor), this was not particularly damaging to the fair use contention because the public had been invited to view the program in its entirety for free. Finally, upon examination of the factual record, the Court concluded that there was inadequate evidence that home taping for time-shifting purposes would have any material adverse impact upon the market for the plaintiffs' programming, either in its initial exhibition or in later exhibition on television (reruns) or even potentially in motion picture theaters.

The four dissenters strongly disagreed with respect to the application and conclusion of the four-factor analysis. Notably, Justice Blackmun, writing for the minority, stressed that the majority asked the wrong question regarding the impact of time-shifting on the market for the work: "The Court has struggled mightily to show that VTR use has not *reduced* the value of the Studios' copyrighted works in their *present* markets. Even if true, that showing only begins the proper inquiry. The development of the VTR has created a new market for the works produced by the Studios."[22] Lower courts in subsequent decisions have

---

S. Co. v. Duncan, 744 F.2d 1490 (11th Cir. 1984). *See also* Campbell v. Acuff–Rose Music, Inc., 510 U.S. 569, 581 (1994) ("[P]arody, like any other use, has to work its way through the relevant factors, and be judged case by case, in light of the ends of the copyright law.").

20.   464 U.S. 417 (1984).

21.   *Id.* at 451.

22.   464 U.S. at 497–98 (Blackmun, J. dissenting).

heeded Justice Blackmun's reminder that the relevant market in cases involving new technological exploitations of works is not only the market for previously-established kinds of exploitation but also, perhaps especially, the emerging market created by the new technological means, a market which may come to rival or even displace the original.[23] It may seem odd at first blush for the copyright owner to control the exploitation of works through means the copyright owner had no hand in devising, but in that respect today's new technologies are no different than ones now old: for example, composers did not invent the radio, but courts recognized that radio broadcasts were public performances for profit (under the 1909 Act), and, accordingly, that broadcasters must acquire licenses from the composers.[24]

The Court divided again (6 to 3) the following year in *Harper & Row Publishers, Inc. v. Nation Enterprises.*[25] There, the defendant publisher of *The Nation* magazine secured a "purloined manuscript" of President Ford's memoirs, about to be published by Harper & Row and excerpted in *Time* magazine; the defendant broke its story about the Ford pardon of Richard Nixon and quoted verbatim some 300 words from the unpublished manuscript. The Court traced the development of the fair use doctrine and noted its nearly nonexistent application to unpublished works under prior copyright law. It rejected the defendant's claim that First Amendment concerns warranted contracting the scope of copyright; Justice O'Connor stressed that "In our haste to disseminate news, it should not be forgotten that the Framers intended copyright itself to be the engine of free expression. By establishing a marketable right to the use of one's expression, copyright supplies the economic incentive to create and disseminate ideas." The Court concluded, instead, that First Amendment interests are already protected under copyright doctrines such as fair use and the idea-expression dichotomy. The Court also rejected the contention that works of public figures are entitled to lesser copyright protection, and ruled against fair use.

The Court acknowledged that news reporting was one of the illustrative uses in the preamble of section 107, but invoked the presumption from the *Sony* case against commercial uses such as *The Nation*'s so that the defendant bore the burden of proving its use to be fair (typically by showing no adverse market impact upon the plaintiff's work).[26] As to the second statutory factor, the Court conceded that "the law generally

---

23. *See, e.g.,* A & M Records, Inc. v. Napster, Inc., 239 F.3d 1004 (9th Cir. 2001), discussed *infra.*

24. *See, e.g.,* M. Witmark & Sons v. L. Bamberger & Co., 291 F. 776 (D.N.J. 1923).

25. 471 U.S. 539 (1985).

26. Given that fair use is an affirmative defense, as to which the defendant bears the burden of persuasion, Infinity Broadcast Corp. v. Kirkwood, 150 F.3d 104, 107 (2d Cir. 1998), it is not clear what Sony's (now largely abandoned) commercial-use presumption in fact adds to the analysis.

recognizes a greater need to disseminate factual works than works of fiction or fantasy,"[27] but it concluded that *The Nation* had copied more than merely objective facts. Moreover, "the fact that a work is unpublished is a critical element of its 'nature',"[28] a "key, though not necessarily determinative factor" against fair use.[29] Although a relatively small part of the Ford manuscript was copied, it comprised a large part of the article in *The Nation* and, most significantly, was qualitatively among the most important parts of the manuscript—its "heart," containing the "most powerful passages," the "dramatic focal points" of great "expressive value." The Court characterized the fourth statutory factor—effect upon the potential market for the copyrighted work—as "undoubtedly the single most important element of fair use."[30] It pointed out that the "scooping" by *The Nation* caused *Time* to cancel its contract with Harper & Row to publish excerpts. Moreover, "[t]his inquiry must take account not only of harm to the original but also of harm to the market for derivative works,"[31] for the statute refers to adverse effect upon the "potential market" for the work.

Thus, after *Sony* and *Harper & Row*, it appeared that there would be a compelling case against fair use should the record show a commercial use by the defendant, or a potentially significant adverse economic impact on the copyrighted work, or an unpublished copyrighted work. Indeed, as to the latter element, a number of court of appeals decisions[32] gave such great weight, in cases involving biographies, to the unpublished nature of letters, diaries and the like—the core source materials of historical and biographical writings—that Congress stepped in in 1992 to add a new closing sentence to section 107: "The fact that a work is unpublished shall not itself bar a finding of fair use if such finding is made upon consideration of all the above factors."

In its most recent foray into the waters of fair use,[33] the Supreme Court used an arguably unappealing set of facts to dispel some misconceptions from the earlier cases and to establish important guidelines that have since informed the analysis of the lower courts. In *Campbell v.*

27. *Harper & Row*, 471 U.S. at 563.

28. *Id.* at 564.

29. *Id.* at 554.

30. *Id.* at 566.

31. *Id.* at 568.

32. *E.g.*, Salinger v. Random House, Inc., 811 F.2d 90 (2d Cir. 1987). *Compare* New Era Pubs. Int'l v. Henry Holt & Co., 873 F.2d 576 (2d Cir.), *reh'g en banc denied*, 884 F.2d 659 (2d Cir. 1989), *with* New Era Pubs. Int'l v. Carol Publ'g Group, 904 F.2d 152 (2d Cir. 1990).

33. Stewart v. Abend, 495 U.S. 207 (1990), involved what the Court found to be the unauthorized marketing by the copyright owners of the well-known motion picture *Rear Window*, over the objection of the owner of copyright in the short mystery story upon which the film was based. The Court rejected the fair use defense: "[A]ll four factors point to unfair use. 'This case presents a classic example of an unfair use: a commercial use of a fictional story that adversely affects the story owner's adaptation rights.'" *Id.* at 238.

Acuff–Rose Music, Inc.,[34] a rap group named 2 Live Crew—after requesting and being denied permission to record a rap parody of the well-known rock song by Roy Orbison, "Oh, Pretty Woman"—recorded it anyway, borrowing the distinctive opening guitar pattern, mimicking the opening "Pretty Woman" phrase in each verse, and adding somewhat salacious lyrics to the rhythm of the original. The court of appeals ruled against fair use, relying heavily upon what clearly appeared to be the Supreme Court cases strongly disfavoring commercial uses and the copying of the "heart" of a copyrighted work.

The Supreme Court unanimously reversed. It held that parody—poking fun at an earlier copyright-protected work, as distinguished from using the copyrighted work as a vehicle to poke fun at some extrinsic happening or individual (satire)—is a form of "criticism or comment" listed in the first sentence of section 107; but that sentence is meant to give only "general guidance" about uses commonly found to be fair. As to the four statutory factors, they must not "be treated in isolation, one from another. All are to be explored, and the results weighed together, in light of the purposes of copyright."[35]

In examining the first factor, the Court downgraded the importance of the defendants' "commercial use," noting that essentially all fair use claims (and the uses enumerated in the first sentence) are made in the for-profit context of publishing and broadcasting. The key issue is whether the defendant has made a "transformative" use: not one that merely supersedes the objects of the earlier work by copying it, but that "adds something new, with a further purpose or different character, altering the first with new expression, meaning, or message."[36] A court must inquire "whether a parodic character may reasonably be perceived," and no attention should be given to whether it is in good or bad taste (an issue that had been mooted in earlier decisions in the lower courts).

As to the second factor, a court must determine whether the copyrighted work falls close "to the core of intended copyright protection" because it is creative (rather than essentially factual): the exemplar "Oh, Pretty Woman" was said to do so. But that factor will count for little in the context of parody because parodies generally skewer more works of fiction and entertainment than of fact.

---

34. 510 U.S. 569 (1994).

35. *Id.* at 578. The Court, through Justice Souter, gave credit to Justice Story, and *Folsom v. Marsh*, 9 F. Cas. 342 (C.C.D. Mass. 1841) (No. 4,901), discussed *supra* page 178, for fashioning decisional criteria that were essentially incorporated by Congress in section 107 nearly 150 years later.

36. *Id.* at 579. The Court borrowed the phrase "transformative use" from an article by Second Circuit Judge Pierre Leval, *Toward a Fair Use Standard*, 103 Harv. L. Rev. 1105, 1111–12 (1990).

The court of appeals had emphasized the third factor, and the taking of the qualitative "heart" of that song, but the Supreme Court— although it acknowledged that "quality and importance" of the copied material should count as well as quantity (a proposition it had already advanced in *Harper & Row*)—observed that the lower court had failed to take account of the special nature of parody. "When parody takes aim at a particular original work, the parody must be able to 'conjure up' at least enough of that original to make the object of its critical wit recognizable. . . . [T]he heart is . . . what most readily conjures up the song for parody, and it is the heart at which parody takes aim. Copying does not become excessive in relation to parodic purpose merely because the portion taken was the original's heart."[37]

As for the fourth factor, and any adverse market impact that was to be "presumed" under *Sony* by virtue of the defendants' commercial use, the *Campbell* decision significantly altered the standard: A presumption of market harm is not applicable to a case involving something beyond "verbatim copying of the original in its entirety,"[38] and thus not to a "transformative" work, particularly for a parody which serves a "different market function." Indeed, by invoking "the rule that there is no protectible derivative market for criticism," the court indicated, as a normative (rather than empirical) matter, that there is no legally cognizable market for parody. "The market for potential derivative uses includes only those that creators of original works would in general develop or license others to develop. Yet the unlikelihood that creators of imaginative works will license critical reviews or lampoons of their own productions removes such uses from the very notion of a potential licensing market."[39] Even were authors likely to license authorized parodies, we would not want authors to restrain unauthorized criticism on the ground that the critique competes with other commentaries for which the author might be paid. One might add that the concept of an authorized parody by its own oxymoronic terms makes a mockery of the parodist's enterprise.

The Court remanded to allow the lower court to consider further evidence of market harm (flowing from rap-music substitution and not from parodic criticism), the amount of copyrighted material taken and what the defendants added to it, and other elements noted by the Court in its opinion. The case subsequently settled.

With its decision in *Campbell*, the Supreme Court on the one hand diluted the litigative presumptions of the earlier cases and emphasized the complementary and interactive nature of the four statutory factors, but pointed toward the "transformative" standard and potential adverse

---

37. *Campbell*, 510 U.S. at 588.　　　**39.** *Id*. at 592.
38. *Id*. at 591.

market harm as of central importance to fair use analysis. The Court also noted that in cases of parody and other critical works in which a fair use defense is found unpersuasive, an injunction need not automatically issue to remedy the infringement; the public's interest in the publication of the later work and the interest of the copyright owner may both be protected by an award of damages. (As we will see in Chapter 9, the court's suggestion regarding the withholding of injunctive relief is bearing more general fruit.)

B. *Fair use and the creation of new works*

With the Supreme Court jurisprudence in mind, it is useful to divide the lower court decisions dealing with fair use into two categories: those in which the defendant has borrowed for the purpose of creating a new work, and those in which the defendant has made and disseminated what are substantially copies of an earlier work with the aid of new technologies. In the former situation, the more permissive attitude toward "transformative" works would be expected to result in more frequent findings of fair use. This has in fact been the case, not only for new works but, perhaps more surprisingly, in some instances of new dissemination, as we will see. In any event, the Supreme Court's emphasis in *Campbell v. Acuff–Rose Music, Inc.*[40] upon the case-by-case determination of fair use claims, and the interwoven nature of the four statutory factors, defy confident predictions of case outcomes.

1. "Transformative use"

Under the first fair use factor, the courts have indeed given great weight to the "transformative" aspects of an otherwise infringing work, but the decisions do not form an altogether coherent pattern. Moreover, contradictions have come to riddle the assessment of whether a work is transformative. Notably, the "transformative" qualities which might weigh in defendant's favor under the first factor might also undermine the author's exclusive right to create or authorize the creation of derivative works. While courts recognize this paradox, their analyses do not consistently offer a satisfactory exit from the impasse. More fundamentally, recent cases evidence a drift from "transformative *work*" to "transformative *purpose*;" in the latter instance, copying of an entire work, without creating a new work, may be excused if the court perceives a sufficient public benefit in the appropriation.

Examples of incoherence regarding transformative *works* are several courts of appeals cases involving parodies. The Ninth Circuit Court of

40. 510 U.S. 569 (1994).

Appeals, rejecting a fair use defense, held that it was not transformative to use the well-known "Cat in the Hat" poem of Dr. Seuss as the basis for a fully rewritten poem telling the story of the O.J. Simpson criminal trial.[41] The Second Circuit also held against a fair use defense on the part of the publisher of a 132–page book containing some 643 newly written trivia questions designed to test its readers' recollection of scenes and events from the *Seinfeld* television series; among other things, the court noted that the trivia game "is not critical of the program, nor does it parody the program; if anything, [it] pays homage to *Seinfeld*."[42] The court also found that the "trivia" market niche is one that the producers of *Seinfeld* might well wish to develop for themselves in the future.

On the other hand, that same court held transformative and a fair use a photograph combining the head of a middle-aged male comic actor with a nude pregnant female body meant to duplicate the Annie Leibovitz cover for *Vanity Fair* magazine showing the actress Demi Moore— even though the doctored photograph was used in an advertisement and only marginally "commented" upon the Leibovitz original.[43] And in *Suntrust Bank v. Houghton Mifflin Co.*,[44] decided in 2001, the Eleventh Circuit upheld the fair use defense of *The Wind Done Gone* (TWDG) against an infringement claim by the owners of copyright in the classic novel *Gone With the Wind* (GWTW). The former novel borrowed 18 characters from GWTW, made only transparent changes in the character names, and for much of the book recounted many of the same incidents—but altogether altered the virtues and vices of the white and the black characters, and made concomitant alterations in the story line, so that "the institutions and values romanticized in GWTW are exposed as corrupt in TWDG."[45] The court characterized TWDG as a parody in the sense of critical commentary, even though it lacked a comedic tone and did not take the form of scholarly or journalistic commentary.

In the cases just evoked, the courts seemed to be struggling with the distinction, enunciated in *Campbell*, between parody, which mocks the copied work, and satire, which copies from the work in order to make fun of or to criticize something else. The Supreme Court recognized the need to copy from the targeted work in the case of a parody, but questioned the claim to fair use in the case of a satire: if the joke is on

---

41. Dr. Seuss Enters., L.P. v. Penguin Books USA, Inc., 109 F.3d 1394 (9th Cir. 1997).

42. Castle Rock Entm't, Inc. v. Carol Publ'g Group, Inc., 150 F.3d 132, 145 (2d Cir. 1998) (quoting lower court); *id.* at 143 (defendant's purpose "is not to expose *Seinfeld*'s 'nothingness,' but to satiate *Seinfeld* fans' passion for the 'nothingness' that *Seinfeld* has elevated into the realm of protectable creative expression."). *Accord,* Rog-

ers v. Koons, 960 F.2d 301 (2d Cir. 1992) (Jeff Koons sculpture based on plaintiff's photograph did not comment on the photograph).

43. Leibovitz v. Paramount Pictures Corp., 137 F.3d 109 (2d Cir. 1998).

44. 268 F.3d 1257 (11th Cir. 2001) (preliminary injunction denied).

45. *Id.* at 1267.

something else, then there is less if any need to copy from the plaintiff's work. As a result, courts often either woodenly applied the distinction (*Dr. Seuss Ents.*), or strained to find a parodic purpose (*Leibovitz*).

More recent appellate court decisions, however, appear less shackled by the distinction. The Ninth Circuit in *Mattel, Inc. v. Walking Mountain Productions*,[46] in upholding the fair use defense, recognized that the defendant's message might both mock the copyrighted work and make a broader social point. In that case, in a series of 78 photographs, titled "Food Chain Barbie," defendant photographer Forsythe depicted a Barbie doll, often without clothes, victimized by a variety of kitchen appliances (and appearing occasionally to enjoy it). Forsythe described the message behind his photographic series as an attempt to "critique the objectification of women associated with [Barbie], and to lambaste the conventional beauty myth and the societal acceptance of women as objects because this is what Barbie embodies."[47] And in *Blanch v. Koons*,[48] the Second Circuit found appropriation artist Jeff Koons's incorporation of a substantial part of plaintiff's advertising photograph into a collage to be a "transformative" commentary because Koons used the "image as fodder for his commentary on the social and aesthetic consequences of mass media," even though Koons's commentary did not take aim at the image itself (indeed, Koons testified that he treated the photograph as a "fact in the world").[49]

Blanch v. Koons also evidences the expansion of "transformativeness" to embrace copying for "an entirely different purpose and meaning,"[50] even when the copying does not significantly alter the copied work. Thus, in *Bill Graham Archives v. Dorling Kindersley Ltd.*,[51] the Second Circuit held "transformative" reduced-sized complete images of posters of the legendary rock band the Grateful Dead by the publisher of a coffee-table-book biography of the group because the book used the images of the posters as "historical artifacts" to document the Dead's concerts, rather than for the posters' original aesthetic purpose.

The documentary/aesthetic distinction has, as we shall see, significantly expanded the application of the fair use exception to new technological uses. But even in more traditional contexts, the distinction in purpose can help ensure that the copyright in a work does not preclude third parties from producing a work *about* the copied work, so long as they do not copy more than needed for the documentary purpose. By

---

46.   353 F.3d 792 (9th Cir. 2003).

47.   *Id.* at 796.

48.   467 F.3d 244 (2d Cir. 2006).

49.   *Id.* at 252. *But see* Cariou v. Prince, 784 F.Supp.2d 337 (S.D.N.Y. 2011) (copying

"the photographs he appropriates for what he perceives to be their truth" without any discernible commentary, held not "transformative").

50.   *Blanch*, 467 F.3d at 253.

51.   448 F.3d 605 (2d Cir. 2006).

contrast, courts discount the assertions of documentary purpose if they perceive that the defendant has reproduced the copied author's "original expression for its inherent entertainment and aesthetic value."[52]

In an influential decision arising in a quite different context—reverse engineering (and thus copying) a computer program embodied in a game console—the Ninth Circuit in *Sega Enterprises, Ltd. v. Accolade, Inc.*[53] upheld the defense of fair use. The defendant's purpose was to create an "intermediate copy" which served as the basis for analysis of the program and ultimately for the design of independently-created video games that could run on plaintiff's game console. Although the Ninth Circuit's opinion predates the rise of "transformative use," its analysis is consistent with both the "work" and the "purpose" prongs of "transformativeness." Reverse engineering of the entire program was the only practicable way for the defendant to discover unprotectible elements (e.g., ideas and methods of operation) that were embedded in the copyrightable "object code" that operated the game console; to rule otherwise would have allowed the plaintiff to preclude public access to its ideas and functional concepts, in violation of the core policies of copyright law. Thus, the purpose of the copying was not to exploit the code as a work of authorship, but to uncover its functionality in order to allow the creation of new works whose expressive aspects did not reproduce plaintiff's code.

2. Market harm

The fourth fair use factor (the impact of the use upon the potential market for the work), albeit after *Campbell* no longer dispositive, remains the other dominant consideration, one often conflated with the first factor; courts tend to equate "transformative" works or purposes with those that do not substitute for the copyright owner's normal markets for the work.[54] Indeed, the Second Circuit has even coined the term "transformative market,"[55] apparently meaning an exploitation that falls outside the copyright owner's zone of exclusivity. The counterpoint to a "transformative market" (favoring fair use) is "a traditional license market," that is, a "traditional, reasonable, or likely to be

52. Warner Bros. v. RDR Books, 575 F. Supp. 2d 513, 544 (S.D.N.Y. 2008) (*Harry Potter Lexicon* "not consistently transformative" because copied too much). *Accord,* Craft v. Kobler, 667 F. Supp. 120, 129 (S.D.N.Y. 1987) (biographer's extracts from Stravinsky's writings held "far too numerous and with too little instructional justification").

53. 977 F.2d 1510 (9th Cir. 1992).

54. Bouchat v. Baltimore Ravens Ltd. P'ship, 619 F.3d 301 (4th Cir. 2010); Perfect 10, Inc. v. Amazon.com, Inc., 508 F.3d 1146 (9th Cir. 2007); Bill Graham Archives v. Dorling Kindersley, Ltd., 448 F.3d 605 (2d Cir. 2006).

55. *Dorling Kindersley,* 448 F.3d at 614–15.

developed market"[56] (disfavoring fair use). What constitutes such a market may be both an empirical question, and, as we saw in *Campbell*, a normative matter. Empirically, courts inquire into whether the plaintiff is currently exploiting the market in which the defendant is engaged, or whether the market is one that similarly situated copyright owners would normally exploit. The latter showing is important in instances where the author has chosen for artistic or other reasons not to develop a particular market. For example, in the case of a novelist who declines to create or authorize a sequel,[57] or of a screenwriter-television producer who refuses to license a trivia quiz book about the show,[58] arguments that unauthorized entrants into those markets cause the creators no harm because they chose to forgo those derivative-works markets prove unavailing because courts recognize both that defendants' uses occupy traditional markets, and that the copyright confers the right to determine the work's artistic as well as its commercial destiny: "It would . . . not serve the ends of the Copyright Act—*i.e.*, to advance the arts—if artists were denied their monopoly over derivative versions of their creative works merely because they made the artistic decision not to saturate those markets with variations of their original."[59]

The inquiry into "traditional license markets" also endeavors to avoid the charge of circularity. Arguably, if the defendant's use is one that copyright owners *could* license, then its unlicensed exploitation cannot be fair use. By focusing on whether license markets in fact exist, or are in imminent prospect,[60] courts seek to follow the direction in the fourth statutory factor to examine the use's impact on the "*potential market for the work*" (emphasis supplied) without overstretching the realm of possible licensing opportunities.

3.   Other considerations

Because section 107 states that in ruling upon a defense of fair use, the factors considered by the court "shall include" the four already discussed here, courts have frequently inferred that they may include

---

56. *Id.* at 614, *quoting* American Geophysical v. Texaco, 60 F.3d 913, 930 (2d Cir. 1994).

57. Salinger v. Colting, 641 F. Supp. 2d 250 (S.D.N.Y. 2009), *vacated on other grounds by* Salinger v. Colting, 607 F.3d 68 (2d Cir. 2010).

58. Castle Rock Entm't, Inc. v. Carol Publ'g Group Inc., 150 F.3d 132 (2d Cir. 1998).

59. *Id.* at 145–46 (quoting lower court, 955 F. Supp. 2d at 272); *id.* ("Although Castle Rock has evidenced little if any interest in exploiting this market for derivative works based on *Seinfeld*, such as by creating and publishing *Seinfeld* trivia books . . ., the copyright law must respect that creative and economic choice.")

60. *See, e.g.*, A & M Records, Inc. v. Napster, Inc. 239 F.3d 1004 (9th Cir. 2001) (examining market harm from the perspective not only of file-sharing's impact on established markets for sales of CDs, but also on the emerging market for licensed downloads).

additional considerations into their analysis. For example, courts have inquired into the "amount and substantiality of the portion used" not only "in relation to the copyrighted work as a whole," but in relation to the defendant's work as well. The Supreme Court, in *Harper & Row Publishers, Inc. v. Nation Enterprises*,[61] pointed out that the 300 words copied from President Ford's 450–page book constituted 13% of the infringing article. Courts have tended to be more lenient when the unauthorized use was "incidental," that is, when the copyright-protected work was captured as part of a larger permissible reproduction or performance, such as a song partially heard in television news footage of a festival event.[62] The Second Circuit Court of Appeals gave thorough consideration to the doctrine of "incidental use"—and the *de minimis* doctrine more generally in copyright—in a case in which a poster of a copyrighted artwork was incorporated in the set of a television program and fleetingly shown.[63] The court nonetheless ruled against fair use. By contrast, a district court in the same Circuit ruled *de minimis* the fleeting incorporation into the set of the Mel Gibson film *What Women Want* of plaintiff's "Silver Slugger" pinball machine that depicted copyrighted designs on its front and sides. Distinguishing the poster case, the court emphasized that the copyrighted work was not readily recognizable and lacked a "qualitative connection" between the plaintiff's work and the film.[64] Some courts have counted it against a defendant invoking fair use that he or she behaved in an ethically objectionable fashion[65]—as exemplified by the Supreme Court's reference to the "purloined manuscript" in *Nation*—although the Court just as readily held in *Campbell* that the defendants' having ignored the copyright owner's denial of a license to record was immaterial, and that whether "parody is in good taste or bad does not and should not matter to fair use."[66]

---

61. 471 U.S. 539 (1985).

62. Italian Book Corp. v. ABC, 458 F. Supp. 65 (S.D.N.Y. 1978). *But see* Schumann v. Albuquerque Corp., 664 F. Supp. 473 (D.N.M. 1987) (broadcast of entire copyrighted songs had "entertainment value").

63. Ringgold v. Black Entm't T.V., Inc., 126 F.3d 70 (2d Cir. 1997) (holding use "decorative" rather than "transformative").

64. Gottlieb Development v. Paramount Pictures Corp., 590 F. Supp. 2d 625 (S.D.N.Y. 2008).

65. NXIVM Corp. v. Ross Inst., 364 F.3d 471 (2d Cir. 2004). By the same token, the plaintiff's attempts to suppress information may favor a finding of fair use. *See, e.g.*, Rosemont Enters. v. Random House, Inc., 366 F.2d 303 (2d Cir. 1966) (attempt to suppress unauthorized biography of Howard Hughes); Online Policy Group v. Diebold, Inc., 337 F. Supp. 2d 1195 (N.D. Cal. 2004) (attempt to prevent publication of internal emails indicating plaintiff knew that its computerized voting machines were unreliable).

66. Campbell v. Acuff–Rose Music, Inc., 510 U.S. 569, 582 (1994).

C. Fair use and new technologies of copying and dissemination

The four factors set forth in section 107 have been applied not only in cases in which the defendant creates a new derivative work but also when it seeks to employ new technologies that permit the efficient duplication and dissemination of the copyrighted work. The fair use defense is then embedded within an assertion that the rights of the copyright owner should be counterbalanced by the public interest in increasingly inexpensive access and resulting intellectual enrichment that the new technologies can afford. More broadly, the defendants in these cases urge that copyright should not impede the development of new technologies and their attendant business models. Key cases have involved videotaping of copyrighted television programs, photocopying of literary materials useful in research and education, and Internet reproduction and transmission of all manner of copyrightable works (particularly musical sound recordings).

1. Videotaping and photocopying

In *Sony Corp. of America v. Universal City Studios, Inc.*,[67] decided by the Supreme Court in 1984, the central issue was whether Sony, the manufacturer of the first commercially successful videotape recorder (VTR), was secondarily liable for alleged infringements on the part of home viewers who taped copyrighted programs and films shown on free broadcast television for later viewing at more convenient times ("time-shifting"). The Court held—over a forceful dissenting opinion for four Justices—that such home videotaping for private and noncommercial use was a fair use, and that Sony could not be held liable; Sony's VTRs were capable of being put to "substantial noninfringing uses." The Court held that noncommercial uses are presumptively fair and presumptively do not adversely affect the market of the copyright owner; and the record showed in any event that there was no such market impact with respect to taping for the purpose of time-shifting. That entire copyrighted programs and films were copied, with no "productive" use (or in today's terminology, "transformative" use) made by the home viewer, "may be helpful in calibrating the balance, but it cannot be wholly determinative."[68]

Several influential decisions of lower courts explored the application of the fair use doctrine to photocopying technologies. Two prototype situations were the making and sale by commercial copy-shops of multiple copies of so-called coursepacks compiled by college professors (using copyright-protected material without consent); and the making of single copies of journal articles for individuals employed to do research for commercial entities. Although these activities would appear commonly to

---

67. 464 U.S. 417 (1984).   **68.** *Id.* at 455 n.40.

advance the public interest, and are mentioned in the first sentence of section 107, indeed quite explicitly (i.e., "teaching (including multiple copies for classroom use), scholarship, or research"), the trend of the few cases is to find these activities, when carried out by commercial entities, not to fall within the fair use privilege. Not surprisingly, there are concurring and dissenting opinions to be reckoned with.

In *Basic Books, Inc. v. Kinko's Graphics Corp.*,[69] the photo-reproduction by the Kinko's company of teaching materials, using substantial portions of copyrighted books—without securing permission from or paying license fees to the copyright owners—was held by the district court in the Southern District of New York not to be a fair use. The court placed particular weight on the profit-making motive of the defendant. Several years later, in *Princeton University Press v. Michigan Document Services, Inc.*,[70] a sharply divided Sixth Circuit sitting en banc reached the same outcome as the *Kinko's* court on similar facts. The majority held, among other things, that the reference in section 107 to "multiple copies for classroom use" was not meant to provide a blanket exemption for such activity (any more than for any of the other activities mentioned there, such as criticism and news reporting); that the for-profit status of the defendant (a negative under the first fair use factor) is not altered by the nonprofit status of the ultimate academic users (teachers and students); that the un-"transformed" verbatim duplication of whole chapters and other large portions of the plaintiff-publishers' books weighed heavily against fair use; and that the photocopying adversely affected not only the publishers' book sales but also the photocopying royalties that they would otherwise be paid by a by-then thriving licensing and collecting agency (the Copyright Clearance Center). (Three separate dissenting opinions emphasized the weight properly to be accorded to educational uses in the fair use framework in particular and, more generally, in promoting the objectives of copyright.)

The principal decision considering, and rejecting, the fair use defense in connection with single photocopies of short journal articles made to assist researchers is that of the Court of Appeals for the Second Circuit in *American Geophysical Union v. Texaco, Inc.*[71] Researchers engaged in developing new chemical products for the Texaco company received copies of scientific-journal tables of contents and indicated which articles they wished to read or to retain in their files for future use, so that the articles could be photocopied for them; in most cases, Texaco paid for two or three subscriptions to each journal in order to make the articles more accessible to its research staff. The court (2 to 1) concluded, *inter alia*, that the use of the photocopies was "archival"

---

69. 758 F. Supp. 1522 (S.D.N.Y. 1991).   **71.** 60 F.3d 913 (2d Cir. 1994).
70. 99 F.3d 1381 (6th Cir. 1996) (en banc).

rather than productive and a substitute for purchasing additional subscriptions (or paying photocopying license fees); that it was hardly "transformative"; that the measure for applying the "amount and substantiality" factor in section 107 was the individual journal article and not the entire journal issue (or volume); and that potential lost license fees were to be taken into account because courts should consider "traditional, reasonable, or likely to be developed markets when examining and assessing a secondary use's 'effect upon the potential market for or value of the copyrighted work.' "[72] While the dissent charged the majority's licensing analysis with circularity, the emergence of a functioning market for photocopy licensing, through the Copyright Clearance Center, may have been dispositive of the market-harm issue.[73]

The photocopying decisions are significant not only for their endorsement of new licensing markets but equally importantly for their recognition that the new technology at issue had changed the nature of the object of inquiry into economic harm. Where once the relevant economic unit was the book or journal issue as a whole, the photocopier's disaggregation of the work into separate chapters or articles (*Texaco*) or even shorter excerpts (*Kinko's*; *Michigan Document*) shifts the focus to smaller compensable units. This phenomenon is not confined to photocopiers or to literary works, as the emergence of a market for "ringtones" (usually 20–30 seconds of a recorded musical composition) attests. As a result, the third factor (amount and substantiality of the portion taken) may come to blend with the fourth, as the "substantiality" of the copied amount may turn on its distinct exploitability.

2. Digital copying and the Internet

Perhaps the most powerful new technology of reproduction of copyrighted works is the computer and in particular the Internet. Not surprisingly, fair use defenses have been asserted in this setting. The Court of Appeals for the Ninth Circuit ruled upon the fair use defense asserted by the compiler of a pictorial (as distinguished from textual) database, who included without consent the copyright-protected photographs displayed on a photographer's website.[74] The court held that small "thumbnail" versions of the photographs could not be enlarged by a computer user with sufficient clarity to result in competitive injury to the photographer.[75] Moreover (although the analysis is debatable), the court held the thumbnail versions to be "transformative" because they

---

72. *Id.* at 930.

73. Paul Goldstein, COPYRIGHT'S HIGHWAY: FROM GUTENBERG TO THE CELESTIAL JUKEBOX 204–07 (Revised Edition, 2003).

74. Kelly v. Arriba Soft Corp., 280 F.3d 934 (9th Cir. 2002).

75. *Id.* at 944.

were meant to be used not for their original aesthetic purposes but rather to be a part of an exhaustive pictorial database.[76]

A later decision involving thumbnail images made and displayed by Google reached a similar conclusion, notwithstanding the plaintiff's claim that in the years following the earlier case a market had emerged for downloading thumbnail images from the display page to cellphones. The Ninth Circuit, not altogether persuasively, rejected as speculative that assertion of economic harm.[77] The court also held that Google's full reproduction and permanent storage of the images in its database was made for the transformative and publicly beneficial purpose of indexing (again, the aesthetic/documentary distinction) and therefore was a fair use.

Confronted with the question whether peer-to-peer file-sharing of copyrighted music recordings is a fair use, however, the Ninth Circuit held that it is not. In *A & M Records, Inc. v. Napster, Inc.*,[78] the Napster website made available free software that could be utilized for the purpose of searching for and copying recordings located on other computer hard-drives, and for the purpose of making accessible to others recordings stored on one's own computer. The contributory liability of Napster depended upon whether the file-sharing computer users were infringing or were engaged in fair uses. (We will discuss contributory liability in the next chapter.) Unlike the videotaping of copyrighted free broadcast television programs for temporary "time-shifting" purposes, earlier found by the Supreme Court to be a fair use,[79] the Ninth Circuit held the Internet-facilitated sharing of music files not to be thus privileged. As for the first factor in section 107, the court found the reproduction and distribution of copyrighted music recordings not to be in any way "transformative"; moreover, the computer user was engaged in a "commercial" use ("[C]ommercial use is demonstrated by a showing that repeated and exploitative unauthorized copies of copyrighted works were made to save the expense of purchasing authorized copies.").[80] The musical compositions and sound recordings were "creative," and file transfer "necessarily 'involves copying the entirety of the copyrighted work.' "[81] Under the fourth factor, the court concluded that Napster causes economic harm to the copyright owners by reducing the sale of music compact disks and by creating obstacles to the copyright owner's

---

76. *Cf.* Bill Graham Archives v. Dorling Kindersley Ltd., 448 F.3d 605 (2d Cir. 2006) (discussed *supra*).

The *Arriba* database-compiler's display on its website of full-size photographic images, however, was determined not to be transformative, and to threaten economic injury to the plaintiff photographer. 280 F.3d at 947–48.

77. Perfect 10, Inc. v. Amazon.com, Inc., 508 F.3d 1146 (9th Cir. 2007).

78. 239 F.3d 1004 (9th Cir. 2001).

79. Sony Corp. of Am. v. Universal City Studios, Inc., 464 U.S. 417 (1984).

80. *Napster*, 239 F.3d at 1015.

81. *Id.* at 1016 (quoting the district court in *Napster*, 114 F. Supp. 2d 896, 912 (N.D. Cal. 2000)).

attempts to enter the market for the legal digital downloading of music for a fee.

This conclusion was confirmed in a lawsuit directly against a home-computer user who downloaded more than 1,300 recorded songs, claiming that this was a fair use because it merely allowed her to "sample" songs with a view toward possible purchase. The Court of Appeals for the Seventh Circuit concluded that the fourth statutory factor cut heavily against the defendant, in view of the lost revenues for the copyright owner resulting from displaced broadcasting royalties and fees for lawful Internet sampling and downloading.[82]

It has also been held not to be a fair use for a website operator ("My MP3.com") to reproduce on its computer servers tens of thousands of compact disks of popular music. These disks could be played over the computer, at or away from home, by subscribers who accessed the website and demonstrated there that they already uploaded the CD (which does not necessarily mean that she in fact owned the disk), or had purchased it from a cooperating online retailer; the avowed objective was to allow "place-shifting" of one's own recordings to a variety of locations in a convenient listening format. The court found a commercial use (through the selling of advertising for the MP3.com website), a nontransformative use, copying of creative recordings in their entirety, and injury to the market for such computer-based access to music that was "likely to be developed" by plaintiff recording companies.[83] One should note, however, that the business model at issue, which involved the entrepreneur's copying of approximately 80,000 CDs, now may be displaced by more evolved "cloud" models, in which the entrepreneur, rather than creating a centralized database of works cross-referenced to multiple customers, separately stores each customer's "collection" and allows access only to the customer's "own" holdings. The "storage" still constitutes a reproduction on the service's site, and therefore a prima facie infringement, but a *Sony*-based consumer-convenience argument here may exert more force. Moreover, as we will see in the next chapter, legislation limiting the liability of host service providers may also insulate these business models at least in part.

The fair use defense was considered and also rejected, outside the context of music dissemination on the Internet, in a case in which the

---

82. BMG Music v. Gonzalez, 430 F.3d 888 (7th Cir. 2005). The court noted that the Supreme Court had assumed in *Metro-Goldwyn–Mayer Studios Inc. v. Grokster, Ltd.*, 545 U.S. 913 (2005), that the file-sharers there were directly infringing the copyright in the music and sound recordings. *BMG Music*, 430 F.3d at 889. Later decisions in suits brought against file-shar-ing end-users have also rejected fair use defenses. *See, e.g.,* Sony BMG Music Entm't v. Tenenbaum, 672 F. Supp. 2d 217 (D. Mass. 2009), *rev'd on other grounds*, Sony BMG Music Entm't v. Tenenbaum, 660 F.3d 487 (1st Cir. 2011).

83. UMG Recordings, Inc. v. MP3.Com, Inc., 92 F. Supp. 2d 349 (S.D.N.Y. 2000).

website, as a springboard for public commentary, duplicated in full the text of copyright-protected newspaper articles (rather than duplicating just the headlines, with links back to the source webpages for full text). Despite the nonprofit and "public-benefit" nature of the copying, and the "predominantly factual" nature of the newspaper articles copied, the court found that the Internet copying was not transformative, that it was full-text, and that it diverted potentially paying users from the newspaper's website and other licensed providers.[84]

By contrast, with the development of search engines, particularly Google, the practice of "crawling" and "scraping" websites for reproduction of extracts in a search report or on a site aggregating links to the indexed content, has refocused the fair use defense as an adjunct to the defense of implied license. Arguably, anyone who posts a website wants that website to be found on the Internet; to be found, one's site has to be "indexed," that is, copied and stored in the search engine's database, as well as partly reproduced in search reports. Copyright owners who do not wish to have their sites copied can "opt out" of being crawled by including an instruction to the search engine's "robot" not to copy the site. Otherwise, in this fully automated process (whose defaults the search engine nonetheless sets), the website will be included. Failure to withdraw completely from the indexing process (there currently appears to be no halfway setting, allowing the "bot" to reproduce some but not all of the content of an open-access webpage) is construed as acceptance of the search engine's terms. The more widespread the practice of implied licensing, the more "fair" it becomes.[85] While the outcome seems reasonable in the context of search reports, it is more problematic with respect to news aggregation sites that copy headlines and full sentences from news organizations' websites.[86] It is also troubling that fair use may be becoming intertwined with implied-license arguments which themselves presume copyright owner acceptance of search engines' unilaterally-imposed design choices.

II. Exemptions and Compulsory Licenses

A. *Library copying*

Section 108 gives to certain libraries the right, despite section 106(1), to make up to three copies and phonorecords of copyrighted works, subject to certain conditions. Most significantly, the library must

---

84. Los Angeles Times v. Free Republic, 54 U.S.P.Q.2d 1453 (C.D. Cal. 2000).

85. *See, e.g.*, Field v. Google, Inc., 412 F. Supp. 2d 1106 (D. Nevada 2006).

86. *Cf.* Barclays Capital Inc. v. Theflyonthewall.com, Inc., 650 F.3d 876 (2d Cir. 2011) (news aggregator Theflyonthewall.com abandoned its fair use defense, conceding copyright liability for its copying).

be open to the public or to specialized researchers, and the copying must not be for commercial advantage. The reproduction must serve one of these purposes: preservation and security of an unpublished work; replacement of a copy or phonorecord that is damaged, deteriorating, lost or stolen (when an unused replacement is unavailable on the market at a fair price), or in an obsolete format; furnishing a single periodical article or a "small part" of a larger work to a person using it for private study, scholarship or research; furnishing to a person for such private use a copy or record of an "entire work, or . . . a substantial part of it" if the work is not available at a fair price.

The library's privileges under section 108 are lost if it "is aware or has substantial reason to believe that it is engaging in the related or concerted reproduction or distribution of multiple copies or phonorecords of the same material" or if it "engages in the systematic reproduction or distribution of single or multiple copies or phonorecords" of articles or "small parts" of works for private use. Thus, if a faculty member, instead of making 150 photocopies of a copyrighted article for her entire class, instructs the students to approach the library separately with requests for individual copies, the library will no doubt be found to have "substantial reason to believe" that it is engaging in the "related or concerted reproduction" of multiple copies of the same copyrighted material. There are other limitations on the library privilege as well, as set out in detail in section 108.

A library can insulate itself altogether against liability for copying done independently on the premises by library users. It need only provide a photocopy machine for unsupervised use by library patrons and place a notice on the machine that the making of copies is subject to the copyright law.[87]

Section 108 has provided guidance to the library community. In effect, it provides a list of free uses that libraries may make of copyrighted materials to preserve their collections and serve their patrons. Section 108 was updated in 1998 to allow preservation and replacement copies to be made in digital form as well as in traditional facsimile form, but copies made in digital form may not be made available outside the library premises. There appear to be no reported decisions construing section 108.

Despite the 1998 amendments, Section 108 has not kept pace with digital developments. The Library of Congress and the U.S. Copyright Office accordingly assembled a "Section 108 Study Group," composed principally of representatives of libraries and archives and of copyright owners, to consider how to update Section 108 for the digital era. The proposals include new exceptions for the preservation of publicly-avail-

---

87. *See* § 108(f)(1).

able "born digital" content such as websites and blogs, as well as individual works disseminated only in digital formats. The Group's final report and recommendations were published in March 2008.[88]

Section 108 does not define the outer limits of lawful library uses; the fair use doctrine remains available in the event that specific section 108 exceptions do not apply.[89] Thus, no negative inference follows from a library's failure to qualify for a particular section 108 privilege. The fair use fall-back has provided the backdrop to recent controversies concerning large-scale scanning of library collections, notably by Google. Scanning a library's entire collection almost certainly exceeds the scope of section 108 preservation copying; nor does section 108 permit making digital preservation copies available online to a remote public.[90] But the scanning and making-available might be fair use depending on how much of the work was disclosed, or, more controversially, depending on whether obtaining authorization to make the work available is futile or unduly burdensome because the work's author or rightholder cannot be found. In the latter case, we encounter the problem of "orphan works" noted in Chapter 5.

As discussed earlier, the consonance of an orphan-works exception with basic U.S. copyright norms and international obligations turns principally on the diligence of the search to locate the author or rightholder. The more superficial the search, the more likely it is to classify as "orphans" works of ascertainable parentage.[91] But in the context of mass digitization, the cost of undertaking a diligent search for each of what may be millions of works may exceed the library's (or most public or commercial partners') resources. Hence the impetus to urge an aggressive approach to fair use, which would stress the public benefit of enhanced access to works of authorship (factor 1), and the absence of market harm to authors who, because they cannot be found, or through their silence are assumed implicitly to approve the digitization, do not come forward to oppose the digitization (factor 4). Because this approach inverts the usual allocation of rights and duties by shifting from the exploiter's obligation to obtain permission to establish instead a duty on the author's part to object,[92] it would require an especially adventurous court to find fair use in a context probably best left to Congress.[93]

---

88. *See* http://www.section108.gov/.

89. *See* sec. 108(f)(4).

90. *See* sec. 108(b)(2), (c)(2).

91. For a perhaps-extreme example, see Authors Guild newsletter, "Found one! We re-unite an author with an 'orphaned work.'" http://blog.authorsguild.org/2011/09/14/found-one-we-re-unite-an-author-with-an-% E2% 80% 9Corphaned-work-% E2% 80% 9D/cite

92. *Cf.* Authors Guild v. Google, Inc., 770 F. Supp. 2d 666, 682 (S.D.N.Y. 2011) (rejecting proposed class-action settlement agreement; "it is incongruous with the purpose of the copyright laws to place the onus on copyright owners to come forward to protect their rights when Google copied their works without first seeking their permission.")

93. *Cf. id.* at 677–678 (solution to orphan works problem a matter for Congress).

B. *Educational, nonprofit and other performances and displays*

Section 110 exempts a variety of public performances and displays, typically in the context of educational and other nonprofit uses.

1. Educational uses

Section 110(1) exempts face-to-face classroom performances or displays of all kinds of copyrighted works for teaching purposes in a nonprofit educational institution. This capacious exception allows both teachers and students to show, recite, play, dance, sing, etc. any kind of work, without limitation as to its nature, in a nonprofit instructional setting. Where the exception applies, it allows maximum flexibility and spontaneity because it imposes no transactions costs on its implementation. Two caveats, however: the exception does not apply to performances of audiovisual works by means of a copy that the teacher or student knows was not lawfully made; and the performance or display must take place as part of instructional activity. Section 110(1) would not exempt the student film club's screening of *Casablanca* or the school musical's performance of *Little Shop of Horrors*.

Section 110(2) as originally enacted in 1976 exempted performances of nondramatic musical and literary works through transmissions on what was then known as instructional television, i.e., basically a nonprofit school transmitting to classrooms or to students whose disabilities prevented them from getting to a classroom. With the advent of the Internet, however, and a fuller appreciation of its extraordinary (and interactive) capabilities for reaching students, even in their homes, with a mix of text, sound, graphics and film, the original text of section 110(2) became unduly confining. In 2002 Congress amended the Copyright Act by enacting the so-called TEACH (Technology, Education and Copyright Harmonization) Act, which enlarges the statutory exemption for uses of copyrighted works in what is now known as "digital distance education"—while attempting to protect the copyright owner against the hazards of unauthorized digital retransmissions. Section 110(2) still shelters transmissions by governmental bodies and accredited nonprofit educational institutions, but it now exempts not only the performance of a nondramatic literary or musical work but also "reasonable and limited portions of any other work" (i.e., dramatic works, motion pictures, television programs) or "display of a work in an amount comparable to that which is typically displayed in the course of a live classroom session." To be exempted, transmissions by an educational institution must be at the direction of an instructor, an integral part of instructional activities and "directly related and of material assistance" thereto, and they must be limited to students officially enrolled in the pertinent course. Moreover, the transmitting institution must, *inter alia*, apply "technological measures" that prevent students from retaining the copyrighted works "for longer than the class session" and that also prevent "unauthorized further dissemination" by the students to others (known as downstream transmissions).

2.   Other Section 110 exceptions

Section 110(3) exempts certain uses of copyrighted works in the course of religious services.

Section 110(4), a particularly significant provision, largely continues the approach of the 1909 Act toward nonprofit performances of music, and adds other nondramatic works (speeches, lectures, poetry). The subsection is elaborate, but its basic thrust is to exempt live performances of such works when there is no commercial purpose, when the performers are not being paid, and when there is no admission charge— or when any admission proceeds "are used exclusively for educational, religious, or charitable purposes and not for private financial gain, except where the copyright owner has served notice of objection to the performance" under certain circumstances stipulated in the subsection. It is this exemption that shelters performances of music and readings of literature in school assembly programs, in amateur performances in public parks, and at school literary and athletic events. The exemption does not apply to performances on college radio stations, for these are "transmissions" that are expressly excluded from the section 110(4) exemption. Nor does this particular exemption apply to nonprofit performances of copyrighted *dramatic* literary or musical works (i.e., plays, operas, musicals).

Section 110(4) has not spawned much litigation, but one recent decision has reached the perhaps reassuring determination that a cell-phone ringtone heard when the phone rings in a public place, albeit a public performance, is exempted under Section 110(4), and therefore cannot be controlled by the owner of the copyright in the musical composition.[94]

Section 110(5) is designed to shelter the playing of radios and televisions in order to create a pleasant atmosphere in restaurants, retail

---

94. In re Cellco Partnership, 663 F. Supp. 2d 363, 374–75 (S.D.N.Y. 2009).

establishments, doctors' offices and the like. Subsection 110(5)(A) has been a part of the statute since its enactment in 1976. It was designed by Congress to endorse the Supreme Court's decision in *Twentieth Century Music Corp. v. Aiken*,[95] holding that the undefined word "performance" in the 1909 Act did not reach the use of simple loudspeakers to amplify radio sounds in a small fast-food restaurant. Subsection 110(5)(A) shelters the "communication of a transmission" from a radio or television set "of a kind commonly used in private homes." Absent this exemption, the broad definition given in section 101 to the right of "public performance" would make it an infringement for a doctor, barber, or bartender to have copyrighted music or dramatic programming emanating from a radio or television set placed in a waiting room, shop, or tavern. With the exemption, simply turning on the set does not infringe. In a situation in which most of some 2,500 retail clothing and shoe stores (all owned by the same parent company) operated in each store a radio receiver with two attached shelf speakers to play music broadcasts, the exemption for a "single" receiving apparatus within each store was deemed to apply.[96]

The exemption is lost, however, if sound-amplification equipment not commonly found in a home is utilized, or if a direct charge is made to see or hear the transmission, or if the transmission "is further transmitted to the public."[97] The exemption applies only to works already being transmitted through a broadcast; it does not embrace, for example, the doctor's playing of music in her waiting room from a compact-disk player; nor does it cover "music on hold" inflicted (via transmission) on phone callers who do not immediately succeed in contacting the human being they seek.

Section 110(5)(B) was added to the statute in 1998 as the Fairness in Music Licensing Act, with a stormy history before and since. As something of a *quid pro quo* for the 20–year extension of the copyright term, which was designed largely to assist the music industry, restaurant and retail-store owners prevailed upon Congress to enlarge the so-called "home-style equipment" exemption just described—and to exempt the "communication by an establishment of a transmission" from radio or television of nondramatic music in a larger area. The music may lawfully be played throughout an eating and drinking establishment of less than 3,750 square feet, and other retail establishments of less than 2,000 square feet—and also throughout even larger establishments based on certain limits as to the number of loudspeakers (even commercial rather than home-style equipment) and television sets. This obviously repre-

---

95.   422 U.S. 151 (1975).

96.   Edison Bros. Stores, Inc. v. Broadcast Music, Inc., 954 F.2d 1419 (8th Cir. 1992).

97.   Sailor Music v. Gap Stores, 668 F.2d 84 (2d Cir. 1982); Broadcast Music, Inc. v. United States Shoe Corp., 678 F.2d 816 (9th Cir. 1982).

sents a significant incursion upon the exclusive public-performance rights of music copyright owners, and was in fact challenged by foreign songwriters and music publishers as a violation of U.S. treaty obligations. A dispute-resolution panel of the World Trade Organization held section 110(5)(B) to be inconsistent with the Berne Convention, but the United States has yet to make revisions needed to avoid trade sanctions, and has instead paid fines to the complainant parties.

Subsections 110(6) through 110(10) exempt certain public performances at state fairs, at stores promoting the sale of records of the copyrighted work or of the radio or television sets communicating the works, in transmissions for the blind or other handicapped persons, and at social functions organized by nonprofit veterans or fraternal organizations. Section 110(11), the "Family Movie Act of 2005," exempts the "making imperceptible," within a private household, of "limited portions" (i.e., sex, profanity, or violence) of a motion picture being viewed there, provided no fixed copy of the altered film is made.

3. First-sale doctrine and direct displays

Despite the exclusive right of the copyright owner to sell or otherwise dispose of copies and phonorecords, the first-sale doctrine (discussed in Chapter 6), set forth in section 109(a), gives an immunity to subsequent owners who transfer title (or lend) to others. And despite the exclusive right of public display, the owner of a copy is free by virtue of section 109(c) to display it "to viewers present at the place where the copy is located." Section 109(b) in turn limits the first-sale doctrine by barring the commercial renting of musical recordings and computer software. Congress's concern was with speedy, inexpensive, and fully accurate duplication by the overnight borrower.

C. Cable television and other retransmissions

Section 111 creates a compulsory license for cable television retransmissions of copyrighted programs that are shown on broadcast television. (Otherwise, such retransmission would be an infringing "public performance" of the program.) The section is extremely elaborate and complex, and does not lend itself to easy summarization.

Section 111 grants a *complete* exemption from liability for cable systems that bring broadcast programming to subscribers who are near the broadcast source (i.e., within the "must carry" area as set out by the Federal Communications Commission) or that are at a sufficiently great distance that the broadcast programming can be received only by cable. If, however, the cable system carries broadcast signals into distant but already served television markets, the compulsory license applies. The cable operator may do so, but it must pay a royalty for the privilege of this compulsory license. The royalty is based principally on the system's receipts and the amount of distantly-originated non-network programming that the cable system retransmits to its subscribers. (The statute in effect assumes that the copyright owner has already been fully compensated by the television network for the broadcasts that are viewed wherever the network is accessible, whether through the originating broadcast or through cable retransmissions.) The statute as enacted in 1976 set forth certain royalty rates, which have since been increased by the Copyright Royalty Tribunal (CRT) and, since the CRT's abolition, these rates are now subject to modification by the Copyright Royalty Judges. The cable system must forward regular statements of account and royalty fees to the Copyright Office, to be later distributed so as to provide fair recompense to owners of copyrighted material retransmitted over cable systems. A cable system that fails to comply with the requirements of the compulsory-license provisions of section 111 will be fully liable for copyright infringement.

Section 111 also exempts from liability the relaying, by a hotel or apartment house, of sounds emanating from a radio or television broadcast into the private lodgings of guests or residents, without any direct charge therefor.

Sections 119 and 122 give satellite transmitters of television broadcasts to private "dish" owners a compulsory license similar to that provided for cable systems under section 111. The compulsory-royalty payments collected from ordinary cable systems and satellite systems have generated for owners of copyrighted television programs an average of $150 million for *each* of the years since 1988.[98]

D. Musical compulsory licenses

1. Mechanical recordings and jukeboxes

Section 115, as already discussed,[99] sets forth the compulsory license for the manufacture and distribution of phonorecords of nondramatic musical works (as distinguished from the sound recordings, the recorded performances of those musical works). Once the music copyright owner allows the distribution in the United States of one recorded version, then any other performers and recording companies may make and distribute

---

98. *See* United States Copyright Office, SATELLITE TELEVISION AND LOCALISM ACT § 302 REPORT 44 n. 117 (2011) ("On average, about $150 million in royalties have been collected annually through the cable and satellite distant signal licenses since their inception. However, the average figure for the last ten years is higher.").

99. *See supra* Chapter 6.

their own ("cover") recordings, upon the payment of royalties and compliance with other statutory obligations. Beginning in 1978 with 2.75 cents per recording of a copyright-protected work, the compulsory royalty that must be paid by the record manufacturer gradually increased by administrative action to 8.5 cents per record (or 1.65 cents per minute of playing time, whichever was larger) during the period 2004–2005, and became 9.1 cents (or 1.75 cents per minute) on January 1, 2006.[100] A rate-setting proceeding by the Copyright Royalty Judges, effective March 1, 2009, retained the rate of 9.1 cents per song (or 1.75 cents per minute) for physical phonorecords.[101] In January 2011, a new rate-setting proceeding was initiated.[102]

These rates pertain to each recording of each copyrighted musical composition, rather than, say, per-recording of the total 10 or 15 tracks on the typical compact disk. The compulsory-license format and rates apply not only to disks and tapes sold to record purchasers in retail establishments but also to the so-called "digital phonorecord deliveries"[103] that can be transmitted through the Internet. Whichever the distribution medium, the recording company invoking the compulsory license is required by the statute to make regular periodic accountings and royalty payments; in the typical situation, these licenses and payments are monitored by the Harry Fox Agency in New York City.

As originally enacted, section 116 of the Copyright Act of 1976 provided another compulsory license relating to nondramatic musical works (but not for sound recordings)—this one for public performances through jukeboxes or, in the language of the statute, "coin-operated phonorecord players." From 1909 through 1977, jukebox operators had been the beneficiaries of what was known as the "jukebox exemption." Jukebox performances, heard at penny arcades in 1909, had become a billion-dollar industry in the 1970s, and Congress took a much-contested step in the 1976 Act by stripping the industry of its total exemption, and affording jukebox operators a compulsory license upon payment to the Copyright Office of an annual fee of $8 per jukebox to cover all of the music recordings placed in the box during the year. The now-defunct Copyright Royalty Tribunal (CRT) gradually increased the per-box annual royalty to $63 effective in 1986. The CRT distributed the royalties to the performing rights societies—ASCAP, BMI and SESAC—which in turn redistributed them to their respective songwriter and music-publisher members.

Because of doubts that the jukebox compulsory license conformed to U.S. obligations under the Berne Convention concerning public-perform-

---

100. *See* 37 C.F.R. § 255.3.
101. 74 Fed. Reg. 4510.
102. 76 Fed. Reg. 590.

103. The phrase is defined in section 115(d).

ance rights of music copyright owners, Congress modified section 116 effective March 1, 1989. Congress now expresses a preference for freely negotiated licenses for jukebox plays; owners of nondramatic music copyrights and owners of coin-operated phonorecord players "may negotiate and agree upon the terms and rates of royalty payments for the performance of such works and the proportionate division of fees paid among copyright owners" (in effect insulating such coordinated treatment from antitrust liability). Only if such negotiations are unsuccessful is there to be resort to the compulsory-license royalty structure, with rates and distributions determined by the Copyright Royalty Judges. Since 1990, voluntary agreements have in fact been negotiated between ASCAP, BMI, and SESAC on one side and the Amusement and Music Operators Association on the other, so that the jukebox compulsory license has essentially been a dormant "back-up" arrangement since that time.

2.   Sound-recording performance and digital-transmission rights

Section 114[104] reiterates the exclusive right of the copyright owner to reproduce (by direct dubbing) the sounds of a sound recording, but expressly provides that an independently fixed imitation of those sounds will not constitute an infringement. Nor will it infringe to give a public performance of the sound recording by playing it in a face-to-face setting (such as by a DJ in a disco) or through an analog transmission (such as in a radio broadcast).

Since 1995, however, it has been an exclusive right of the sound-recording copyright owner, under section 106(6), "to perform the copyrighted work publicly by means of a digital audio transmission" such as to a subscriber to a digital-audio radio service or, most significantly, to an Internet user. (Such public performances of the musical works that are covered by separate copyrights are regulated by other statutory provisions.) Despite the broad language of this grant to the sound-recording copyright owner, elaborate provisions in subsections 114(d) through 114(j) provide for certain limitations upon this "digital audio transmission" right. For example, there is a complete exemption for nonsubscription digital transmissions (free digital radio broadcasts); and a compulsory license—with royalty rates to be set, absent successful private negotiation, by the Copyright Royalty Judges—is afforded for most subscription transmissions and for most Internet transmissions (most commonly through the "streaming" or "webcasting" of copyrighted sound recordings). In the compulsory-license situations, the license will be lost if the transmissions are of a nature that pose a significant risk of digital copying, by the subscriber or Internet user, that would

---

104.   *See supra* Chapter 6.

substitute for direct purchases of the recordings (such as when the transmitting entity makes available an advance listing of its record plays or when it plays within a three-hour period several selections from the same sound recording or featured artist).[105]

The payment structure established under section 114(g)(2) further develops the approach, initiated in the Audio Home Recording Act (see *supra* Chapter 6), of guaranteeing featured and nonfeatured performers a certain percentage of the proceeds from the compulsory license. First, the statute divides the proceeds 50%–50% between the performers and the copyright owner of the exclusive right of digital public performance, usually the sound-recording producer. Next, the statute separates non-featured from featured performers, reserving 5% of the receipts to funds managed by the two musicians' unions (sharing equally), the American Federation of Musicians and the American Federation of Radio and Television Artists. The remaining 45% goes to the featured recording artists. By contrast, if the digital public performance comes within the copyright owner's full exclusive right, for example, an interactive on-demand stream, section 114(g)(1) states that the performers, both featured and nonfeatured, will be paid whatever their contracts provide. As a result, if the digital transmission, such as a webcast, comes within the compulsory license, the performers may be better remunerated than under the "full" exclusive right. Ironically, then, performers may be better off with less copyright than with more; full rights guarantee the performers no participation in proceeds while rights diminished by the compulsory license assure a royalty set-aside for the recording artists.

E. Other exempted uses

Section 112 gives persons entitled to make certain public performances or displays, pursuant to contract or statutory provisions, the additional right to make an "ephemeral recording" of the copyrighted work either for archival purposes, or simply for the purpose of facilitating the performance or display, provided, in the latter case, that the recordings are promptly thereafter destroyed.

Section 113, as already discussed,[106] allows certain uses of pictorial, graphic, and sculptural works, particularly as they relate to useful articles. Section 113(d) sets out special limitations on the rights of creators of "works of visual art" with respect to the incorporation of those works in buildings. Notwithstanding these creators' coverage by the Visual Artists' Rights Act, section 113(d) allows building owners,

---

105. *See generally* Arista Records, LLC v. Launch Media, Inc., 578 F.3d 148 (2d Cir. 2009) (analyzing transmissions coming within the "sound recording performance complement").

106. *See supra* Chapter 2.

under elaborately detailed circumstances, to remove or even destroy the artworks installed on their property. Section 120 also concerns buildings; it provides for certain exemptions to the exclusive rights of copyright owners of "architectural works," including the right to photograph or make other two-dimensional representations of such works when they are visible from public places, and the right of the owner of a copyright-protected building to make alterations to it, and even to destroy it. The Section 120 exemption for two-dimensional depictions does not extend to three-dimensional representations, and it applies only to publicly visible architectural works, not to publicly displayed pictorial, graphic or sculptural works. Thus, the architect retains exclusive rights to authorize the reproduction of her work in the form of paperweights, snowglobes, maquettes and other 3–D formats. And the creator of a mural or a sculpture visible from the public way still controls the right to authorize commercial photographs and drawings focusing on the work (as a practical matter the artist is unlikely to enforce her rights against tourist snapshots).

Section 117(a) exempts certain reproductions of computer programs that would otherwise violate subsections 106(1) or 106(2). The "owner" of a copy of a computer program (e.g., one who purchases the program for use in one's home or business) may make a copy or adaptation of the program for "archival purposes" (as a safeguard against damage or destruction) or when such reproduction or adaptation is "an essential step in the utilization of the computer program in conjunction with a machine." The latter exemption—which most typically allows the program-copy owner and computer operator to load the program (e.g., as encoded on a disk or downloaded to computer memory) into the computer in order to use it for its intended purpose—is needed because loading from a medium of storage into computer memory is technically the making of a "copy" of the copyrighted program.[107] For much the same reason, Congress found it to be an unobjectionable use of a computer program—and so created an express exemption in section 117(c)—"for the owner or lessee of a machine to make or authorize the making of a copy of a computer program if such copy is made solely by virtue of the activation of a machine that lawfully contains an authorized copy of the computer program, for purposes only of maintenance or repair of that machine," subject to certain limited restrictions.

Finally, Section 118 as written in 1976 gave to public radio and television broadcasters a compulsory license to perform nondramatic music and to display works of art upon the payment of certain royalties. This format was later subordinated by section 118(b) to license agreements voluntarily negotiated between such "public broadcast entities"

---

107. Vault Corp. v. Quaid Software Ltd., 847 F.2d 255 (5th Cir. 1988).

and such music and graphic copyright owners. These agreements—expressly sheltered by section 118 from the antitrust laws—may establish "the terms and rates of royalty payments and the proportionate division of fees paid among" those owners. Failing such voluntary agreements, the Copyright Royalty Judges, appointed by the Librarian of Congress, are to set terms and rates.

Chapter 8

SECONDARY LIABILITY: GENERAL PRINCIPLES AND IN DIGITAL COMMUNICATIONS

With the evolution of digital communications, the means of reproducing and disseminating copyrighted works increasingly leave the control of copyright owners and traditional commercial distribution intermediaries. Websites and peer-to-peer ("P2P") and other technologies allow members of the public to copy and publicly communicate works of authorship. This does not mean that dissemination intermediaries have vanished from the copyright landscape, but rather that we have new kinds of intermediaries who do not themselves distribute copyrighted content but give their customers the means to copy and make works available to the public. The principal economic actor in this scenario is not likely to be the member of the public but rather the infringement-enabling entrepreneur. Accordingly, copyright owners will endeavor to establish the liability of the entrepreneurs, particularly when it would be costly and complicated to proceed against a host of direct infringers, as is the situation with Internet copying.[1]

I. General Principles

A. *Varieties of secondary liability*

A copyright owner may bring infringement actions not only against the person actually engaging in the unauthorized exercise of one of the exclusive rights in section 106, but also against "contributory" and "vicarious" infringers. The Copyright Act makes no specific provision for thus extending the range of liability,[2] but these doctrines have been a

---

1. As Judge Posner bluntly stated in *In re Aimster Copyright Litigation*:

The [digital file] swappers, who are ignorant or more commonly disdainful of copyright and in any event discount the likelihood of being sued or prosecuted for copyright infringement, are the direct infringers. But firms that facilitate their infringement, even if they are not themselves infringers because they are not making copies of the music that is shared, may be liable to the copyright owners as contributory infringers. Recognizing the impracticability or futility of a copyright owner's suing a multitude of individual infringers ('chasing individual consumers is time consuming and is a teaspoon solution to an ocean problem,'), the law allows a copyright holder to sue a contributor to the infringement instead, in effect as an aider and abettor.

334 F.3d 643, 645 (7th Cir. 2003) (citation omitted).

2. Section 106, however, provides for the exclusive rights "to do *and to authorize*" (emphasis added). The legislative histo-

211

part of our copyright jurisprudence for many decades.[3] As the Supreme Court has summarized these bases for derivative liability, "[o]ne infringes contributorily by intentionally inducing or encouraging direct infringement, and infringes vicariously by profiting from direct infringement while declining to exercise the right to stop or limit it."[4] In addition, one who supplies the means to infringe and knows of the use to which the means will be put (or turns a blind eye) can also be held liable for contributory infringement.[5] Willful facilitation of infringement may lead to a finding of "intentional inducement" of infringement.[6]

1. Contributory infringement

The Supreme Court endorsed and applied the law of contributory copyright liability in *Sony Corp. of America v. Universal City Studios, Inc.*[7] The plaintiff film studio contended that the manufacturer-distributor of a popular brand of videotape recorder was responsible for contributory infringement, based on the direct infringements allegedly committed by the home-tapers. The Court, in effect, concluded that even though contributory liability is not mentioned in the Copyright Act (unlike the specific provision therefor in the patent statute[8]), it is encompassed within section 106, which gives the copyright owner the exclusive right not only to make copies but "to authorize" others to make copies. Moreover, contributory liability is akin to such liability in tort cases more generally, which treat a person who knowingly participates in or furthers a tortious act as jointly and severally liable with the primary tortfeasor. The Court essentially endorsed the definition contained in an earlier and still frequently cited decision of the Court of Appeals for the Second Circuit: "[O]ne who, with knowledge of the infringing activity, induces, causes, or materially contributes to the infringing conduct of another, may be held liable as a 'contributory' infringer."[9]

In the cases that initially followed the Second Circuit's encapsulation of the doctrine, the relationship between the supplier and the user of the means was sufficiently close that there could be little doubt of either the knowledge or the nexus between the means and the infringe-

ry indicates that Congress intended "authorization" to cover at least contributory infringement. See H.R. Rep. No. 94–1476 at 61.

3. *See, e.g.,* Polygram Int'l Publ'g, Inc. v. Nevada/TIG, Inc., 855 F. Supp. 1314 (D. Mass. 1994); Demetriades v. Kaufmann, 690 F. Supp. 289 (S.D.N.Y. 1988).

4. MGM v. Grokster, 545 U.S. 913, 930 (2005) (citations omitted). For detailed analysis of the tort law bases for secondary liability in copyright law, see Alfred C. Yen, *Third-Party Copyright Liability After* Grokster, 91 MINN. L. REV. 184 (2006).

5. *See generally* Paul Goldstein, GOLDSTEIN ON COPYRIGHT § 8.1 (3d ed. 2005).

6. *Grokster*, 545 U.S. 913.

7. 464 U.S. 417 (1984).

8. *See* 35 U.S.C. §§ 271(b), (c).

9. Gershwin Publ'g Corp. v. Columbia Artists Mgmt., Inc., 443 F.2d 1159, 1162 (2d Cir. 1971).

ment.[10] For example, in the "make-a-tape" case, a record shop rented phonorecords to customers who would also purchase blank tape and then use a recording machine on the store premises to copy the rented recording onto the blank tape.[11] The store owner's knowledge of the likely use of the blank tape was patent. By contrast, when the infringement-facilitating device leaves the direct control of the facilitator, so that he no longer knows in fact what his customers are up to, contributory infringement may be more difficult to establish. That, in essence, was the problem posed in *Sony*.

Sony could well anticipate that consumers would use the videotape recorder's record function to copy protected television programs, but once the device was out of the manufacturer's hands, it could neither know precisely what the end users were doing, nor limit their use to permissible copying. The Supreme Court in *Sony* therefore cautioned that the manufacturers and sellers of videotape machines could not be liable merely because they had constructive knowledge that their purchasers *might* use the equipment to make infringing copies. Borrowing from the so-called "staple article" exception in patent law,[12] the Court held that selling the videotape recorders would not constitute contributory infringement "if the product is widely used for legitimate, unobjectionable purposes. Indeed it need merely be capable of substantial noninfringing uses."[13] Because many copyright owners of television programs did not object to home videotaping, and because the court had held that even unauthorized home videotaping, of free broadcast television programs for time-shifting purposes, is a fair use,[14] the Court concluded that "the Betamax is, therefore, capable of substantial noninfringing uses. Sony's sale of such equipment to the general public does not constitute contributory infringement of respondents' copyrights."[15]

2. Vicarious liability

Vicarious liability, on the other hand, can be imposed on persons who do not "induce, cause or materially contribute to" direct infringe-

---

10. *See* Goldstein, *supra* note 5 (advancing the general proposition that "the closer the defendant's acts are to the infringing activity, the stronger will be the inference that the defendant knew of the activity").

11. Elektra Records Co. v. Gem Elec. Distribs., Inc., 360 F. Supp. 821, 821 (E.D.N.Y. 1973); *see also* A & M Records, Inc. v. Abdallah, 948 F. Supp. 1449, 1453–54 (C.D. Cal. 1996) (sale of custom-length blank tape timed to correspond to particular sound recordings); RCA Records v. All-Fast Sys., Inc., 594 F. Supp. 335, 336–37 (S.D.N.Y. 1984) (defendant's employees

used 'Rezound' cassette recorder to make copies of sound recordings on customers' request).

12. 35 U.S.C. § 271(c).

13. Sony Corp. of Am. v. Universal City Studios, Inc., 464 U.S. 417, 442 (1984).

14. *See supra*, Chapter 7.

15. *Sony*, 464 U.S. at 456. Moreover, on the record in the case, the "primary use" of the VTR was for time-shifting. *Id.* at 493 (Blackmun, J., dissenting).

ment or indeed who do not even know that another is involved in infringing activity. Again, as in the law of torts generally, vicarious copyright liability can be imposed on the basis of principles akin to those underpinning so-called "enterprise liability," as exemplified in the doctrine of *respondeat superior*. In a seminal case on the issue, *Shapiro, Bernstein & Co. v. H.L. Green Co.*, the Court of Appeals for the Second Circuit held:

> When the right and ability to supervise coalesce with an obvious and direct financial interest in the exploitation of copyrighted materials—even in the absence of actual knowledge that the copyright monopoly is being impaired—the purposes of copyright law may be best effectuated by the imposition of liability upon the beneficiary of that exploitation.[16]

In that case, the court imposed liability for the sales of unlawfully made phonograph records upon the proprietor of a department store, as well as upon the record concessionaire actually doing the selling within the store; the store owner had the right to supervise the concessionaire and to share in its gross receipts from the sale of records.[17]

3.   Judicial development of the bases of secondary liability

These two theories of secondary liability were brought to bear in an influential decision of the Court of Appeals for the Ninth Circuit, *Fonovisa, Inc. v. Cherry Auction, Inc.*[18] The plaintiff held copyrights in Hispanic music recordings, and claimed infringement on the part of the operators of a flea market (or "swap meet") where third-party vendors routinely sold counterfeit recordings. The vendors rented space for their booths, and Cherry Auction advertised, supplied parking and refreshments (from which it derived income, to add to its admissions fees), and retained the right to exclude any vendor for any reason. The trial court had dismissed the complaint, but the court of appeals viewed the allegations as sufficient to sustain secondary-infringement claims. After a thorough review of the precedents, the court of appeals held that Cherry Auction was vicariously liable for the vendors' directly infringing record sales, because through its right to terminate vendors it had the

---

16. Shapiro, Bernstein & Co. v. H.L. Green Co., 316 F.2d 304, 307 (2d Cir. 1963).

17. In an effort to apply or extend the principle of vicarious liability (often with a view toward finding more solvent defendants), plaintiffs have named as defendants such entities as radio stations on which allegedly pirated merchandise is advertised, as well as sponsors of allegedly infringing broadcasts. *See* Screen Gems–Columbia Music, Inc. v. Mark–Fi Records, Inc., 256 F. Supp. 399 (S.D.N.Y. 1966) (advertising agency); Davis v. E.I. DuPont de Nemours & Co., 240 F. Supp. 612 (S.D.N.Y. 1965) (sponsor of television show and its advertising agency).

18. 76 F.3d 259 (9th Cir. 1996). *See also* Arista Records, Inc. v. Flea World, Inc., 2006 WL 842883 (D.N.J. 2006).

ability to control their activities, and because it reaped "substantial financial benefits from admission fees, concession stand sales and parking fees, all of which flow directly from customers who want to buy the counterfeit recordings at bargain basement prices."[19] The court also found sufficient allegations of contributory infringement because Cherry Auction allegedly knew of the directly infringing sales and because it provided the "site and facilities" (i.e., space, utilities, parking, advertising, plumbing and customers) for those infringements.

It was only a matter of time before these principles and precedents were applied so as to determine whether there was secondary infringement on the part of website operators—such as Napster, StreamCast, and Grokster—that have provided file-sharing software that can be used to facilitate the unauthorized exchange of music recordings on the Internet. The first important decision was that of the Court of Appeals for the Ninth Circuit in *A & M Records, Inc. v. Napster, Inc.*[20] There the court concluded that individual Napster users were infringing (by duplicating and distributing copyright-protected music and recordings) and were not engaging in fair use, and that Napster, Inc. was secondarily liable. There was contributory infringement: "Napster has actual knowledge that specific infringing material is available using its system, that it could block access to the system by suppliers of the infringing material, and that it failed to remove the material,"[21] and Napster provided the "site and facilities" to assist finding and downloading the recordings. As for vicarious infringement, Napster had the ability to locate infringing material on its search indices and the right to terminate users' access to the system; it also stood to derive ever-increasing advertising revenues as more users were drawn to its website through the appeal of the infringing music.[22]

Napster had invoked *Sony* for the proposition that its service was "capable of substantial noninfringing use" because not all the files were copied without authorization, and because peer-to-peer architecture could in the future spawn more non-infringing uses. The Ninth Circuit agreed that *Sony* required taking into account the service's capacity for future lawful use but nonetheless held Napster a contributory infringer.[23] Glossing *Sony*, the *Napster* court held that courts should inquire into non-infringing uses when the distributor of the device lacks actual

---

19. *Id.* at 263.

20. 239 F.3d 1004 (9th Cir. 2001).

21. *Id.* at 1022.

22. In a later case in which the defendant's file-sharing technology was somewhat different, the Seventh Circuit reached essentially the same conclusion concerning

contributory liability as did the *Napster* court, and reserved judgment on the question of vicarious liability. In re Aimster Copyright Litig., 334 F.3d 643 (7th Cir. 2003).

23. *Napster*, 239 F.3d at 1020–22.

knowledge of and control over specific infringements.[24] Where, however, it is possible to segregate and prevent infringing uses, it is not appropriate to exculpate the entire system by virtue of its capacity for non-infringing uses. In other words, the consequences to technology of enforcing copyright rules were different in *Sony* and in *Napster*. *Sony* presented the court with an all-or-nothing challenge: either the device would be enjoined, frustrating legitimate uses, or no liability would attach, despite the infringements the device enabled. In *Napster*, by contrast, the service could disable infringing uses by blocking access to listings of protected files, while allowing permissible uses to continue. *Napster* thus transformed *Sony* into an inquiry into knowledge of and ability to prevent specific infringements.[25]

Of course, the *Napster* rule set out the instructions for its own demise: if Napster was liable because it could maintain control over its users' activities, then the next device or service would be sure to make it difficult, if not impossible, for the service to exercise control.[26] So were born the P2P file-sharing enterprise Kazaa, and its U.S. licensees, Grokster and Streamcast (dba Morpheus). Unlike Napster, these services had no centralized directory; they dispersed information about file locations across computer "nodes" around the world. Users could find each other, but the services disclaimed the ability to prevent infringements as they were occurring. In the *Grokster* case, songwriters, record producers, and motion picture producers alleged that the Grokster and Morpheus file-sharing networks should be held liable for facilitating the commission of massive amounts of copyright infringement by the end-users who employed the defendants' P2P software to copy and redistribute films and sound recordings to each others' hard drives. Although it recognized that Grokster and Morpheus had intentionally built their systems to defeat copyright enforcement, the Ninth Circuit held that without the ability to prevent specific infringements, the services could not be liable.[27] The court scarcely considered whether the services enabled substantial non-infringing use; it acknowledged that 90% of the uses were infringing, but observed in a footnote that 10% could be substantial, particularly when the 10% referenced hundreds of thousands of uses.[28]

24. *Id.* at 1021.

25. For a criticism of the Ninth Circuit's approach, *see* GOLDSTEIN, *supra* note 5, § 8.1.2.

26. For a trenchant analysis of the cat-and-mouse story of the contributory infringement cases see Rebecca Giblin, CODE WARS: 10 YEARS OF P2P SOFTWARE LITIGATION (2011) (explaining why technological developments and legal doctrines have produced the paradox that every time a copyright

owner has alleged the legal liability of a P2P network entrepreneur, the copyright owner has prevailed in court; yet unauthorized P2P file sharing persists, if anything, more virulently than before).

27. MGM Studios, Inc. v. Grokster Ltd., 380 F.3d 1154, 1165–66 (9th Cir. 2004), *rev'd*, 545 U.S. 913 (2005).

28. *See id.* at 1162 n.10. That the other 90% would be even more extensive seems not to have troubled the court.

A unanimous U.S. Supreme Court reversed. It held that the Ninth Circuit had misapplied the *Sony* standard, or, more accurately, that the Ninth Circuit did not appreciate that the *Sony* standard does not even come into play when the defendant is "actively inducing" copyright infringement.[29] That is, a device might well be capable of substantial non-infringing uses. But if it can be shown that the distributor *intended* users to employ the device in order to infringe copyright, then the distributor will be liable as a matter of basic tort principles. The Court thus reinterpreted *Sony* as a case articulating a standard for assessing liability when the copyright owner cannot prove that the device distributor sought to foster infringement.

This approach enabled the Court to avoid determining how the *Sony* "substantial noninfringing use" test would apply in the case before it.[30] Rather, the Court—buttressed by the Patent Act provision imposing liability upon "[w]hoever actively induces infringement"[31]—held instead that "one who distributes a device with the object of promoting its use to infringe copyright, as shown by clear expression or other affirmative steps taken to foster infringement, is liable for the resulting acts of infringement by third parties."[32]

The Court set out three "features" probative of intent to induce infringement: (1) the defendant explicitly promoted the infringement-enabling virtues of its device; (2) the defendant failed to filter out infringing uses; (3) defendant's business plan depended on a high volume of infringement.[33] In *Grokster*, all three elements were easily demonstrated. The defendants had sent out emails extolling P2P copying, and had "aim[ed] to satisfy a known source of demand for copyright infringement, the market comprising former Napster users."[34] One of the defendants not only declined to devise its own filters; it blocked third-party filters. And the defendants' business plans depended on advertisers, whose rates would turn on the volume of users encountering the ads. The more the defendants could attract visitors, the better for their businesses, and the prospect of free music attracts more visitors than paid music. Taken together, these factors demonstrated a clear intention

---

29. *Grokster*, 545 U.S. at 934–35.

30. Six Justices who joined in the unanimous Court opinion did, however, opine as to how the *Sony* test would apply on the record before them, with three finding contributory liability and three finding none.

31. 35 U.S.C. § 271(b). The Court had previously applied an inducement test to determine contributory liability for trademark infringement. *See* Inwood Labs. v. Ives Labs., 456 U.S. 844, 854 (1982). Unlike *Sony*, *Inwood Laboratories* did not purport to draw guidance from the Patent Act.

Compare Inwood Labs., 456 U.S. 844, *with* Sony Corp. of Am. v. Universal City Studios, 464 U.S. 417 (1984).

32. *Grokster*, 545 U.S. at 918–919.

33. *Id.* at 939–40.

34. *Id.* at 939. *See also* Sverker Högberg, Note, *The Search for Intent–Based Doctrines of Secondary Liability in Copyright Law*, 106 COLUM. L. REV. 909, 952–53 (2006) (discussing the post-*Grokster* dangers of targeting a "risky demographic").

to foster infringement. As the Court declared: "The unlawful objective is unmistakable."[35]

The Court rejected the defendants' contention that a finding of secondary liability would significantly interfere with the development of new electronic technologies: "The inducement rule ... premises liability on purposeful, culpable expression and conduct, and thus does nothing to compromise legitimate commerce or discourage innovation having a lawful promise."[36]

4. Whither Secondary Liability for Copyright Infringement?

Having ruled that bad intent, if proved, suffices to establish liability for infringements thus induced, the full Court declined to analyze what the standard for contributory infringement would be when intent to foster infringement cannot be shown. As a result, it remains unknown whether *Sony*'s "substantial noninfringing use" standard means that the principal use of the device or service at issue *in fact* serves noninfringing ends,[37] or whether it suffices that a potential noninfringing use of the technology underlying the device or service *could become* significant.[38] Nonetheless, it may not matter what proportion of noninfringing use allows an entrepreneur to enter *Sony*'s safety zone because the *Grokster* inducement standard may displace inquiries into the substantiality of noninfringing uses:[39] Where a device or service facilitates infringement on a massive scale, its distributor may well be found to have intended that result.[40] Moreover, *Grokster*'s emphasis on bad intent

35. *Grokster*, 545 U.S. at 940. On remand the district court entered a permanent injunction against Streamcast's continued distribution of the Morpheus software, 518 F. Supp. 2d 1197 (C.D.Cal. 2007).

36. *Grokster*, 545 U.S. at 937.

37. *Id.* at 942–4, (Ginsburg, J. concurring)

38. *Id.* at 954–55 (Breyer. J. concurring)

39. *Cf.* Peter S. Menell & David Nimmer, *Legal Realism in Action: Indirect Copyright Liability's Continuing Tort Framework and* Sony's *De Facto Demise*, 55 UCLA L. Rev. 143, 172–77 (2007) (surveying post-*Sony* caselaw and business practices to show that the "merely capable of substantial non infringing use" standard was rarely observed in practice); Peter S. Menell & David Nimmer, *Unwinding Sony*, 95 CAL. L. REV. 941, 993 (2007) (arguing "capable of substantial non-infringing use"

standard rests "on a faulty [historical] foundation").

40. In *Sony*, for example, the VTR manufacturer certainly intended to provide the means to tape television programs at home, and even promoted the VTR's utility in building a home library of copied programs (*Grokster* feature 1); it also declined to equip the VTR with a "jammer" to prevent unauthorized copying (*Grokster* feature 2). But, on the record in the case, most of the unauthorized copying was of a kind (timeshifting and erasure of free broadcast television) that a majority of the Supreme Court found noninfringing. This suggests that size does matter. In fact, at least one court has explicitly concluded that the respective magnitude of infringing and noninfringing uses is a factor in determining whether a defendant can be held liable for inducement. *See* Monotype Imaging, Inc. v. Bitstream, Inc., 376 F. Supp. 2d 877, 887 (N.D. Ill. 2005); *see also* Columbia Pictures Indus., Inc. v. Fung, No. CV 06–05578SVW,

leaves open the possibility that inducement may still be found even when the bad actor operates on a more modest scale, particularly when the defendant declines to take steps to prevent infringement because its business model is infringement-dependent.

If profit-motivated failure to filter promotes an inference of intent to induce infringement, then perhaps implementation of copyright filters warrants the opposite inference, of non-intent to encourage infringement. While failure to filter may not of itself prove bad intent, the entrepreneur who does filter may defeat inferences of intent to induce infringement. Filtering therefore may afford a federal common law "safe harbor" from future inducement claims.[41] But, as we will see immediately below, federal statutory safe harbors may relieve the entrepreneur who qualifies as a "service provider" from any obligation to take affirmative steps to avoid infringement.

II. Service Provider Liability

Issues of secondary copyright infringement are also raised when the defendant is one step more removed from the direct infringement than in the cases just discussed—in which the defendants consciously designed and distributed software that was used, and was largely meant to be used, to make illicit copies and phonorecords. What, if any, liability is there, on the part of Internet service providers (ISPs) that allow home computer users to connect to the Internet and to post and exchange all manner of potentially copyright-protected materials? These ISPs provide an appealing target for copyright infringement lawsuits, when the alternative would often be cumbersome suits against individuals. ISPs accordingly have, thanks to the 1998 "Digital Millennium Copyright Act" (DMCA), largely succeeded in insulating themselves from most copyright liability. We will first consider the principal pre-DMCA judicial decision on ISP liability, which in fact inspired the legislation that we will then examine.

2009 WL 6355911, at *14 (C.D. Cal. 2009) (finding inducement liability where company's "business model depend[ed] on massive infringing use").

It remains unclear, however, whether an internet service provider who arguably passively facilitates infringement on a massive scale is immunized by virtue of the section 512 "safe harbors" (discussed in the next section).

41. *See* Tim Wu, *The Copyright Paradox*: *Understanding* Grokster, 2005 Sup. Ct. Rev. 229, 247 (stating that "one might also infer from [the] language [barring liability based solely on failure to filter] that *Grokster* creates a kind of safe harbor that may

prove important. It may be read to suggest that a product that *does* filter is presumptively not a product that is intended to promote infringement, even if it does, in practice, facilitate infringement"). An early post-*Grokster* decision appears to bear this out. *See Monotype Imaging*, 376 F. Supp. 2d 877 (finding no inducement because, inter alia, defendant submitted evidence that it had taken steps to avoid the infringing use of its compatible type fonts). The court also found that "unlike in *Grokster*, there is no evidence in the record to show that Bitstream's business was benefited by increasing the number of infringing uses of [its product]." *Id.* at 889.

Perhaps the most influential pre–1998 court decision is *Religious Technology Center v. Netcom On–Line Communication Services, Inc.*[42] The plaintiff, a unit within the Church of Scientology, finding that a disgruntled former member, Erlich, had posted certain unpublished Church documents on an online "bulletin board," brought a copyright infringement action against the operator of the bulletin board and the ISP that provided online access to the bulletin board and to the Internet more generally. The court held that the ISP (Netcom) could be liable as a contributory infringer if, after receiving a "take-down notice" from the Church, it could reasonably have known of the copyright-protected status of the posted documents, and it allowed the messages to remain on its system and to be further distributed to servers worldwide. The court also found, with respect to vicarious liability, that Netcom had a history of policing its users' postings and suspending some (for obscenity, commercial advertising and the like); but that it derived no economic benefits from Erlich's infringement.

A. *The statutory safe harbor regime*

Although the *Netcom* case and others like it exonerated ISPs from direct liability when they acted as "mere conduits" for Internet communications, the prospect of even indirect liability for contributory infringement spurred service providers to lobby Congress for exemptions from copyright liability and remedies. In 1998 Congress passed the Digital Millennium Copyright Act (DMCA), which added section 512 to the Copyright Act.[43] This section exempts online service and access providers from liability for damages for copyright infringement, and significantly reduces the scope of injunctive relief, if the providers meet the Act's cumulative tests establishing the independence of the providers from the infringing content they transmit, host or link to. Failure to comply with § 512 does not of itself subject the service provider to liability for copyright infringement; section 512 offers a safe harbor, but a nonqualifying provider must still be proved to have infringed, and may still invoke traditional copyright and other defenses.[44]

Section 512 divides the universe of service providers into four categories: (a) those who merely transmit third-party content "through an automatic technical process without selection of the material by the service provider" (often referred to as "mere conduits"); (b) "system caching" of third-party content if the "intermediate and temporary storage" of the material "is carried out through an automatic technical process for the purpose of making the material available to users of the

42. 907 F. Supp. 1361 (N.D. Cal. 1995).   **44.** *Id.* § 512(*l*).
43. 17 U.S.C. § 512.

system or network who … request access to the material" from the third party that initiated its transmission; (c) hosts of third-party content residing on systems or networks at the direction of users and (d) "information location tools," such as search engines that link to websites.[45]

While mere-conduit service providers in most instances receive immunity from monetary liability and injunctive relief,[46] host service providers are susceptible to "take-down notices"[47] from copyright owners and an obligation under stipulated circumstances to remove the allegedly offending material from its network. A similar regime applies to search engines. If the provider of the link to an allegedly infringing site does not know and is not aware of the presence of infringing material on the linked site, and, upon proper notification from the copyright owner, acts expeditiously to remove the link, the provider will not be liable for damages, and will be subject to limited injunctive relief. Section 512 does *not*, however, alleviate the liability of those who *originate* content on a website. Finally, it is worth observing that § 512 addresses only liability for copyright infringement. It affords no safe harbor from liability for transmitting, hosting or linking to content that violates other rights, including intellectual property rights such as trademarks.[48] The ensuing analysis will consider the copyright liability regime established for service providers that host third-party content.

B.   *Hosting Third–Party Content: The Application of the Exemption*

Section 512(c) sets forth cumulative prerequisites to a hosting service provider's qualification for exemption from direct or vicarious liability for copyright infringement. First, the host must be a "service

---

45. *Id.* § 512(a), (b), (c), (d). In all cases section 512(i)(1)(A) requires qualifying service providers to implement a policy for terminating the accounts of repeat infringers.

46. *Id.* § 512(a), (j)(1)(B).

47. *See generally* Rossi v. Motion Picture Ass'n of Am., 391 F.3d 1000 (9th Cir. 2004); ALS Scan, Inc. v. RemarQ Cmtys., Inc., 239 F.3d 619 (4th Cir. 2001).

48. Because sound recordings first fixed before February 15, 1972 are not covered by the 1976 Copyright Act, but only by state law, see sec. 301(c), section 512 by its own terms does not afford service providers a safe harbor for hosting unauthorized phonorecords of pre–1972 sound recordings. At least one court, however, has (probably incorrectly) stated that section 512 applies to both state and federal copyright claims. *See* Capitol Records v. MP3Tunes LLC, No. 07 Civ. 9931 (WHP), 2011 WL 5104616 at *10 (S.D.N.Y. Oct. 25, 2011). Because some States protect pre–1972 sound recordings through unfair competition rather than copyright claims, *see, e.g.*, Columbia Broadcasting v. Melody Recordings, Inc., 341 A.2d 348 (N.J. Super. Ct. App. Div. 1975), however, the court's interpretation would mean that section 512's application depends on the state in which the service provider is located. It seems unlikely, to say the least, that Congress could have intended such a result.

provider." Section 512's definition of "service provider" is exceedingly vague; the term "means a provider of online services or network access or the operator of facilities therefor".[49] "Online services" are not defined. The case law has generally interpreted "service provider" extremely broadly, to cover not only Internet-specific businesses, but a variety of traditional businesses' Internet operations, such as online auctions,[50] online real estate listings,[51] and an online pornography age-verification service.[52]

Second, section 512(c) absolves a host service provider from liability "for infringement of copyright by reason of the storage at the direction of a user of material that resides on a system or network controlled or operated by or for the service provider . . .".[53] At first blush, it might appear that a website, as opposed to a server which hosts websites, cannot be "a system or network controlled or operated by or for the service provider" and therefore that section 512 does not protect the operators of websites that host content posted by end-users. But the website might be part of a system controlled by the website operator, so this element probably does not screen out "user-generated content" (UGC) sites. Nonetheless, a UGC site cannot bootstrap all of its activities to the user-posted content: § 512 exculpates *"storage* at the direction of a user";[54] it does not suspend liability for other acts in which the service provider might engage independently of or even with respect to the user-posted content.[55] That said, courts have ruled that section 512(c) does not require the host service provider to restrict its activities to the mere storage of user-posted content.[56] As the Ninth Circuit has stressed, section 512 assumes that users will be able to access content posted to host websites; thus, the websites must be permitted to transmit the stored content to the requesting user; to limit section 512(c) to the sole act of storage would effectively nullify the safe harbor.[57] To the extent

---

49. § 512(k)(1)(B).

50. Hendrickson v. eBay, Inc., 165 F. Supp. 2d 1082 (C.D. Cal. 2001) (but parties did not dispute whether eBay was a 'service provider' within the meaning of the statute).

51. Costar Group Inc. v. Loopnet, Inc., 164 F. Supp. 2d 688, 701 (D. Md. 2001) (" 'Online services' is surely broad enough to encompass the type of service provided by LoopNet that is at issue here.").

52. Perfect 10, Inc. v. Cybernet Ventures, Inc., 213 F. Supp. 2d 1146, 1175 (C.D. Cal. 2002) (assuming defendant qualified as a service provider, but admitting that it "has found no discussion [in prior case law] of this definition's limits").

53. 17 U.S.C. § 512(c)(1) (2000).

54. *Id.* (emphasis added).

55. *Cf.* Costar Group Inc. v. Loopnet, Inc., 164 F. Supp. 2d 688 (D. Md. 2001) ("The legislative history indicates that [the actions protected by § 512(c) do] not include [the action of uploading] material 'that resides on the system or network operated by or for the service provider through its own acts or decisions and not at the direction of a user.' " (quoting H.R. REP. No. 105–551, at 53 (1998)).

56. *See* UMG Recordings, Inc. v. Shelter Capital Partners, LLC, 667 F.3d 1022 (9th Cir. 2011); Io v. Veoh, 586 F. Supp. 2d 1132 (N.D. Cal. 2008).

57. *UMG Recordings*, 101 U.S.P.Q.2d at 1008 and n.8.

the storage-plus activity is not closely related to the storage, the service provider would lose the safe harbor only with respect to the activities that exceeded the bounds of " 'storage' and allied functions"; any excess would not disqualify those activities that came within those bounds.[58]

The remaining criteria echo the common law rules regarding vicarious liability and contributory infringement. One set of criteria addresses the financial benefit derived from the hosted content, the other looks to the host provider's level of knowledge that the third-party content is infringing.

1. No direct financial benefit

The service provider must not "receive a financial benefit directly attributable to the infringing activity, in a case in which the service provider has the right and ability to control such activity."[59] With respect to the nexus between the infringement and the benefit to the website, if the website accepted advertising targeted to the infringing content, the benefit would surely be "direct". Moreover, as we shall see, if the website knew the content was infringing, it would be obliged to remove the material even without notification by the rightholder.[60] Assume, however, that the relationship between infringement and the benefit is more attenuated. For example, the website accepts advertising; the rates charged are a function of the popularity of the material alongside which the ads appear. Or, the website accepts advertising, but the advertisements appear randomly; the rates are the same whatever the content in connection with which the ads appear. The overall popularity of the website will, however, influence the amount of money the website operator can charge for ads. If it is true that free (unauthorized) copyrighted content is a "draw,"[61] then making ad rates turn on the popularity of portions of the website may foster too close a relationship

---

58. Viacom Int'l Inc. v. YouTube, Inc., 718 F. Supp. 2d 514 (S.D.N.Y. 2010).

59. § 512(c)(1)(B). This standard adopts the common law test for vicarious liability enunciated in copyright cases involving digital as well as traditional infringements. See, e.g., Perfect 10, Inc. v. CCBill LLC, 481 F.3d 751, 766–767 (9th Cir. 2007) (common law standards and § 512(c)(1)(B) standards are the same); A & M Records v. Napster, Inc., 239 F.3d 1004, 1022–1023 (9th Cir. 2001); Costar Group Inc. v. Loopnet, Inc., 164 F. Supp. 2d 688, 704 (D. Md. 2001), aff'd, 373 F.3d 544 (4th Cir. 2004) (DMCA provides no safe harbor for vicarious in-

fringement because it codifies both elements of vicarious liability.)

60. See 17 USC § 512(c)(1)(A)(i).

61. See, e.g., Fonovisa v. Cherry Auction, Inc., 76 F.3d 259, 263 (9th Cir. 1996); UMG Recordings, Inc. v. Sinnott, 300 F. Supp. 2d 993, 1002–1003 (E.D. Cal. 2004) (finding defendant received a benefit from increased revenue at concession stands and on-site go-kart track); Arista Records, Inc. v. Mp3Board, Inc., No. 00 Civ. 4660 (SHS), 2002 WL 1997918, at *11 (S.D.N.Y. Aug. 29, 2002) ('direct financial interest' prong satisfied when infringing works acted as draw and defendant received substantial amount of advertising tied to number of users).

between the infringements and the financial benefit. By contrast, in the second scenario the financial benefit may be too attenuated;[62] it might be necessary to show that the presence of free unauthorized content makes the site as a whole more attractive than it would be without that content. Put another way, the copyright owner may need to show that the free unauthorized content is in fact "drawing" users to the site.[63]

2. Right and Ability to Control Infringing Activity

Even if the "direct financial benefit" standard is met, the service provider will not be disqualified from the safe harbor unless it also had the "right and ability to control" the infringing activity. Some courts have found that the ability to block access to infringing uses of a website does not of itself mean that an online service provider has the "right and ability to control" for the purposes of § 512.[64] For these courts, since section 512(c)(1)(C) already conditions qualification for the safe harbor on expeditious removal of the infringing content once the service provider is properly notified of its existence, the "right and ability to control" under § 512(c)(1)(B) must mean something more than a subsequent ability to block access.[65] "Something more" might mean an ability to intervene before the infringing content is placed on the website.[66] But this plus factor presents its own anomalies: if the service provider must be more closely implicated in the user's activities in order to have the requisite control, then the service provider would already be disqualified on the § 512(c)(1)(A) ground that the service thereby acquires forbidden knowledge of the user's activities. Given these paradoxes, it may make most sense to interpret "right and ability to control" consistently with the common law of vicarious liability. In the common law context, courts will rule that a defendant online service provider has the "right and

---

62. *Cf.* Aitken, Hazen, Hoffman, Miller, P.C. v. Empire Constr. Co., 542 F. Supp. 252, 262 (D. Neb. 1982) (building company built building based on plaintiff's architectural works without permission, but lumber company and engineer employed by building company who received fixed fees for constructing building held not vicariously liable).

63. *See Costar Group*, 164 F. Supp. 2d at 704–705 (stating that an *in*direct benefit that infringements may provide to a website 'does not fit within the plain language of the statute').

64. *See, e.g.*, Hendrickson v. eBay, Inc., 165 F. Supp. 2d 1082, 1093–1094 (C.D. Cal. 2001); Costar Group Inc. v. Loopnet, Inc.,

164 F. Supp. 2d 688, 704–705 (D. Md. 2001).

65. *See Hendrickson*, 165 F. Supp. 2d at 1093–1094; *Costar Group*, 164 F. Supp. 2d at 704 n.9.

66. *See* Tur v. YouTube, Inc., No. CV064436 FMC AJWX, 2007 WL 1893635, at *3 (C.D. Cal. June 20, 2007) ('[T]he requirement [of 'something more'] presupposes some antecedent ability to limit or filter copyrighted material.' (citations omitted)); Perfect 10, Inc. v. Cybernet Ventures, Inc., 213 F. Supp. 2d 1146, 1181–1182 (C.D. Cal. 2002) ('Here Cybernet prescreens sites, gives them extensive advice, prohibits the proliferation of identical sites, and in the variety of ways mentioned earlier exhibits precisely this slightly difficult to define "something more".').

ability to control" an infringing activity if it can block attempts to use its online service for infringing activities.[67]

3. Knowledge standard

The host must "not have actual knowledge that the material or an activity using the material on the system or network is infringing", and it must not be "aware of facts or circumstances from which infringing activity is apparent"; this latter test is sometimes referred to as the "red flag" standard.[68] Once the host becomes "aware" of infringing activity, it must act "expeditiously to remove, or disable access to, the material."[69] Most importantly, in the absence of prior awareness, but upon proper notification by the copyright owner, the service provider must respond "expeditiously to remove, or disable access to" the allegedly infringing material.[70] Accordingly, section 512(c)(2) requires that a service provider, in order to benefit from the reduction in liability, designate, and provide contact information concerning, an agent to receive notification of claimed infringements. Under § 512, the qualifying service provider incurs no general burden of anticipating or preventing infringement;[71] it need only react to notices of infringement that the copyright holders uncover.

Because one may foresee that at least some of the content the notified service provider takes down will promptly reappear, hydra-like, the question arises at what point, if any, the service provider becomes

67. *See, e.g.,* A & M Records, Inc. v. Napster, Inc., 239 F.3d 1004, 1023–1024 (9th Cir. 2001) (although *Napster* was decided after enactment of sec. 512, the court held that Napster did not qualify for the statutory safe harbour, and therefore applied common law rules of vicarious liability); Religious Tech. Ctr. v. Netcom On–Line Comm. Servs., Inc., 907 F. Supp. 1361, 1375–1376 (N.D. Cal. 1995).

68. *See, e.g.,* Perfect 10, Inc. v. CCBill LLC, 481 F.3d 751, 763 (9th Cir. 2007).

69. 17 U.S.C. § 512(c)(1)(A)(iii) (2006).

70. *Id.* § 512(c)(1)(C).

71. *Id.* § 512(m)(1) (stating that availability of the safe harbor is not conditioned on 'a service provider monitoring its service or affirmatively seeking facts indicating infringing activity'). Section 512(i)(1)(B) does make 'accommodat[ion of] ... standard technical measures' a prerequisite to qualifying for the statutory safe harbors. Arguably, filtering technology might be such a measure. The definition of 'standard techni-

cal measures', however, suggests that the present state of filtering technologies may not suffice, principally because there is not yet an inter-industry consensus regarding the design and implementation of filtering measures. See § 512(i)(2). Section 512(i)(2) states:

(2) Definition—As used in this subsection, the term 'standard technical measures' means technical measures that are used by copyright owners to identify or protect copyrighted works and—

(A) have been developed pursuant to a broad consensus of copyright owners and service providers in an open, fair, voluntary, multi-industry standards process;

(B) are available to any person on reasonable and nondiscriminatory terms; and

(C) do not impose substantial costs on service providers or substantial burdens on their systems or networks.

disqualifyingly "aware" that the contested content is making repeat appearances, so that some obligation to forestall specific infringements may attach. So far, the caselaw interpreting the statutory "red flag" standard suggests the flag may need to be an immense crimson banner before any service-provider obligation to intervene of its own accord comes into play. "General knowledge that infringement is 'ubiquitous' does not impose a duty on the service provider to monitor or search its service for infringements."[72] Although the point is debatable, it has been held that even repeated take-down notices identifying the same specific unauthorized content do not give rise to sufficient awareness.[73]

4. Notice and take down . . . and put back

Copyright owners alleging that the service provider is hosting infringements must send the provider's agent a signed, written communication identifying the work infringed, the material alleged to be infringing and its location; a statement that the complaining party has a good faith belief that the use is unauthorized; and a sworn statement that the information contained in the notification is believed to be accurate.

Upon receiving the notification, the provider must "expeditiously" remove or block access to the alleged infringing material, or else face the full range of liability should the author prevail in an infringement suit. But the provider who removes or blocks the material must also so notify the posting user; the user may then send a "counter notification" (whose contents the law prescribes).[74] In that event, the service must send the counter notification to the person who notified the service of the alleged infringement, and must inform that person that the service will replace the material in ten business days. The copyright owner must within that time "file[] an action seeking a court order to restrain the subscriber from engaging in infringing activity relating to the material on the service provider's system or network."[75] If the copyright owner does not initiate the action, and so inform the service provider's designated agent, then the service provider must put back the material "not less than 10, nor more than 14, business days following receipt of the counter notice. . . ."[76]

Because section 512(c) in effect affords copyright owners do-it-yourself injunctive relief, the purpose of these provisions is to ensure that § 512(c) does not make it *too* easy for copyright owners to compel the removal of allegedly infringing material without judicial process.

---

72. Viacom Int'l Inc. v. YouTube, Inc., 718 F. Supp. 2d 514, 525 (S.D.N.Y. 2010).

73. *Id.* at 524, *citing* UMG Recordings, Inc. v. Veoh Networks, Inc., 665 F. Supp. 2d 1099, 1108 (C.D. Cal. 2009).

74. *See* 17 U.S.C. § 512(g)(3).

75. *Id.* § 512(g)(2)(C).

76. *Id.*

Section 512(c) encourages providers who have received notice to take down the material immediately, since the text insulates service providers who comply with the statutory requirements from suit by persons (including the website operator or posting user) disgruntled at the removal of the material from the server.[77] From the point of view of authors and copyright owners, the strong incentives to remove material may offer an effective means of enforcement, since the author's first goal will often be to get the material taken down before it can be copied/disseminated further.

On the other hand, there is the risk that timorous service providers will remove material whose posting was not infringing, for example, because the posting constituted fair use. Hence the opportunity for the posting user to demand that the material be "put back," and a corresponding obligation for the copyright owner to initiate judicial proceedings if the copyright owner wishes to ensure that the "take down" of the material remain in effect. Moreover, any person who knowingly misrepresents that material or activity is infringing will be subject to damages incurred by any person injured as a result of the service provider's removal of the material.[78] Courts have, in fact, awarded significant damages and attorney's fees against copyright owners found to have abused the notice-and-takedown system by demanding removal of content that the courts deemed clear fair uses.[79]

A user who sends a counter-notification must include his "name, address, and telephone number, and a statement that the subscriber consents to the jurisdiction of [the] Federal District Court for the judicial district in which the address is located, or if the subscriber's address is outside of the United States, for any judicial district in which the service provider may be found . . . ."[80] The service provider must communicate the counter-notification to the copyright owner. In the case of a user who does not send a counter-notification, but whom the copyright owner nonetheless seeks to pursue, § 512(h) provides for issuance of a subpoena to compel the service provider to disclose the identity of the user. The copyright owner must present the prescribed documentation to the clerk of "any United States district court." Upon issuance of the subpoena, the service provider must "expeditiously disclose" the requested information.

---

77. *See id.* § 512(g)(1).

78. *See id.* § 512(f).

79. *See, e.g.*, Online Policy Group v. Diebold, Inc., 337 F. Supp. 2d 1195 (N.D. Cal. 2004) ($125,000 in damages and attorneys fees); *see also* Lenz v. Universal Music Corp., 572 F. Supp. 2d 1150 (N.D.Cal. 2008)

(holding damages available to recompense for the "financial and personal expenses associated with responding to the claim of infringement"). *Cf.* Rossi v. Motion Picture Association of America, 391 F.3d 1000 (9th Cir. 2004) (mistaken take-down notices sent in good faith; no damages awarded).

80. 17 U.S.C. § 512(g)(3)(D).

5. Remedies Available Against Hosts and Conduit Transmitters of Infringing Content

Section 512 bars any award of damages against any service provider that complies with the statute's criteria. Section 512(j) sets forth the limited circumstances under which injunctive relief will be available against a complying service provider. The court may order the host or caching provider to block access to the infringing material, and to terminate the account of the subscriber who uploaded the infringing material. By contrast, if the service provider merely transmits the infringing material, the court may order the service to terminate the subscriber, but may not order the service to block access to the material, with one important exception. When the material resides on a site located outside the U.S., a court may order the U.S. access provider to block access to that site.[81] This exception is consistent with the overall scheme of the Online Liability Limitation Act, which diminishes liability in accordance with the degree to which the service provider is implicated in content it hosts or transmits. When the service merely transmits, Congress has, as a general matter, oriented the copyright owner's pursuit toward the host (as well as toward the primary infringer). But if the host is off-shore, there is a greater probability that the host will not comply, or at least that it will be more difficult and time-consuming to obtain an order against the host from a foreign jurisdiction (particularly if that jurisdiction is a "copyright haven"). In that case, the only meaningful relief will be from the U.S. participants in the communication, hence the court's power to order local access providers to block foreign sites (but not to order local access providers to block local sites; the latter order is properly directed against the site itself).[82]

---

81. *See id.* § 512(j)(1)(B)(ii).

82. *Cf.* United States v. Rojadirecta.com, No. 11–cv–4139–PAC, 2011 WL 2428753 (S.D.N.Y. June 17, 2011) (Immigrations and Customs Enforcement seizure of domain name hosting links to infringing broadcasts of live sporting events).

Chapter 9

ENFORCEMENT OF COPYRIGHT

I. Jurisdictional and Procedural Issues

A. *Subject Matter Jurisdiction*

Jurisdiction to hear actions "arising under any Act of Congress relating to . . . copyrights" is given exclusively to federal courts pursuant to 28 U.S.C. § 1338(a). The typical infringement action therefore cannot be brought in a state court. In what appears to be an unprecedented holding, the Indiana Supreme Court held that in a contract action brought by a publisher against an author, in which the author files a counterclaim for copyright infringement, a state court may hear and decide the copyright counterclaim.[1] The 2011 "Leahy–Smith America Invents Act" has now "legislatively overruled" such results by amending section 1338(a) to provide: "No State court shall have jurisdiction over any claim for relief arising under any Act of Congress relating to patents, plant variety protection, or copyrights."[2] Thus the assertion of copyright infringement by means of a counterclaim will lead to the case's removal to a federal court. On the other hand, this amendment would not seem to reach those situations in which the defense requires interpretation of the Copyright Act, but the defendant raises no countervailing claim of copyright infringement, for example if the defendant asserts that the claim is preempted under section 301 of the 1976 Act (see Chapter 10, *infra*). Congress, therefore, has not entirely eliminated state courts from ruling on copyright questions. Nonetheless, the principal prior source of state court subject matter jurisdiction, so-called common-law copyright claims relating to unpublished works, has now largely vanished because section 301 of the 1976 Act has abolished state copyright law, except with respect to sound recordings fixed before February 15, 1972.

With respect to federal subject matter jurisdiction, it is sometimes difficult to determine whether a claim "arises under" the federal Copyright Act, particularly when the principal issue to be determined relates to contract interpretation or disputed ownership. Federal jurisdiction will be exclusive if the action is for copyright infringement or if its determination turns on an interpretation or application of the federal Copyright Act. In a frequently cited passage from the opinion of Judge

---

1. Green v. Hendrickson Publishers, Inc., 770 N.E.2d 784 (Ind. 2002).

2. Pub. L. 112–29, 125 Stat. 284, 112th Cong. 1st sess. (2011) sec. 19.

Friendly in *T.B. Harms v. Eliscu*, the Court of Appeals for the Second Circuit stated:

> Mindful of the hazards of formulation in this treacherous area, we think that an action "arises under" the Copyright Act if and only if the complaint is for a remedy expressly granted by the Act, e.g., a suit for infringement or for the statutory royalties for record production, or asserts a claim requiring construction of the Act ... or, at the very least and perhaps more doubtfully, presents a case where a distinctive policy of the Act requires that federal principles control the disposition of the claim. The general interest that copyrights, like all other forms of property, should be enjoyed by their true owner is not enough to meet this last test.[3]

Even if a dispute over title must be resolved antecedent to determining infringement and remedies, and the title dispute turns on contract construction, a federal court will have jurisdiction.[4] Moreover, as suggested in the *Harms* quotation, if the only dispute before the court relates to disputed title, even that will provide a basis for exclusive federal jurisdiction if the dispute turns on application of statutorily defined terms such as "work made for hire" or "joint work."[5] But if, for example, co-ownership is conceded, and the only issue is the division of royalties pursuant to principles of contract or equity, that is simply a matter of state law and does not provide a basis for federal jurisdiction.[6] The same is true if the plaintiff's complaint raises only the question whether a license has been effectively terminated because of misconduct on the part of the other party to the agreement.[7]

As with any federal court action, a substantial copyright claim will carry with it supplemental jurisdiction to hear state-law claims that are significantly related.

B. Personal jurisdiction

The usual rules that obtain in federal actions concerning the determination of personal jurisdiction over the defendant and proper venue

---

3. 339 F.2d 823, 828 (2d Cir. 1964) (citations omitted). This formulation has been more recently endorsed in, *e.g.*, 1mage Software, Inc. v. Reynolds & Reynolds, Co. 459 F.3d 1044 (4th Cir. 2006); Scandinavian Satellite Sys., AS v. Prime TV Ltd., 291 F.3d 839 (D.C. Cir. 2002); and Bassett v. Mashantucket Pequot Tribe, 204 F.3d 343 (2d Cir. 2000).

4. Vestron, Inc. v. Home Box Office, Inc., 839 F.2d 1380 (9th Cir. 1988).

5. Lieberman v. Estate of Chayefsky, 535 F. Supp. 90 (S.D.N.Y. 1982). *See also* Goodman v. Lee, 815 F.2d 1030 (5th Cir. 1987).

6. Gaiman v. McFarlane, 360 F.3d 644 (7th Cir. 2004).

7. Scholastic Entm't, Inc. v. Fox Entm't Group, Inc., 336 F.3d 982 (9th Cir. 2003).

also apply in copyright cases. Under Federal Rule of Civil Procedure 4(k)(1), the federal district court's basis for personal jurisdiction over the defendant follows that of the state courts in the state in which the federal district court is located. Fed. R. Civ. P. 4(k)(2) also permits federal courts to assert personal jurisdiction when the claim arises under federal law, no State has jurisdiction, and "exercising jurisdiction is consistent with the United States Constitution and laws." In *Graduate Mgt. Admission Council v. Raju*,[8] the defendant—the operator of a website in India—carried on its website the text of questions from GMAT examinations, whose copyright was owned by the Virginia plaintiff. The federal court, although holding that jurisdiction could not properly be asserted under the Virginia state long-arm statute because of lack of sufficient business activities within the state, found that there was an independent source of federal *in personam* jurisdiction under Federal Rule 4(k)(2).[9] Many state long-arm statutes authorize assertion of personal jurisdiction over an out-of-state actor who has committed a tort outside the state which causes harm in the state; some states further require that the in-state injury have been foreseeable, and that the defendant derive substantial income from interstate commerce. Given the ease with which works may be communicated to the forum from far-flung points of origin via the Internet, the "tort out/impact in" basis of jurisdiction is likely to be invoked with increasing frequency against alleged infringers operating from elsewhere in the U.S. or from abroad.

In *Penguin Group (USA) Inc. v. American Buddha*,[10] the New York Court of Appeals, on a question certified from the Second Circuit, considered whether, in a New York publisher's copyright infringement action, a court situated in New York could assert personal jurisdiction under the New York "long arm" statute over the operator of an "online library" whose business or servers were located in Arizona or Colorado. While the case concerned a defendant from another U.S. state, the court's analysis would appear to apply equally to a defendant from a foreign State. The New York statute, N.Y. C.P.L.R. § 302(a)(3)(ii), authorizes personal jurisdiction over an out-of-state defendant with no other contacts with New York, who, "commits a tortious act outside of the state that causes an injury to a person or property within the state, provided that the party . . . expects or reasonably should expect the act

---

8. 241 F. Supp. 2d 589 (E.D. Va. 2003),

9. *See also* Metro–Goldwyn–Mayer Studios v. Grokster, Ltd., 243 F. Supp. 2d 1073 (C.D.Cal.2003) (upholding under California "minimum contacts" standards personal jurisdiction over KaZaA, an Australian–Vanuatan entrepreneur of peer-to-peer file-sharing software; Fed. R. Civ. P. 4(k)(2) adduced as an alternative basis for personal jurisdiction). As the *Raju* and *Kazaa* cases

indicate, Rule 4(k)(2) may assume increasing importance in the context of the Internet, which may spawn copyright infringements nation-wide in impact yet lacking sufficient "minimum contacts" with any particular state.

10. 16 N.Y.3d 295, 921 N.Y.S.2d 171, 946 N.E.2d 159 (N.Y. 2011).

to have consequences in the state and derives substantial revenue from interstate or international commerce." Jurisdiction turned on whether the defendant's copyright-infringing activities in Arizona or Colorado "caused the requisite injury in New York." The complaint apparently specifically alleged neither that the defendant distributed works in New York by making them available for downloading by New York residents, nor that New York residents had engaged in infringing downloads caused by defendant's website offer. As a result, no act of infringement (through reproduction or distribution) occurred in New York, though a New York resident allegedly sustained the impact of the out-of-state act.

The New York Court of Appeals held the "situs of injury for purposes of determining long-arm jurisdiction under N.Y. C.P.L.R. § 302 (a) (3) (ii) ... [is] the residence or location of the principal place of business of the copyright holder." Although plaintiff's residence in the forum generally does not, standing alone, suffice to make the forum the place of injury, the court held that the "convergence" of "the function and nature of the Internet and the diverse ownership rights enjoyed by copyright holders situated in New York" "tipped the balance" toward siting the injury in New York.

> [T]he alleged injury in this case involves online infringement that is dispersed throughout the country and perhaps the world. In cases of this nature, identifying the situs of injury is not as simple as turning to "the place where plaintiff lost business" because there is no singular location that fits that description.
>
> As a result, although it may make sense in traditional commercial tort cases to equate a plaintiff's injury with the place where its business is lost or threatened, it is illogical to extend that concept to online copyright infringement cases where the place of uploading is inconsequential and it is difficult, if not impossible, to correlate lost sales to a particular geographic area. In short, the out-of-state location of the infringing conduct carries less weight in the jurisdictional inquiry in circumstances alleging digital piracy and is therefore not dispositive.[11]

The court stressed that the NYCPLR's additional prerequisites of substantial revenue from interstate or international commerce, and of foreseeability of the in-state injury, together with constitutional norms of "minimum contacts," ensured that "our decision today does not open a Pandora's box allowing any nondomiciliary accused of digital copyright

11. 16 N.Y.3d at 305.

infringement to be haled into a New York court when the plaintiff is a New York copyright owner of a printed literary work."[12]

C. *Applicable Law*

1. Cross-border copyright infringement: When U.S. law applies

As the *American Buddha* case (just discussed) illustrates, cross-border copyright infringement, while not new with the Internet (consider broadcasting and cross-border "signal bleed"[13]), may be becoming increasingly prevalent given the ease with which digital files may be sent to and from anywhere in the world. If a digital file is uploaded from outside the U.S. to a U.S.-based website, has a copyright infringement occurred in the U.S.? If the file resides on an off-shore website, but is streamed to or downloaded by U.S. users, or is offered to U.S. users for streaming or downloading, has a copyright infringement occurred in the U.S.? What if the allegedly infringing communication originates in the U.S. but culminates abroad?

The Ninth Circuit in *Subafilms, Ltd. v. MGM–Pathé Communications Co.*,[14] held that no U.S. copyright violation occurred when the U.S.-resident defendant, operating from its Los Angeles offices, allegedly directed its agents in Mexico to exhibit motion pictures without the copyright owner's permission. The court declined the plaintiff's invitation to interpret the "to authorize" prong of section 106 ("exclusive rights to do or to authorize") to cover the authorization from the U.S. of an allegedly copyright-infringing act abroad. Thus, mere "authorization" does not establish a distinct infringing act; the allegedly infringing conduct that is "authorized," such as public performance of the films, must also occur in the U.S. By contrast, where an initiating act takes place here, U.S. copyright law may reach the foreign culmination of the infringement if the initial act that occurred in the U.S. was itself a copyright infringement. Thus, in several cases involving the making in the U.S. of an infringing "root copy" of a work that was subsequently transmitted outside the U.S. or distributed in copies outside the U.S., courts have found that the initial U.S. infringement justified awarding

---

12. *Id.* at 307. One may nonetheless query whether the additional prerequisites are not both under- and over-inclusive. Overinclusive because once a work is made available on the Internet, it is foreseeable that it can be accessed anywhere in the U.S. (or the world). Under-inclusive because not all internet infringers derive substantial revenue from interstate or international commerce; indeed some may derive no revenue at all. In the latter instance, however,

the section 512 notice-and-takedown procedure (discussed *supra* chapter 8) may afford sufficient relief.

13. *Cf.* Allarcom Pay Television, Ltd. v. General Instr. Corp., 69 F.3d 381, 387 (9th Cir. 1995) (holding U.S. copyright law did not apply to television programming broadcast from the United States to Canada).

14. 24 F.3d 1088 (9th Cir. 1994) (en banc).

relief for the ensuing acts of public performance or distribution that occurred abroad.[15]

In the reverse scenario, in which the point of origin of the communication is outside the U.S. but the actual or intended recipients of the copies, the public performance, or the public display are located in the U.S., courts have readily found that an act of infringement, to which U.S. law applied, takes place in the U.S. Thus, in *Shropshire v. Canning*,[16] the Canadian defendant uploaded an infringing copy of a video to YouTube's website in U.S.; the court found that the copying of the video onto YouTube's U.S.-based server and its public performance of the video from the server constituted acts of infringement occurring in the U.S. In *Twentieth Century Fox Film Corp. v. iCraveTV*,[17] iCrave TV, a Toronto-based website, converted into videostreaming format the broadcast signals from U.S. television programming received across the border, and made the programming available to U.S. viewers via its Canadian website. The court found that the alleged infringement occurred in the United States when U.S. citizens "received and viewed defendants' streaming of the copyrighted materials," without plaintiffs' authorization, even though the streaming began in Canada. The receipt of the transmissions in the U.S. constituted public performances under U.S. copyright law.

2. Application of foreign copyright laws

When the infringement takes place wholly abroad, *Subafilms* instructs that U.S. copyright law will not apply, even when the parties are U.S. residents. The non-applicability of U.S. law, however, does not mean that no infringement claim may be pursued in U.S. courts: in recent years there has been an increasing willingness on the part of the U.S. courts to consider claims of infringement committed on foreign soil

15. *See, e.g.,* Update Art Inc. v. Modiin Publ'g Ltd., 843 F.2d 67 (2d Cir. 1988) (publication in Israel of photograph of poster; initial copy of photograph allegedly made in U.S. and sent to Israel for further copying and distribution); Peter Rosenbaum Photography v. Otto Doosan Mail Order, Ltd., 76 U.S.P.Q.2d 1759 (N.D. Ill. 2005) ("predicate act" of infringement of photograph in U.S. when source copy of photographs reproduced in catalogs in Japan and Korea was made in the U.S.); Sheldon v. Metro–Goldwyn Pictures Corp., 106 F.2d 45 (2d Cir. 1939), *aff'd*, 309 U.S. 390 (1940) (distribution in Canada of motion picture held to infringe plaintiff's play); *see also* L.A. News Serv. v. Reuters Television, 149 F.3d 987, 991 (9th Cir. 1998) (unauthorized transmission of film footage from New York to Europe and Africa violates no rights under U.S. law because those transmissions do not constitute "completed act of infringement" within the U.S.; but damages awarded for the extraterritorial transmissions because those transmissions were made from unauthorized copies of the footage that had been made in New York, following an unauthorized transmission of the film from Los Angeles to New York).

16. No. 10 CV–01941–LHK, 2011 WL 3667492 (N.D. Cal. Aug. 22, 2011).

17. No. 00–121, 2000 WL 255989 (W.D. Pa. Feb. 8, 2000).

and to apply foreign copyright law. In other words, infringement actions are increasingly viewed as "transitory" (rather than "local"), as much as an action in tort or for breach of contract. If there is personal jurisdiction over the defendant and a basis for subject-matter jurisdiction (diversity of citizenship, even if not a federal question), it has been held that "[A] copyright owner may sue an infringer in United States courts even though the only alleged infringement occurred in another country. Under the territoriality principle, the copyright law of the other country, and not United States copyright law, will govern the action in the United States."[18]

In *Boosey & Hawkes Music Publishers, Ltd. v. Walt Disney Co.,*[19] in which the assignees of Igor Stravinsky challenged the rights of Disney to market videocassettes of the well-known film *Fantasia*, containing the composer's *The Rite of Spring*, copyright infringements were asserted under the laws of 18 foreign nations. In 1998 the Court of Appeals for the Second Circuit held that the federal district court in New York should not dismiss the case because of *forum non conveniens*, but should rather be prepared to hear the case and apply foreign law. That same court, the same year, held that it is particularly appropriate to apply foreign law (in that case, Russia's) with respect to the matter of copyright ownership (as distinguished from the issue of infringement) when at issue were the respective rights of Russian newspaper reporters and publishers.[20]

D. Standing: Who may sue

The 1976 Act defines "infringer of the copyright" and accords rights to institute infringement actions. Section 501(a) provides that "Anyone who violates any of the exclusive rights of the copyright owner as provided by sections 106 through 122, or who imports copies or phonorecords into the United States in violation of section 602, is an infringer

18. Armstrong v. Virgin Records, 91 F. Supp. 2d 628 (S.D.N.Y. 2000) (alleged infringements in England). *See also* London Film Productions, Ltd. v. Intercontinental Communications, Inc., 580 F. Supp. 47 (S.D.N.Y. 1984) (British films allegedly infringed in Chile, Venezuela, Peru, Ecuador, Costa Rica and Panama).

For a striking example of adjudication of multiple-territory copyright claims, see *Monroig v. RMM Records & Video Corp.*, 196 F.R.D. 214, 220 (D.P.R. 2000), in which plaintiff's song was modified and reproduced without authorization in phonorecords and on the sound track of a film distributed in Puerto Rico, Venezuela, Chile, Panama, Nicaragua, Costa Rica, Guatemala, Ecuador, Peru, Mexico, Spain, Portugal, Japan, Uruguay and Colombia. Plaintiff did not receive authorship credit as the composer. The court found violations not only of the songwriter's reproduction rights under the U.S. Copyright Act, but also of his moral rights in each of the countries of distribution. The court awarded $5,000,000 for the combined foreign moral rights violations.

19. 145 F.3d 481 (2d Cir. 1998).

20. Itar–Tass Russian News Agency v. Russian Kurier, Inc., 153 F.3d 82 (2d Cir. 1998).

of the copyright." Section 501(a), particularly when read in conjunction with section 201(d)(2), makes clear what had been a source of confusion under the prior law. Under section 201(d)(2), any of the exclusive rights in section 106 may be transferred and owned separately, and the "owner of any particular exclusive right is entitled, to the extent of that right, to all of the protection and remedies accorded to the copyright owner by this title." Copyright ownership is thus said to be "divisible" under the 1976 Copyright Act.

Divisibility of copyright has implications regarding who can bring an action for copyright infringement. Section 501(b) states that "The legal or beneficial owner of an exclusive right under a copyright is entitled . . . to institute an action for any infringement of that particular right committed while he or she is the owner of it." Thus, if novelist *A* transfers her hardcover publication rights to *B*, her paperback rights to *C*, her translation rights to *D*, and her motion picture rights to *E*, each of those persons—provided the transfers were exclusive—may bring an infringement action against any other person who, without authorization, is exercising the particular exclusive right held. Because, in any one of these infringement actions, *A*'s interests will likely be affected—and perhaps so too will the interests of some or all of the other hypothetical characters—section 501(b) provides that the court may (and sometimes must) direct the plaintiff to give these others notice, and "may require the joinder, and shall permit the intervention, of any person having or claiming an interest in the copyright."

By conferring the right to sue on the "legal *or beneficial* owner" (emphasis supplied), the statute also gives standing to authors even after they have assigned their rights, if the authors maintain a continuing financial interest in their works. If, for example, a novelist or songwriter conveys copyright under an agreement providing for the payment of royalties based on sales, the transferee publisher is the legal copyright owner, but the novelist or songwriter is regarded as the beneficial owner and may bring an action even if the publisher does not.[21]

A person holding a *nonexclusive* license to exercise one or more of the rights set forth in section 106 may not sue for infringement. Thus, an action for infringement resulting from the unauthorized public performance of a popular song must be brought by the copyright owner, typically a music publishing company, and may not be brought by the performing rights society of which the songwriter or publisher is a

---

21. H.R. Rep. No. 94–1476, at 159 (1976). The beneficial owner may himself, however, be an infringer of the copyright held by the legal owner if he fails to secure the consent of the latter to copying or to preparing a derivative work. Fantasy, Inc. v. Fogerty, 654 F. Supp. 1129 (N.D. Cal. 1987).

member, such as ASCAP or BMI (even though the society will be conducting the litigation in all of its details).[22]

Courts have recently rejected claims by non-copyright owners to whom the copyright owners have assigned a purported right to bring an infringement action. In one instance, the author, a screenwriter, was not a copyright owner because her script was a work for hire. The Ninth Circuit, *en banc*, held ineffective the producer's assignment to her of a right to sue another producer whose television program allegedly infringed the screenplay, when the assigning producer did not also grant her an ownership interest in the screenplay.[23] In a less sympathetic context, in *Righthaven, LLC v. Democratic Underground, LLC*,[24] Righthaven obtained assignments of copyright from online news sources and initiated infringement actions against third parties whose websites copied the assignor's articles in whole or in part. A user of Democratic Underground's website posted a comment on the site that incorporated extracts from a Las Vegas Review–Journal article. Righthaven then obtained an assignment of the copyright from the Review–Journal and sued Democratic Underground for copyright infringement. The court ruled that Righthaven lacked standing, because Righthaven had acquired nothing more than a right to sue. The assignor Las Vegas Review–Journal's retention in fact of full control over the copyright in its article meant that Righthaven was not a "copyright owner."

E.   *Registration as a prerequisite to suit*

Prior to March 1, 1989, it was a requirement of an infringement action that the copyright in the allegedly infringed work be registered in the Copyright Office (typically by the plaintiff copyright owner). As a result of U.S. adherence to the Berne Convention, implementing legislation eliminated this prerequisite to suit—but only for works initially published in *other* nations that are members of the Berne Union. Works initially published in the United States must still be registered with the Copyright Office prior to suit.[25] This two-tiered system of registration has been criticized on the ground that it operates to the disadvantage of U.S. authors and publishers.

Even apart from the requirement of registration as a condition of suit, the Copyright Act affords sufficient incentives to registration such

---

22.   Ocasek v. Hegglund, 116 F.R.D. 154 (D. Wyo. 1987); Broadcast Music, Inc. v. CBS, Inc., 421 F. Supp. 592 (S.D.N.Y. 1983).

23.   Silvers v. Sony Pictures Entertainment, Inc., 402 F.3d 881 (9th Cir. *en banc* 2005).

24.   791 F. Supp. 2d 968 (D. Nev. 2011). *See also* Righthaven, LLC v. Hoehn, 792 F. Supp. 2d 1138 (D. Nev. 2011); Righthaven, LLC v. Wolf, 100 U.S.P.Q.2d 1476 (D. Colo. 2011).

25.   For a discussion of how the courts have administered this requirement, see *supra* Chapter 5, pages 118–20.

that it is common for copyright owners (at least of published works) to register their copyright long before there is any hint of litigation. If, for example, registration is made before a work is published or within five years after it is published, the certificate of registration "shall constitute prima facie evidence of the validity of the copyright and of the facts stated in the certificate."[26] This can be a significant aid to a plaintiff in proving copyright ownership, the originality of the work, the validity of the copyright, and priority of publication. Prompt registration is also a means of ensuring that in any possible future litigation the plaintiff will be eligible to claim attorney's fees and statutory damages.[27]

In some instances, the Copyright Office may choose not to register a person's claim of copyright, perhaps because the work is regarded as lacking in original authorship. In those cases in which the plaintiff must allege registration (which continue to be the overwhelming number of copyright infringement actions), the statute deals with the Register of Copyright's nonregistration by permitting the lawsuit—after the plaintiff has made proper efforts to register the copyright—but requiring the plaintiff to serve the Register with a copy of the complaint. In such cases, the Register is afforded the opportunity to become a party to the action with respect to the issue of registrability.[28]

F.   Limitations on liability: statute of limitations and sovereign immunity

There are two important limitations on exposure to copyright liability. The first is section 507 of the Copyright Act, which sets forth a period of limitations of three years for civil proceedings and five years for criminal proceedings. The running of the statute is "tolled" during any period of fraudulent concealment of the infringement or, more generally, when a reasonable person in the plaintiff's shoes would not have discovered the infringement.[29] Does "discovery" imply a duty to seek out infringements? Arguably, a reasonable person could regularly search the internet to look for websites carrying her work. The court in *Mackie v. Hipple*,[30] in an action involving an unauthorized photograph of a publicly displayed sculpture, declined to adopt such a rule, observing that the defendant "presents no case law indicating that [the plaintiff sculptor] had an affirmative duty to police the internet and stock photography agencies to find infringing copies of his work."[31]

26.   17 U.S.C. § 410(c).

27.   *See supra* pp. 120–21; 17 U.S.C. § 412.

28.   17 U.S.C. § 411(a).

29.   Taylor v. Meirick, 712 F.2d 1112 (7th Cir. 1983).

30.   96 U.S.P.Q.2d 1932 (W.D. Wash. 2010).

31.   The "duty to police" defense, albeit for now unsuccessful, might be seen in the larger context of defenses that endeavor to shift to authors and copyright owners the

The courts are divided, however, on the question whether repeated acts of infringement—the latest of which may be minor and may occur long after the principal infringements have ceased—should be treated as a single "continuing" wrong, such that the plaintiff may sue for all infringing acts so long as the most recent one falls within the three-year statutory period.[32] Courts also divide over the availability of a laches defense to a claim brought within the statutory limitations period.[33]

A second, and controversial, limitation on copyright liability is the doctrine of sovereign immunity. The Eleventh Amendment to the Constitution prevents federal courts from hearing claims against states. Although the Supreme Court has held that Congress has the power to abrogate that immunity, the scope of that congressional power has been the subject of evolving and not altogether clear standards since the 1980s (accompanied by sharp divisions within the Court). The Court held in 1989 that Congress could abrogate the immunity of the states in substantive areas falling within Article I of the Constitution, such as interstate commerce and patents and copyrights.[34] However, the intention to make states liable for money damages had to be manifested in very explicit statutory language,[35] and in 1990 Congress added a new section 511 explicitly providing that the state, the state instrumentality, or their employees "shall not be immune, under the Eleventh Amendment of the Constitution of the United States or any other doctrine of sovereign immunity" from suit in a federal court for copyright infringement, and that the full range of remedies ordinarily available against private defendants is also available in such suits.

Congress' clarification did not long survive. In 1999, the Court addressed whether it was constitutional for Congress to subject the states to patent-infringement or trademark-infringement liability by means of provisions that were essentially the same as those added to the Copyright Act in 1990. In the two *Florida Prepaid Postsecondary* cases, the Court considered the Commerce and Patent Clauses of the Constitution, as well as the Fourteenth Amendment, which empowers Congress to enact legislation implementing the constitutional ban on state deprivation of "property" without due process of law. The Court held, 5 to 4,

---

burden of objecting to unauthorized exploitations, thus inverting the normal copyright rule requiring would-be exploiters to obtain the rightholder's permission. *See* discussion *supra* Chapter 7 at page 198 (fair use and implied licenses).

32. *Compare Meirick*, 712 F.2d 1112 ("continuing wrong"), *with* Roley v. New World Pictures, Ltd., 19 F.3d 479 (9th Cir. 1994) (rejecting a "rolling statute of limitations").

33. *Compare* Lyons Partnership LP v. Morris Costumes Inc., 243 F.3d 789 (4th Cir. 2001), *with* Chirco v. Crosswinds Communities, Inc., 474 F.3d 227 (6th Cir. 2007); Danjac LLC v. Sony Corp., 263 F.3d 942 (9th Cir. 2001).

34. Pennsylvania v. Union Gas Co., 491 U.S. 1 (1989).

35. Atascadero State Hosp. v. Scanlon, 473 U.S. 234 (1985).

that on the facts presented none of those constitutional sources empowered Congress to abrogate the immunity of the states against federal-court actions for damages for patent or trademark infringement.[36]

The following year, in *Chavez v. Arte Publico Press*,[37] the *Florida Prepaid* Patent Act decision was held dispositive by the Court of Appeals for the Fifth Circuit in an action for copyright infringement by an author against the University of Houston, a state agency. The court held that the 1990 amendments to the Copyright Act purporting to render states fully liable for copyright infringement, including damages, exceeded Congress's power under both Article I and the Fourteenth Amendment. (Under generally prevailing sovereign-immunity jurisprudence, there is no bar to the issuance of injunctions against state instrumentalities or to judgments for damages against state officials in their individual capacity.[38])

Given the broad use of copyrighted materials by state instrumentalities—libraries,[39] schools, universities, as well as the wide range of typical executive and administrative agencies—their immunity against damages actions creates a major gap in the enforcement of the copyright laws, especially with the compounding inequity of the states' ability to enforce those laws against private parties.

II. Remedies

A. *Injunctions*

Injunctive relief, both temporary and final, has been traditionally issued in copyright actions and is expressly provided for in section 502 of the 1976 Copyright Act. In copyright, as in other cases, the plaintiff must show that four factors weigh in its favor: irreparable harm, inadequacy of money damages, balance of hardships, and public interest. Nonetheless, it had commonly been held that once the plaintiff establishes a prima facie case of a valid copyright and its infringement, irreparable injury would be presumed and a temporary injunction would

---

36. College Sav. Bank v. Florida Prepaid Postsecondary Educ. Expense Bd., 527 U.S. 666 (1999) (Lanham Trademark Act); Florida Prepaid Postsecondary Educ. Expense Bd. v. College Sav. Bank, 527 U.S. 627 (1999) (Patent Act).

37. 204 F.3d 601 (5th Cir. 2000).

38. Richard H. Fallon, Jr., *The "Conservative" Paths of the Rehnquist Court's Federalism Decisions*, 69 U. CHI. L. REV. 429, 459 (2002) ("Nearly without exception, state officials can be sued for prospective

injunctive relief, and they can often be sued for damages in their official capacities.")

39. When the University of Michigan permitted Google to scan its entire collection of in-copyright books, it did so in part because the University faced no liability for damages and it received a valuable service in return. *See* Rebecca Tushnet, *My Library: Copyright and the Role of Institutions in a Peer-to-Peer World*, 53 UCLA L. REV. 997, 1020 (2006) (discussing Michigan's "sovereign immunity against monetary damages for copyright claims").

issue.[40] So too, a permanent injunction had commonly issued when copyright validity and infringement were ultimately found: it was normally assumed that compensatory relief would not adequately redress the injury, often because it is difficult to assess, and that the infringement will likely continue in the future unless enjoined.[41]

The Supreme Court has, however, urged circumspection in the issuance of injunctions—at least in those cases in which the infringing material makes its own "transformative" literary, artistic or musical contribution. In such cases, the interests of the copyright owner and of the public (in having access to the infringing work) may be best served by limiting the remedy to one for damages.[42] More recently, in a patent case, *eBay Inc. v. MercExchange, LLC*,[43] the Supreme Court held that a permanent injunction should not automatically flow from a finding of patent infringement without scrutiny of the four factors.

Subsequent to *eBay*, some lower courts have concluded that the Supreme Court has generally raised the standard of requisite harm for issuance of a preliminary, as well as a permanent, injunction. Thus, in *Salinger v. Colting*,[44] the Second Circuit affirmed the district court's holding that "J.D. California"—the pseudonymous author of *60 Years Later: Coming Through the Rye*, an unauthorized sequel to J.D. Salinger's *The Catcher in the Rye*—was unlikely to succeed on the merits of his fair use defense of parody or other transformative use. Nonetheless, the Second Circuit held that recent Supreme Court decisions abrogated prior Second Circuit precedent presuming irreparable harm once the court has found a likelihood of success on the merits of a copyright infringement claim, and therefore reversed the district court's entry of a preliminary injunction.[45]

If automatic entry of a preliminary injunction upon a showing of likelihood of success on the merits, or of a permanent injunction following a full hearing on the merits, may have given insufficient weight to the public benefit defendant's additional creative contributions could have conferred, one may nonetheless find the opposite trend problematic. The prospect that an increasing number of courts will determine that the author's interests can be adequately protected through a judicial decree allowing continued distribution and exhibition upon the payment

---

40. Apple Computer, Inc. v. Formula Int'l, Inc., 725 F.2d 521 (9th Cir. 1984).

41. *See, e.g.*, Bridgeport Music, Inc. v. Justin Combs Pub., 507 F.3d 470 (6th Cir. 2007); Walt Disney Co. v. Powell, 897 F.2d 565 (D.C. Cir. 1990).

42. Campbell v. Acuff–Rose Music, Inc., 510 U.S. 569 (1994); New York Times Co. v. Tasini, 533 U.S. 483 (2001).

43. 547 U.S. 388 (2006).

44. 607 F.3d 68 (2d Cir. 2010).

45. *See also* Vergara Hermosilla v. Coca–Cola Co., 717 F. Supp. 2d 1297 (S.D. Fla. 2010) (declining to prohibit exploitation of the plaintiff's Spanish-language version of the song, but ordering the defendant to credit the plaintiff as the author of the version).

of a reasonable royalty raises two concerns. The first is institutional: is it appropriate for a court of equity systematically to impose judicially created compulsory licenses in lieu of the statutory injunctive remedy? Second, copyright is a property right; the right to prevent third parties from exploiting the work, including by making unauthorized derivative works (whose production will necessarily entail creative value-added), is the essence of the "exclusive right." Denial of injunctive relief undermines the ability to control both the market and the artistic destiny of the work, yet that control may provide the core incentives that promote the production of works of authorship.[46] It remains to be seen, in any event, how courts assess the four factors, in particular whether the "public interest" factor takes into account not only the benefits of access to the defendant's infringing work, but also the detriment to the value of the author's creation.

In addition to enjoining further distribution or communication of the infringing work, the court may also order, pursuant to section 503, the impounding and the reasonable disposition (including the destruction) of all infringing copies and phonorecords and of the devices used to manufacture them.

B. *Damages*

Perhaps the most intricate, and most important, remedial section of the statute is section 504, which spells out in detail the circumstances under which damages and profits may be awarded. The Act provides for the award of either *actual* damages and any additional profits, or what are known as *statutory* damages.

1. Actual Damages and Profits

In order to dispel the confusion that had existed under the 1909 Act regarding the possible duplicative award of actual damages and profits, section 502 of the 1976 Act provides:

---

46. *See, e.g.,* Salinger v. Colting, 641 F. Supp. 2d 250, 268 (S.D.N.Y. 2009), *rev'd on other grounds,* 607 F.3d 68 (2d Cir. 2010) (rejecting argument that Colting's entry into the market for sequels that Salinger declined to exploit was fair use):

This approach is also consistent with the purposes of copyright in "promot[ing] the Progress of Science and useful Arts ...," U.S. Const., Art. I, § 8, cl. 8, because some artists may be further incentivized to create original works due to the availability of the right not to produce any sequels. This might be the case if, for instance, an author's artistic vision includes leaving certain portions or aspects of his character's story to the varied imaginations of his readers, or if he hopes that his readers will engage in discussion and speculation as to what happened subsequently. Just as licensing of derivatives is an important economic incentive to the creation of originals, so too will the right *not* to license derivatives sometimes act as an incentive to the creation of originals.

The copyright owner is entitled to recover the actual damages suffered by him or her as a result of the infringement, and any profits of the infringer that are attributable to the infringement and are not taken into account in computing the actual damages. In establishing the infringer's profits, the copyright owner is required to present proof only of the infringer's gross revenue, and the infringer is required to prove his or her deductible expenses and the elements of profit attributable to factors other than the copyrighted work.

The principal purpose of the statutory provision is to avoid double-counting in the computation of monetary remedies. Thus, if the copyright owner marketed its copyrighted wares only east of the Mississippi River at a profit of $1 per unit, and the infringer marketed its infringing wares from coast to coast at a profit of 50 cents per unit, a court should award damages measured by the loss of $1 for each of the plaintiff's displaced east-region sales and the infringer's profits measured by 50 cents for each of the west-region sales. A frequently used measure of the plaintiff's damages is the reasonable value that the defendant would have paid for a license to use the copyrighted material legally.[47] It is, of course, sometimes difficult to determine which of the defendant's sales should be treated as causing a direct economic loss to the plaintiff (i.e., damages) and which should be treated exclusively as generating noncumulative profits for the defendant.[48]

Once the court separates out the defendant's profits, it is at least as difficult to determine which of those profits "are attributable to the infringement." All that the plaintiff need do is prove the defendant's gross profits derived from the enterprise of which the infringement is a part. The burden then shifts to the defendant to reduce the award of profits, which can be done in two different ways.

The defendant may show that its profits were derived from elements of its activities other than the infringement. A motion picture producer who has made illicit use of a copyrighted novel can show, for instance, that the bulk of its box-office (and video sale and rental) receipts can be traced to its starring players, its original plot elements, its cinematography and special effects, its advertising campaign, and the like.[49] The defendant may also show—whether or not its gross profits were attributable to noninfringing elements—that its venture in fact was so costly as to eliminate most or all of its profits. Thus, even if an infringing

---

47. On Davis v. The Gap, Inc., 246 F.3d 152 (2d Cir. 2001).

48. *See* Taylor v. Meirick, 712 F.2d 1112 (7th Cir. 1983).

49. *See* Sheldon v. Metro–Goldwyn Pictures Corp., 309 U.S. 390 (1940). *See gener-*

ally Caffey v. Cook, 409 F. Supp. 2d 484 (S.D.N.Y. 2006), for a thorough discussion of the noninfringing elements contributing to profits, as well as the costs of a theatrical production.

theatrical production is based word-for-word on a copyrighted dramatic text, the defendant can attempt to prove that the salaries of the performers, the cost of renting the theater, the cost of advertising and the like were so high as totally to absorb its box-office receipts. In such a case, it would be proper for the court to award no profits—although it would of course be perfectly appropriate for the court to award damages as measured by the reasonable value of a license to perform the play publicly, or as measured by the lost opportunity to market the script to a film producer (because of the bad press received by the infringing theatrical performance).

Two decisions by the Court of Appeals for the Ninth Circuit, in which the court had to make difficult determinations in assessing the defendant's profits, are illustrative. In one case, the infringing brewing company used the plaintiff's music as a minor accompaniment pattern in a beer commercial.[50] In another, the infringer was a hotel and gambling enterprise that used the plaintiff's music in one part of a multi-scene musical revue in the hotel theater.[51] The court's decisions should be examined for thoughtful suggestions as to how to assess the plaintiffs' possible claims, respectively, to all of the brewer's profits on the advertised beer and to all of the profits from the hotel's gambling operations that were presumably fueled in part by those who attended the nearby musical theater. In a later case raising the issue, the Court of Appeals for the Second Circuit observed:

> [I]f a publisher published an anthology of poetry which contained a poem covered by the plaintiff's copyright, we do not think the plaintiff's statutory burden would be discharged by submitting the publisher's gross revenue resulting from its publication of hundreds of titles, including trade books, textbooks, cookbooks, etc. In our view, the owner's burden would require evidence of the revenues realized from the sale of the anthology containing the infringing poem. The publisher would then bear the burden of proving its costs attributable to the anthology and the extent to which its profits from the sale of the anthology were attributable to factors other than the infringing poem, including particularly the other poems contained in the volume.... [T]he statutory term "infringer's gross revenue" should not be construed so broadly as to include revenue from lines of business that were unrelated to the act of infringement.[52]

50. Cream Records, Inc. v. Jos. Schlitz Brewing Co., 754 F.2d 826 (9th Cir. 1985).

51. Frank Music Corp. v. Metro–Goldwyn–Mayer, Inc., 772 F.2d 505 (9th Cir. 1985).

52. *The Gap*, 246 F.3d at 160. *See also* Mackie v. Rieser, 296 F.3d 909 (9th Cir. 2002) (copyrighted sculpture was depicted in symphony orchestra brochure, without permission; sculptor unsuccessfully based

In making all of these calculations, courts are obviously often reduced to engaging in approximations. It is commonly held that "Any doubt as to the computation of costs or profits is to be resolved in favor of the plaintiff."[53]

2.　Statutory Damages

As an alternative to an award of actual damages and profits, section 504(c)(1) gives to the plaintiff the right to "elect, at any time before final judgment is rendered, to recover . . . an award of statutory damages for all infringements involved in the action, with respect to any one work . . . in a sum of not less than $750 or more than $30,000 as the court considers just." Such an award is referred to as "statutory damages." The Supreme Court has held—based on constitutional law and history— that when an infringement case is being tried to a jury, all issues pertinent to the award of statutory damages are to be decided by a jury.[54] Statutory damages (and attorney's fees) are available only if the work was registered with the copyright office before the infringement occurred or if, in the case of a published work, the post-infringement registration of the copyright was effected within three months following publication.[55] The registration precondition to statutory damages applies to U.S. and to foreign works alike.[56]

Statutory damages provide a vindication of the copyright owner's interest when litigation would otherwise appear largely futile even though just. For example, in some cases of copyright infringement, such as the occasional unauthorized music performance in a restaurant or nightclub, proof of actual damages and profits may be difficult or nonexistent—despite the acknowledged violation of the plaintiff's rights. Such cases are appropriate for the award of statutory damages. In addition the purpose of the statutory-damage remedy is largely deterrent and even punitive. Indeed, under section 504(c)(2), the court has the discretion to award as much as $150,000 per work infringed, upon determining that the infringement was committed "willfully" (which is generally understood to require proof that the defendant knew it was violating the law). For that reason it is generally regarded as inappropri-

---

claim for profits upon the orchestra's gross box-office income for the musical season).

53.　*Frank Music Corp.*, 772 F.2d at 514.

54.　Feltner v. Columbia Pictures Television, Inc., 523 U.S. 340 (1998). *But cf.* BMG Music v. Gonzalez, 430 F.3d 888 (7th Cir. 2005) (no right to a jury determination of damages award when plaintiff requests minimum statutory damages award for will-

ful infringement because no dispute of fact regarding amount to award).

55.　17 U.S.C. § 412.

56.　*See, e.g.*, Elsevier B.V. v. United-Health Group, Inc., 93 U.S.P.Q.2d 1408 (S.D.N.Y. 2010); Football Association Premier League Ltd. v. YouTube, Inc., 633 F. Supp. 2d 159 (S.D.N.Y. 2009).

ate to award punitive damages in an infringement action in which statutory damages are sought.[57]

If the defendant has willfully infringed a large number of works, the total statutory damage award may be so elevated as to seem excessive, particularly if the infringer is not large and wealthy.[58] The problem may have been most acutely posed in the P2P file-sharing cases, in which two juries have awarded over $500,000 against each of two individual file-sharers. Although the awards came within the statutory range, indeed were not at the top of the scale for willful infringement, both courts found the total awards to be vastly disproportionate. In *Capitol Records v. Thomas–Rasset*,[59] the court applied *remittitur* to reduce the jury's award of statutory damages from $80,000 per sound recording infringed to $2,250 (three times the statutory minimum per work infringed). In *Sony BMG Music Entertainment v. Tenenbaum*,[60] the district court had held the jury's award of $22,500 for each of 30 recorded songs, for a total award of $675,000, to violate due process; the First Circuit reversed, on the ground that, rather than reaching a constitutional issue, the district court should have applied *remittitur*.

Although the plaintiff need not offer proof of actual damages or profits to secure statutory damages, the court of course may—and generally does—take account of such proof in making an award of statutory damages. It should be noted that the general statutory range of $750 to $30,000 applies not to each infringement of an exclusive right, but rather to each work infringed by the defendant, regardless of the number of infringements. Thus, if a nightclub without a performance license stages twice-nightly performances of 10 songs over a period of four months, the court can make only 10 statutory-damage awards, one for each copyrighted song. Similarly, if the defendant violates both the reproduction and the public performance rights in a given work (for example, by providing a work both for downloading and for streaming), the court may make only one award of statutory damages.

Section 504(c) further contains the total award by expressly providing that "For the purposes of this subsection, all the parts of a compilation or derivative work constitute one work." Copying without consent all of the songs on a record album would most likely give rise to a single award of statutory damages (at least where the songs have been selected and organized for inclusion in the album), while copying and marketing

---

57. *The Gap*, 246 F.3d 152.

58. *See generally* Pamela Samuelson & Tara Wheatland, *Statutory Damages in Copyright Law: A Remedy in Need of Reform*, 51 WILLIAM & MARY L. REV. 439 (2009).

59. 680 F. Supp. 2d 1045 (D. Minn. 2010).

60. 721 F. Supp. 2d 85 (D.Mass. 2010), rev'd, 660 F.3d 487 (1st Cir. 2011).

DVDs containing several television shows from a single season would most likely give rise to multiple awards.[61]

Just as the statute provides for an award of statutory damages five times as great as the usual amount in the case of willful infringement, section 504(c) also provides for reductions below the statutory "floor" in certain cases of demonstrated innocent infringement. If the infringer can prove that he or she "was not aware and had no reason to believe that his or her acts constituted an infringement," the court may reduce the award to as little as $200. (Since the effective date of the Berne Convention Implementation Act, March 1, 1989—abandoning the requirement of a notice on each copy in order to preserve the copyright—this has been the principal remaining statutory inducement to copyright owners to place a conspicuous copyright notice on their works.) And statutory damages may be remitted by the court completely if the defendant reasonably believed that his or her use was a fair use under section 107 and the defendant was an employee of a nonprofit school or library, acting in the scope of employment (or was, under certain conditions, a public broadcaster).

C. Costs and Attorney's Fees

As a final element of compensatory relief, a court has the discretion, under section 505, to award costs to either party and to award a reasonable attorney's fee to the prevailing party. Recall that, under section 412, pre-infringement registration (or registration within the three-month post-publication grace period) is a prerequisite to an award of attorney's fees.

In 1994, the Supreme Court, in *Fogerty v. Fantasy, Inc.*,[62] addressed a question that had divided the circuits: whether attorney's fees are more readily to be awarded to successful plaintiffs (in order to encourage the litigation of meritorious claims of copyright infringement, which promotes the public interest in creativity) or whether a more evenhanded standard should be applied. The Supreme Court endorsed the latter view, noting that in order to serve "the purpose of enriching the general public through access to creative works, ... defendants who seek to advance a variety of meritorious copyright defenses should be encour-

---

61. *Compare* Bryant v. Media Right Productions, 603 F.3d 135 (2d Cir. 2010) (ten songs each on record albums "Songs for Dogs" and "Songs for Cats": each album constitutes a single work for purposes of statutory damages), *with* WB Music Corp. v. RTV Comm. Group, Inc., 445 F.3d 538, 541 (2d Cir. 2006) (songs on album had been separately released; held to be sepa-rate works for purposes of statutory damages); MCA T.V., Ltd. v. Feltner, 89 F.3d 766 (11th Cir. 1996); Twin Peaks Prods., Inc. v. Publications Int'l Ltd., 996 F.2d 1366, 1381 (2d Cir. 1993) (both finding each episode of television series to be separate work).

62.   510 U.S. 517 (1994).

aged to litigate them to the same extent that plaintiffs are encouraged to litigate meritorious claims of infringement."[63] The Court, however, rejected the argument that the prevailing party should routinely be awarded attorney's fees, as is true under the "British Rule." Rather, the Court concluded that the language of the Copyright Act makes it clear that such fees are to be awarded to prevailing parties only as a matter of the court's discretion, based upon such factors as frivolousness, motive, objective unreasonableness, and the need in certain cases to advance considerations of compensation and deterrence (so long as applied even-handedly to prevailing plaintiffs and defendants).[64]

D. Criminal Liability

In rare cases, copyright infringement may result in the imposition of criminal liability under section 506. Under section 506(a), the government must prove that the infringement was willful (understood to mean that there is awareness of illegal activity) and either "for purposes of commercial advantage or private financial gain" or "by the reproduction or distribution, including by electronic means" of copies or phonorecords—during any 180–day period—with a total retail value of more than $1,000. The punishment is set forth in 18 U.S.C. § 2319, and involves a sliding-scale of fines and imprisonment based on the total value of the goods involved and the frequency with which the offense has been committed. The court also has the discretion to order the forfeiture and destruction of all infringing copies or phonorecords and of devices used in the infringement. Subsections 506(c), (d) and (e), respectively, set forth the crimes of fraudulent placement of a copyright notice, fraudulent removal of a copyright notice, and false statements of material fact in a copyright registration application. (It appears, however, that no criminal prosecutions have been brought on the basis of these provisions.) As already noted, the statute of limitations for criminal proceedings under the Copyright Act is five years (compared with three years in civil infringement cases).

In 2005, Congress added Section 506(a)(1)(C), extending criminal liability to the willful infringement "by the distribution of a work being prepared for commercial distribution, by making it available on a computer network accessible to members of the public" if the infringer knew or should have known that the work was intended for commercial distribution. Penalties for such infringement include fines, up to 3 years imprisonment for a first offense, and up to 5 years imprisonment for a

---

63. *Id.* at 527.

64. *Id.* at 534 & n.19. *See* Gonzales v. Transfer Techs., Inc., 301 F.3d 608, 610 (7th Cir. 2002) (in the interest of deter-rence, "the prevailing party in a copyright case in which the monetary stakes are small should have a presumptive entitlement to an award of attorneys' fees").

second offense (or up to 6 and 10 years, respectively, if the offense is committed for commercial advantage or private financial gain).

The same year, Congress also made it a crime to "use an audiovisual recording device to transmit or make a copy of" all or part of a copyrighted motion picture or other audiovisual work from a performance in a "motion picture exhibition facility."[65] The penalties for violation include fines, up to 3 years imprisonment for a first offense, and up to 6 years imprisonment for a subsequent offense.

As will be seen immediately below, the Digital Millennium Copyright Act of 1998 imposed certain prohibitions upon the circumvention of anti-copying devices and the removal of "copyright management information." (Sections 1201, 1202 of the Act.) Although violation is technically not a copyright infringement, these prohibitions are embraced within Title 17 of the U.S. Code; section 1203 sets out civil remedies, and section 1204 further provides that violations that are willful and for purposes of "commercial advantage or private financial gain" can result in criminal liability.

III. Technological Protection Measures and Copyright Management Information

Given the speed with which the Internet can be used both to reproduce near-perfect copies and phonorecords and to transmit them around the world, Congress concluded it was important to support the efforts of copyright owners to prevent infringement at the outset, rather than merely to seek judicial relief afterward. Of course, digital dissemination of copyrighted works also poses opportunities, notably in reducing the costs of producing hardcopies and distributing them through "bricks and mortar" stores. Congress perceived that the development of a digital marketplace would require building copyright-owner confidence that digital dissemination would not result in rampant unauthorized redistribution. The Digital Millennium Copyright Act (DMCA) was added to the Copyright Act in 1998. Its purpose (apart from the secondary-liability provisions discussed in the previous Chapter), in section 1201, is to promote lawful digital dissemination by ensuring that "technological protection measures" that copyright owners choose to apply to their works—such as scrambling or encrypting digital versions of recordings, films and books—are not circumvented without proper authorization. Such technological protection measures are intended to prevent usable copies of the copyright-protected work from being copied, stored or transmitted to others.

65. 18 U.S.C. § 2319B.

A. Technological Protection Measures: The structure of section 1201

Section 1201(a) provides that "no person shall circumvent a technological protection measure that effectively controls access to a work" protected by copyright, and that "no person shall manufacture, import, offer to the public, provide or otherwise traffic in any technology, product, service, device, component, or part thereof" that (among other things) is "primarily designed or produced" for the purpose of circumvention or is knowingly marketed for use in circumvention. While section 1201(a) thus forbids circumvention of what is known as "access-protection" technology, section 1201(b) imposes comparable proscriptions upon "copy-protection" technology. Violations of section 1201 are not technically infringements of copyright,[66] but sections 1203 and 1204 impose civil and criminal liability, respectively, much like that for copyright infringement.

Section 1201 thus defines three new violations: (a)(1) to circumvent technological protection measures that control access to copyrighted works; (a)(2) to manufacture, disseminate or offer, etc., devices or services, etc., that circumvent access controls, and (b) to manufacture, disseminate, or offer, etc., devices or services, etc., that circumvent a technological measure that "effectively protects a right of the copyright owner...." It is important to appreciate that the violation occurs with the prohibited acts; it is not necessary to prove that the dissemination of circumvention devices resulted in specific infringements or that the purpose of circumventing an access control was to commit an infringing act.[67] On the other hand, section 1201 also sets out a long, disparate (and somewhat incoherent) list of exceptions to the prohibition on circumvention of access controls.[68]

To appreciate the scope of section 1201, it is necessary to inquire further into the subject matter of its protection, into the acts it prohibits, and into its accommodation of copyright exceptions.

1. Subject matter protected

Section 1201 covers two different kinds of protective measures, those that "effectively control access to a work protected under this title

---

66. Nor is registration of copyright in the technologically protected work a prerequisite to an anticircumvention claim, *see* I.M.S. Inquiry Mgmt. v. Berkshire Info. Sys., 307 F. Supp. 2d 521 (S.D.N.Y. 2004).

67. *See, e.g.*, MDY Indus. v. Blizzard Entm't, Inc., 629 F.3d 928 (9th Cir. 2010), discussed *infra*.

68. 17 U.S.C. § 1201(d)-(j) (1998).

[the Copyright Act],"[69] and those that "effectively protect a right of a copyright owner,"[70] i.e., that protect against copying and communicating to the public. Judicial decisions construing section 1201 have considered what it means to protect "effectively." They also have addressed whether the object of the access control measure is a "work protected under this title."

With respect to effective protection, the courts are unanimous that "effective" protection does not mean protection that is especially difficult to crack.[71] In *Lexmark v. Static Controls Corp.*, a decision concerning the circumvention of a code controlling access to the functions of a computer printer, however, the Sixth Circuit Court of Appeals observed that because the printer-engine program was accessible by other means, the lock-out code could not be deemed "effective."[72]

The *Lexmark* case is most significant for its analysis of the second issue—whether the technological measure controls access to a work protected under the Copyright Act. In notorious but, happily, unsuccessful attempts to leverage the DMCA into protecting the "aftermarket" for spare and replacement parts, the producers of printers and cartridges, in one case, and of garage-door openers, in the other,[73] asserted that rival printer-cartridge and door-opener manufacturers had violated the DMCA's prohibition on circumvention of access controls. In both cases, the spare part in question would not interact with the host device unless the host device recognized the spare part as authorized to function together with the host device. If the spare part entered the appropriate authentication sequence or, in the terms of a frequently used metaphor, engaged in the "secret handshake" with the host device, then the host would be "fooled" into "thinking" that it was working with a component made by the same producer and would allow the component to perform its intended function. The "secret handshake" thus made it possible for

69. 17 U.S.C. § 1201(a).

70. *Id.* at § 1201(b).

71. 321 Studios v. MGM, 307 F. Supp. 2d 1085, 1095 (N.D. Cal. 2004); Universal City Studios v. Reimerdes, 111 F. Supp. 2d 294, 317–18 (S.D.N.Y. 2000), *aff'd sub nom*, Universal City Studios, Inc. v. Corley, 273 F.3d 429 (2d Cir. 2001) (observing that the defense that DVD protection code did not "effectively" protect DVDs because a Norwegian teenager easily cracked it "would gut the statute if it were adopted"); Sony Computer Entertainment v. Divineo, 457 F. Supp. 2d 957 (N.D. Cal. 2006) (rejecting contention that wide availability of circumvention devices makes a technological protection measure "ineffective").

72. Lexmark Int'l. v. Static Control Components, Inc., 387 F.3d 522, 547 (6th Cir. 2004). On remand from the Federal Circuit, the District Court in Storage Technology Corp. v. Custom Hardware Eng'g & Consulting, No. 02–12102–RWZ, 2006 WL 1766434 (D. Mass. 2006), followed the 6th Circuit in ruling that when access to the copyrighted work (in this instance, computer code) is otherwise available (in this instance on floppy disks), a measure controlling access by some other means is not "effective." *See also* MDY Indus. v. Blizzard Entm't, Inc., 629 F.3d 928, 953 (9th Cir. 2010) (holding access control ineffective because it only prevented access in certain circumstances).

73. Chamberlain Group v. Skylink Techs., 381 F.3d 1178 (Fed. Cir. 2004).

a rival printer cartridge to substitute for the printer producer's own replacement cartridges, and for a "universal garage door opener" to open the remote-controlled garage doors installed by a rival company.

Since neither printer cartridges nor garage doors are copyrighted works, one might query the basis on which 1201 could have applied. The plaintiffs emphasized that computer programs control the functioning of these devices, and computer programs are copyrighted works. The extraordinary consequence of plaintiffs' reasoning would have been that any useful object whose workings are controlled by computer programs can come within the scope of section 1201 if the object's producer makes access to those programs subject to an authentication sequence. As a policy matter, this result is inconceivable. Among other things, Congress has persistently declined to legislate design protection, in part because of its inability to resolve the spare-parts issue;[74] Congress is unlikely to have sought the result of an exceptionally strong design-protection regime through the stealthy means of the DMCA.

Policy aside, the text of section 1201 does not require protecting against the circumvention of the authentication sequence that controls access to the copyrightable computer program that controls the functioning of the consumer product. The *Lexmark* court reviewed earlier "secret handshake" cases, involving access to transmissions of recordings of musical works, to videogames and to motion pictures on DVDs.[75] The court underscored that all of those cases involved circumvention of access to computer programs that were "conduit[s] to protectable expression."[76] In the printer cartridge case, by contrast, operating the computer program did not make it possible to see, hear or otherwise engage with a work of authorship. Rather, "the program's output is purely functional: [it] 'controls a number of operations' in the Lexmark printer."[77]

2. Nature of the access that the measure controls

If the technological protection measure must control access to a nonfunctional copyrighted work, does the access also have to be related to the exercise of rights under copyright? The court in *Chamberlain v. Skylink* garage door opener controversy also declined to protect the authentication sequence against circumvention, but arrived at that result by addressing the *purpose* of the access that the technological

---

74. *See* 17 U.S.C. §§ 1301–1302 (2000), for the closest Congress has come, setting out a *sui generis* regime limited to the protection of boat-hull designs.

75. *See, e.g.*, RealNetworks v. Streambox, 2000 WL 127311 (W.D. Wash. Jan. 18, 2000) (one of the first decisions to find violations of technological protection measures, in that case both access and copy controls).

76. *Lexmark*, 387 F.3d at 547–48.

77. *Id.* at 548.

measure controls. The court interpolated into section 1201 a require-ment that the protection against circumvention of an access control be related to protection against infringement. To the extent that access controls forestall infringement, for example, by making unauthorized copies unplayable and therefore futile, the access control comes within the scope of section 1201. But the court determined that if the uses that the access control cuts off are not infringing uses, then the access control is not one that section 1201 was designed to protect.[78] While this distinction makes some sense in the case of garage-door openers, as applied to access controls that are "conduits" to works of authorship, the proposition is in some tension with Congress's goals in prohibiting the circumvention of those technological measures. The *Chamberlain* court worried that interpreting section 1201 to create an independent violation for circumventing access controls (or disseminating access circumvention devices) would "effectively create two distinct copyright regimes," one tied to the traditional rights of copyright owners (section 1201(b)), and the other allowing copyright owners "unlimited rights to hold circum-ventors liable under § 1201(a) merely for accessing that work, even if that access enabled only rights that the Copyright Act grants to the public."[79]

But, as the Ninth Circuit observed in *MDY Indus., LLC v. Blizzard Ent. Inc.*,[80] a controversy involving the online multi-player videogame "World of Warcraft," there is considerable evidence from the text and from the legislative history that Congress did intend to create an additional copyright regime based on the control over access to digitally distributed works of authorship. The text indicates that the "access" that section 1201(a) protects goes beyond traditional copyright preroga-tives; it distinguishes "access" from a "right of the copyright owner under this title." The legislative history shows that the DMCA was designed in part specifically to foster a variety of business models offering the public a diversity of levels of access, for a diversity of prices. The Ninth Circuit quoted the report of the House Commerce Committee:

> [A]n increasing number of intellectual property works are being distributed using a "client-server" model, where the work is effectively "borrowed" by the user.... To operate in this new environment, content providers will need both the technology to make new uses possible and the legal framework to ensure they can protect their work from piracy.[81]

---

78. *Chamberlain*, 381 F.3d at 1197–1201. *Accord*, Storage Tech. Corp. v. Custom Hardware Eng'g & Consulting, Inc., 421 F.3d 1307 (Fed. Cir. 2005).

79. *Chamberlain*, 381 F.3d at 1200–01.

80. 629 F.3d 928 (9th Cir. 2010)

81. 629 F.3d at 947–48, *quoting* H.R. REP. No. 105–551, pt. 2, at 23 (1998).

Thus, the "access" that section 1201(a) protects goes beyond traditional copyright prerogatives. The difference in scope becomes apparent if one compares the consequences of protecting a measure controlling "... access to a *work* ..." with a measure controlling "... access to a *copy* of a work...." The latter corresponds to "access" in the copyright sense of the right to distribute copies of the work; the former is the new right introduced in the DMCA. In a pay-per-view scheme, the home viewing is not a public performance; circumventing an access protection to view the film more times than paid for does not violate a "right of the copyright owner." Legal protection of the access measure thus gives the copyright owner control over consumer activities not reached by traditional copyright rights.

3.   Acts prohibited

Section 1201 prohibits the *act* of circumventing an access control and the *"trafficking"* in devices that circumvent either access controls or "rights" controls. It does not prohibit the act of circumventing a rights control, in part because the results of that act will be directly infringing (or will qualify for an exception), and in part because the most economically significant act is the distribution of the device that will allow the end-user to circumvent.

a.   Act of circumvention

While most of the cases involve devices that circumvent access and/or rights controls, a few cases have raised the question what it means to "circumvent" an access control. Although some courts have held that an unauthorized person's use of an actual password does not "circumvent,"[82] this interpretation appears inconsistent with the statute. Section 1201(a)(3)(A) defines "to circumvent" as "to descramble a scrambled work, to decrypt an encrypted work, or otherwise to avoid, bypass, remove, deactivate, or impair a technological measure, *without the authority of the copyright owner*" (emphasis supplied). Entry of the password "deactivates" the measure that restricts access;[83] if the password is employed by an unauthorized user, then the deactivation will not have occurred with the copyright owner's authority.[84]

---

82. IMS Inquiry Mgmt. Sys. v. Berkshire Info. Mgmt. Sys., 307 F. Supp. 2d 521 (S.D.N.Y. 2003). *Accord*, Egilman v. Keller & Heckman, 401 F. Supp. 2d 105 (D.D.C. 2005).

83. A password-controlled access measure fits the statutory definition of a technological measure that effectively controls access to a work. *See* 17 U.S.C. § 1201(a)(3)(B).

84. *See, e.g., Blizzard,* 629 F.3d at 943; 321 Studios v. MGM, 307 F. Supp. 2d 1085, 1098 (N.D. Cal. 2004) ("while 321's software does use the authorized key to access the DVD, it does not have authority to use this key, as licensed DVD players do, and it

b. Trafficking in circumvention devices

Section 1201(a)'s core application can be illustrated by the 2001 decision of the Court of Appeals for the Second Circuit in *Universal City Studios, Inc. v. Corley.*[85] There, the plaintiffs were eight major motion picture studios that had incorporated in their DVD versions of their copyrighted films a Content Scramble System (CSS), which prevented making copies of the DVDs, or playing them on devices lacking licensed decryption technology, or transmitting them on the Internet. The defendants posted a computer program designed to circumvent CSS (DeCSS) on their website and linked to other sites that also made DeCSS generally available. The court readily found the defendants to have violated section 1201(a)(2) ("trafficking") of the DMCA, by offering and providing on their website circumvention software that was "primarily designed" for the purpose of circumventing the CSS "technological measure that effectively controls access to a work" protected by copyright. The court also found that the defendants and DeCSS did not fall within any of the several statutory exemptions, and that the finding of liability and the issuance of an injunction did not violate the First Amendment.[86]

4.   Exceptions to circumvention of access controls

The DMCA provides a variety of exceptions to the bans upon circumvention, including for reverse engineering, encryption research and security testing.[87] The § 1201(f) exception for reverse engineering permits the circumvention of access controls for the sole purpose of creating non-infringing interoperable programs. This provision appears to offer a significant safety valve, notably because it also permits both development of devices necessary to effect the permitted reverse engineering, and distribution of the fruits of the permitted reverse engineering.[88]

therefore avoids and bypasses [the] CSS [access control].").

85. 273 F.3d 429 (2d Cir. 2001).

86. In a criminal prosecution arising from the Internet distribution of software designed to circumvent the access-protection technology used on e-books marketed on the Internet, the district court upheld section 1201(a) against a series of constitutional challenges, including vagueness, the "limited times" provision of the Copyright and Patent Clause, and the limits upon

Congress's power to regulate interstate commerce. *See* United States v. Elcom, Ltd., 203 F. Supp. 2d 1111 (N.D. Cal. 2002).

87. *See, e.g.,* Jane C. Ginsburg, *Copyright Legislation for the "Digital Millennium,"* 23 COLUM. J.L. & ARTS 137, 148–52 (1999), for a fuller description of these, and the other, exceptions to 17 U.S.C. § 1201(a) (2000).

88. *See* § 1201(f)(2)(3). The case law construing § 1201(f) remains fairly sparse. *See* Davidson & Assoc. v. Internet Gateway,

5. Copyright Office rulemaking

While the exceptions to section 1201(a) are multiple, they are also very narrowly defined and do not invite expansive judicial construction.[89] As a result, Congress instructed the Librarian of Congress, in consultation with the Register of Copyrights, to conduct a rulemaking every three years, both to identify particular "classes of works" whose users would be "adversely affected by the prohibition . . . in their ability to make noninfringing uses under this title," and to suspend the application of the prohibition on the act of access control circumvention as to those works until the next rulemaking period.[90] The burden of proving the need for the exemption falls on the proponent.[91] Each rulemaking is *de novo*: a class identified in a prior rulemaking is not automatically reinstated; the Copyright Office must determine whether a need for an exemption continues to be demonstrated. It is important to recognize, moreover, that the prohibitions against trafficking in access circumvention devices continue to apply.

A detailed discussion of the excepted classes is beyond the scope of this volume,[92] as is an analysis of other potential bases for exceptions, particularly to accommodate First Amendment concerns.[93] For present purposes it suffices to say that the excepted classes have expanded over time, ranging from obsolete formats and devices, to cover certain educational uses, and, perhaps most importantly and recently, cellphones. One such exemption allows owners of cellphones to switch phone-service networks while retaining their hardware. The need for this cellphone exception arose because of arguable misuse of the anti-circumvention protections to achieve a goal the statute was not designed to achieve. Proprietors of wireless networks appear to have been bootstrapping access to their network service to protection of the technological measure that controls access to the software which causes the cellphone to function in connection with the service. The second cellphone exemption

334 F. Supp. 2d 1164 (E.D. Mo. 2004), *aff'd*, 422 F.3d 630 (8th Cir. 2005) (rejecting application of exception).

89. *See* 17 U.S.C. § 1201(a)(1)(B)-(E) (2000).

90. 17 U.S.C. § 1201(a)(1)(C) (2000). For a fuller discussion, *see* June Besek, *Anti-Circumvention Laws and Copyright: A Report From the Kernochan Center for Law, Media and the Arts,* 27 Colum. J.L. & Arts 389, 416–23 (2004).

91. *See* Library of Congress, Copyright Office, 37 C.F.R. Part 201, [Docket No. RM 2005–11], Exemption to Prohibition on Circumvention of Copyright Protection Systems for Access Control Technologies at 5 [hereafter 2006 Rulemaking], http://www.copyright.gov/1201/docs/fedreg_notice.pdf.

92. For fuller discussions, *see, e.g.,* Robert A. Gorman, Jane C. Ginsburg and R. Anthony Reese, COPYRIGHT: CASES AND MATERIALS 1106–11 (8th ed. 2011); the rulemakings are available on the Copyright Office website: http://www.copyright.gov/1201/

93. *See, e.g.,* Jane C. Ginsburg, *The Pros and Cons of Strengthening Intellectual Property Protection: Technological Protection Measures and Section 1201 of the U.S. Copyright Act,* 16 INFORMATION & COMMUNICATIONS TECHNOLOGY LAW 191 (2007).

covers the activity colloquially known as "jailbreaking," or, in the words of the Rulemaking, "Computer programs that enable wireless telephone handsets to execute software applications, where circumvention is accomplished for the sole purpose of enabling interoperability of such applications, when they have been lawfully obtained, with computer programs on the telephone handset."[94] Although the exception is phrased in general terms, it was prompted by a particular use of an access control: Apple's design of the iPhone to prevent the running of third-party applications that Apple had not approved.

B. *Copyright Management Information*

Section 1202 of the DMCA is designed to encourage the copyright owner to embed important copyright-related information in digital copies and phonorecords, including the names of the author and copyright owner and the terms and conditions for use of the work. This is known as copyright management information (CMI). Section 1202 prohibits knowingly providing false CMI with the intent to facilitate or conceal copyright infringement, as well as furthering the removal or alteration of CMI with reasonable grounds for knowing this will facilitate or conceal an infringement.[95]

How effectively § 1202 achieves the desired reliability and accuracy of information relevant to proper identification of works and to electronic (or other) transactions in rights under copyright is debatable. Section 1202 may fall short in at least one respect. Linking the violation of the copyright management information provisions to copyright infringement does not effectively achieve the objective of ensuring the accuracy and reliability of a key component of copyright management information— proper identification of the author (as opposed to the copyright holder). Apart from the § 106A right of attribution with respect to works of visual art (see *supra* Chapter 6), there is no right *under copyright* to be credited as the author of a work. By contrast, there is a right under the Berne Convention to authorship credit. (*See* art. 6[bis].) This means that willfully removing or altering the author's name is not in itself copyright infringement. This gap in § 1202's coverage disserves the general public interest in knowing who is the author of the work. Congress recognized the public benefit of authorship credit, since § 1202(c)'s definition of copyright management information includes "the name of, and other identifying information about, the author of a work." Section 1202 does not oblige the rights owner to attach copyright management information

---

94. 75 Fed. Reg. 43825, 43828 (July 27, 2010).

95. For cases illustrating the difficulty of securing relief under section 1202(b), *see*

Gordon v. Nextel Communications, 345 F.3d 922 (6th Cir. 2003); Schiffer Publishing, Ltd. v. Chronicle Books, LLC, 76 U.S.P.Q.2d 1493 (E.D. Pa. 2005).

to distributions of the work, but if the rights holder does attach copyright management information, then it would be appropriate to interpret the statute to require that the information include the name of the author. Thus understood, § 1202 expresses a public policy favoring author identification as part of a reliable system of dissemination (especially electronic distribution) of copyrighted works. But as the judicial interpretation of § 1202 suggests, Congress may not have drafted this provision in a way that sufficiently implements either authors' interests or the more general interest in ensuring accurate information about a work of authorship.

1. Judicial application of section 1202

The caselaw has addressed three issues: What is "copyright management information"? Where must copyright management information appear in order to be protected? and What level of knowledge or intent violates section 1202?

a. *What is Copyright Management Information?*

Regarding the first question, courts have divided over whether only identifying information that is part of an "automated copyright protection or management system" can be deemed CMI protected under section 1202.[96] The controversy seems misplaced, for the text of section 1202 plainly envisions a broad application for CMI; section 1202(c)(2) defines CMI as "any of the following information conveyed in connection with copies or phonorecords of a work or performances or displays of a work, including in digital form, except that such term does not include any personally identifying information about a user of a work or of a copy, phonorecord, performance, or display of a work." The specification of "including in digital form" clearly means that information not in digital form is also covered. Some courts nonetheless justified their improbable reading of "including" to mean "only if" (and in addition, only if the digital information is part of a rights management system) on the ground that section 1202 was enacted as part of the Digital Millennium Copyright Act; that the title of the chapter to which § 1201 and § 1202 belong is "Copyright Protection and Management *Systems*"; and that Congress's goal in section 1202 was to foster electronic commerce. As the Court of Appeals for the Third Circuit recognized, however, the fact that section 1202 emerged from a context of legislative responses to

---

96. *Compare* IQ Group v. Wiesner Pub., LLC, 409 F. Supp. 2d 587 (D.N.J. 2006); Textile Secrets Int'l, Inc. v. Ya–Ya Brand, Inc., 524 F. Supp. 2d 1184, 1198 (CD. Cal. 2007) (CMI must be related to automated system), *with* Murphy v. Millennium Radio Group LLC, 650 F.3d 295 (3d Cir. 2011); Agence France Presse v. Morel, 769 F. Supp. 2d 295 (S.D.N.Y. 2011) (declining to read such a limitation into section 1202).

the challenges of digital communications neither precludes a more general role for CMI, nor compels such a substantial rewriting of the definition.

A broad reading of CMI to include identifying information on analog as well as digital copies, and whether or not in connection with a rights-management "system," could mean that removal or alteration of a copyright notice, or of an author's byline, even from analog copies, violates section 1202. Removal standing alone, however, does not suffice to make out such a violation. It is also necessary to consider what "conveyed in connection with copies or phonorecords of a work or performances or displays of a work" means, and, most importantly, whether the CMI claimant can surpass the statute's high threshold for proving the requisite intent. In any event, as a matter of public policy, imposition of civil liability[97] for the willful removal or alteration of copyright notices or author bylines with the intention to facilitate copyright infringement seems like a sanction consonant with the interests both of authors and their audiences.

b. Location of Copyright Management Information

Regarding the location of CMI, some courts have interpreted "in connection with" to require that the identifying information be embedded in the copy or phonorecord of the work,[98] while others have rejected such a narrow view.[99] Again the language of the statute does not command incorporation of the CMI in the work: "conveyed in connection with" does not mean "on copies," and if a "performance of a work" is involved, embedding may not be possible. Similarly, if the object of the transaction is a display of an artwork, its creator, understandably, may not wish to embed CMI in the image. If the goal is to provide reliable information regarding the identity of the work, of its author, and of the terms and conditions of its exploitation, it would seem that providing the information in ways that do not imperil the integrity of the work could still meet Congress's objectives.

---

97. Section 506(d) imposes a maximum fine of $2500 for the removal or alteration of a copyright notice with fraudulent intent. Section 1204(a) provides for far more substantial fines for violating sections 1201 or 1202.

98. Kelly v. Arriba Soft Corp., 77 F. Supp. 2d 1116 (C.D.Cal.1999), *aff'd*, 336 F.3d 811 (9th Cir. 2003) (information on photographer's webpage, not on individual photographs); Schiffer Pub., Ltd. v. Chronicle Books, LLC, 73 U.S.P.Q.2d 1090 (E.D. Pa. 2004) (information on inside cover of book, not on individual photographs)

99. BanxCorp v. Costco Wholesale Corp., 723 F. Supp. 2d 596 (S.D.N.Y. 2010); *See also* Agence France Presse v. Morel, 769 F. Supp. 2d 295 (S.D.N.Y. 2011) (citing *BanxCorp* in declining to decide significance of CMI location on motion to dismiss).

c. *Knowledge standard*

Finally, many CMI claims are likely to founder on the statutory double intent standard. Under § 1202(b), the wrongful act is not simply removing the information, or distributing or publicly performing or displaying the work without the information. The statute also requires that those who distribute, perform or display the work (1) have known that the information was removed or altered without the copyright owner's authorization, *and* (2) that those who remove or alter the information, or who distribute or perform works whose information has been removed or altered, do so "knowing, or ... having reasonable grounds to know that it will induce, enable, facilitate, or conceal an infringement of any right under this title." Thus, even intentional removal or alteration of CMI is not unlawful if the copyright owner cannot show that the person who removed or altered the information knew that the removal would encourage or facilitate copyright infringement.[100]

The cases suggest that the second level of intent is most likely to be established when the defendant, having removed or altered the CMI, distributes the work without the accompanying information (or with altered information) to third parties, who will in turn make the work available to the public. Thus, in *McClatchey v. AP*,[101] in rejecting the AP's motion for summary judgment, the court held:

> Under Plaintiff's version of the facts, AP intentionally cropped the copyright notice out of the picture before distributing it to subscribers. This appears to be precisely the conduct to which Section 1202(b) is directed. As Plaintiff notes, the nature of APs' business is to provide stories and pictures for use by its members and subscribers. Thus, a reasonable factfinder could conclude that by cropping out the copyright notice, Defendant had the requisite intent to induce, enable, facilitate or conceal infringement.

By contrast, where the person removing the CMI has directly distributed the work to the public, it may be more difficult to show that the removal or alteration will facilitate copyright infringement, because it may be necessary to show that the distributor knew or should have known that end-consumer recipients would be induced by the absence or alteration of the CMI to infringe the work. Because the end-user's infringement need not be intentional,[102] one can imagine some scenarios

---

100. *See, e.g.,* Gordon v. Nextel Comms., 345 F.3d 922 (6th Cir. 2003); *Kelly,* 77 F. Supp. 2d 1116; *Schiffer,* 73 U.S.P.Q.2d 1090.

101. 82 U.S.P.Q.2d 1190 (W.D. Pa. 2007). *See also Banxcorp,* 723 F. Supp. 2d 596; Jacobsen v. Katzer, 609 F. Supp. 2d 925 (N.D. Cal. 2009).

102. *See, e.g.,* Sheldon v. MGM Pictures Corp., 81 F.2d 49 (2d Cir. 1936); Bright Tunes Music Corp. v. Harrisongs Music, Ltd., 420 F. Supp. 177 (S.D.N.Y. 1976).

that might meet this test, for example, affixing a false Creative Commons or similar notice authorizing free redistribution of the work. Nonetheless, on the whole, section 1202 does not seem the most effective vehicle to ensure the reliability of information about the work and its licensing.

Chapter 10

STATE LAW AND ITS PREEMPTION

I. State Anti–Copying Laws

Throughout the history of copyright law in the United States, the laws of the several states—under a variety of legal theories—have afforded protection against the unauthorized copying or other use of the intellectual creations of others. Most significantly, until 1978, state law generally forbade the unauthorized first printing or public distribution of an unpublished work. This was known as common-law copyright, typically afforded by judicial development but sometimes by state statute. Since the amendment of the Copyright Act, effective January 1, 1978, which extended federal protection to all works from the moment they are "fixed in a tangible medium of expression,"[1] federal copyright has automatically attached even to unpublished works. Under the terms of section 301 of the Act, "no person is entitled to any such right or equivalent right in any such work under the common law or statutes of any State." Because state common-law copyright afforded relief against conduct—copying or public distribution pure and simple—that is exactly the same as that proscribed by the 1976 Act, Congress determined that the exclusive rights, limitations, remedies, and federal jurisdiction that are provided through the federal Act should preempt state copyright law.

There are, however, a number of other state theories that bar one person's unauthorized use of another's intellectual product. State laws of unfair competition forbid one person's "passing off" his or her own work as having been created by another. This theory is frequently applied to prevent the use of a popular title or a character (or character name) to identify another person's work. State trademark law is an application of the doctrine of "passing off" to goods and services, the labeling of which would cause confusion in the consumer marketplace. Another branch of unfair competition law is known as "misappropriation." The converse of passing off, misappropriation prevents one person from representing expressly or impliedly to be his or her own a work actually created by another person; the layman labels this as plagiarism, but the law has called this kind of typically unattributed copying "misappropriation" (or sometimes, "reverse passing-off"). "Misappropriation" has also come to mean unauthorized copying plain and simple, without the issue of authorship attribution. The Supreme Court decision in *International*

1. 17 U.S.C. § 102(a).

262

News Service v. Associated Press,[2] rendered as an elaboration of federal tort law in the early years of the twentieth century (pre-*Erie*[3]), articulated this doctrine and its underlying rationale, and inspired state courts in developing their own local laws of unfair competition.

States also bar copying or other unauthorized uses of intellectual creations when such use would be in breach of contract or in breach of trust or some other fiduciary relationship. The reproduction or other use of a person's unpublished and carefully guarded industrial formulae, business schemes, or customer lists may run afoul of a state's trade secret laws. The publishing of another's work might also be forbidden under various state tort theories—such as the right of privacy (e.g., when *A* writes a love letter to *B*, who publishes it), defamation (e.g., when *A* writes *B* a letter stating scurrilous things about *C*, and *B* publishes that letter), and the right of publicity (e.g., when *A*'s name and image are used in advertising or on merchandise).

In addition to these state laws against copying the work of another, federal laws may often be available. The federal Patent Act[4] bars the use or sale of products, processes, or designs of useful articles for which a federal patent has been issued. Under the federal trademark statute, the Lanham Act,[5] phrases and pictorial works can be registered if they have come to identify goods or services, and federal actions may be brought to forbid their copying, if that copying is likely to confuse consumers regarding the source or endorsement of the goods or services. Even unregistered works are protected against copying under section 43(a) of the Lanham Act if their use in connection with goods and services in interstate commerce could be viewed as a

> false designation of origin, false or misleading description of fact, or false or misleading representation of fact, which ... is likely to cause confusion, or to cause mistake, or to deceive ... as to the origin, sponsorship, or approval of his or her goods, services, or commercial activities by another person.[6]

This section creates, in effect, a federal statutory law of unfair competition.

A. *Federal Preemption*

When relief is sought under state law against unauthorized use of literary, artistic, or musical creations, a question arises as to the compatibility of state relief with the federal Copyright Act. For a state to forbid

---

2. 248 U.S. 215 (1918).

3. Erie R.R. Co. v. Tompkins, 304 U.S. 64 (1938) (abolishing "federal common law" in diversity cases).

4. 35 U.S.C. §§ 101 et seq.

5. 15 U.S.C. §§ 1051 et seq.

6. *Id.* § 1125(a)(1)(A).

copying permitted under federal law, or for a state to permit copying that federal law proscribes, would equally raise questions of compliance with the Supremacy Clause of the Constitution, Article VI, Clause 2.

In a number of significant cases that arose prior to the 1976 Copyright Act, the Supreme Court dealt with claims that state anti-copying laws were preempted because of their incompatibility with either the patent or copyright law of the United States. In two well-known companion cases decided in 1964, the Court overturned, as inconsistent with federal patent law, the application of a state unfair competition law that would have forbidden the copying and marketing of lighting fixtures for which utility and design patents were unavailable or had expired. The Court stated its holding in broad terms:

> [W]hen an article is unprotected by a patent or a copyright, state law may not forbid others to copy that article. To forbid copying would interfere with the federal policy, found in Art. I, § 8, cl. 8, of the Constitution and in the implementing federal statutes, of allowing free access to copy whatever the federal patent and copyright laws leave in the public domain.[7]

The Court made clear that it had no objection to state law "which requires those who make and sell copies to take precautions to identify their products as their own,"[8] i.e., state labeling laws forbidding unfair competition in the form of "passing off."

In a later decision pointing in a somewhat different direction, the Supreme Court upheld a state law making it a crime to "pirate" (by directly dubbing sounds from) recordings manufactured by others, at a time when the federal Copyright Act had not yet extended copyright protection to "sound recordings." In *Goldstein v. California*,[9] decided in 1973, the Court concluded that Congress's omission of sound recordings was not intended to prevent states from enacting anti-piracy laws, because much potentially copyrightable subject matter is amenable to "local" regulation and because Congress had (in the time period pertinent to the case) left the matter of protection for sound recordings "unattended."

II. Preemption under the 1976 Copyright Act

Congress did not leave the general issue of preemption of state anti-copying laws unattended for long. In the 1976 Copyright Act, Congress

---

7. Compco Corp. v. Day–Brite Lighting, Inc., 376 U.S. 234, 237 (1964) (citing Sears, Roebuck & Co. v. Stiffel Co., 376 U.S. 225 (1964)). The Court reiterated these views in

Bonito Boats, Inc. v. Thunder Craft Boats, Inc., 489 U.S. 141 (1989).

8. *Compco*, 376 U.S. at 238.

9. 412 U.S. 546 (1973).

incorporated elaborate preemption provisions in section 301. Section 301(a) provides:

> On and after January 1, 1978, all legal or equitable rights that are equivalent to any of the exclusive rights within the general scope of copyright as specified by section 106 in works of authorship that are fixed in a tangible medium of expression and come within the subject matter of copyright as specified by sections 102 and 103, whether created before or after that date and whether published or unpublished, are governed exclusively by this title. Thereafter, no person is entitled to any such right or equivalent right in any such work under the common law or statutes of any State.

In section 301(b), Congress reiterated that state rights and remedies are not annulled or limited if they relate to subject matter falling outside section 102 and 103, including "unfixed" works, or if the rights afforded by state law are not "equivalent to" the rights accorded by section 106.[10] In a provision whose importance may increase with the so-called "long tail" of older works newly made available online, section 301(c) states:

> With respect to sound recordings fixed before February 15, 1972, any rights or remedies under the common law or statutes of any State shall not be annulled or limited by this title until February 15, 2067. The preemptive provisions of subsection (a) shall apply to any such rights and remedies pertaining to any cause of action arising from undertakings commenced on and after February 15, 2067. Notwithstanding the provisions of section 303, no sound recording fixed before February 15, 1972, shall be subject to copyright under this title before, on, or after February 15, 2067.

Thus, state protection for pre–1972 sound recordings—a significant category covering, for example, most Beatles recordings, many Motown recordings, and for classical music lovers, Maria Callas recordings—is expressly left available until the end of 2067. While not displacing state law, section 301(c) does not establish that common law copyright or other coverage in fact existed in every state, although it appears that, in addition to centers of sound recording production, such as New York and California, most other states protect sound recordings by statute and/or common law as well.[11]

----

10. Also sheltered against preemption are state causes of action arising before January 1, 1978 (long since barred by the three-year statute of limitations in section 507(b) of the Copyright Act).

11. *See* 2 Melville B. Nimmer & David Nimmer, NIMMER ON COPYRIGHT, § 8C.03[B],[C] at 8C–7 to 8C–9 (2011) (most states today protect sound recordings made before 1972); Peter Jaszi & Nick Lewis, PROTECTION FOR PRE-1972 SOUND RECORD-

To make it clear that preemption is intended only of state laws, section 301(d) provides: "Nothing in this title annuls or limits any rights or remedies under any other Federal statute." Accordingly, it is still possible to seek anti-copying relief under, say, federal design-patent law to protect the shape of useful articles, or under the Lanham Act to bar the use of words or pictures that confuse the public regarding the source of goods or services.[12]

A. Works within the scope of Federal copyright

Section 301 clearly preempts what was known as common-law copyright: the right of first publication of, typically, a literary or musical manuscript. State laws that are *not* preempted fall into two categories. First are anti-copying laws that relate to works not within the subject matter of copyright; the principal statutory example of this is a work not fixed in a tangible medium of expression. Thus, if a work is communicated by the author only in "live" form—such as an improvised lecture or comedy routine—the unauthorized copying of that work (e.g., by shorthand notation or by tape recording) or the unauthorized performance of that work can be forbidden by state law. To that extent, it can be said that common-law copyright continues to exist, but only with respect to works that have not been "fixed" (or that have been fixed without the author's consent).

Pursuant to U.S. treaty obligations, the Copyright Act was amended in 1994 to add section 1101 which protects a live musical performance against unauthorized fixation, the distribution of copies or phonorecords of the unauthorized fixation, or the transmission of the performance to the public. (See discussion, *supra*, Chapter 2.) This unique example of federal protection of an unfixed work (granting in effect a federal right of first fixation) was sustained against constitutional attack by the Court of Appeals for the Eleventh Circuit, and the federal district court for the Central District of California.[13] Both courts found section 1101 to be

INGS UNDER STATE LAW AND ITS IMPACT ON USE BY NON PROFIT INSTITUTIONS: A 10–STATE ANALYSIS (2009), *available at*: http://www.clir.org/pubs/abstract/pub146abst.html. *But see* Michael Erlinger, *An Analog Solution in a Digital World: Providing Federal Copyright Protection for Pre-1972 Sound Recordings*, 16 UCLA ENT. L. REV. 45, 49 (2009) (recognizing that before the 1970s, "[t]he states ... provided neither universal recognition nor uniform enforcement of any right in sound recordings"). A Copyright Office study released in December 2011 has recommended that pre–1972 sound recordings be brought within the subject matter of federal copyright law, *see Federal Copyright*

Protection for Pre–1972 Sound Recordings: A Report of the Register of Copyrights, http://www.copyright.gov/docs/sound/pre–72–report.pdf

12. *But see* Dastar Corp. v. Twentieth Century Fox Film, 539 U.S. 23 (2003) (Lanham Act is narrowly construed so as to deny relief for unattributed copying of video footage; "origin" of "goods" interpreted to mean physical goods, not "intellectual goods").

13. United States v. Moghadam, 175 F.3d 1269 (11th Cir. 1999); Kiss Catalog, Ltd. v. Passport Int'l Prods., Inc., 405 F. Supp. 2d 1169 (C.D. Cal. 2005). *See also*

supported by the Interstate Commerce Clause. Section 1101(d) expressly provides that state common-law or statutory remedies for unauthorized transmission, fixation and distribution of live musical performances are not preempted.

Related to performers' fixation rights are their rights in their names and images. These are typically the subject matter of state right-of-publicity laws. But sometimes the subject matter of the state claim and of federal rights may overlap, for example, when a performer or celebrity claims publicity rights in her image, but the image is captured in a photograph in which another person owns the copyright. Exploitation of the photograph without the permission of the person depicted in the photograph remains actionable at state law.[14] By contrast, performers' publicity-right claims in their fixed vocal or visual performances have been held preempted when the performances are fully captured in an authorized sound recording or audiovisual work.[15]

Given the wide range of the categories of works listed in sections 102 and 103, it is difficult to imagine any fixed work that falls outside the scope of the federal act. Nonetheless, the statute, or unambiguous legislative history, makes it clear that certain components within the covered categories are not eligible for federal copyright protection. The most obvious example is "any idea, procedure, process, system, method of operation, concept, principle, or discovery, regardless of the form in which it is described, explained, illustrated, or embodied in such work," which section 102(b) declares unprotected. Some courts had concluded that because Congress excluded ideas and concepts from the subject matter of copyright, it follows that states may outlaw their copying.[16] Most courts, however, take what would appear to be the clearly correct view, that Congress in section 102(b) was articulating an affirmative policy of making ideas and concepts available for all to copy, such that state anti-copying laws embracing such subject matter would be inconsistent with the federal scheme.[17] As the Court of Appeals for the Fourth

---

United States v. Martignon, 492 F.3d 140 (2d Cir. 2007) (sustaining criminal statute in 18 U.S.C. § 2319A(a)(1),(3)).

14. See, e.g., Toney v. L'Oreal USA, Inc., 406 F.3d 905 (7th Cir. 2005). Cf. Facenda v. N.F.L. Films, Inc., 542 F.3d 1007, 1031–32 (3d Cir. 2008) (holding right of publicity action was not preempted where plaintiff had consented to use of his voice in one product and defendant had subsequently used his voice in a different product).

15. See, e.g., Jules Jordan Video v. 144942 Canada Inc., 617 F.3d 1146 (9th Cir. 2010); Laws v. Sony, 448 F.3d 1134 (9th Cir. 2006).

16. E.g., Dunlap v. G & L Holding Group, Inc., 381 F.3d 1285 (11th Cir. 2004); Past Pluto Prods. Corp. v. Dana, 627 F. Supp. 1435 (S.D.N.Y. 1986). See also Storch Enters. v. Mergenthaler Linotype, 202 U.S.P.Q. 623 (E.D.N.Y. 1979) (state protection against copying of typeface, despite legislative history showing Congress's desire not to afford protection).

17. E.g., Harper & Row Publishers, Inc. v. Nation Enters., 723 F.2d 195 (2d Cir. 1983), rev'd on other grounds, 471 U.S. 539 (1985).

Circuit concluded, denying state relief for the alleged copying of ideas and methods developed in a Ph.D. dissertation, the "scope" (i.e., subject matter) of the Copyright Act and its "protection" are not synonymous: "[T]he shadow actually cast by the Act's preemption is notably broader than the wing of its protection."[18]

B. Equivalence of State law with rights under Federal copyright

Even if a work is within the categories of federally copyrightable subject matter and is fixed in a tangible medium of expression, a state may forbid unauthorized use of such works provided that such use is not "equivalent to any of the exclusive rights within the general scope of copyright as specified by section 106." If, for example, a state were to attempt to forbid the copying or the public performance of a "fixed" dramatic work, the defendant could properly move to dismiss on the ground of preemption under section 301 of the Copyright Act. If, however, the state's ban on copying or public performance rests upon a theory that is not "equivalent" to federal copyright, state jurisdiction and law can be effective.

Section 301 does not expressly itemize the "nonpreempted" state causes of action. Nonetheless, an earlier version of the copyright revision bill did,[19] and the itemization is useful, for despite some confusing subsequent legislative history (in the form of a colloquy on the floor of the House of Representatives), there is good reason to believe that the deletion of the list from the bill was not intended as a repudiation. Included in the earlier version, as nonequivalent and nonpreempted state claims, were "rights against misappropriation not equivalent to any of such exclusive rights [in section 106], breaches of contract, breaches of trust, trespass, conversion, invasion of privacy, defamation, and deceptive trade practices such as passing off and false representation."

What appears to link these nonpreempted state claims is the presence of a significant element in the theory of relief that goes beyond "mere" copying or public performance (or some other right set forth in section 106 of the Copyright Act). As has been stated by the Court of Appeals for the Second Circuit:

---

18. United States *ex rel.* Berge v. Board of Trustees of Univ. of Ala., 104 F.3d 1453, 1463 (4th Cir. 1997). *See also* Wrench LLC v. Taco Bell Corp., 256 F.3d 446, 455 (6th Cir. 2001) ("We join our sister circuits in holding that the scope of the Copyright Act's subject matter is broader than the scope of the Act's protections.").

19. *See* H.R. Rep. No. 94–1476, at 131–32 (1976).

When a right defined by state law may be abridged by an act which, in and of itself, would infringe one of the exclusive rights, the state law in question must be deemed preempted. Conversely, when a state law violation is predicated upon an act incorporating elements beyond mere reproduction or the like, the rights involved are not equivalent and preemption will not occur.[20]

This has come to be known as the "extra element" test for non-preemption.[21]

Thus, a plaintiff's claim that the defendant has copied a work in violation of a contractual promise, or in violation of an obligation of trust imposed by the state law of fiduciary obligations, is based on a state policy different from the economic-incentive policy underlying the Copyright Act; there are additional elements (above and beyond the copyright claim) to be proved to establish the state cause of action, and state remedies can protect interests beyond those protected by copyright.[22] Moreover, state relief in such contract and fiduciary cases reaches the conduct of only one or a very limited number of persons bound to the plaintiff in the special relationship; the state anti-copying relief does not bar members of the public more generally.[23] For example, the Ninth Circuit has reaffirmed that federal copyright law does not preempt breach-of-contract claims by plaintiffs who "pitched" proposals for motion pictures to studios that allegedly agreed to compensate the proposer if the studio took up the idea.[24] Some courts, however, have been more inclined than others to find preemption in situations in which the alleged contract breach is nothing more than the reproduction of expressive materials.[25]

Preservation of state contract claims may be particularly problematic when the contract does not confirm an arms-length negotiation between parties who have engaged in a course of dealing, as in many of the idea-submission cases, but instead is a form contract generally

20. *Harper & Row*, 723 F.2d at 200.

21. *E.g.*, Wrench LLC v. Taco Bell Corp., 256 F.3d 446 (6th Cir. 2001). This test has been criticized as conclusory. *See* Ritchie v. Williams, 395 F.3d 283 (6th Cir. 2005).

22. ProCD, Inc. v. Zeidenberg, 86 F.3d 1447 (7th Cir. 1996); Acorn Structures, Inc. v. Swantz, 846 F.2d 923 (4th Cir. 1988); Smith v. Weinstein, 578 F. Supp. 1297 (S.D.N.Y.), *aff'd without opinion*, 738 F.2d 419 (2d Cir. 1984). *See* Computer Assocs. Int'l, Inc. v. Altai, Inc., 982 F.2d 693 (2d Cir. 1992) (trade secret).

23. *See ProCD*, 86 F.3d 1447, for a particularly thoughtful—if not uncontroversial—analysis. The court enforced, on a state contract theory, the terms of a so-called shrinkwrap license wrapped with a mass-distributed CD–ROM and barring commercial use of the largely uncopyrighted material (white-page telephone information) embedded thereon.

24. Montz v. Pilgrim Films & Television, Inc., 623 F.3d 912 (9th Cir. 2010).

25. *Taco Bell*, 256 F.3d 446; Kabehie v. Zoland, 125 Cal. Rptr.2d 721 (Cal. Ct. App. 2002).

imposing the terms on a take-it-or-leave-it basis. More troublesome still are the "shrinkwrap" or "click on" licenses whose pervasiveness may reduce to mere formalism the difference between a "contract right" good only against parties in privity, and a "property right" good against the world. In *Pro CD v. Zeidenberg*, in which the Seventh Circuit upheld a shrinkwrap license that prohibited the redissemination of public-domain white-pages listings, the court emphasized the difference between property and contract rights, and posited that a third party who came upon an abandoned copy of the CD and loaded it into his computer would not be bound by the terms of the shrinkwrap license.[26] But if the CD or online file required clicking assent to the terms of use in order to access the content, then all users are in "privity" with the content-purveyor, and the contract becomes the functional equivalent of a copyright.

This does not necessarily mean that the contract should be deemed preempted, for its enforcement may not necessarily contravene copyright policies. In *ProCD*, for example, the shrinkwrap license enabled the information provider to price discriminate, offering the white-pages information to consumers for a lower price, provided they did not resell the information, and offering resellable information to professionals at a higher price. The price-discrimination thus made the information more affordable to general consumers. Disqualifying the contract would not have advanced the general copyright goal to promote the progress of knowledge, if the result would have been to put the content out of reach of the general consumer. But this beneficent characterization may not apply to all mass-market online agreements that give the provider greater rights than those available under the copyright law (or that contract out of a variety of limitations on copyright protection). But courts have yet to articulate clear guidelines for determining whether a mass-market contract accompanying the dissemination of a work within the general scope of copyright should be ruled preempted.[27]

Conversion of a physical manuscript—the wrongful assertion of ownership in the tangible property—could give rise to an unpreempted state cause of action, but conversion of "literary" property in the manuscript would be preempted, for the latter is essentially another name for copyright protection.[28] That is also true for a claim of "interfer-

---

26. *ProCD*, 86 F.3d at 1450–1451.

27. *See, e.g.*, Bowers v. Baystate Tech. 320 F.3d 1317, 1324–26 (Fed. Cir. 2003) (holding specific shrinkwrap license implicated an "extra element" precluding Copyright Act preemption); Recursion Software v. Interactive Intelligence, Inc., 425 F. Supp. 2d 756, 768 (holding "clickwrap" contract claim not preempted without reaching issue of whether *all* such claims

are not preempted). *See also* Guy A. Rub, *Contracting Around Copyright: The Uneasy Case for Unbundling of Rights in Creative Works*, 78 U. Chi. L. Rev. 257 (2011) (arguing that "from an economic efficiency perspective it is difficult to defend the *ProCD* rule.").

28. Ehat v. Tanner, 780 F.2d 876 (10th Cir. 1985).

ence with contractual relationships" when the interference takes the form of a third person's refusal to print the plaintiff's book because the defendant has already marketed an unauthorized copy; the refusal to print is simply an element of the plaintiff's damages that are compensable in a copyright-infringement action.[29] Similarly, the plaintiff will ordinarily not be able to avoid the preemptive thrust of section 301 by claiming under the state anti-copying law that the defendant had acted intentionally, or had been unjustly enriched by tapping into the plaintiff's effort and expense, or had behaved in a "commercially immoral" manner.[30] Although none of these elements of the claim is technically a requisite for a copyright claim under section 106, they are generally regarded as incidental to and not markedly different in substance from a claim for infringement.[31]

It remains to be seen whether courts will uphold state claims that are framed as "misappropriation not equivalent to any of [the] exclusive rights" in section 106 (borrowing the language that had appeared in the earlier copyright revision bill). It is, for example, doubtful whether a modern-day equivalent of the theory fashioned by the Supreme Court in *International News Service v. Associated Press*[32]—reaping where one had not sown in the reporting of uncopyrightable news—could be sustained against a preemption defense by a state (or federal) court applying state tort law.[33] But if the state misappropriation tort is narrowly enough circumscribed, it may survive preemption because it is not equivalent to copyright. So the Second Circuit Court of Appeals held in *National Basketball Ass'n v. Motorola, Inc.*,[34] when it stated "that only a narrow 'hot-news' misappropriation claim survives preemption for actions concerning material within the realm of copyright."[35] In the court's view, such a nonpreempted claim would have to have the following elements:

> (i) the plaintiff generates or collects information at some cost or expense; (ii) the value of the information is highly time-sensitive; (iii) the defendant's use of the information constitutes free-

---

29. Harper & Row Publishers, Inc. v. Nation Enters., 723 F.2d 195 (2d Cir. 1983), *rev'd on other grounds*, 471 U.S. 539 (1985).

30. *E.g.*, Mayer v. Josiah Wedgwood & Sons, 601 F. Supp. 1523 (S.D.N.Y. 1985).

31. For all such "equivalent" and preempted state claims, some federal courts have applied the doctrine of "complete preemption," which results not only in a dismissal, but also in a "recharacterization" of the state claims as federal copyright claims, which thus fall within the exclusive (and removal) jurisdiction of the federal courts. *See* Ritchie v. Williams, 395 F.3d 283 (6th Cir. 2005).

32. 248 U.S. 215 (1918).

33. *See, e.g.*, Barclays Capital, Inc. v. Theflyonthewall.com, 650 F.3d 876 (2d Cir. 2011) (electronic newsletter's copying of another electronic service's stock-market information and predictions). The House Report, however, contemplates the non-preemption of state misappropriation laws that bar the unauthorized use of electronic means to steal a computer database. H.R. Rep. No. 94–1476, at 133 (1976) (citing *International News*).

34. 105 F.3d 841 (2d Cir. 1997).

35. *Id.* at 852.

riding on the plaintiff's costly efforts to generate or collect it; (iv) the defendant's use of the information is in direct competition with a product or service offered by the plaintiff; (v) the ability of other parties to free-ride on the efforts of the plaintiff would so reduce the incentive to produce the product or service that its existence or quality would be substantially threatened.[36]

In the *Motorola* case, the claim failed because the defendant did not "free ride" off of the NBA's information-gathering—actually, information-generation, because the disputed subject matter was real-time sports scores—but rather independently generated the information by recording the scores of the games as they were played.

Where free-riding can be shown, the "heat" of the "hot news" may be the key element that sets it apart from ordinarily preempted claims in information. That said, when, in *Barclays Capital, Inc. v. Theflyonthewall.com*,[37] the Second Circuit returned to the *Motorola* test in a controversy between online services for stock-market information and predictions, a context in which the news' elevated temperature was the essence of its value, a majority held that the plaintiff news service failed the test. The court distinguished *INS*, where the defendant newswire took credit for the AP's news-gathering; in the case before it, Theflyonthewall.com attributed the copied predictions to their source; indeed that the predictions were Barclays' constituted much of their value. Disputing Barclays' charge of free-riding, the majority introduced the dubious distinction between the copying of news that the plaintiff has *gathered* (as AP had) and news that the plaintiff has *created* (Barclays' predictions). The distinction in any event leaves open the prospect of nonpreempted state misappropriation claims in digital online contexts more closely analogous to *INS v. AP*, for example, when a news source's headlines and first sentences are "scraped" for reproduction by a "news aggregation" service.[38]

C.   *"Conflict" preemption*

Although the bulk of the decided cases dealing with the issue of preemption of state law focus, naturally enough, upon the application of the explicit preemption provisions in section 301 of the Copyright Act, a number of cases have invoked a broader theory of preemption based upon a conflict with some substantive term or policy of the federal statute. As with preemption situations generally, beyond copyright, the

36.   *Id.* (citations omitted).

37.   *Supra*, note 33.

38.   *See, e.g.*, Associated Press v. All Headline News Corp., 608 F. Supp. 2d 454 (S.D.N.Y. 2009). Of course, if the copying from the news sources takes more than a *de minimis* amount of expression, a copyright claim will lie and the state claim will be preempted.

question for the court is whether the federal policies reflected in some provision of the Copyright Act would be "set at naught, or its benefits denied" by the application of state law, or whether state law "stands as an obstacle to the accomplishment and execution of the full purposes and objectives of Congress."[39]

This "conflict preemption" might concern such issues as ownership and transfers of rights—matters that do not raise issues of "equivalence" to the exclusive rights set forth in section 106. For example, a state statute purporting to give copyright ownership to an employee who had prepared a literary work within the scope of his employment would disrupt the allocation of ownership rights dictated by Congress and would thus be an obstacle to the policies reflected in the Copyright Act. So too would a state law that would enforce an author's transfer of a copyright despite the absence of a signed writing. By contrast, although federal law does not require *non*exclusive transfers to be in writing, a state statute of frauds which required a writing for transactions whose value exceeds $500 would probably not conflict with the federal scheme if applied to a nonexclusive license priced above the statute of frauds' threshold.

Some courts are more willing than others to effect an "accommodation" of the federal and state laws, and thus to deny that the state law is preempted. One example derives from the community-property laws in eight states, which raise the question whether the initial copyright ownership given by the Copyright Act to the "author" of a work must be shared in some way with that author's spouse. Despite arguments that such a forced sharing would dilute and conflict with federal policy, which is designed to ensure financial rewards that foster creativity, it has been held that state law resulting in co-ownership of the copyright is not preempted; the non-author spouse will share equally in the proceeds from copyrighted works created during the marriage (and even from post-divorce derivative works), although the author-spouse alone will have the right to "manage" the copyright through licensing and transfers.[40]

39. For a comprehensive treatment of the issue, *see* Foley v. Luster, 249 F.3d 1281 (11th Cir. 2001) (Florida law regarding indemnification is not preempted as applied to joint copyright infringers).

40. Rodrigue v. Rodrigue, 218 F.3d 432 (5th Cir. 2000) (applying Louisiana law); In re Marriage of Susan M. & Frederick L. Worth, 241 Cal. Rptr. 135 (1st Dist. 1987) (applying California law, leaving open the question of licensing and transfer rights).

TABLE OF CASES

References are to Pages.

INDEX

References are to Pages

287

†